ON THE FRONTIERS OF SCIENCE

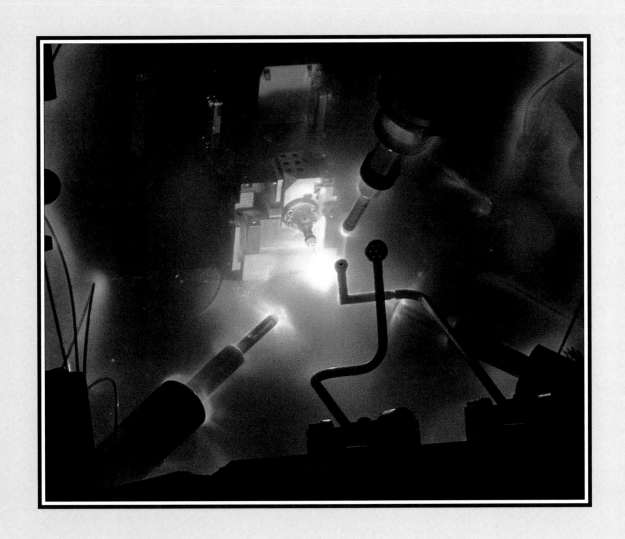

ON THE FRONTIERS OF SCIENCE

How Scientists See Our Future

CONTRIBUTING EDITORS
Nigel Calder and John Newell

Facts On File®
New York • Oxford

Advisors
Professor Jack Good
Professor André Lebeau
Professor James Lovelock

Contributing Editors
Nigel Calder (chapters 7,23)
John Newell (10,11,12)

Contributors
Michael Allaby (6)
Dr Alan Baddeley (17)
Peter Beer (3)
Dr Susan Blackmore (16)
Dr Francis Creed (15)
Professor Paul Davies (1,2,4)
Dr Bernard Dixon (12,14)
Professor John Ebling (22)
Professor Hugh Freeman (19)
Dr Andrew Greenshaw (20)
Dr Trevor Harley (18)
Dr Robin Holliday (13)
Dr Anthony Martin (4)
Professor M.D. Papagiannis (5)
Dr Mark Ridley (21)
Dr Trevor Robbins (17)
Professor J.V. Smith (8)
Lloyd Timberlake (9)
Professor Sir David Weatherall (11,
10)

AN EQUINOX BOOK

Planned and produced by:
Equinox (Oxford) Ltd,
Musterlin House,
Jordan Hill Road
Oxford OX2 8DP

Published in the United States of
America by Facts on File, Inc.,
460 Park Avenue South,
New York, N.Y. 10016

**Library of Congress
Cataloging-in-Publication Data**
On the Frontiers of Science: How
Scientists see our Future.
Contributing editors, Nigel Calder
and John Newell.

p.   cm.
Bibliography: p.
Includes index.
1. Science
I. Calder, Nigel
II. Newell, John
0158.5.F764 1989   8931623
500--dc20   CIP
ISBN 0-8160-2205-4

Introductory pictures (pages 1–8)
1 Laser system (◊ page 44)
2–3 Satellite image of lower Rhône
(◊ page 77)
4–5 Research into sleep (◊ page 187)
7 Packaging pharmaceuticals
(◊ page 143)
8 Space Shuttle (◊ page 42)

Printed in Spain by Heraclio
Fournier SA, Vitoria

Contents

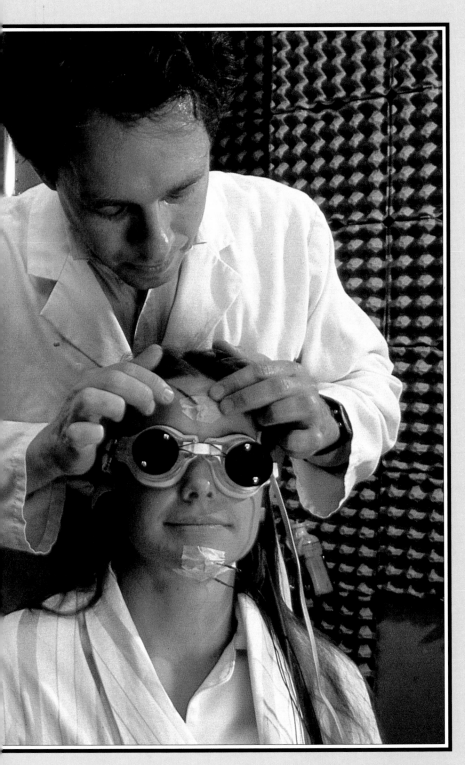

Introduction

Science is running ahead of people. Over the past 30 years, the gap has widened between the scientists out in front at the frontiers of knowledge and the rest of us who want to know what they are doing. It has widened fastest in the exciting, strategic areas. In the last few years science has spurted ahead, for example, in understanding the genes which help to trigger cancer, in discovering new materials that will conduct electricity with virtually no resistance, and in revealing how the development of early embryos is controlled. In such areas of rapid growth, all of which in different ways will affect our lives in years ahead, even the most intelligent, educated lay person has been left behind. Even scientists find themselves in this group. The fastest-moving areas of knowledge, such as biotechnology, are amalgams of several of the old disciplines and so each biotechnologist is having to learn new disciplines from scratch. In this respect the scientist is in the same position as the lay person in much of his or her work.

This book therefore aims to reflect the state of the art in most of the major spheres of science today. An editorial team of distinguished scientists and specialist science writers has picked out the key areas of endeavor, and simplified the concepts that underlie developments at the leading edge of science. We begin with the modern view of the universe as a whole, then look at astronomy and at space research, at space travel, the paradoxes of time travel, and the search for other intelligences beyond the Earth. Then we turn to our own planet, examining it first as an organic whole, in terms of planetary ecology, and then looking at the need to safeguard Mother Earth. The focus tightens further onto the nature of life, the newly-discovered ability to reshape life through genetic engineering, and the interaction of genetics and disease, with gene therapy now on the horizon. The second part of the book opens with a review of some wider issues concerning human health: new therapies, fringe medicine, and how far research on aging can give hope of longer life and an end to senility. Then we turn to mind-body interactions, and to the study of the mind – language, consciousness, new advances in psychiatry and the disturbing (but exciting) prospects for mood control. The last section of the book is concerned with understanding, improving, and ultimately, perhaps, even replacing humans.

Developments in the physical sciences

In the physical sciences, concepts such as grand unification theory (the ability to speak in the same "language" of the four forces that hold the universe together) are intellectually beautiful as well as essential to science. Our species can hardly be said to have come of age if we still talk of gravitation in one mathematical language, and about electromagnetism and the force which holds subatomic particles together in another, as if they existed in separate universes. This book also reveals some of the strange possibilities that confront us through modern cosmology, for example, the notion that most of the universe has already disappeared into black holes, that we are watching the long-drawn-out end of an epic in which many of the actors have already left the stage.

After the great adventure of the Apollo program, space exploration is now in a quieter phase. Much debate about investment treats "space" as if it were a single entity, but it can be viewed as an arena for several totally different scientific activities. One of these, communications, is already paying off. Another, the search for and survey of Earth's resources, will pay off massively in the near future. Yet another, space astronomy, offers great intellectual but no commercial rewards. To put people into space is of little or no practical use for any of these activities; and it would add vastly to their cost. Yet explorations of space are still often talked of as if they must involve people directly. Here the different strands of these efforts in space are disentangled, helping us to adopt a healthy skepticism for powerful lobbies while not denying the deep instinct that drives us to explore beyond our own planet.

Developments in the biological sciences

There is perhaps less need to disentangle the environmental issues concerning our own Earth. After the disaster at Chernobyl in 1986, most people are aware of the dangers of nuclear power. There is increasing awareness too of the threats and problems posed by over-use of chlorofluorocarbons that thin the ozone layer, power station and vehicle exhausts that lead to acid rain and the burning of fossil fuels that is slowly warming up the world, changing climate and weather. On the other hand, what have been largely lacking are explanations which go beyond instant journalism to set out the true magnitude not only of these problems but of the new problems that will be brought about by attempts to solve them. There are no easy answers. It is becoming mercilessly clear that what is done in one part of the world may have its long-term effects in another. Some of these complexities are discussed here in a series of briefings in planetary ecology. These should make it easier to decide which environmental issues are truly fighting issues, where governments are dragging their feet, and which problems may have been exaggerated.

Medicine is about to make a great leap forward. There are thousands of diseases caused by genetic defects in single genes, most of which will with luck be amenable to gene therapy. Genetic engineering will allow the cure of conditions which today condemn millions of infants to short and progressively more crippled lives and sometimes horrible deaths. It will allow the genetic defects which cause these conditions to be screened out of the population without the trauma of repeated abortions. How this will be done – is being done – and the ethical quandaries as well as undoubted blessings that the new techniques bring in their wake, are explained here in a way intended to enable the reader to follow the current controversies.

Some will feel that topics such as "alternative medicine" have no place in a book like this. But precisely because there is a vast interest in and thirst for such therapy, it is right to spell out what it can and cannot do. The discovery of receptors for stress hormones on the white cells that defend us against disease demands that we look afresh at the complex interactions between mind and body. The review here of contemporary knowledge of the mind also reveals the extent to which brain chemistry and genetics are now becoming mingled with social factors as the perceived complex causes of mental illnesses. An examination of the potential for improving, and ultimately replacing, humans shows that specialists in biotechnology and new sciences such as protein engineering are increasingly working together, to create devices, and perhaps ultimately creatures, which are part flesh and part metal or silicon. The barriers between life and non-life are melting and dissolving, as are those between many scientific disciplines.

Looking to the future

Using their expositions as a springboard, our contributors invite the reader to join them in imaginative leaps into the future, to see where we shall be in 30 and in 300 years' time. This is a risky game, but it is more than science fiction. Many of the research projects in laboratories today are clearly pointed toward outcomes in 30 years or so. Many of them, perhaps most, will not reach their targets. Unexpected things will go wrong along the way. Meanwhile other targets will be set up following new discoveries.

However, such predictions do tell us where science today wants to go tomorrow. The same is true for the exciting 300-year speculations. Some will doubtless prove very mistaken, yet our knowledge of life and the universe is already sufficient in some areas to make sensible guesses at the long-term future – mainly by assuming that science will have completely broken down barriers to achievement over huge areas.

1

A Theory of Everything

Fundamental particles...The four basic forces of nature...Progress toward a grand unified theory...Superstrings and supersymmetry...Testing for traces of the superforce...Black holes...Time travel

To most people it is obvious that the world is an organized unity. Wherever we look, from the innermost recesses of the atom to the far-flung galaxies, we encounter harmony and order. In spite of this, in our present state of knowledge, nature's varied phenomena require a multiplicity of different descriptions – a theory of gravitation, a theory of electromagnetism, and so on. Many theoretical physicists believe, however, that underlying this multiplicity is a unified description of nature – a theory of everything. If we possessed such a theory, then all natural phenomena would be seen to flow from a single fundamental principle. It is an idea that is as compelling as it is elusive. The last few years have seen dramatic progress in the quest for a theory of everything, and some theorists are optimistic that we may have the complete theory worked out in 30 years. Such a prospect has been heralded as nothing less than "the end of theoretical physics" by Professor Stephen Hawking of Cambridge, England.

The search for the fundamental building blocks

The ancient Greek philosophers Leucippus and Democritus asserted that all matter is ultimately composed of elementary particles. These "atoms" were supposed to be truly fundamental, in the sense of being indestructible and indivisible.

What we today call an atom is not an elementary particle at all, but a composite body consisting of a compact nucleus surrounded by a swarm of electrons. The nucleus is in turn composed of protons and neutrons. In addition, large numbers of other subatomic particles, not found in ordinary matter, have been discovered in cosmic rays or produced in the laboratory by colliding protons or electrons at high energy. Dozens of different kinds have been catalogued.

In spite of this proliferation, the organization of the subatomic world is actually quite simple once it is realized that all the nuclear particles – the proton and neutron and the many other particles associated with them – are composed of smaller units called quarks. The quarks combine together in pairs or trios to make the nuclear particles. To account for all the known nuclear particles there must be six different varieties of quarks. They are given the whimsical names up, down, strange, charm, top, and bottom.

All other particles are apparently elementary in their own right, and are not made of quarks. These generally lighter particles are the electron and two heavier particles that resemble it, and three species of so-called neutrinos. Collectively they are known as leptons ("light ones"). There are thus six varieties of leptons to go with the six varieties of quarks. (In addition, for each variety of particle there is a corresponding antiparticle in which all its qualities except mass are reversed.) Most theorists believe that these twelve particles are the basic building blocks of all matter – the elementary particles of the ancient Greeks.

▲ *Stephen Hawking is a mathematical physicist who holds the Lucasian Chair at Cambridge, once occupied by Isaac Newton. Like Newton, Hawking works on the theory of gravitation. He is searching for a mathematical formulation which will allow gravitation and quantum physics to be united consistently.*

▼ *The quest for truly fundamental particles of matter runs alongside that for a unified description of nature. The ancient Greeks' "indivisible" atom is now believed to be made of electrons and nuclear particles (protons and neutrons) that are made of combinations of two or three "fundamental particles" called quarks.*

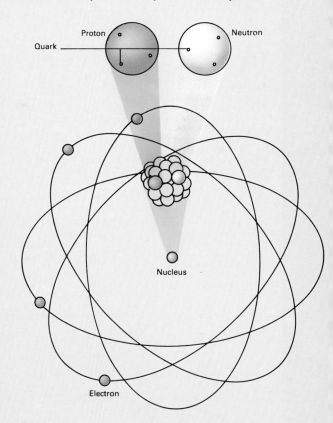

Quark — Proton Neutron

Nucleus

Electron

10

The force between the fundamental particles of matter can be envisaged as being conveyed by yet more "messenger particles"

The forces of nature

Matter on its own is inert. To activate it, forces must act between the particles. In spite of the extraordinary richness of natural phenomena, all known forces can be reduced to just four basic types: gravitation, electromagnetism and two nuclear forces known simply as weak and strong. Gravity keeps our feet on the ground and keeps the Earth in orbit round the Sun. It is the universal cosmic cohesive force, binding planet to star, star to galaxy and galaxy to galaxy. Electromagnetism accounts for all other forces that we encounter in the everyday world. In particular it binds atoms together chemically to make all the substances of our bodies and the objects around us.

The weak nuclear force is rather inconspicuous. It causes certain radioactive decay processes (such as beta decay), but once in a while it produces a truly spectacular event. One such was witnessed on February 26, 1987, when a star was seen to explode in the Large Magellanic Cloud – a mini-galaxy about 150,000 light years away. The event was a so-called supernova, in which the core of an aging star collapses catastrophically, releasing a huge pulse of neutrinos. With only the weak force at their disposal, these neutrinos blast the outer layers of the star into the surrounding space, wrecking it completely and producing a burst of luminosity. The activities of the strong nuclear force are apparent to us every day in the form of the heat and light that come from the Sun. The core of the Sun is a nuclear furnace, wherein reactions driven by the strong force liberate large quantities of energy. It is the same energy that is released during nuclear explosions.

Not all particles feel all the forces. The quarks do, but all the leptons are impervious to the strong force. Among the leptons, the neutrinos are not subject to the electromagnetic force either. All twelve quarks and leptons feel the weak and gravitational forces.

The weak force has three different messenger particles, called W^+, W^-, and Z. The Z particle is identical to the photon, except that it has an enormous mass (the photon is massless). The two W particles are also massive, and they carry electric charge. The strong force acts between quarks. Because quarks can combine together in threes, the strong force is a three-body force (rather than a two-body force as with the other). This makes matters more complicated still, and it is necessary for there to be eight different messenger particles, collectively known as gluons. One of the unusual features of gluon exchange is that it produces a force that *grows* rather than diminishes with distance. This ensures that the quarks remain permanently confined within the nuclear particles: isolated quarks are forbidden.

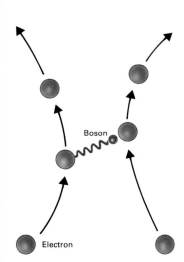

▲ *At the subatomic level, when particles push and pull on each other they exchange energy in packets (quanta) which can themselves be envisaged as particles. Here the force acts between two electrons. The "messenger particle" or boson (which for electromagnetism is called a photon) is created by one electron, and transmits the force to the other electron, which then absorbs it. For gravitation something similar occurs; its messenger particle is called the graviton.*

▶ *Physicists identify just four fundamental forces of nature. Two are familiar in daily life – electro-magnetism and gravitation. The other two are confined to atomic nuclei. The strengths and ranges of the forces vary widely, as do the particles affected by them. Only gravitation acts on all particles in nature.*

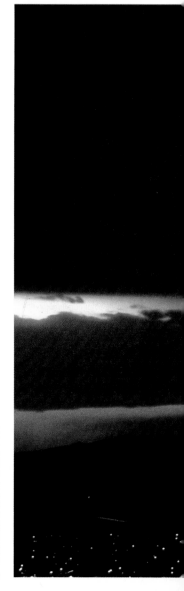

▼ *Electromagnetic forces can manifest themselves in spectacular ways, as in this lightning strike. The fundamental force between individual electrons in clouds and on the ground accumulates to produce a huge electromotive force, unleashed as lightning.*

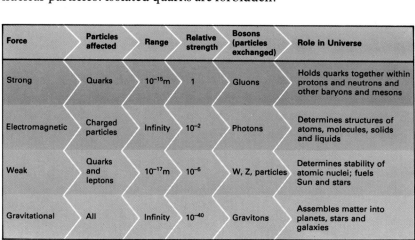

Force	Particles affected	Range	Relative strength	Bosons (particles exchanged)	Role in Universe
Strong	Quarks	10^{-15}m	1	Gluons	Holds quarks together within protons and neutrons and other baryons and mesons
Electromagnetic	Charged particles	Infinity	10^{-2}	Photons	Determines structures of atoms, molecules, solids and liquids
Weak	Quarks and leptons	10^{-17}m	10^{-5}	W, Z, particles	Determines stability of atomic nuclei; fuels Sun and stars
Gravitational	All	Infinity	10^{-40}	Gravitons	Assembles matter into planets, stars and galaxies

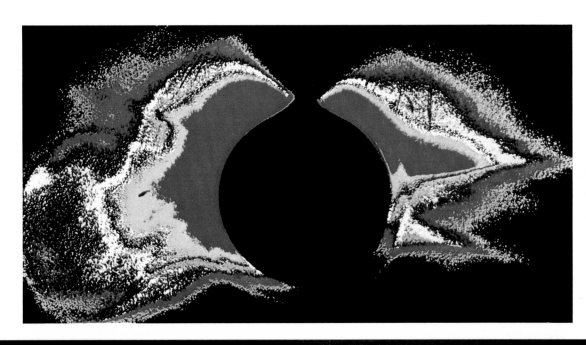

◄ This color-coded photograph of the Sun's tenuous corona, or outer atmosphere, was taken from Skylab. The corona light owes its existence to all four fundamental forces. The light itself is electromagnetic radiation. The energy that produces it comes from nuclear processes deep within the Sun, involving the weak and strong forces. Finally, the corona is held in place by the Sun's gravitation.

The search for a unified theory

The first step on the road to a unified theory was taken in the mid-19th century by the British scientists Michael Faraday (1791-1867) and James Clerk Maxwell (1831-1879), who demonstrated that electricity and magnetism are not independent forces, but parts of a unified electromagnetic force. Faraday suspected a link with gravity too, but his experiments to look for electrical effects in falling bodies were without success.

It was not until 1920 that the idea of linking electromagnetism and gravity resurfaced. At that time a new theory of gravitation had been proposed by Albert Einstein (1879-1955), called the general theory of relativity. It was a replacement of Newton's theory, which had stood unchallenged since 1687. Inspired by Einstein's work, a young German mathematician named Theodore Kaluza was seized by a curious idea. The theory of relativity links space and time together to form a four-dimensional space-time continuum. What would happen, mused Kaluza, if general relativity were formulated in *five* rather than four dimensions? This is what Kaluza did, and to everyone's astonishment it was discovered that five-dimensional gravity obeys the same laws as four-dimensional gravity as well as Maxwell's laws for the electromagnetic field. In other words, gravitation and electromagnetism are automatically unified in five dimensions, where electromagnetism is merely a component of gravity!

The only drawback of the theory concerns the extra dimension. Why don't we see it? An ingenious answer was provided by Oskar Klein. A hosepipe viewed from afar looks like a wiggly line, i.e. one-dimensional. However, on closer inspection it can be seen as a narrow tube. It is, in fact, two-dimensional, and what was taken to be a point on the line is actually a little circle going around the tube. In the same way, reasoned Klein, what we normally regard as a point in three-dimensional space could in reality be a little circle going around a fourth space dimension. Thus Kaluza's extra dimension might well exist, but be impossible to detect because it is closed (circular) and rolled up to a very small circumference. In spite of these bizarre overtones, it seems probable that in future a "theory of everything" will make use of the idea of unseen higher dimensions.

Another vital strand in the unification program which will play a central role in the search for a theory of everything is an appeal to symmetry. Symmetry is familiar in art and architecture, and in natural objects such as snowflakes. Physicists are increasingly finding that certain deep and abstract mathematical symmetries underlie the world of subatomic particles and the forces that act on them.

▲ *Abdus Salam (above) and fellow 1979 Nobel physics laureates Sheldon Glashow and Steven Weinberg suspected a link between the electromagnetic and weak forces. Experiments confirmed their prediction that certain weak-force effects would "spill over" into electromagnetism. They also showed that at very high energies the two forces would effectively merge, and three new messenger particles would appear: W^+, W^-, and Z. These were discovered in the early 1980s.*

▼ *Although nature manifests four distinct forces, physicists believe that each may be part of a smaller number of more primitive forces. At high energy, the electromagnetic and weak forces appear to merge into a single "electroweak" force. Some "grand unified theories" suggest that a further amalgamation takes place between the electroweak and strong forces at as yet unattained energies. The most ambitious unification schemes envisage an amalgamation of all four forces into a single "superforce" at ultra-high levels of energy.*

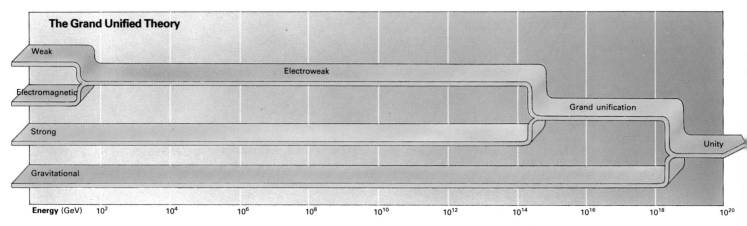

The Grand Unified Theory

Weak

Electroweak

Electromagnetic

Grand unification

Strong

Unity

Gravitational

Energy (GeV) 10^2 10^4 10^6 10^8 10^{10} 10^{12} 10^{14} 10^{16} 10^{18} 10^{20}

Hard on the heels of the electromagnetic-weak theory, enunciated by Glashow, Salam and Weinberg in the 1960s, came more ambitious theoretical attempts to bring in the strong force too. These so-called grand unified theories, or GUTs, employ the powerful concept of gauge symmetry, in a suitably embracing form to encompass three forces. GUTs not only provide models for the amalgamation of three forces, they also unify quarks and leptons. Quarks are the source of the strong force, while leptons are the source of the weak force (♦ page 10). A common description of these forces "mixes" weak and strong activity, and this effectively "mixes" the identities of quarks and leptons, enabling quarks to change into leptons. Thus, the two great classes of fundamental particles are unified in GUTs.

Experimental tests for GUTs are concentrating on two possibilities. One has to do with the ability of quarks to turn into leptons. This effect can lead protons to decay into positrons (the antiparticles of electrons). Theory predicts that on average only one proton in at least 10^{32} will decay per year: spotting proton decay is a formidable task. The second line of attack is to search for magnetic monopoles – particles that carry isolated north or south magnetic poles. All ordinary magnets are dipoles (north and south), but GUTs predict that monopoles must exist too.

▼ Physicists search for proton decay by surrounding a tank of water with photon detectors. A decay event produces a minute flash of light (photons), which can be used to reconstruct a picture of the event electronically, as in the simulation shown below. The short yellow track (center left) represents the positron, the green fork two photons. The entire experiment is performed in a deep mine to eliminate spurious events caused by cosmic rays.

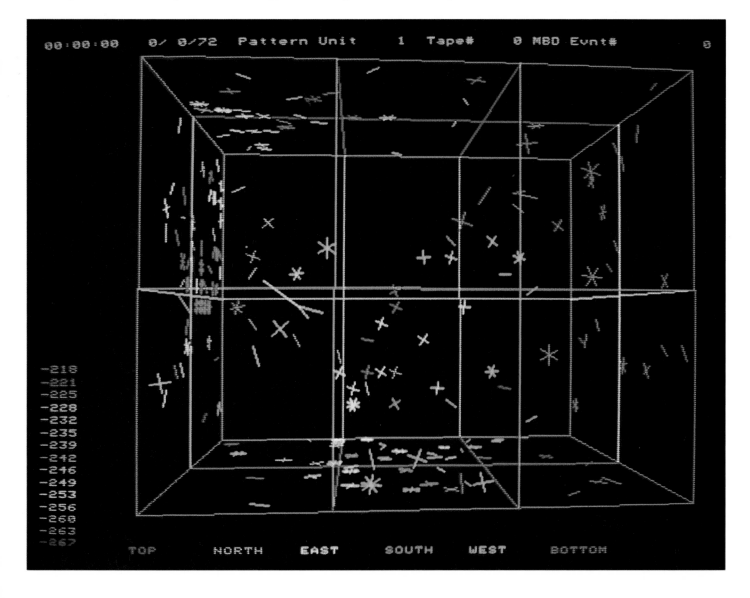

If the "superstring" theory of fundamental particles lives up to its promise, it will be possible to propose one mathematical "superlaw" of nature

Toward a theory of everything

While they wait for the experimenters, the theorists have been pushing ahead to formulate a general theory of everything. The final step is to combine something like GUTs with gravitation, thus unifying all four of nature's forces. But it seems we can do even better than that. It may be possible to unify a theory of the forces with a theory of particles.

To do this, it is necessary to make use of a still more powerful abstract symmetry known, appropriately enough, as supersymmetry. Supersymmetry is a way of grouping together particles that hitherto belonged to completely different camps. It so happens that all particles of matter possess an internal motion called spin. Roughly speaking, quarks and leptons are like little spinning tops, except that the amount of spin they carry is identical and unalterable. For historical reasons this amount is referred to as a half unit.

Messenger particles (◀ page 12) also spin, but they have either 1 or 2 units of spin. This seemingly minor difference turns out to have the most profound consequences for the behavior of the particles. There is a sharp physical division between exact-integer spin particles and half-integer spin particles. What supersymmetry does is to combine both these disparate classes into a common mathematical scheme. It suggests that, in a sense, particles of matter and messenger particles are really all part of a single supersymmetric family. Thus supersymmetry unifies matter and force into a common theme.

But what about gravitation – the missing force? The key development here may well rest with an audacious conjecture advanced a few years ago. Suppose the fundamental objects of the world are not particles at all, but something more complicated? One possibility is loops of string. The idea of modeling particles as strings is an old one. If the string wiggles one way, particle A results; if it wiggles another way, that manifests itself as particle B.

What turned the string model into a world-beater was the amazing discovery that if the strings' activity were made supersymmetric, then a particular wiggle gives the messenger particle of gravity. In other words, if supersymmetry is put into string theory, what emerges is gravity! The euphoria occasioned by this discovery has been astonishing. An army of theorists is currently exploring the mathematics of these "superstrings" in the confident expectation that they will provide the ultimate "theory of everything".

One distinctive feature of the superstrings is that they live in ten space-time dimensions; this is uniquely picked out by the theory. Thus one has to "roll up" six extra dimensions in the manner of Kaluza and Klein (◀ page 12). Major mathematical results need to be proved before it is known whether this can be done satisfactorily. Superstrings have been described as a 21st-century theory that has dropped by accident into the 20th century, and the supporting mathematics has not yet been formulated. Here is something which is destined to see significant advances in the next 30 years.

If the superstring theory lives up to its promise it will signal the end of at least a major part of theoretical physics, namely the two-and-a-half-millennia reductionist program of attempting to build the world from a small number of simple things or "atoms" (◀ page 9). If the theory succeeds in describing all the known particles and forces, and yielding correct values for such things as the masses of all the particles and the relative strengths of the forces, then it will be possible to write down a single "superlaw", a simple, all-embracing mathematical principle from which all of nature ultimately flows.

▲ When nuclei are collided at very high speed, they fleetingly recreate the conditions in the primeval universe in the first microsecond. This photograph, from the Super Proton Synchrotron machine at CERN, shows tracks of subnuclear debris left when sulfur nuclei were impacted against a lead target. Energies released at the moment of the collision are so high that the individual identities of nuclear particles are lost: a fireball of careering quarks is formed. These then recombine into jets of fast-moving protons and other subnuclear particles.

► Although subatomic particles cannot be seen directly, they can leave tracks in a device called a bubble chamber. By applying a magnetic field, the tracks can be curved, and the shapes used to identify the particles responsible by their masses and electric charges. If a high-energy particle such as a proton enters the chamber, it will collide with a resident nucleus and produce a whole shower of particles, as shown in this photograph from Fermilab, Chicago, Illinois.

▲ **Professor Michael Green (above) of London University and John Schwarz of California Institute of Technology are architects of the "superstring" theory.**

▼ **This large-scale view of the universe reveals how galaxies aggregate into clusters, filaments and sheets. This distinct "frothy" structure remains a challenge to theorists. The square gaps are artificial.**

Testing grand theories

Of course, it is far too soon to proclaim that "superstrings" are the answer. In 300 years the concepts of physics might bear as little resemblance to present ideas as superstrings do to the atoms of ancient Greece. But whatever the outcome, we are beginning to see what a theory of everything might be like, how it might be formulated. It seems unlikely that our descendants will revert to theories that treat the different aspects of nature as independent.

The real burden in the next three centuries will not be the development of fancy mathematics, but the experimental testing of these ambitious theories. All current thinking about total unification assumes that the effects of linking all the forces and particles together will only become manifest at energies that are some trillion times greater than those currently attainable in particle accelerators. Probably we shall never reach such energies directly.

If this is the case, it might seem hopeless for us ever to test our theories of everything. There remains, however, a curious possibility. According to modern cosmology, the universe was born amid an intense burst of heat energy, popularly known as the Big Bang. For a tiny fraction of a second, temperatures were achieved in that primeval fire greatly in excess of anything in the universe today. If the forces of nature really are part of a unified scheme, then for a fleeting moment the superforce will have reigned supreme. As the universe rapidly expanded and cooled, the individual forces would have separated out one by one, so that by the end of the first microsecond, the pattern of forces and the identities of the subatomic particles would have assumed the forms familiar to us today.

The successive transitions from a unified superforce to the separated individual forces would

have produced many interesting physical effects. According to one theory, the universe would have undergone a period of accelerating expansion known as "inflation", causing the Big Bang to grow even more violent. Other processes might well have produced exotic objects such as magnetic monopoles (♦ page 14) or cosmic strings.

A cosmic string is a frozen relic which traps in a narrow tube the primeval fields that permeated the cosmos in the Big Bang. Such strings are not permitted to have ends, so they must either extend to infinity or form closed loops. One theory predicts that the early universe was replete with whirling string loops. Their motion would have generated vast quantities of gravitational waves. The resulting energy drain would cause the frenetic wriggling to abate. The quiescent loops would then act as foci or "seeds" for the growth of galaxies and galactic clusters, thereby perhaps explaining the large-scale structure of the universe.

An alternative theory envisages the strings carrying a colossal electric current. The magnetic field generated by the current would be so great that it would blow huge voids in the primeval cosmic plasma. In consequence, the displaced material would lie in vast shells, where it would fragment into galaxies. Thus, one might expect a "frothy" cosmos, full of empty bubbles.

Many of the byproducts of the superforce would have vanished in the maelstrom of the Big Bang, but some of them should have survived to populate the universe today. Cosmologists are currently busy searching for evidence of these primeval entities. It is an awesome thought that if discovered, they would be a living trace of the activities of the superforce during the first brief flash of existence that some call the Creation.

Limits of Astronomy

2

*The telescope or timescope...A "horizon" in space...
A technique for observing the structure of the
universe...The destiny of the universe: "Big Crunch"
or gradual burnout?...Black holes and other ultimate
limits*

Ever since human beings first turned their heads skyward and gazed with curiosity at the stars, the mysteries of the universe have held a special fascination. Today, astronomy is a billion-dollar science. An array of special instruments – optical, infrared and radio telescopes, satellites sensitive to X-rays and gamma rays, neutrino detectors deep underground – peers into the depths of space, gathering information about the most far-flung objects in the cosmos. Already, this observing power takes astronomers close to the so-called "edge" of the observable universe.

The idea of an edge is, however, misleading. There is no suggestion that the universe has any sort of boundary. Indeed, it may well extend to infinity. Of more significance is the fact that the light (and radio) waves whereby astronomers observe the distant regions of the cosmos travel at a finite speed, so a telescope is also a "timescope". We see these regions as they were billions of years ago when the light was emitted.

▲ *The Hubble Space Telescope awaits launch by the Shuttle. Once in orbit, this instrument will be free of the disturbances caused by the Earth's atmosphere, and hence have the power to reveal a much finer level of detail than ground-based telescopes. It will consequently be able to peer much farther into the universe.*

◄ *In the desert at Socorro, New Mexico, 27 radio telescopes are linked into a "Very Large Array". The VLA can act like a single antenna dish 27km in diameter, and permits greater resolution of detail than is possible with a single radio telescope. The incoming radio waves from distant sources are merged electronically, and an image reconstructed from the data.*

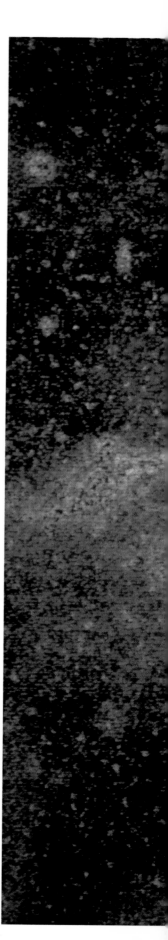

Reconstructing the Big Bang

All available evidence suggests that the entire universe originated in a huge and sudden explosion. Known as the Big Bang, this outburst occurred about 15 billion years ago, and the universe is still expanding as a result. It follows that, however powerful our instruments, we can never see more than 15 billion light years into space, for that takes us back to the point of origin. There is thus a sort of "horizon" in space. This does not imply that nothing lies beyond, any more than the horizon on Earth implies that we can see the edge of the Earth. But it does mean that we are approaching one particular absolute limit of astronomy.

Probing ever closer to the horizon amounts to probing closer to the Big Bang itself. Cosmologists believe that the Big Bang was the origin of space and time as well as matter, so, again, it represents an absolute limit beyond which we cannot push, however far our science and technology advance. Reconstructing the events that occurred during the first microseconds of the cosmos is a major branch of cosmology, and one that will develop rapidly over the next 30 years.

Vital clues about the primeval phase will come from advances in high-energy particle physics. The collision of subatomic particles at enormous speed simulates the conditions that must have prevailed during the first microsecond of the universe. The planned Superconducting Supercollider (SSC), a gargantuan American accelerator many kilometers in diameter, will push back the frontier to within a trillionth of a second of the initial Creation event.

Impressive though this seems, many theorists are interested in events at still earlier moments. It is probable that the basic structure of the cosmos, as well as its contents, was laid down even before the first million-trillion-trillionth of a second had elapsed. Will these epochs be probed by yet bigger accelerators built in future centuries? Many experts think not. The SSC probably represents the limit of foreseeable accelerator technology. Only if physicists find some totally new way of concentrating huge amounts of energy will we be able to simulate the condition of the universe during its most formative stage. In contrast, continuing progress can be expected on the astronomical front. One example of this will be the observation of cosmic heat radiation as a means of investigating the structure of the universe.

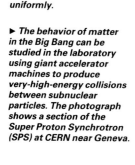

▶ *In this color-coded photograph of a typical cluster of galaxies, in the constellation of Pavo, the pink objects are the brightest, the blue are the faintest. The smaller objects are mostly foreground stars in our own galaxy. Faint halos of gas surround the galaxies. Such clusters form the "atoms" of the cosmos; they tend to aggregate into superclusters, sheets, and filaments, sometimes surrounding huge voids. Only on the largest of scales is matter distributed uniformly.*

▶ *The behavior of matter in the Big Bang can be studied in the laboratory using giant accelerator machines to produce very-high-energy collisions between subnuclear particles. The photograph shows a section of the Super Proton Synchrotron (SPS) at CERN near Geneva.*

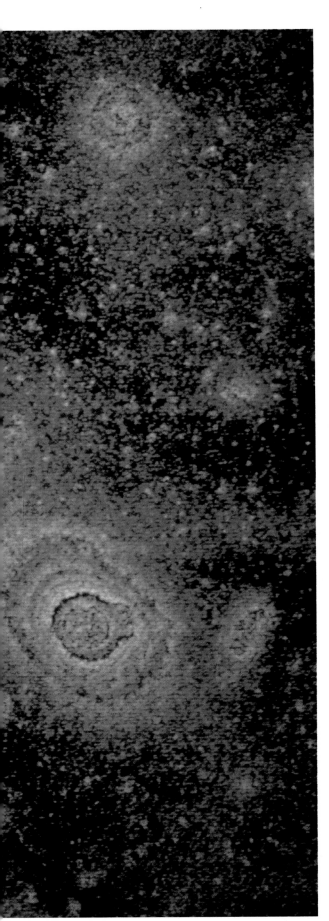

Studying the structure of the universe

The architecture of the universe has been described as "frothy" or "bubbly". Matter is not distributed evenly throughout space. Stars and gas are arranged into galaxies, and the galaxies themselves cluster together into groups. Then these galactic clusters aggregate into superclusters. There are also huge "voids" many millions of light years across with hardly a galaxy to be found. Among other patterns which can be discerned are filaments and sheets of galaxies.

A key technique for observing this structure is to measure carefully the smoothness of the heat radiation that fills all space. This radiation is another relic of the Big Bang, and it has been traveling to us across space more or less without interference since the intensely hot primeval phase. Any irregularities in the universe leave an imprint on the temperature of the cosmic heat radiation. At present, little or no variation in temperature has been found across the sky, but improving satellite technology will enable us to increase the sensitivity to the point where temperature corrugations will appear.

▼ The Sun and stars burn by nuclear fusion. European attempts to achieve controlled fusion reactions in the laboratory rest with this machine, called JET (Joint European Torus). Inside, an intensely hot plasma can briefly simulate the conditions at the center of the Sun.

Weighing the universe is the key to understanding its ultimate destiny

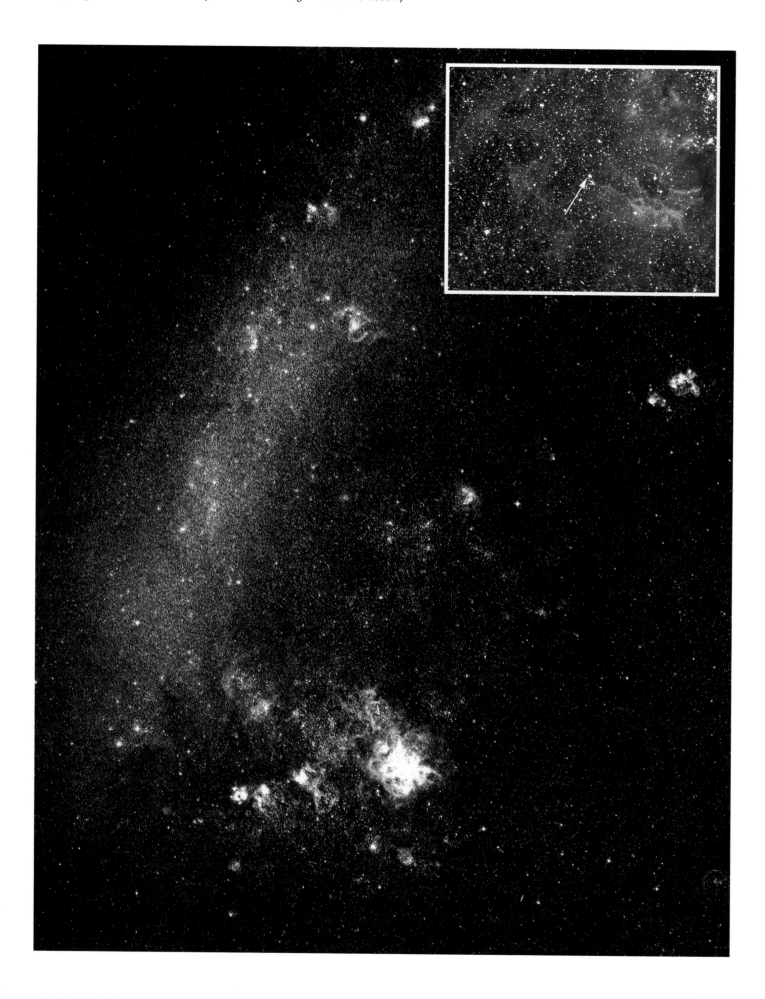

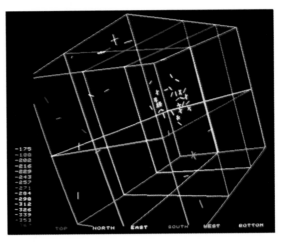

◄ *An electronically-reconstructed image of a neutrino (actually an antineutrino) event from the LMC supernova. The neutrino struck a proton in the water tank of the IMB detector (⧫ page 13), producing a positron (antielectron). The motion of the positron is represented in this electronic display by the yellow crosses.*

◄▲ *Visible to the naked eye in the Southern Hemisphere is a mini-galaxy close to our own called the Large Magellanic Cloud (LMC). On February 23, 1987 a star in the LMC (inset) was observed to explode (above). The event is known as a supernova, and it occurs when an aging massive star exhausts its fuel. The stellar core collapses, releasing a huge burst of neutrinos, which blasts the outer layers of the star into space. The explosive energy causes the shattered star to glow brighter than a billion suns. Coinciding with the LMC flare-up, particle physicists working below ground, searching for proton decay, saw instead a transient pulse of neutrinos. In spite of their star-smashing quality, neutrinos are exceedingly ephemeral entities. Most pass right through the Earth unhindered. Astronomers believe that the entire universe is bathed in neutrinos from the Big Bang, and from normal stars and supernovae.*

Are we moving toward the end of time?

The key determinant of the universe's age is its weight. The Big Bang flung the cosmic material apart, but the outward flight is continually opposed by the force of gravity. Every year the rate of cosmic expansion falls a bit as the gravity of the cosmic material restrains it. A simple calculation reveals that if there is enough mass in the universe, the expansion will eventually come to a complete halt and contraction will ensue. In that case the universe will shrink faster and faster, imploding on itself in a monstrous cataclysm that terminates in the total obliteration of space, time and matter. This awesome event is known as the "Big Crunch", and is rather like the Big Bang in reverse. If this scenario causes alarm, the alternative is no more reassuring. A universe which goes on expanding for ever is doomed to slow degeneration and eventual death, as all sources of free energy run out. All the stars are destined to burn out; it is certain that after eons of time the cosmos would be reduced to a cold, dark, almost totally empty space.

To decide which of these fates lies in store astronomers have attempted to weigh the universe to see if its gravitating power is sufficient to arrest the expansion. A simple head count of stars and gas clouds gives a value of only about one percent of the critical weight, but astronomers guess that for every gram of visible matter there are at least ten grams of invisible matter. The main problem is that nobody at present knows what this invisible matter is. Suggestions range from black holes, to dim stars, to exotic subatomic particles coughed out by the Big Bang, among them the ghostly neutrinos, thought to be the most common objects in the universe. Particle physicists have identified a whole range of other similar particles – gravitinos, photinos, axinos – that could provide enough "missing mass" to halt the cosmic expansion. Detecting and totting up all these products of the Big Bang is well-nigh impossible in the coming decades, but the particle theorists may be able to deduce their properties, enabling an accurate sum to be performed.

In the absence of information about these unseen particles, astronomers can attempt to weigh the universe directly from the way it moves. For example, stars orbit in galaxies faster than they should if the only mass were the visible material. Our own Milky Way, for example, is known to have a massive halo of unknown matter around it. Also, galaxies in clusters are seen to fall together faster than they should if the only mass present were the known mass of the galaxies. And the slowdown of the overall cosmic expansion is a measure of the total gravitating content. We can expect a great improvement in the precise measurement of all these effects over the next 30 years.

See also
Limits of Astronomy 17-22
The Space Agenda 23-40
Moving Around in Space 41-54

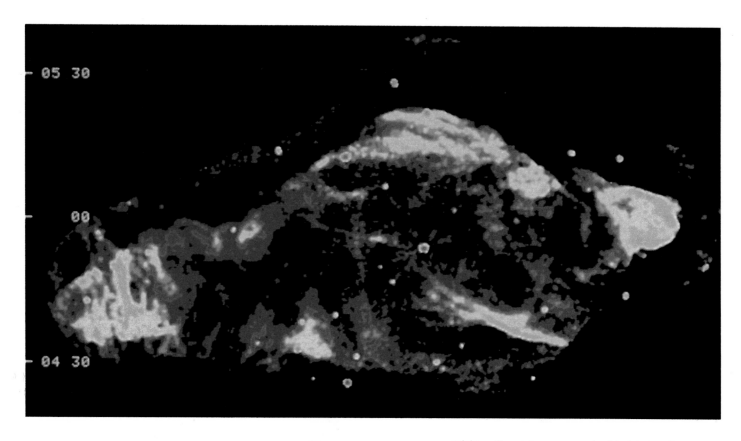

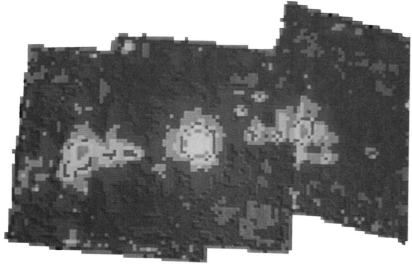

▲ **Astronomers are puzzled by a weird object called SS 433, which might be a supernova remnant, perhaps in the form of a black hole surrounded by gas. The top photograph shows a color-coded radio map of this region. Below is an X-ray image: SS 433 is the central white spot.**

Black holes and other monstrosities

Whatever befalls the universe as a whole, scientists know that local regions of the cosmos are vulnerable to a miniature version of the Big Crunch. The overwhelming power of gravity is capable of crushing individual stars and imploding them into black holes. Inside a black hole, matter is squeezed out of existence at a so-called space-time singularity, where space and time come to an end.

Black holes are believed to lie in the centers of a whole range of astronomical objects that are currently being discovered. The mysterious quasars provide a good example. These are incredibly compact, exceedingly energetic objects that tend to flare up and emit vast quantities of radiation. Quasars might well contain supermassive black holes. As surrounding gaseous material falls into the holes, enormous quantities of energy are released that give the quasars the appearance of exploding violently.

Similar effects could be occurring in certain "disturbed" galaxies that seem to be ejecting spurts of material at very high speed, or emitting intense quantities of radio waves or X-rays. On a smaller scale, within our own Galaxy are objects such as the enigmatic SS 433, a sort of mini-quasar. Here too, jets of high-energy material are streaming out, and gravity could again be the power source, either in the form of a black hole, or some other collapsed object such as a neutron star.

As well as improved conventional telescopes, the next 30 years should see the advent of "gravity wave" telescopes. Violent gravitational disturbances, such as the collapse of a star to form a black hole, set up ripples of gravitation that spread out through space in the form of waves. Although incredibly weak, this gravitational radiation could eventually provide as much information as electromagnetic radiation. To detect it, astronomers have to be able to measure minute quivering motions in delicately suspended metal bars or systems of mirrors. A typical stellar implosion in our Galaxy will shake these instruments by no more than a thousandth of the radius of an atomic nucleus. Incredibly, however, the technology to spot this is already becoming available.

Looking 300 years ahead, it is almost impossible to forecast the shape of astronomy. Undoubtedly many new objects will have been discovered that will require new physics for their proper understanding. New instruments will provide the sort of information that is as yet undreamt of by scientists.

The Space Agenda

3

From Sputnik 1 to the Moon landings...Exploring the planets...Giotto...A new impetus to space exploration... Telescopes...Space stations...Industrialization of space... Permanent colonies in Earth orbit...Bases on planets... "Glasnost" in space?...Motives for exploring space

On October 4, 1957 a tiny man-made object the size of a football changed man's perception of space for ever. It was of course Sputnik 1 – the first artificial satellite. The little more than 30 years since then have seen an astonishing catalog of achievement. Twelve men have walked on the surface of the Moon; unmanned spaceprobes have visited all but two of the planets; and there has been a fleeting but dramatic encounter with a comet. Yet every mission provides as many questions as answers: there is still so much to learn. We have taken only the first steps on a long road of exploration. The following pages chart something of the achievements so far, and look ahead to the time when man will truly be "man in space".

The shockwave that Sputnik 1 sent through the United States was redoubled four years later on April 12, 1961. On that day the Russian Yuri Gagarin became the first main in space and the first to go into orbit. Even though Alan Shephard safely made a 15-minute suborbital flight the next month, it was not enough. Something had to be done to restore the United States' self-esteem and faith in their engineers and scientists. On May 25, 1961, John F. Kennedy gave expression to this sentiment when he announced that "This nation should commit itself to achieve the goal, before the decade is out, of landing a man on the Moon and returning him safely to Earth."

First brief encounters with the Moon
The USA's commitment to land a man on the Moon before the 1960s were out was one of the boldest possible; yet, astonishingly, it was achieved with five months to spare. On Christmas Eve 1968, Apollo 8 with its three-man crew was orbiting the Moon; and none who experienced it will ever forget the night of July 19-20, 1969, when Neil Armstrong and Buzz Aldrin walked on the Moon – while Mike Collins circled patiently overhead. In the meantime, both superpowers had sent a whole series of unmanned probes to photograph and eventually land on the Moon. After Apollo 11, six more crews set off for the Moon: one – Apollo 13 – was rather lucky to return unhurt; the others reached their target, and brought back several hundred kilos of very expensive moonrock. But by 1972 public interest had almost vanished, and both space powers seemed content to leave the Moon for the foreseeable future.

▲ *Geologist Harrison Schmitt, the only scientist in six crews who landed on the Moon, took part in the final mission, Apollo 17. The Apollo program was an historic item on the Space Agenda. How long before we return to our nearest neighbor in Space?*

◄ *Part of the Belgian, Dutch, French and English coasts photographed from Spacelab in November, 1985 by Dutch astronaut Wubbo Ockels. This 7-day science mission to near-Earth orbit pointed the way for later, longer missions and, eventually, permanent space stations.*

Voyager 2's encounter with Neptune will conclude an epic 12-year mission in space

Venus and Mars

Exploration of the Solar System began in earnest in 1961, when the Soviet Union launched its first probe to Venus. This failed, and it was left to the United States National Aeronautics and Space Administration's Mariner 2 in December 1962 to become the first successful planetary probe. But throughout the 1960s the Soviet Union launched more Venera probes, and scored several firsts. In October 1967 Venera 4 managed to penetrate the hot, dense atmosphere of Venus to land on the surface and send radio signals back for over an hour.

NASA's Mariner 4 was the first probe to reach Mars, flying past in July 1965 and returning 11 photographs of the surface. Two more Mariner craft flew by 1969, followed by the first Mars orbiter, Mariner 9, in 1971. Two Soviet orbiters dropped landers on the surface at around the same time, but they were engulfed in great dust storms. In 1974 the Russians attempted landings again with four probes, one of which, Mars 5, was a success.

For the Russians, part of the problem at that time was unreliable technology. They turned their attention for a while to Venus, which is nearer to the Earth than Mars. In 1975 Veneras 9 and 10 returned from orbit the first pictures of the planet's surface, and were followed by further missions in 1978. They were joined by two Pioneer Venus orbiters. In 1982, two more Veneras sent back surface pictures and radar maps.

It was NASA's Viking mission that achieved the first successful landing on Mars, in 1976. Two orbiters dropped landers on the surface, and the amazing pictures they returned show an arid, red-brown desert landscape. No sign of life was detected, but many mysteries remain. Both the United States and the Soviet Union are planning to return to Mars in the near future to find out more (◆ pages 28, 29).

The giant planets

The launch of the Voyager probes to the distant, giant worlds of Jupiter and Saturn, and the astonishing pictures they sent back, recaptured some of the excitement lost when the Moon program ended in 1972. Jupiter, by far the largest of the planets, with a mass more than 300 times that of the Earth, was first inspected by the tiny Pioneer 10 spacecraft launched in 1973 on a voyage which has no end – for Pioneer has now left the Solar System and is voyaging on toward the stars. No living being is ever likely to encounter it in the vastness of space – but just in case, it carries a little plaque engraved with a man, a woman and a diagram of our Solar System. Pioneer told us a great deal about the giant planets but their real beauty was revealed in the striking images sent back by the two much larger Voyager spacecraft as they swept past Jupiter. For the first time we saw striking close-up views of the tiny worlds of Jupiter's principal satellites. Then the Voyagers journeyed on past Saturn and its rings for still more spectacular images.

Uranus and beyond

Voyager 2's passage by Saturn was close enough to pull it into a new path – set for encounter with two more distant planets, Uranus and Neptune. Three-and-a-half years later, in January, 1986, Voyager passed through the ring system of Uranus, and set off for its last encounter – with Neptune, due in August, 1989. If that, too, succeeds it will conclude an epic of space exploration: a 12-year mission, sending signals and images back from the furthest edge of the Solar System, from every known planet except tiny Pluto.

▶▶ On August 20, 1977, Voyager 2 set off from Cape Canaveral on its 12-year mission to the outer planets, Jupiter, Saturn, Uranus and Neptune. The artist's impression (far right) shows Voyager 2 nearing Uranus on January 24, 1986. The large dish antenna is for radio communication across some 4.5bn km. Other instruments are for magnetic and optical observations. Within a few hours Voyager swept past the planet and through the plane of its ring system. The cloud-belts forecast in the picture were not in fact found: Uranus appeared as a featureless blue disk. The planet has no solid surface, and is covered with a dense, poisonous atmosphere. It has at least 9 rings and 5 small satellites.

◄ The surface of Mars, seen from the unmanned Viking 2 space probe. The horizon is tilted because one of Viking's feet landed on a rock. The soil samples scooped up and analyzed by the onboard laboratory provided inconclusive results. The biological tests gave no proof of life; but some doubts remain.

▶ *Europe's space scientists prepare to take the first-ever close-up look at a comet: the scene inside the European Space Agency's Operations Centre (ESOC), Darmstadt, West Germany, as Giotto neared Halley's Comet. Screens show the radio tracking network, Giotto, and returning data.*

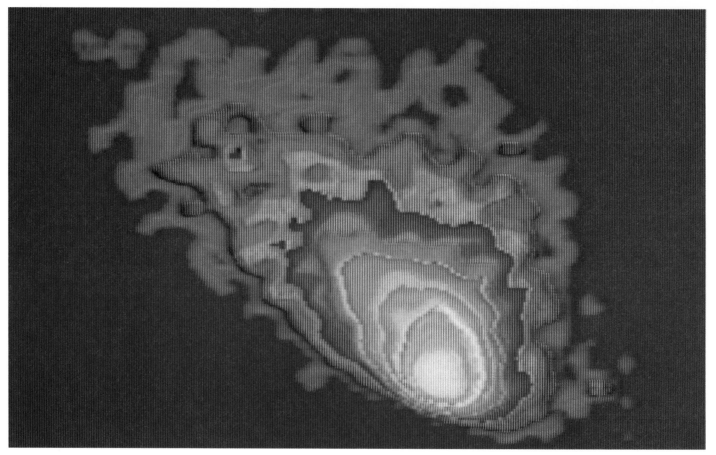

Mission to a comet

The one space mission of recent years that really gripped the public's imagination was the encounter with Halley's Comet. It may not be the most spectacular but this is the one comet about which most people have heard. Orbiting the Sun every 76 years, its return in 1985-1986 gave astronomers their first-ever opportunity to get a close look at a comet. Europe's space scientists made the running, as the United States' plans were shelved on cost grounds; and while Soviet and Japanese satellites did observe Halley's Comet from a distance, only Giotto, designed and built by the European Space Agency and its member countries, came really close.

The probe was launched in July, 1985 and after an eight-month journey it flashed across the comet's path on the night of March 13, 1986. "Flashed" is no exaggeration: Giotto's speed relative to the comet nucleus was much faster than that of a rifle bullet. The minutes before closest encounter were among the most tense since men walked on the Moon: the big worry was whether Giotto would be destroyed, or its delicate instruments put out of action, by the impact at devastating speed of a few particles of the thick cloud of dust surrounding the comet. A grain of sand at that speed could tear a hole right through the protective shielding. At first all went well and the images sent back grew larger and clearer on the screens as Giotto rushed closer to the comet. Although a comet appears large, it is in reality just a huge, thin cloud of vapor and ice crystals reflecting the Sun's light. At its center is the only solid part, a tiny nucleus a few kilometers across. In order to reveal any detail, Giotto had to send pictures back from a distance of 1,000 kilometers or less. The closest approach was about 500 kilometers and the scientists almost won their gamble. Giotto got to within 1,000 kilometers when the picture on the screens shook, then vanished. Particle impacts had knocked the camera out of alignment. Some 20 minutes later contact was regained, but while other instruments worked, no more pictures were returned.

Even so, it was a triumph: enough images and other data had been sent back to give astronomers a better idea than ever before of a comet's nature. The general conclusion favored the "dirty snowball" theory.

Giotto is still in orbit around the Sun, and there are plans to try for another comet encounter in a few years' time, but it remains uncertain whether the cameras can be made to work again. Further missions to other comets are therefore included among the space scientists' plans for the future.

A new impetus in space exploration

After a dramatic start, the exploration of space has lost momentum. The Space Shuttle tragedy in 1986 and other launcher failures set the United States' program back at least three years. There seemed also to have been a loss of drive, almost of interest. Now, however, things are changing again. The United States, Europe and the Soviet Union all have ambitious programs for the next 15 years.

In the United States, the new commitment stems from the acceptance in principle of the 1986 report of the National Commission on Space charged with redefining the nation's space aims. The report, *Pioneering the Space Frontier*, makes fascinating reading. It reaffirms Kennedy's goal of leadership in space (◀ page 23), and calls for a return to the Moon, manned flight eventually to Mars and, as a first step, the building of a large, permanently-manned space station. In the near future, there will be more robot missions to the planets.

◀ The closest-ever view of a comet, a computer-enhanced image of Halley's Comet, as seen by Giotto from a distance of less than 1,000km. The images were full of surprises: the nucleus was far darker than had been expected – its surface is made up of sooty deposits left behind when some of the ice that makes up the comet – which is like a giant dirty snowball – is evaporated by the Sun's heat. The ice crystals, spread over millions of kilometers, form the comet's tail.

◀ January 28, 1986, a bleak day in the story of space: 7 astronauts perish as the Space Shuttle "Challenger" explodes in a ball of fire just 73 seconds after lift-off. The disaster gave rise to endless inquiry and soul-searching. Had safety been sacrificed by pushing the program ahead too fast? It was a tremendous blow – but President Reagan at once reaffirmed US commitment to the exploration of space.

The planets revisited

The first robot mission to be featured in NASA's firm plans is Magellan, a new voyage to Venus. After launch in October, 1989 this is due to reach Venus after a four-month journey and send back the first high-resolution radar map of the planet's surface, forever hidden from our eyes beneath a thick blanket of cloud. Within a year of Magellan, two other planetary missions are due to be launched by the Space Shuttle: Galileo, a new probe to Jupiter, and the first of a new series of manned Spacelab flights. But for astronomers the real excitement centers on the long-delayed launch of the Hubble Space Telescope.

Later in the 1990s while much of the United States' space energies will go into the development of the space station, there will be other planetary missions. A further look at a comet, a mission to the asteroid belt, and the development of a Mars lander which will carry with it a mobile laboratory, the Mars Rover, are all under study.

Return to Mars

It will not be long before Mars and its satellites come under close scrutiny again. In July, 1988 the Soviet Union came back into the game with the launch of their two Phobos missions, named for the Martian satellite of the same name, their principal target. The mission program includes a detailed three-month study from low orbit, looking at the surface and identifying potential landing-sites, using laser beams to examine the texture, and low swoops to drop instrument packages onto the surface. Phobos – an irregular-shaped rock only a few kilometers across – offers intriguing possibilities as a future landing-site or even a semi-permanent base. Its very small gravity means that it will actually take less energy, and therefore less fuel, to land a rocket there and bring it back than was needed to go to the Moon and return. The Soviet space scientists intend to follow up this first Mars mission with others to land on its surface – probably carrying Mars Rovers – and eventually, around 1998, they have an ambitious plan to land an unmanned spacecraft to scoop up samples and return them to Earth.

Europe in space

In Europe, too, things are moving again. There has always been a strong desire to keep a foothold in the new technology through a lively program of research and exploration. Much of that has been in fields which offer good practical returns: communications and Earth-observation satellites (the French SPOT is the highest-definition civilian "eye in the sky"). Scientific exploration has also been a strong thread, the most dramatic example being the successful Giotto mission to Halley's Comet (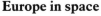 page 26). Now the European Space Agency, backed enthusiastically by most of its member states, has launched a bold new program with four main themes: Columbus, Hermes, Ariane 5 and a series of science satellites.

Columbus is Europe's contribution to the NASA Space Station (♦ page 32). While Americans will build and operate most of the station, ESA will provide one of the four laboratory modules that form the central structure. Europe will also build a separate polar platform – a satellite to fly scientific instruments in orbit above the Earth's poles. The unmanned science satellites due to be launched during the 1990s include the HIPPARCOS telescope (♦ page 31) and the ISO (Infrared Space Observatory), the most powerful telescope of its kind yet designed. Also planned is a cluster of satellites to study the Sun's magnetic field, and the joint ESA/NASA project, Ulysses.

▲ The Ulysses space probe undergoes final trials at the European Space Agency's test center in the Netherlands. Ulysses will be launched on the US Space Shuttle in 1990. Unlike any other space probe, it will leave the ecliptic – the plane containing the Sun and planets – and soar millions of kilometers above the Sun to study it from over its poles.

▼ Hermes, Europe's proposed man-carrying shuttle, is seen in this impression being launched by the very powerful Ariane 5 which is being developed for the mid-1990s. Hermes, strongly favored by the French, is without doubt the most controversial part of Europe's space program. A miniature Space Shuttle, it will carry a crew of 3.

◄ *An Ariane 3, Europe's main commercial satellite launcher, on the pad at Kourou, French Guiana. June, 1988 saw the first flight of the more powerful Ariane 4, which will become ESA's principal workhorse.*

▼ *NASA's Mars Observer will be launched in 1992 from the Transfer Orbit Stage (TOS). After deployment from the Space Shuttle, the TOS will fire its engine for just over 2 minutes to reach escape velocity. The moment of separation (below) will come 20 minutes later, as the Observer sets off on its long journey.*

Telescopes in space

The difficulties, and the cost, of putting large telescopes into Earth orbit are tremendous – so why do it? In a word, the reason is our atmosphere. It not only enables us to breathe, but protects our skins from the most harmful of the Sun's rays, the ultraviolet wavelengths. But, earthbound astronomers can never "see" ultraviolet light from the stars nor indeed, most of the infrared radiation and X-rays. In fact astronomers can peer through just a few small gaps in the curtain which conceals much of the electromagnetic spectrum of signals. The atmosphere even distorts the visible light that it does let through. Air is not perfectly transparent, nor is it pure: it bends and absorbs light, and the dust it contains scatters the light. Like a restless ocean, the atmosphere is forever in motion. All in all, doing astronomy from the ground is like trying to see the outside world from the bottom of a none-too-clean swimming-pool.

As soon as rockets and spacecraft became available, astronomers clamored to fly instruments on them to detect wavelengths more or less "invisible" from the Earth's surface. Over the past 20 or so years, the first attempts have been made to work in all these wavebands, and some basic maps of the universe's X-ray and infrared radiation sources made. The Infra Red Astronomy Satellite (IRAS) flown by British, Dutch and United States astronomers in 1983 was particularly successful.

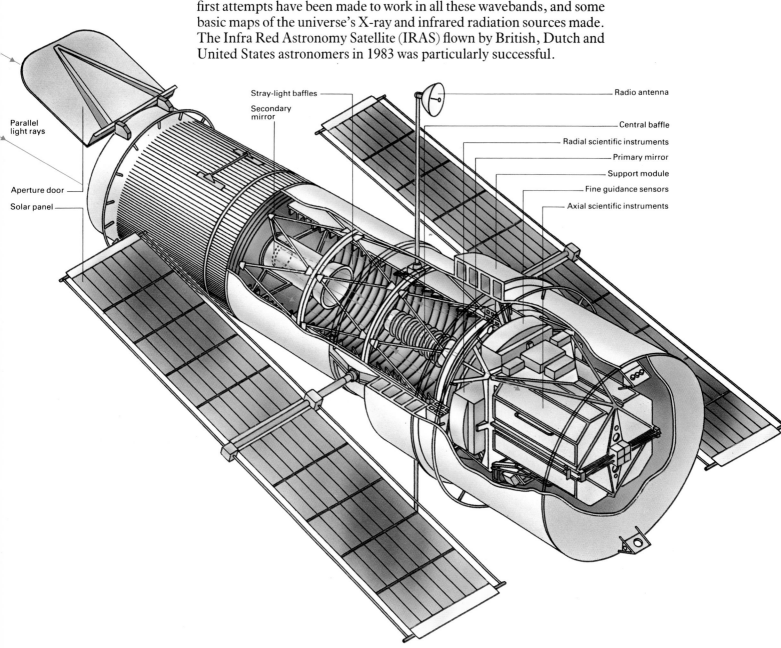

Parallel light rays

Aperture door

Solar panel

Stray-light baffles

Secondary mirror

Radio antenna

Central baffle

Radial scientific instruments

Primary mirror

Support module

Fine guidance sensors

Axial scientific instruments

Probing the galaxies

Over the next few years better and more powerful instruments are planned which will open new windows on the universe. But first to fly are two instruments designed to work with visible light. The Hubble Space Telescope (HST) is the largest space astronomy instrument yet built – more than 14 meters long. A joint project of United States and European astronomers, it would have flown on the Space Shuttle in 1986 but for the Challenger tragedy. Its great advantage lies in the extreme sharpness of its images. A good telescope on a high mountain site may achieve a resolution of about one second of arc (roughly a three-thousandth of a degree). Such sharpness of image is roughly equivalent to being able to read the headlines in a newspaper from a distance of one kilometer. The Hubble Space Telescope is expected to do about 10 times better – reading the "fine print" in the paper. It should reveal new and unsuspected detail in the most distant galaxies.

Mapping the heavens

Two thousand years ago the Greek astronomer Hipparchus made the first real map of the heavens, showing the positions of the 800 brightest stars. Ever since, astronomers have sought to improve on his work, and today hundreds of thousands of stars are mapped, with a completeness and accuracy limited only by the atmosphere. The science of astrometry – mapping the heavens – will take its greatest stride forward with the launch in 1989 of HIPPARCOS (the name is an acronym), the aptly-named star-mapping satellite built by Europe's astronomers.

HIPPARCOS will do more than measure the positions of the 120,000 brightest stars selected for inclusion in its control catalog. During its two-and-a-half years' mission it will measure each one several times, and detect the very small movements over the period. These will give the stars' real movements in the sky. The apparent motion backward and forward every six months, as the Earth moves in its yearly journey round the Sun – the parallax – is a measure of the star's distance from Earth. So HIPPARCOS will give the positions, distances and motions of all 120,000 stars with never before attainable accuracy. The astronomers' dream of the best-ever star map – a map for the 21st century – is nearing achievement.

▼ *The Optical Telescope Assembly – seen here on its final assembly stand at the Perkin-Elmer works in Connecticut, USA – is the heart of the billion-dollar Hubble Space Telescope. Precautions including dust screens and workers' protective clothing ensure that not a scrap of dust reaches the delicate optical surfaces.*

◄ *The Hubble Space Telescope is much the largest space-astronomy instrument yet built. The telescope assembly houses the 2.4-meter diameter primary mirror (not large compared with the biggest on Earth), which is of great light-gathering power. Coupled to it, a battery of instruments will wring the last bit of information from the light received.*

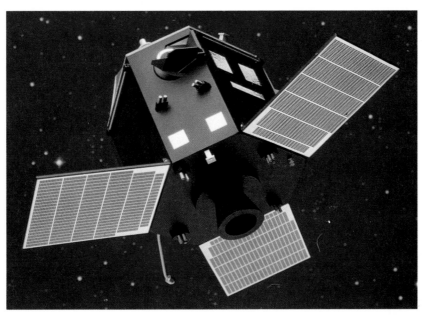

◄ *HIPPARCOS, star-mapper extraordinary: this small but astonishingly accurate telescope is seen as it will appear in orbit. Each star image produces a pulse of current in a sensitive photodetector, enabling its brightness and position to be computed with great precision. HIPPARCOS could measure the size of a golfball held up in London, from the distance of New York.*

Lightweight structures used in space would buckle and collapse under gravity on Earth's surface

Space stations – bases in orbit

Manned bases in Earth orbit have been central to the space enthusiast's dream for decades. Their most significant feature, permanent manning, 24 hours a day, 365 days a year, will give them maximum flexibility to meet new and still-unforeseen tasks or emergencies. For however good our robots become (and they have become very good indeed: witness the exploration of the planets), human beings are still the most adaptable all-purpose machines. Space stations will be unsurpassed laboratories for all kinds of observations in astronomy, meteorology and earth resources. Microgravity experiments and small-scale production of crystals or pharmaceuticals can also take place there in low-gravity factories alongside the main space station. Above all, such platforms are an essential stepping-stone to planetary exploration.

The space enthusiast's dreams are now taking solid shape. The Soviet Union, after years of steady preparation, already has its first space station, Mir: rudimentary, but capable of much expansion and improvement (page 34). After years of indecision, the United States is going ahead too. President Reagan ordered planning to start in 1984, and – provided Congress continues to approve the substantial cost – NASA should be ready to start "cutting metal" quite soon.

How will the space station be built? Its mass of several hundred tonnes makes it essential to assemble it in orbit from smaller units within the 30-tonne lifting capacity of the Space Shuttle. Starting, it is hoped, in 1994 it will take about a dozen flights to carry into orbit the main elements of the station, and another half-dozen to bring up supplies and equipment. By 1996, if all goes well, the first permanent crew of four astronauts will be in place. The cost of all this is estimated at some $15 billion: a lot of money, but much less than the Apollo Moon program. Europe, Japan and Canada will contribute units. In the mid- to late 1990s, the serious work can begin – and there seems to be no reason why the station, continually altered and added to as requirements change, should not continue in use for decades, in the absence of both gravitational stress and atmospheric corrosion.

▼▶ *When planning of the US Space Station began, many designs were considered. Early proposals (right) included a T-shaped structure in 1982 and the 1984 "triangular" plan. The absence of gravity means that lighter, less rigid-looking structures are possible, and consequently the dual-keel concept evolved (below). When built in the mid-1990s, the Space Station will probably be a somewhat simpler form of that shown here. The main laboratories and living units (a full crew will be 8) are in the four central cylindrical units, each about the size of a railway carriage. They are interconnected by linking units, each with several hatches and docking-ports. Smaller storage and experiment areas are also attached. Stretching nearly 100m into space, a light lattice framework supports an array of radio antennae, scientific experiments and solar panels to provide power of at least 75kw.*

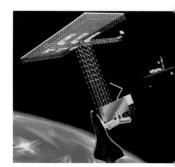

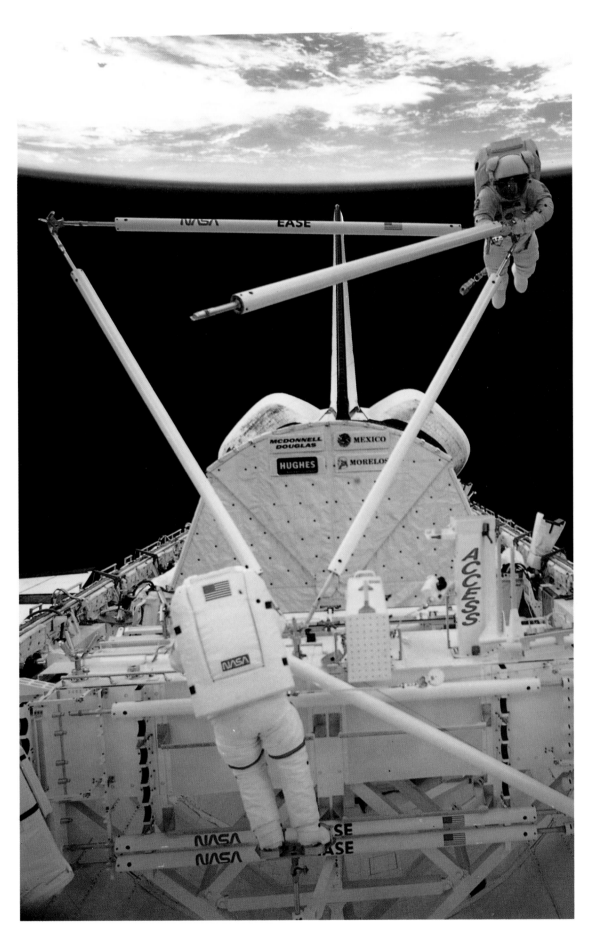

◄ Shuttle astronauts
practice space assembly
techniques. The Space
Station will weigh
hundreds of tonnes. Major
units, such as the living and
laboratory modules, will be
taken up complete in the
Shuttle's cargo bay, but the
huge lattice framework
must be assembled in space
like a giant construction
toy. Some of the work will
be done by a remote-
controlled manipulator arm,
the rest by free-flying,
spacesuited astronauts.

The powerful "Energia" launcher may get Soviet cosmonauts to Mars before the year 2010

Living on the station

*We already have a good idea, from the United States'
Skylab and, more importantly, from the Soviet
Union's long-endurance orbit flights, what kind of
conditions the crews will face during their stints in
space, probably for three months at a time. The
problem of weightlessness, the need for regular
exercise, and the trials of living in rather cramped
surroundings (but no more so than those faced by a
submarine crew!) are now familiar. In one respect –
the fight against boredom – there should be less
difficulty. The larger size of the station, the possibility
of frequent EVAs (extra-vehicular activities), and the
challenge of this new venture, should see to that.
Finally, what if emergency strikes – a systems
failure, or perhaps serious illness or accident to one
of the crew? For this, studies are in hand for a space
lifeboat – a capsule able to return independently of
any Earth-launched rescue mission.*

Mir and after: the Soviet perspective

In February, 1986, the Soviet Union launched a new spacecraft that was their first step in the permanent colonization of space. The orbiting laboratory Mir ("peace") and its systems were tested out by a two-man crew and soon declared operational. Since February, 1987 Mir has been permanently occupied by a succession of cosmonaut crews, including Yuri Romanenko, whose 326-day stay set a new duration record for manned spaceflight. More significantly for future plans, in May, 1987 the Soviet Union also tested the most powerful launcher ever built, Energia ("Energy"). Its launching capacity and the continual operation of Mir will eventually enable Soviet cosmonauts to reach Mars.

The purpose of the Soviet space program has often been misunderstood. In the early days, Khrushchev undoubtedly saw space as a propaganda weapon. But having lost the race to the Moon, the aim of the Soviet Union became more modest: to develop the use of space stations in Earth orbit. A succession of seven Salyut space laboratories gave them a lead in just this area, each one building on experience from the previous ones. The Soviet philosophy is of slow, continual evolution and in a sense, they have never thrown away anything that works – merely adding to and developing the technology. Thus the Soyuz transport vehicle still in use today is a variant of the very first one launched in 1967. And Mir is a descendant of Salyut.

However, when the technology does not work, the space scientists of the Soviet Union start again. The race to the Moon was lost because the heavy-lift launcher then being developed never became operational. So Energia was developed from scratch. Its potential is enormous, particularly when compared with the other launchers in use today: Europe's Ariane can launch 5-8 tonnes into orbit; the Space Shuttle can lift 30 tonnes; but Energia could launch 200 tonnes. So a mere handful of launches a year could build up a large station in space.

In the near future, Mir will form the nucleus of a large complex to which several other modules will be added. Already an astronomical observatory, Kvant ("quantum") is in place, and other units will follow every few months – an accomodation unit, an engineering laboratory, a biomedical unit and so on. This enlarged space station will then be serviced by a new reusable space shuttle, similar to but a little smaller than that of NASA. Launched on Energia, it will regularly ferry crews and supplies to Mir by the mid-1990s.

Industry in orbit

The Soviet Union was quick to see the practical value of space. They make constant use of weather and remote-sensing satellites to plan agricultural production, for instance. They performed the first welding experiments in space, and have developed elaborate pharmaceutical and metallurgical production equipment on the Salyut and Mir craft. Some western observers are convinced that their long-term aim is the large-scale industrialization of space.

By converting sunlight into infrared radiation, the Sun's energy could be sent back to Earth in a concentrated laser beam. On the ground, vast arrays of solar cells would convert the incoming energy into hundreds of megawatts of electrical power to feed vast solar-power stations. The Soviet Union might thus meet the pressing energy shortages of the next century. Such plans may seem like science fiction, but there is a telling precedent. Within five years of Sputnik 1, the Soviet Union had launched the first animal safely into space, the first probes to the Moon and Venus, and the first human being to fly in orbit.

◄ Link-up in space: the Soyuz space transport vehicle, workhorse of the Soviet program, photographed from a porthole of the specially adapted Apollo spacecraft that took part in the historic Soviet-US space link-up of July, 1975. Perhaps that brief encounter was a forerunner of things to come?

◄ West German Ulf Merbold works on Spacelab 1, carried into orbit by the Space Shuttle in November, 1983. Spacelab was brought back to Earth after a 10-day flight and refurbished. The Spacelab flights were NASA's first serious attempt to do biomedical and microgravity experiments in orbit.

Colonies in space

The idea of men and women working and living in large, self-supporting orbiting space colonies has long been a favorite of science-fiction writers, but its acceptance as a serious scientific possibility is surprisingly recent, and owes its genesis primarily to one man, the Princeton physicist, Professor Gerard O'Neill.

In theory a space habitat – as the colonies are often called – could be established in stable orbit almost anywhere in space. A low Earth orbit (at some 300 kilometers), like that of the planned Space Station, has the advantage of being relatively easy to reach, but with the serious drawback of orbiting the Earth every two hours or so. The geostationary orbit, 36,000 kilometers above the Earth's surface, has more attractions: a habitat there would enjoy a 24-hour day and night cycle, as we do, and remain always above the same point on Earth. The favored location is much further out, at a point on the Moon's orbit. This is the so-called "fifth Lagrange point" (L5), named for its discoverer, the French mathematician J.L. Lagrange (1736-1813). At this point, the Earth's and Moon's gravitational fields are in balance, and an object placed there is completely stable. To get there from the Moon, say, or to leave the habitat, requires the minimum energy.

Building the colony

A key part of O'Neill's idea is that there is no need to bring all the material for the colony up from Earth. Much of it could be mined and prepared for use at a Moon base, and then hurled out to the L5 point by a kind of space gun called a mass driver. This uses powerful magnetic fields to accelerate a sled or bucket containing the load to a very high speed; the cargo is then released and hurled into space just as a stone is flung from a catapult. This idea is no mere flight of fancy, as small versions of the device have already been built. Furthermore, on the Moon gravity is only one-sixth what it is on Earth. Using a mass driver, the large amount of materials needed could be assembled at the chosen point in orbit for a small fraction of the energy needed to bring it out from Earth. A similar system might be used to power space vehicles (◆ page 94).

"Island One"

There is of course a minimum size below which no habitat could be made even moderately self-supporting. O'Neill suggests we should start with a habitat, which he calls "Island One", able to support a population of a few thousand people – 10,000 at most. The size of such an "island" works out to be surprisingly small: a sphere less than 500 meters in diameter – only 4-5 times the largest dimension of the Space Station that the United States is already planning for the 1990s. The inside surface of such a sphere would provide rather more living-space for each inhabitant than many towns on Earth today, as well as enough space for the intensive cultivation of the necessary food crops.

Sufficient space, imaginative landscaping, an atmosphere as near to Earth's own as we choose to make it (but without the pollution!) and an Earth-like artificial gravity could all be provided. The gravity field would be produced by making the whole sphere rotate about twice a minute. Tests on volunteers have already shown that most people can adapt quite well to that rate of rotation, but anything more tends to cause discomfort. This is another factor limiting the minimum size of island, as the smaller it is, the faster it must spin to produce normal gravity. (For discussion of the much larger "world ships", ◆ page 52.)

▲ *A large laboratory and observatory complex is portrayed in this artist's impression of a possible development from the Space Station (seen in the background). From there, more and bigger laboratories and even manufacturing facilities would lead – according to some predictions – to a major leap forward, to the establishment of whole self-supporting communities in space.*

▶ *Why live in space? Human nature has always been to colonize new territories, sooner or later, once they have been discovered. There could be some very practical reasons, but these are unlikely to include the more efficient running of business communities indicated ironically in this vision. Low-gravity factories could carry on the manufacture of valuable crystals and other materials in a way impossible on Earth. Perhaps more importantly, huge platforms gathering solar energy and beaming it down to Earth are seriously being considered as one possible answer to any future energy crisis. By far the cheapest place to make them would be a factory in or alongside a space colony.*

Planetary bases

Perhaps the most important space development in the 21st century will be the construction of bases on the planets. It will not be easy; and there are only a handful of worlds that could conceivably be colonized. Mercury and Venus are too hot, the outer planets too cold. Only the Moon, Mars and its moons, and maybe the asteroids remain to be considered. Aware of losing their lead in space, many in the United States' space community feel that such bases should be their long-term goal.

There are two schools of thought in the United States about where the first base might be established. Scientists at the Johnson Space Center in Houston, Texas, favor a "lunar initiative", starting with mining operations on this nearest possible planetary base. The lunar soil would yield both hydrogen and oxygen, and could be used to make an ideal concrete. Engineering studies suggest there is no reason why a base on the Moon could not be created remarkably quickly.

On the other hand, there is a strong "Mars first" lobby that argues for a direct attack on the problems of landing men on the red planet. Mars is seen as a politically attractive goal, given that the Russians have already made clear their interest in going there. Their Energia booster and experience of long stays in space undoubtedly give them a head start. But the Mars project, fascinating though it is, could all too easily lead to another unnecessary and wasteful space race – a race, moreover, in which undue risks might be taken just to keep ahead. That was the view, too, of the influential study by Sally Ride and her group: they favored the stepwise approach - first the Space Station, then a Moon base, and, considerably later, on to Mars.

Glasnost in space?

There is one fascinating possibility, unthinkable even a few years ago, but not to be ruled out in today's climate of glasnost and arms treaties: a cooperative program between the superpowers to bring about results that, pursued separately, would strain either to the limit. Both countries have tremendous strengths in space: the Soviet Union in heavy lift capability, in space medicine and living; the United States in automation and communications. Together they could make a Mars base a reality sooner rather than later - perhaps even by the year 2010.

Planet-base technology

The first essential needed to create a viable base is a reliable, low-cost transportation system. An Earth-orbiting space station seems vital as a staging point. Improved shuttles of a new generation would ferry crews and materials up there; and for the journeys from there to the Moon (or indeed Mars) new, more efficient vehicles must be developed. The first basic living and working units could then be transported up relatively quickly. "Over the first few flights," says the Ride report, "the outpost would grow to include a living area, a research area, a lunar rover, small machines to mine lunar soil, and a pilot plant for extraction of oxygen from the rock." All this might be in the years 2000 to 2005, by which time the outpost could support five people for several weeks at a time. In the next phase, people could be virtually "at home on the Moon", with closed-loop life-support systems and a working oxygen plant to enable up to 30 people to stay for months at a time. But whatever the space scientists go for first, it is virtually certain that, just as Everest was climbed "because it was there", so one day next century people will land on Mars, and begin to establish some sort of foothold there.

▼ A manned base on the Martian moon Phobos might look like this. The lights of bases on the planet can be seen in the background, above the approaching spacecraft. Low gravity would make Phobos a good base for the exploration of Mars. More clues to its suitability as a base will be returned during 1989 by the first Soviet unmanned missions to Phobos, which left Earth in 1988.

▼ This artist's impression shows a "Mars station" in orbit above the red planet. The vehicle is adapted from the Space Station, the central modules of which are clearly visible. The smaller satellite is moving off to act as a communications relay for Earth. A station like this could be built up in Mars orbit, or assembled near the Earth and boosted out to Mars, using basically existing technology.

▶ Former shuttle astronaut Dr Sally Ride was the USA's first woman in space. She headed the 1987 NASA study group which like the National Commission (◊ page 27), recommended a bold program of space exploration. President Reagan liked the idea, and his parting gift to NASA was a $100m budget to develop some of the necessary technology: cargo vehicles, space robots and Moon mining.

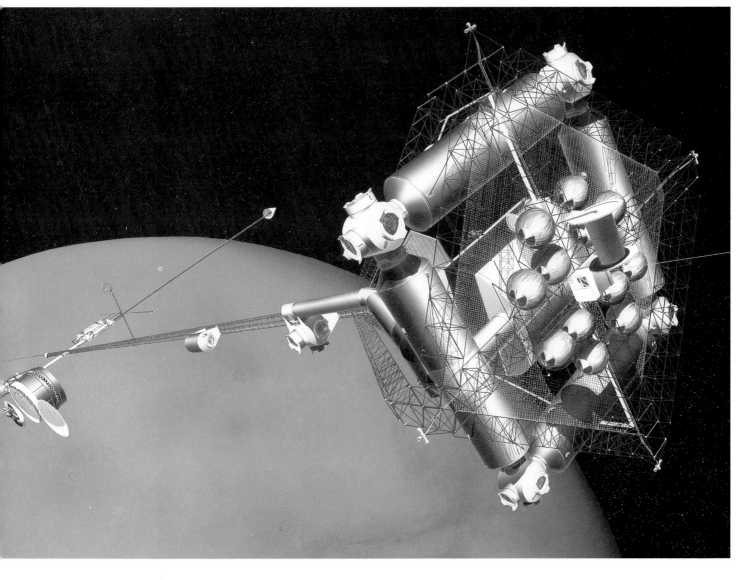

Extending the agenda

The next 10-15 years will see a wide range of unmanned missions. Not only will vastly more powerful telescopes be flown in orbit; unmanned probes will revisit the major planets, starting with the 1988-1989 missions to Phobos and continuing with a return trip to Jupiter, and visits to asteroids and comets. Both Soviet and American space stations will certainly develop substantially – an almost essential prelude to manned flight across the Solar System, such as the planned flights to Mars around the end of the century. How quickly it will all happen must depend on economics and politics – but happen it will.

However, looking further ahead, the crystal ball is inevitably more clouded. Will there ever be planetary bases, and even artificial cities in orbit? Many who have been closely involved with the opening-up of space believe that they too will come about, though setting dates for the various stages is well-nigh impossible. These tasks will be immensely difficult and challenging; but the same is true of projects such as building Concorde, tunneling under the English Channel, or indeed putting man on the Moon. Few today would use the word "impossible". In the

words of that doyen of space visionaries, Arthur C. Clarke, "forecasts are often too optimistic in the short term, but too pessimistic in the long."

How strong is the will to go on? Leaving aside all question of humanity's innate striving to conquer new heights (and that is a very powerful motivation), there may well be very strong practical reasons, for example, shortage of living-space, in the centuries to come. Much sooner than that, the inevitable energy shortage of the next century will have to be overcome by bold new means. Some experts are convinced that giant solar platforms in space will provide one of the most effective ways of meeting our energy needs without harming the environment.

Finally there is the political dimension. These great projects will surely be beyond the resources of any one power, however single-minded. If the opening-up of the last few years continues, it will surely lead to a new recognition of what could be achieved by a major joint effort. So shall we – or rather, our descendants – see a move away from achievements for national success and prestige, and toward achievement for Planet Earth? If that comes about – and perhaps only if it does – we shall at last truly shake off the bonds of Earth.

► **As ever more complex and costly equipment goes into orbit, on-site repairs will be necessary. Here, astronauts Dale Gardner and Joseph Allen have retrieved the damaged Westar VI communications satellite, to be brought back on the Shuttle for repair and eventual resale – Gardner's "For Sale" sign makes joking reference to this.**

Moving Around in Space

4

The need for new propulsion systems...An "ideal" launch vehicle...HOTOL...Solar sailing...Solar cells, microwave and laser power...Ion thrusters...Nuclear propulsion, continuous and pulsed...Project Daedalus...Time travel...The antimatter rocket... The interstellar ramjet...Traveling into the past...Self-contained world ships

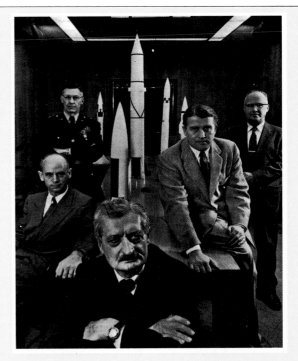

There is no shortage of ideas for the colonization of the Solar System and mankind's expansion out into space. However, for any of these to become more than just dreams, ways must be found to provide methods of cheap, reliable and efficient propulsion. The use of chemical rockets presents a serious limitation to human occupation of outer space. These rockets are very expensive. For example, many large modern communication satellites used for television and telephone relay cost a lot less to make than the price the operators have to pay to get them launched into space. To break out of this situation, where the cost of launch limits the rate of expansion and utilization of space, much less expensive launch vehicles must be developed. In addition, the energy from the chemical reaction used to provide the thrust of the rocket is limited. More and more propellant is needed, the further a mission is to be sent or the faster a spacecraft is to travel. To avoid this state of affairs, advanced, nonchemical propulsion systems with higher energy exhausts and higher exhaust velocities are required.

▲ *The early developments in rockets were carried out in Germany. The pioneer Hermann Oberth is front center, with Wernher von Braun directly to the right behind him.*

▼ *A Soviet rocket on its way to the launch pad at Baikonur. The largest part of the launch mass of a chemical rocket is the propellant that is expelled.*

Economic access to space

In order to be able fully to exploit the space environment, current systems have to be replaced. To achieve cost-effective access to Earth orbit, in order to lay the foundations for expansion beyond, something approaching an "ideal" launch vehicle is needed. This would be single-stage, fully recoverable and reusable. These characteristics, together with a modest size, would keep the costs of development and use to a minimum. The vehicle should be capable of remote control, so that it has no need to be permanently manned. It should be easy to handle on the ground and capable of a quick turnaround, in a manner very similar to modern-day airliners.

For such a vehicle, as hardware costs are reduced through re-usability, the launch preparations and operational costs become proportionately more important. Propellant costs are always a relatively small part of the total launch cost, and do not affect the launch economics greatly.

Such a system will not only revolutionize the market potential of space, but will also stimulate and encourage increased utilization. The launching of large masses into orbit will no longer be dominated by vehicle costs, but will be determined by the value of the payloads themselves. The manned exploration of space will become a relatively inexpensive endeavor, instead of the complex and costly exercise it is at present. The stage will be set for future expansion outward away from the Earth.

▶ *It is estimated that HOTOL will reduce the cost of attaining low Earth orbit by at least a factor of 5. This economy of operation, coupled with quick reaction and a rapid turnaround capability, could revolutionize the spaceflight scene from the year 2000 onward. In addition, however, HOTOL technology is forward-looking, with ample potential for development beyond the cheap and effective spacecraft launcher which it is presently planned to be.*

◀ *Manned space flight, with systems such as the US Space Shuttle, involves the use of wholly or partially expendable launch vehicles, large ground-support teams and long periods between flights. An analogy would be airline travel based on the idea of throwing the plane away after every transatlantic crossing, needing 500 air traffic controllers and ground crew to look after the plane while it is in flight, and then having to wait 2 months before another flight can take place.*

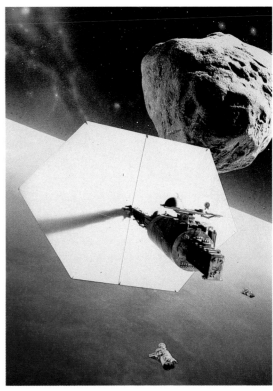

An air-breathing launch vehicle

The HOTOL (Horizontal Take Off and Landing) launch vehicle is in the early stages of development in the United Kingdom. It is based upon a new type of rocket engine which allows the oxygen in the atmosphere to be burnt with onboard hydrogen. This reduces the amount of propellant that the vehicle has to carry and allows the use of wings to optimize the flight profile. The take-off speed is about 540 kilometers/hour and a runway length of 2,500 meters is needed. The vehicle climbs at an angle of 24 degrees, going supersonic after two minutes and clearing commercial airspace about 2.5 minutes after that. At an altitude of 26 kilometers, traveling at five times the speed of sound and nine minutes into the flight, the use of oxygen in the air is no longer efficient. The vehicle switches over to oxygen carried on-board and continues into orbit at an operational altitude of some 300 kilometers.

HOTOL reenters at a very high angle of about 80 degrees, reducing as the speed falls. It commences a hypersonic glide at 25 kilometers. The large wing and low mass allow relatively low temperatures to be maintained and metal-alloy skins will suffice for the protection of the underside of the vehicle. The hypersonic lift-to-drag ratio of HOTOL during entry, more than twice that of the Space Shuttle, gives it a high cross-range capability. This would be sufficient to allow a European landing from launch into an equatorial orbit. The final-approach and landing techniques are similar to the Shuttle, but gentler: touchdown speed is just over 300 kilometers/hour and ground roll less than 2 kilometers.

A one-hour HOTOL passenger flight from Europe to Australia is a distinct possibility and little imagination is needed to identify other important uses for this remarkable aerospace plane.

Solar sailing

Away from Earth orbit, solar sailing is a possible method of dispensing with propellant altogether, and thus of avoiding the penalties of excessive takeoff mass at the same time.

Sunlight falling upon any object exerts a pressure on it, creating a force in the direction opposite to that from which the sunlight is coming. In space, where gravitational forces are small and there is no atmospheric drag to resist motion, even the very tiny forces that solar pressure produces are enough to move a spacecraft. Over time the forces, acting steadily, will allow quite respectable vehicle velocities to be built up.

Operations in toward the Sun would encounter an increasingly strong force, although conditions for the "solar sail" would also become more severe. Movement away from the Sun would have the problem of decreasing intensity of sunlight, and of the pressure that it exerts. Either the propulsive forces would be allowed to decrease, and the efficiency of the method would fall, or the area of the solar sail would have to be increased, to maintain a constant thrust from the system.

The Sun could be replaced as the source of light by the type of high-power laser used to beam energy to an onboard electric propulsion system. In this case, rather than increasing the area of the sail, the power output of the laser system could be increased. This could be achieved either by increasing the output of a single laser, or by building an array of lasers and switching them in one by one as the vehicle accelerates away from the base.

This concept has, in principle, unlimited scope for reaching very high velocities and is one of the methods suggested for an engine to drive spacecraft out of the Solar System and toward the stars.

▲ Solar-sail vehicles will have large mirror-type collectors attached with long cables. They will be similar in dimension to the power receivers discussed on page 45, but masses will be much lower, as the forces and thermal loads experienced will be considerably less.

Prospects are good for achieving laser-transmitter powers of over one gigawatt in the next few decades

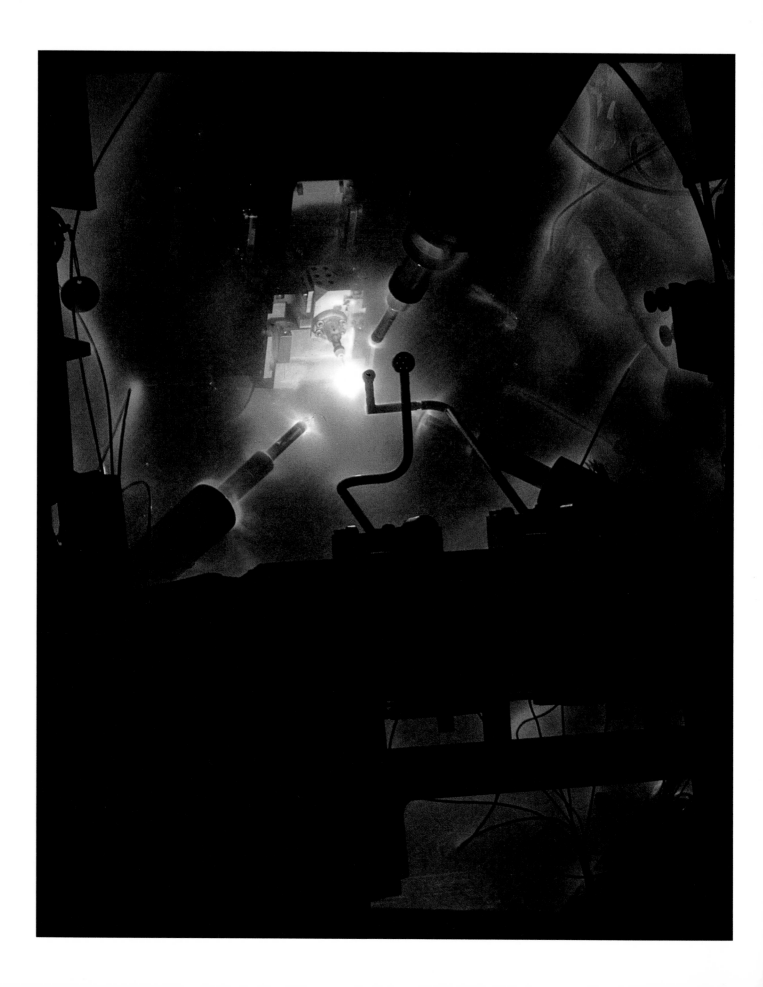

Electric propulsion

The use of economic, efficient ground-launch vehicles is only part of the requirement for opening up space. The same ideals apply in orbit. The spacecraft must be reusable, making return journeys or acting as shuttle from one place to another. The rocket engines that will be used must also have high exhaust velocities, to avoid large propellant fractions.

One method of achieving a high exhaust velocity is not to use chemicals as the source of the energy in the exhaust, but to use onboard power supplies to accelerate charged particles, or ions, to high velocities. The propellant gas is carried in the neutral atomic form, which can be turned into a positively charged particle simply by removing an electron, a process which requires a modest amount of energy. These ions can then be attracted by electric fields, with a strength of several kilovolts or more, and accelerated to velocities of at least 30-40 kilometers per second. This is more than chemical reactions are capable of, and requires a much lower mass of propellant. Nevertheless this mass has to be taken into account. For large spacecraft, with power demands of tens of kilowatts or more, this supply will represent a costly investment.

The standard source of spacecraft power at present is solar cells, which convert sunlight into electricity. The usefulness of such cells is quite limited, however. At distances much closer to the Sun than the Earth's orbit, excessive temperatures cause permanent damage to the cells. As the distance away from the Sun increases, so the intensity of sunlight falls, and the cells become less efficient. Solar electric propulsion is therefore applicable only to missions in Earth orbit, in the space around the Moon, and at distances from the Sun out to about three times Earth orbit.

An alternative method of powering an electric propulsion system is to beam the power to a vehicle from a remote power-generating facility. This has the effect of removing any power system from the vehicle, apart from the onboard energy-receiving equipment. The energy can be transmitted in the form of either microwaves or light. The efficiency of a microwave system will be greater than that of a laser system, but its transmission and receiving dishes will generally be very large. Typically a radius of a few tens of kilometers is needed to receive microwave power over a distance of a few hundred thousand kilometers.

Laser systems will be much smaller, with collector diameters of only a few tens of kilometers for power transmission over distances equivalent to that of the Earth from the Sun. However, there is little benefit to be gained by using a laser unless its power density at the spacecraft is substantially greater than sunlight. For Earth-Sun distances this implies that laser transmitter powers of over one gigawatt (one billion watts) are required. Rapid advances in laser and pulsed-power technologies, partly in military programs, make the prospects for lasers in this power-range good over the next few decades.

Even with large power lasers, the spacecraft receivers must increase in size as the distance between them and the power station increases, because of the spreading out of the laser beam. The third method of powering electric propulsion systems, nuclear power from fission reactions, avoids this and leads to much more compact vehicles. A fission power reactor with appropriate shielding is carried on board, and used to generate electricity to run the propulsion system. The operation of such systems is not, of course, constrained by distance from the Sun, and the operational life-time of the reactor will be set by the durability of the reactor itself.

▲ The first space test of a lightweight solar panel. The panel, shown during deployment from the Shuttle in 1984, can be re-stored after use. Future systems will cost less than current arrays, and weigh 10 times less than at present.

◄ The Antares laser system at Los Alamos National Laboratory in the United States. Initially dedicated to nuclear fusion studies by inertial confinement, this carbon dioxide laser has found new application in the development of space-based defense systems, as part of the US Strategic Defense Initiative (SDI). Future research will expand the duration and energy of Antares' pulse and spread the beam to irradiate larger target areas.

▲ A full-size ion thruster designed for orbit control of space vehicles. The ions are expelled through the holes in the grid at the top of the thruster. Magnets around the side of the main chamber improve efficiency by helping the processes that create the ions from the neutral propellant gas fed into the chamber. Power supplies on board the spacecraft provide the energy to accelerate the particles. Solar arrays can be used to provide tens of kilowatts but larger powers will require the use of nuclear reactors.

Nuclear propulsion

Nuclear power has been suggested (◀ page 45) as one method of providing the energy in a rocket exhaust, indirectly, using it to generate the electricity to drive an ion engine. The power released by the atom can also be used directly to energize propellant and provide thrust. While this concept does not produce such high exhaust velocities (only about 3-4 times that of chemical rockets), it does have the advantage over electric propulsion and solar sailing of providing a high thrust. (Nuclear power also has the advantage over solar sailing of not being limited in its operation by distance from the Sun.) The methods already discussed require long propulsion times to build up their speed, whereas a nuclear propulsion system needs a much shorter period under thrust. This would be important for missions to the Moon, and to the nearer planets such as Mars and Venus. For more distant journeys to the outer planets, a high thrust would not give any significant advantage in terms of mission duration.

One type of nuclear propulsion is to use a continuous nuclear fission reactor to provide the heat to accelerate a propellant, and thus provide the thrust. A light gas, usually hydrogen, is passed through the core of a fissioning reactor, where the nuclear energy given off is transferred to the gas, thus accelerating it. It is then ejected out of a rocket nozzle in the conventional manner. The limitations to the exhaust velocities in such systems are set by material properties, particularly materials' resistance to very high temperatures, and by the efficiency with which the energy can be coupled into the flowing stream of gas.

The materials problem can be greatly alleviated by the use of pulsed propulsion methods rather than the continuous type of propulsion system assumed so far. In this concept, a nuclear charge is ejected from the vehicle and detonated some way behind. The products from the explosion expand out into space, and some of them are intercepted by a pusher plate on the bottom of the spacecraft. The time over which they interact is very small, and does not create any severe heating or deterioration of the plate. Shock absorbers are used to damp out the accelerating pulse from the explosion, and the sequence is repeated a number of times to build up the speed.

Some erosion of the plate does take place, of course, and this sets the limit to the exhaust velocity that can be attained. This is impressively high, however, at around 40-50 kilometers per second, and with a high thrust level. If a magnetic field is produced parallel to the pusher plate and used to decelerate the products of the explosion, thus shielding the plate from damage, then much higher exhaust velocities are possible. The system limit now depends upon how much propellant is used to moderate the nuclear detonation, and slow down the reaction products. Exhaust velocities of 100-200 kilometers per second should be attainable, although with reduced thrust level.

Considerable effort has been expended upon this system. The best-known study was Project Orion, which undertook a research program between 1957 and 1965. Fission bombs with an explosive yield of about one kilotonne were used in this concept. Testing on the ground, using conventional high-explosive charges and a scaled-down model, impressively proved the propulsion concept. The vehicle had good performance characteristics and potential on paper, but further study of this type of nuclear propulsion system was effectively stopped by the signing of the nuclear test-ban treaty which, although specifically aimed to reduce nuclear weapons proliferation, prevented any testing of a vehicle using internally triggered nuclear bombs.

▲ *An artist's impression of a free-flying power station. The Space Shuttle is docked, receiving additional power on a long-duration flight. The solar arrays at the top convert sunlight into electricity. Nuclear power reactors can provide much larger amounts of power and result in more compact systems.*

▲▶ *Daedalus passes Neptune and its moon Triton (above) on the way out of the Solar System into interstellar space. The first stage of the starship, shown in this artist's impression firing to produce thrust, is jettisoned after all its fuel is used. The second stage travels to the target on its own. This is shown in the engineering drawing (right), where the different components of the vehicle are identified. The engine is at the bottom, with fuel tanks directly above it. The payload, containing computers, probes, scientific instruments and systems to repair any faults, is located at the front of the starship.*

The first probe outside the Solar System

The first type of rocket engine to be used outside the Solar System will be based upon the nuclear-pulse propulsion concept, and indeed studies have already been carried out on such a vehicle to probe nearby planetary systems.

One study group was formed in 1973 by the British Interplanetary Society; they investigated a simple interstellar mission in an exercise called Project Daedalus. The major limiting factor for the mission was known to be in the area of propulsion, and a simple, undecelerated, unmanned stellar fly-by of Barnard's Star, at distance of approximately six light years from the Sun, was chosen.

The vehicle consisted of a two-stage nuclear pulse rocket capable of traversing the distance in about 50 years. The mass at engine ignition was about 54,000 tonnes, of which 50,000 tonnes would be propellants. At the end of the boost phase the vehicle would be travelling at about 12 percent of the speed of light. The total mission would involve about 20 years for the design, manufacture and checking-out of the vehicle, some 50 years in flight time, and 6-9 years in order to transmit information back to the Solar System.

The propulsion system used electron beams to implode small pellets of deuterium and helium 3 to conditions under which fusion reactions took place. The energies released by fission were not considered great enough for a starship, and other fusion fuels released too many damaging neutrons.

Helium 3 is a very rare isotope with a natural abundance of about 1 part in 100,000. However, 17 percent of the atmosphere of Jupiter is helium, and there is enough of the isotope to fuel millions of Daedalus vehicles. It was suggested that separation plants should be floated in the atmosphere beneath hot-air balloons to process and collect the atmospheric gases for use as propellant.

At the end of its flight to Barnard's Star, the starship releases a series of sub-probes to fan out and fly through any planetary system that may be present. The information collected by these probes, together with all the data gathered by the starship itself, will then be transmitted back to Earth where it will be received by a large radio telescope.

In order to ensure that the starship functions for the required 50 years, two mobile robot systems are provided to maintain and repair any parts of the vehicle that fail during the long voyage.

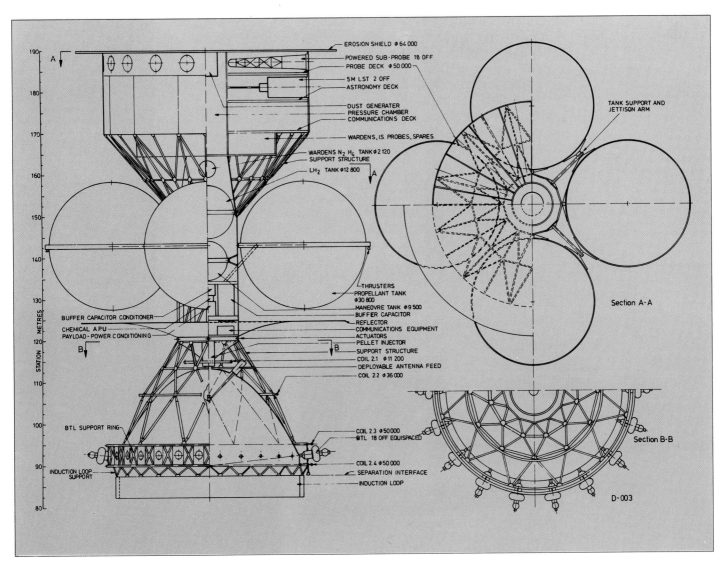

An astronaut traveling close to the speed of light could theoretically make a 10-year trip round the galaxy and return to find Earth 1,000,000 years older

The limits of time travel

Relativity weaves space, time and matter into a unity and leads to a number of effects that cause distortions of time. Perhaps the best known is the "twins effect". An astronaut who leaves Earth and travels at high speed to some distant star finds on his or her return that s/he has aged less than the twin left behind. What has happened?

During the journey, time passes more slowly in the spacecraft than on Earth, However, the astronaut is quite unaware of this, because thought processes – like everything else – are equally slowed. As far as s/he is concerned, time passes normally, and s/he is surprised to find on returning that events on Earth have "got ahead".

The size of the effect depends on the spacecraft's speed. In the theory of relativity the speed of light plays a key role, and the magnitude of the time-stretching effect being described here is determined by how close the spacecraft can approach the speed of light. To take an example, at 99 percent of the speed of light, a journey to the nearest star and back takes about nine years as far as the Earth twin is concerned, but to the astronaut the round-trip time is only about 16 months. If the speed is 99.9 percent of the speed of light the journey time from Earth remains more or less the same, but for the astronaut it is reduced to about five months.

When the astronaut returns to Earth s/he arrives to find everything several years ahead of his or her own time. In effect, s/he has traveled into the future. In principle, by extending the journey time and getting very close to the speed of light the astronaut could travel hundreds or even thousands of years into the future this way. A trip around the galaxy might take 10 years of spacecraft time, but the astronaut would return to Earth one million years after leaving it!

Can we expect future spacecraft to reach an appreciable fraction of the speed of light so that the twins effect would become noticeable? Without the effect, the duration of interstellar voyages would be unacceptably long. The problem is that the speed of light is very great – about 300,000 kilometers per second. It takes light only a second or so to reach the moon from Earth. Our current spacecraft take several days. Clearly we have a long way to go before space travel near the speed of light is a reality. Nevertheless, if a suitable power source can be found there is no reason why the technological obstacles cannot be overcome within 300 years.

Another way to travel into the future is to use gravity, because gravity

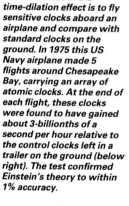

▼ *A direct test of the time-dilation effect is to fly sensitive clocks aboard an airplane and compare with standard clocks on the ground. In 1975 this US Navy airplane made 5 flights around Chesapeake Bay, carrying an array of atomic clocks. At the end of each flight, these clocks were found to have gained about 3-billionths of a second per hour relative to the control clocks left in a trailer on the ground (below right). The test confirmed Einstein's theory to within 1% accuracy.*

▶ *A color-coded "snapshot" of tracks of fast-moving atomic particles traced in a bubble chamber. Some of these particles are produced in the upper layers of the atmosphere by cosmic rays, and would not reach the bubble chamber at all were it not for the time-dilation effect. This effect greatly extends the lifetime of the particles, and enables them to travel some way through the atmosphere before decaying.*

▼ *In this artist's impression of a black hole silhouetted against the Milky Way, light beams from stars behind the hole are bent around it by the intense gravity and clothe the black disk in a bright halo. An in-falling asteroid is torn apart as it plunges toward the hole.*

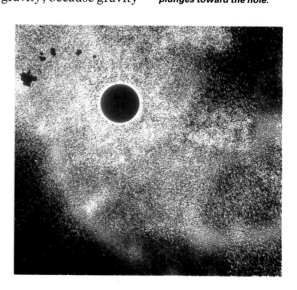

slows time. It is possible to observe clocks in gravity-free space running very slightly faster than those on Earth. It is even possible to measure the time discrepancy between the top and bottom of a tower using ultra-sensitive nuclear clocks. Over a human lifetime, the effect causes a mountain dweller to travel about a picosecond (10^{-12} seconds) into the future ahead of a coastal dweller.

Although these effects are minute, they increase dramatically near very strongly gravitating objects. On the surface of a neutron star, for example, where gravity is billions of times greater than on Earth, time can run at half the rate it does on Earth. The ultimate timewarp occurs near a black hole. At the surface of the hole, time essentially stands still relative to Earth. For an observer who crosses into the hole, it takes just a split-second of his own time for the entire infinite future of the external universe to pass by! Even if we possessed the technology, it is improbable that anyone would be foolish enough to journey close to a black hole. Apart from anything else, the spacecraft (and astronauts) would be subject to huge differential forces that would rip them to pieces before the time-dilation effect became significant. This is one form of time travel that will remain fictional even 300 years hence.

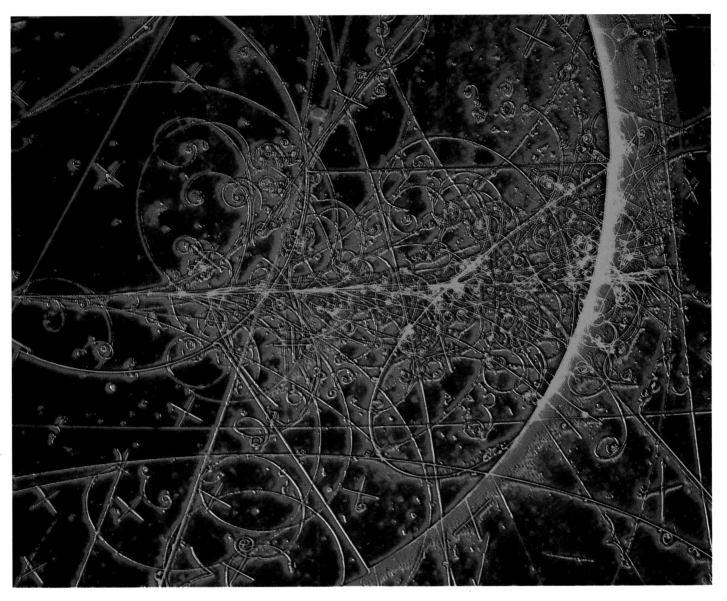

Interstellar travel will demand much more ambitious methods than those used to date within the Solar System

The antimatter rocket

The ultimate rocket propulsion system is the photon rocket, where matter is completely annihilated and the resultant energy is radiated away to produce thrust. There is no possibility, with our present-day knowledge of physics, of a vehicle containing its own energy source and propellant being better than this.

To achieve sensible propellant loads, mass must be converted very efficiently into energy. Nuclear processes liberate less than one percent of the available mass as energy, and hence it is often proposed that matter-antimatter reactions, such as the proton-antiproton reaction, should provide the energy. Antimatter is totally absent from our part of the universe and would have to be manufactured. The process needs an amount of energy at least equal to double the mass of antimatter produced. The cost of production and energies required make onboard production unfeasible. However, even assuming production of antimatter prior to the trip, another problem is that of storage. Solid walls would result in the annihilation process occurring. Storage in a magnetic field, or as a magnetically levitated antimetal, may be possible answers. A further problem is that of radiating the energy away from the vehicle very efficiently, as the deposition of a small amount would result in the rapid vaporization of the vehicle.

The interstellar ramjet

Another vehicle capable of relativistic speed (◀ page 49) is the interstellar ramjet, conceived as a way to avoid vehicles having to carry their own fuel and propellant. All the propulsion system consumables come from outside the vehicle, and its range and speed are unlimited. The system has enormous potential.

Interstellar space is filled with hydrogen gas, some in the neutral and some in the ionized form. This gas is collected by an intake on the ramjet and is fed into a reactor which converts some of the mass into energy in fusion reactions. This energy is used to accelerate the unconverted matter rearward to provide thrust. Operation at highly-relativistic velocities in a region of high hydrogen density needs an intake radius of 2,000 kilometers. Such large sizes rule out the use of solid materials, as the structural densities would be far too high. The surface of such intakes would be continually heated and eroded by the bombardment of high-energy particles and would rapidly fracture and begin to break up. For this reason the intake is usually envisaged as a magnetic type, in which hydrogen ions are collected by the magnetic field and fed into the reactor mouth at the front of the vehicle. If the hydrogen in space is not ionized, this can be easily accomplished by shining a laser beam ahead of the ramjet, causing photonization to occur.

Is travel into the past forbidden?

Although travel into the future, whether by motion or gravitation, is a reality, there is a snag. It is not possible to do it and get back again. Travel backward in time seems to be forbidden. Why is this?

According to the theory of relativity, if an object can travel faster than light it can travel backward in time. However, the theory forbids any object from breaking the light barrier. The object just gets heavier and heavier, and has to push ever harder to increase the speed. In experiments with subatomic particles, this escalating-mass effect is very noticeable, and particle accelerators have to be designed to take it into account. There is no way one can push on through the speed of light. There is no reason to suppose this conclusion will change in the future – it seems to be a deep principle of nature, and not just a technological limitation.

There is another reason why travel into the past appears to be forbidden, whatever new scientific discoveries may await us. This objection is a philosophical rather than a physical one. It concerns some well-known paradoxes familiar to fans of the *Dr Who* television series. Consider the case of a time-traveler who goes back to the year before he was born and kills his mother. What happens? If his mother is dead, then he will never be born. But if he isn't born he is not able to embark upon the time travel, and hence he is not able to kill his mother. But if his mother is not killed, then the time-traveller is born! This self-contradictory nonsense would seem to scupper the whole idea of travel into the past.

The same problem besets any attempt to communicate with the past using signals. Suppose a machine is constructed that can send messages backward in time. It would then be possible to arrange for a self-destruct device to be fitted and programmed in the following way. A signal is transmitted at two o'clock into the machine's own past, to be received one hour earlier, at one o'clock. If a signal is received at one o'clock, the machine explodes. A moment's thought shows that the machine falls into the same paradox as the time-traveler. If a signal is received, the machine is destroyed. But then it is incapable of transmitting the message at two o'clock. In which case, no signal is received, so the machine does not explode. But if it doesn't explode, the signal is sent…

In spite of these grave problems about sending signals to the past, it is still possible for some entities to travel backward in time. The theory of relativity makes no statement that forbids faster-than-light travel as such. Although ordinary bodies are not allowed through the light barrier, there might be particles which only travel faster than light. For these "tachyons", the light barrier operates the other way – they cannot cross it from the high-speed side.

If tachyons exist, then to some observers they will effectively go backward in time. To avoid the foregoing paradoxes it is essential that we are unable to interact with tachyons in a controlled way enabling us to send a message. This would be the case if tachyons and ordinary particles affected each other only randomly, for example.

At the time of writing, there is no positive evidence for the existence of tachyons and some theorists believe that the whole idea is nonsense. Nevertheless, they are taken seriously enough for searches to have been made for them. These searches have concentrated on the products of high-energy particle reactions. As the experimenters explore ever-higher energies in the coming decades it may just be that a tachyon will show up. If so, the future will never be the same again.

◄ *An artist's impression of an interstellar ramjet or "ramscoop" starship. Instead of carrying a large amount of fuel on board, ram-propelled spaceships would use the hydrogen atoms which are scattered through space. These atoms would be collected by huge magnetic fields, generated by equipment on the starship, which would extend large distances in front of the vehicle to gather up the fuel needed to burn in the engines. The magnetic fields would exert large forces on the structure of the starship, setting a limit to the field strengths that can be used. This, in turn, would limit the amount of fuel that can be collected, and hence the efficiency of this method. However, very large velocities may be possible.*

World ships

The use of fast starships for interstellar flight has received a good deal of attention, but an alternative is the use of much slower ships. Such a vehicle would leave its planetary system carrying a community whose objective was simply to live a normal existence, such that future generations would have the option of exploring or colonizing other planets as they were encountered. These vehicles would have coast velocities of a fraction of a percent of the speed of light, and to compensate for the resulting long journey times they must increase in size to such an extent that they should be considered to be small worlds in their own right. World ships must be large enough to be self-sufficient for times measured in thousands of years, with populations measured in hundreds of thousands. They will probably travel together in fleets of at least a few tens in number, to take advantage of the increased stability which this larger ecological and cultural diversity should provide.

The simplest structure capable of allowing the travelers to take their basic culture and environment with them is a rotating cylinder with the occupants on the interior. Since the mechanical stresses involved limit the dimensions, materials such as high-strength steel would be used for the outside shell. The elements required (iron, nickel, cobalt, titanium, aluminum) are all available in large quantities in the asteroid belt. The cylinder would have a radius of about 10 kilometers and a length of about 115 kilometers. The ship would rotate to give a gravitational attraction at the inside surface equal to that of the Earth. The total ship population would be around 700,000.

The mass of the world ship structure, the soil and the atmosphere (obtained either from the home planet or a gas-giant planet) is estimated to amount to some 550 billion tonnes. While this picture of a world ship is obviously heavily biased toward the anthropocentric viewpoint, it does at least give an indication of the scale of engineering which must be considered in such an undertaking.

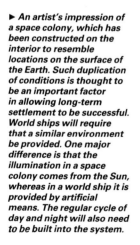

▶ *An artist's impression of a space colony, which has been constructed on the interior to resemble locations on the surface of the Earth. Such duplication of conditions is thought to be an important factor in allowing long-term settlement to be successful. World ships will require that a similar environment be provided. One major difference is that the illumination in a space colony comes from the Sun, whereas in a world ship it is provided by artificial means. The regular cycle of day and night will also need to be built into the system.*

In order to propel a vehicle the size of a world ship the engine power would need to be about a million times the entire artificial power output of the Earth. Since a world ship must be able to command such engine power at any time, even when light years and millennia away from home, the power source must be on-board. The only practical mechanism currently known is the external nuclear pulse rocket (◀ page 46). Calculations indicate that for such a vehicle departure mass is about 2,700 billion tonnes of which some 2,150 billion tonnes is nuclear fuel and propellant. The world ship would carry pulse charges containing about 80 billion tonnes of deuterium, a quantity readily available in the atmospheres of gas-giant planets.

The quantities of propellants for rocket vehicles are limited to the availability of hydrogen and helium within the Solar System. Even assuming very limited mining of deuterium, structural materials would appear to be the constraining factor. The availability of the constituents of steel in the asteroids has been estimated to be sufficient to construct about 170,000 world ships. This figure represents an unrealistic upper limit. The actual capacity for world-ship construction will be governed by the means available to mine, sort and enrich asteroidal material of the quality being employed at the time purely for uses within the Solar System. Once a Solar System-based civilization could construct world ships in sufficient numbers, the Galaxy would be open to colonization and exploitation.

▼ *The achievement of the capability of constructing world ships in quantities of several hundred should not represent a technological or economic strain upon a Solar System-wide community. Given a stop in any planetary system, such as that shown in this futuristic impression of a "long-range pioneer fleet", it would be possible to refuel, and assuming adequate onboard manufacturing capability, new tankage and pulse triggers could be made in the new system, ready for departure on a continuing journey to unexplored stars and their planetary systems. Voyages throughout the whole Galaxy may be possible.*

The way forward

The rate at which humans occupy the Solar System depends critically on the development of economic and efficient propulsion systems, in sufficiently wide variety to meet the demands of different classes of vehicle.

For launch from Earth into orbit, to establish the first permanently manned space bases and lunar colonies, a fully reuseable, single-stage-to-orbit, air-breathing system must be developed. If this does not prove to be possible, for whatever reason, then the exploitation and exploration of space will still proceed, but at a reduced rate and at an increased cost.

Once in orbit, there are a wide range of propulsion systems that can be used, only some of which have been discussed above. The different systems will probably find application in different regions of the Solar System, depending upon the level of technical development and the availability of power in sufficient quantity.

For operations in Earth orbit it is likely that ion-drive systems (◀ page 45), either powered by solar arrays or by power beamed to them from remote power stations, will prove to be the workhorses of space development. They will act as space tugs, moving ever-increasing quantities of material into a range of orbits, in support of human operations.

For travel to the Moon such ion drives will be used for cargo transport, but it is likely that nuclear fission propulsion systems (◀ page 46) will be developed for manned missions. With their higher thrust they will reduce the trip times to acceptably low durations.

The same considerations will apply once mankind moves further out into the Solar System. For cargoes, where the trip times are not of primary importance, ion drives powered by onboard nuclear reactors, or by power beamed from remote stations, will be used for propulsion. For missions where more rapid trip times are demanded, nuclear-fission propulsion and nuclear-pulse propulsion systems will be used increasingly.

Still further in the future, spacecraft will be propelled from the Solar System into interstellar space at ever-increasing speeds. It is likely that laser-driven light sails (◀ page 45) and nuclear-pulse propulsion based upon the use of fission explosions (◀ page 46) will propel the first serious attempt to penetrate the regions outside the Solar System in a meaningful and determined manner. By the time that this happens, the System itself should be populated with a wide variety of space vehicles, performing different missions in a variety of different ways. The antimatter rocket and "ramscoop" rocket or ramjet are two projects being investigated to support true interstellar exploration (◀ page 50). These varied space vehicles will have two things in common, however – economy and efficiency.

▼ *A Shuttle astronaut, supported by the remote manipulator arm, checking a test of an erectable space structure. Many future tasks to be carried out in Earth orbit will rely upon the construction of large structures in space. The regular presence of humans in space, and their ability to carry out such tasks, will be one major determining factor in the exploitation of Earth orbit, and of the Solar System in the longer term.*

Other Intelligences

5

Bioastronomy, a new field of science...Visitors from space...The universe apparently predisposed to life...The radio Search for Extra-Terrestrial Intelligence (SETI)...Recent SETI developments...Implications of discovering other intelligences

The idea that life and intelligence might exist in other parts of the universe is indeed very old. Around 400 BC, for example, the Greek philosopher Metrodorus of Chios was writing that "It seems impossible in a large field to have only one shaft of wheat and in the infinite universe only one living world." However, it has not been possible to start any serious searches for extraterrestrial life or for extraterrestrial intelligence until the second half of the present century, because such searches had to await the development of radio astronomy and space exploration, both of which have experienced spectacular growth in the last 30-40 years. Thus, a very old concern of mankind has finally become an exciting new field of science, called "bioastronomy". In 1982, the International Astronomical Union, representing all the astronomers of the world, established a new commission, Bioastronomy: Search for Extraterrestrial Life, with Michael D.Papagiannis, professor of astronomy at Boston University, as its first president.

Panspermia and UFOs

The idea that life may exist in many other places in the universe has long been popular with laymen and scientists alike. Soon after Charles Darwin put forward his theory of evolution, Hermann Richter proposed that the first living organisms had come to the Earth from space and for this reason he named them "cosmozoa". In 1901 the Swedish chemist Svante Arrhenius (1859-1927) proposed a more sophisticated version of this theory which he named "panspermia", which in Greek means "germs everywhere". This theory advocates that spores (single cells in a hibernation) are floating freely in the vast expanses of our galaxy and are responsible for the origin of life on planets that have the proper conditions, which essentially are liquid water, as does the Earth. Though this possibility cannot be completely excluded, in reality it does not make the origin of life any easier to explain, because if life could have originated somewhere else in our galaxy, it could as easily have started on Earth.

The British biologists Francis Crick and Leslie Orgel proposed in the 1970s an alternative possibility which they named "directed panspermia". According to this version, the first microorganisms were sent to Earth using special space probes by another advanced stellar civilization. Stretching it even further, probably with tongue in cheek, the American astronomer Tom Gold has suggested the idea of an "accidental panspermia" according to which the first microorganisms were inadvertently left behind, together with their garbage, by extraterrestrial travelers who had made a brief stopover on Earth. Finally, in recent years the British astronomer Fred Hoyle and Indian mathematician Chandra Wickramasinghe have suggested that the Earth is being invaded continuously, even today, by microorganisms from outer space, which are responsible for certain widespread diseases, such as flu epidemics. However, the data on which they based their conclusions have been strongly challenged by many other scientists.

The same skepticism has been expressed by most scientists about visits by extraterrestrials, both past (ancient astronauts) and current (UFOs), which are very popular with the public and which has accumulated a voluminous literature since World War II. The problem with all these reports, some of which have been filed by well-qualified people, is that the original observations cannot be repeated by other scientists to confirm the initial results, which is an absolute requirement for scientific acceptance. At this stage, then, all we can say about the UFOs is that "absence of evidence is not evidence of absence", and hope that, if indeed there is some truth to all these stories, our modern technology will allow us to obtain scientifically verifiable evidence in the near future.

◄ **UFOs photographed over Montreal in Canada on August 5, 1973. Most UFO sightings can be explained as balloons, planets etc. The UFO cult and media interest have led to many false reports. It is hard to pick out the few genuine unexplained events.**

The universe is well predisposed to the complex phenomenon of life

Scientific grounds for the search

Earlier this century, large telescopes revealed that we live in a large galaxy called the Milky Way that has about 300 billion stars (suns), and that the visible universe has 10-100 billion galaxies. Hence the number of stars in the visible universe is a truly astronomical number with 22 zeros. A significant fraction of these stars are similar to our own Sun and therefore they could also have around them planets like the Earth, where life could originate and evolve to high intelligence.

The rocks and the metals of the Earth, as well as the nitrogen and the oxygen in our atmosphere and the oxygen of the water, are all more recent products of the universe that are continuously being manufactured in the cataclysmic explosions of massive stars that are called supernovae. In this category belong practically all of the chemical elements which we call collectively "heavy elements", but which account for only about 2 percent of the total mass of the universe. The other 98 percent is hydrogen and helium produced during the explosive start (Big Bang) of the universe.

It is interesting that oxygen, carbon and nitrogen, which in that order are the three most common of the heavy elements, together with

▼ *Looking toward the center of our own galaxy. The Milky Way is so called because viewed from the Earth as it orbits the Sun, a minor star about two-thirds of the way out along one of our galaxy's spiral arms, the flat disk of the Galaxy appears edge-on as a lighter-colored "milky" band which sweeps across the night sky.*

hydrogen, which is by far the most common element of the universe, make up also about 98 percent of the biomass of the Earth (the mass of all living organisms), about three-quarters of which is in the form of water. Water is an ideal medium for the complex chemistry of life and since it consists of hydrogen and oxygen which have a great affinity for each other, it must be the most common molecule in the universe. It appears, therefore, that the universe is favorably predisposed to the formation of planets like the Earth and to a water-based life of carbon, oxygen, hydrogen and nitrogen like ours.

The universe is also a system operating at essentially three levels of temperature: the very high temperatures of the stars, the intermediate temperatures of the planets, and the very low temperature of the vast spaces of our expanding universe. A planet like the Earth absorbs high-quality energy from the Sun and uses it to build complex chemical structures of importance to life (prebiotic chemistry, photosynthesis, etc.).

Once life gets started, it grows in complexity, which allows it to cope with more complex environments, and in intelligence, which allows it to make the proper choices in a complicated world. The growth of intelligence in many cases is bound to lead to science and technology, which give tremendous advantages to those that possess them. It seems, therefore, that it is scientifically justified to search for extraterrestrial intelligence (a task which is usually abbreviated to SETI), because even though these other stellar civilizations might be physically very different from us, we will be speaking the same scientific language, since the language of science is universal.

The Arecibo message

1 Binary numbers 1-40
2 Atomic numbers of hydrogen, carbon, nitrogen, oxygen and phosphorus
3 Chemical formulas for sugars and bases in nucleotides of DNA molecule
4 Number of nucleotides in human DNA
5 Double helix of DNA
6 Human being
7 Height of human being
8 Size of human population
9 Solar System with Earth displaced toward human being
10 Arecibo telescope
11 Diameter of telescope

▼ *The radio message (below left) sent from the Arecibo telescope (◊ page 60) in 1974 consists of 1,679 digits converted into a pictogram crowded with scientific information about the Earth and its inhabitants and demonstrating our state of scientific knowledge, by arranging them in 73 lines of 23 digits each (1679 is only divisble by 73 and 23). Voyagers 1 and 2 (◊ page 24) carry audiovisual disks (below right) containing speech, music, digitally encoded pictures and a message from US President Jimmy Carter.*

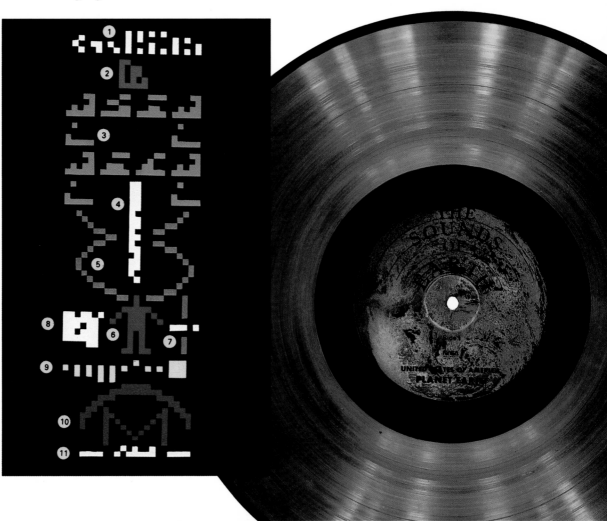

Some of the giant planets and their larger satellites have a chemistry similar to that on Earth when life's precursors, organic compounds, were being formed

The search for life in our Solar System

The first exploration of practically all of our Solar System has been completed, looking at every step for the possible presence of life. Mercury has been found to lack an atmosphere and due to its close proximity to the Sun it is too hot for life. Venus, on which the Soviet Union has landed several space probes, was also found to be too hot with temperatures around 455°C, where even lead would melt. It also has an extremely high atmospheric pressure (about the same as swimming at a depth of 900 meters), and not a drop of water. Consequently, the presence of life on Venus is extremely unlikely.

When the Viking probes landed on Mars in 1976 carrying with them laboratories to test the Martian soil for life, hopes were high of discovering signs of life, but unfortunately the results proved negative. The two Viking landers scooped some of the topsoil of Mars and carried out biological experiments with it which, in spite of some early positive signs, proved ultimately negative. They also studied the carbon content of the topsoil, which was found to be practically zero. (Carbon is the basis of life on Earth and because of its very special properties it is likely to be the basis of life almost everywhere.)

Mars has a lot of water, but all of it is ice, because with its very thin atmosphere (less than 1 percent of the Earth's) any liquid water would evaporate instantly into the near vacuum that surrounds it. There is evidence, however, that during its long history Mars might have had periods with liquid water on its surface, as seen, for example, from the river-like features. Such periods might have followed major volcanic eruptions that could have created a temporary atmosphere, and therefore Mars might have had intervals with life on it.

The Pioneer and Voyager fly-by missions to the giant planets revealed that in their atmospheres (and that of some of their larger satellites, such as Titan, the giant moon of Saturn), an active pre-biotic chemistry is going on, creating complex organic compounds that in the case of the Earth led to life.

So far, liquid water – a basic prerequisite of life – has been found nowhere outside Earth. The only possible exception could be Europa, the second of the four large (Galilean) moons of Jupiter, which appears to be covered by a thick layer of ice with many long cracks. It is speculated that underneath the ice layer there might be liquid water heated by the strong tidal forces of Jupiter, which is 300 times more massive than the Earth. The fact that no sunlight can penetrate the thick layer of ice over Europa does not in itself prohibit life. On Earth, marine life in the deep oceanic trenches, unreached by sunlight, gets its energy from sulfur compounds that stream out from oceanic vents in the crust.

The overall picture obtained so far from the exploration of our Solar System is that the chemical evolution that led to life on Earth, has gone on in several other parts of our Solar System (some pieces of asteroids, falling on Earth as meteorites, have been found to contain amino acids and nitrogen bases that are important components of all living organisms). It is still continuing on certain of the planets and moons of our Solar System. We cannot yet completely exclude the possibility that life might have existed on Mars at some time in its past history, or that it might exist today in an underground ocean on Europa. However, in the absence of definite evidence of the liquid water which seems to be a basic requirement for the existence of life, we must conclude that, the chances of finding extraterrestrial life on any other planet or moon of our Solar System appear to be very low.

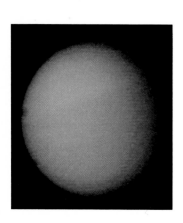

▲ *Titan, the giant moon of Saturn. The missions of Pioneer and Voyager spacecraft, flying close by the giant planets of the Solar System and their surprisingly varied moons, found no evidence of life. But on Titan active chemistry is in progress, at present creating some of the complex organic compounds which, on Earth and perhaps elsewhere, formed the building blocks for the emergence of life.*

▶ *A mosaic composed of 102 pictures of Mars taken from the Viking orbiter spacecraft as it orbited the planet. It covers almost a complete hemisphere and shows ancient rivers and volcanoes clearly. The center shows the system of canyons named the Vallus Marineris, up to 8km deep. Dried-up river channels run north from north-central canyons. Many of them flowed into a basin named Acidalia Planitia, the dark area in the extreme north of the picture. The three Tharsis volcanoes, each about 25km high, are visible as dark red spots in the west. South of the Vallus Marineris is very ancient terrain little changed by geological events and so preserving craters formed by impacts long ago.*

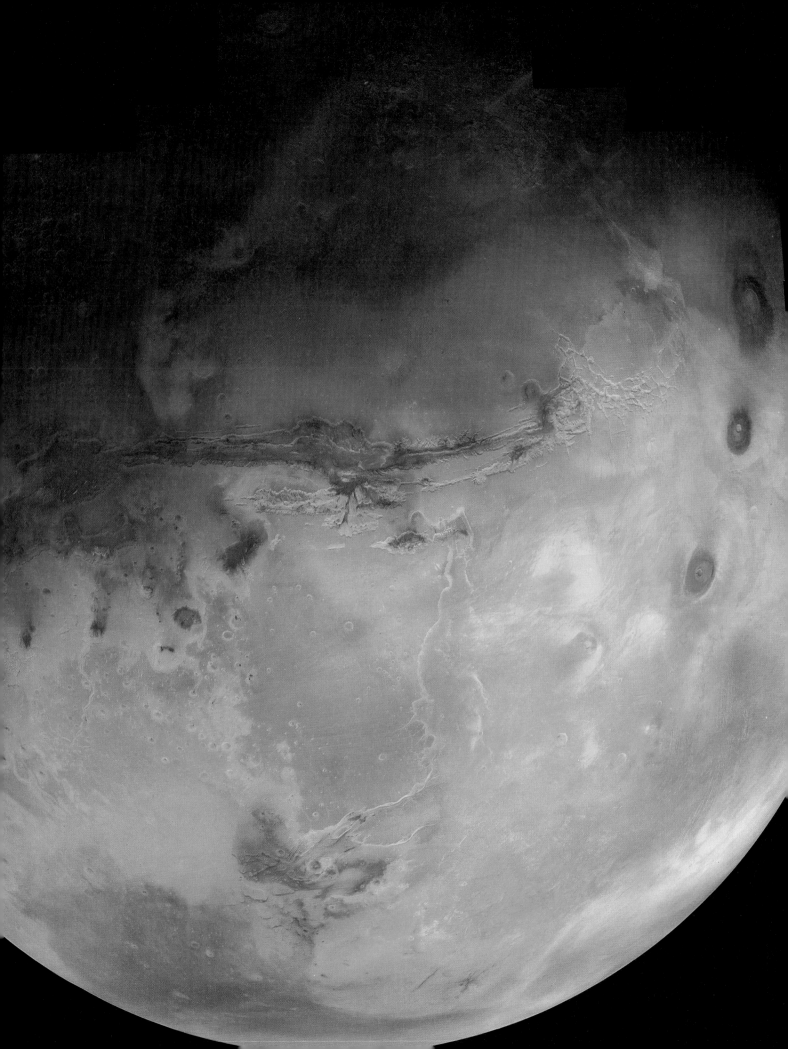

The search for extraterrestrial intelligences will be much more effective if conducted from space observatories away from the disturbance of Earth's atmosphere

The technological basis for SETI projects

Due to the large distances that separate the stars, it is at present beyond our means to search for primitive life on planets of other solar systems. However, some day in the future, using major astronomical instruments in space or on the far side of the Moon, we might be able to study the spectra of such extrasolar planets and look for evidence of life, such as the presence of an oxygen atmosphere, which as on Earth must be the byproduct of photosynthesis carried out by living organisms.

The search for planets around other stars is a very exciting, but also a very difficult, area of astronomical research. Trying to see a planet like the Earth orbiting around a nearby star like the Sun (which is bound to be at least 5-10 light years away) is like trying to resolve two objects only 2 millimeters apart at a distance of 1 kilometer. Furthermore, the luminosity of the Sun so overpowers the dim light of the planet, that it is like trying to see a firefly sitting on the edge of a powerful searchlight. However, the expectation is that in the early part of the next century we shall have a reasonably good understanding of the presence of planets, including small ones like the Earth, around the different stars in the vicinity of our Sun, and hence we will have a far better understanding of how common Earth-like planets might be in the universe. We do have now, however, the technology to search for advanced technological civilizations in other solar systems, which could easily communicate with us by radio waves.

All of the chemical elements and most molecules (water, ammonia, methane, etc.) emit or absorb at characteristic frequencies or wavelengths (the two being interrelated) of the electromagnetic spectrum, which includes X-rays, ultraviolet, visible and infrared light, and radio waves. These spectral lines become the signatures of these atoms and molecules that allow us to identify their presence at cosmic distances. Optical spectroscopy was initiated toward the end of the last century, but radio spectroscopy had to wait for the development of

▲ *Highly accurate measurements of the distance to the Moon have been made by directing laser beams at reflectors left behind on the Moon by astronauts, and measuring the time for the beam's return journey. Laser beams may be used for short-distance communication in space because of their high communications capacities. But the absorption of light by dust or gas makes them less suitable over longer distances.*

▼ *The 300-meter radio telescope at Arecibo, Puerto Rico, is built in a natural bowl among hills and cannot be steered. Its ability to locate and track different objects therefore depends on the natural movement of the Earth. The instrument could exchange radio messages with a similar instrument anywhere in the Milky Way, and one such message has already been sent from Arecibo (◀ page 57).*

radio astronomy in the 1930s. In 1951 Ewen and Purcell of Harvard University discovered the first radio line, the spectral line of atomic hydrogen at a wavelength of 21 centimeters (or at a radio frequency of 1,420 GHz). Subsequent work has led to the discovery of more than 100 such radio lines and to the identification of a wide range of organic compounds in interstellar space, which show that the chemistry of life is universal.

Soon after the discovery of the hydrogen radio line, in a 1959 paper in *Nature*, Cocconi and Morrison proposed to start searching for radio signals from other stellar civilizations, employing the hydrogen frequency which at the time was still the only known radio line. The rationale was that it was a universally-known frequency and therefore would be the top choice, at least for the initial contact. Shortly after, in the spring of 1960, Frank Drake carried out the first radio search for extraterrestrial intelligence (SETI), which he named Project Ozma after the Princess in the story of *The Wizard of Oz*. Drake used the hydrogen frequency to look for signals from two nearby, Sun-like stars, Epsilon Eridani and Tau Ceti, and devoted about 200 hours to this first search. It heralded many more, conducted all over the world.

▼ *Beta Pictoris is a star in the constellation of The Painter with a disk of material around it (here seen edge-on) which may be a planetary system like the Solar System. The material appears to be the same as that making up the Earth and the Sun's other planets. The disk may be only a few hundred million years old, one-tenth the age of the Solar System. Beta Pictoris is at least 50 times as bright as the Sun and is evolving far more quickly. Planets may already have formed from the disk. The search for planets is at an early stage, but instruments on the Infra-Red Astronomy Satellite (IRAS) have detected infrared sources around at least 40 stars which may represent planets being formed.*

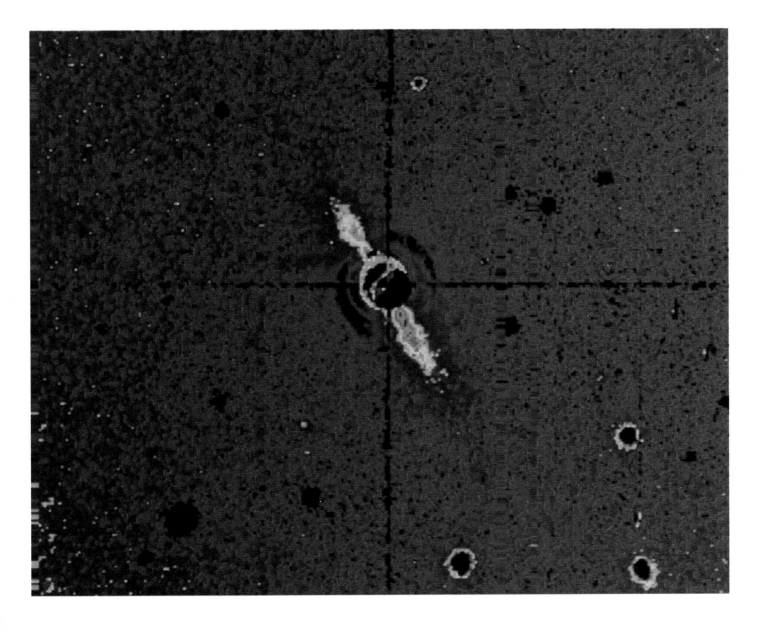

Beyond the "magic frequencies"

Since 1960, more than 50 SETI projects have been conducted, involving 200,000 search hours, using most of the major radio telescopes of the world, and with the active participation of the United States, Soviet Union, Australia, Canada, France, Germany, United Kingdom, Argentina and Japan. Most of these searches were conducted at the hydrogen line (◀ page 61), although other lines, such as those of hydroxyl (OH) around 18 centimeters, have also been used. There are now two telescopes dedicated to SETI. The older of the two, in operation since 1973, is the large radio telescope of Ohio State University near Columbus, Ohio, while the newer one, which has been in operation since 1983, is the Harvard-Smithsonian radio telescope near Boston, Massachusetts.

All these searches, conducted at both the hydrogen line and other select frequencies, and examining several hundreds of stars that resemble our Sun or sweeping the sky for many years, have unfortunately produced no positive results. This does not mean that we are getting close to exhausting our search of space because, by concentrating only on these so-called "magic frequencies", a colossally larger range of frequencies where radio signals could also be transmitted with equal ease, has been left unexplored. For this reason, in the 1970s NASA decided to develop a far more sophisticated long-term program to search over a much wider range of frequencies. This new approach became possible only thanks to a new generation of instruments called multi-channel spectrum analyzers (MCSAs), which can check out simultaneously millions of adjacent frequencies.

This new project, which is called the NASA SETI program, will have two components, the targeted search and the all-sky survey. The targeted search will examine close to 1,000 different targets, of which about 800 will be sun-like stars up to a distance of 82 light years. It will focus in the frequency range of the "water hole", which is the range between the lines of hydrogen (H) and of hydroxyl (OH). The targeted search will use some of the largest radio telescopes on Earth and will examine each target with very high-sensitivity and also with very high-frequency resolution, dividing the whole range of the water hole into about one billion distinct frequencies.

The all-sky survey will sweep the whole sky, covering the large celestial regions left out by the targeted search. It will also cover the whole "microwave window" of Earth, the range between 1 and 10 gigahertz within which radio waves with no significant galactic interference can pass through the atmosphere of Earth. It will, however, have a 30 times lower frequency-resolution and a considerably lower sensitivity since it will use primarily moderate-size radio telescopes. Nevertheless it will complement the targeted search and together the two will comprise the first truly comprehensive search of the whole sky using the whole radio spectrum. The NASA SETI program is expected to start around 1995 and will last for about 10 years, because it will have to use the different radio telescopes only on a part-time basis. To implement this program, NASA with the help of Stanford University is now building an MCSA with 8 million channels, and is also preparing special computer programs (algorithms) to separate weak radio signals from the "noise" background, including signals with a changing frequency (Doppler effect) transmitted from an approaching or a receding source. This MCSA with the Arecibo radio telescope will be able to do the 200 hours of the first search that Drake carried out in 1960 (◀ page 61) in just one-thousandth of a second.

▲ *Nikolai Kardashev is a pioneer of SETI (the search for extraterrestrial intelligence) in the Soviet Union, which plans to use a radio telescope, built far from other radio installations to avoid interference, to seek out ET broadcasts, starting in 1990.*

▶ *The 26-meter radio telescope in Harvard, Massachusetts is used to listen for signals from alien civilizations. It is fully automated and operates 24 hours a day, 365 days a year. Together with an Ohio State University instrument, the Harvard telescope accumulates around 17,000 SETI hours every year.*

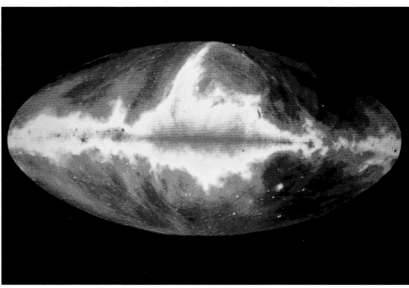

▲ A map of the whole sky, as seen from the surface of the Earth by radio telescopes at the 73-meter wavelength. The red horizontal band is the plane of the Milky Way, our own galaxy. The view of the sky is constructed in the same way as projections of the surface of the Earth in terrestrial maps, but the sphere of the sky is seen from the Earth as the center, looking outward.

◄ A radar map of the northern hemisphere of Venus. This map was constructed by radio waves transmitted to the planet by the 300-meter radio telescope at Arecibo in Puerto Rico used as a radar dish, reflected from the planet, and returned to Earth. The amount of detail it contains shows how much information can be contained even in a passively-reflected signal.

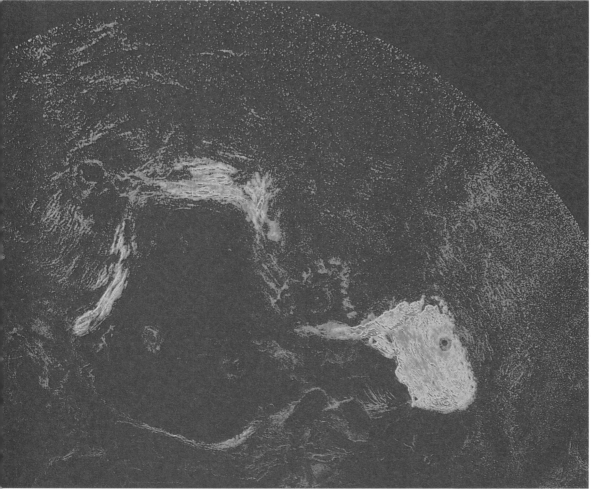

A look into the future

If our civilization can maintain its current technological progress, we can anticipate that over the next 100 years we shall carry out a thorough search for life in our Solar System, and conduct a detailed search for radio and probably for optical and infrared signals in every direction, after which we shall be able to say if there are any planets with biological activity around any of the closer stars. We shall therefore be able to give reasonably accurate answers to the following questions: is life on Earth a unique phenomenon, or are we one of many planets where life has managed to develop, and is our technological civilization a very rare occurrence among the billions of stars of our galaxy, or does our galaxy have an active society of stellar civilizations which we shall be invited to join?

The responses to both questions are of fundamental importance to our civilization. If there existed such a galactic society and if we were invited to join it, this would certainly be a historical landmark in the evolution of mankind. If, on the other hand, we were to conclude that there is no one else out there, then we should be bound to realize how unique our civilization is and how important it is to preserve it, in the hope that some day we might become the pioneers that would populate the whole galaxy with intelligent life. Furthermore, if we were to find that primitive life does exist in many solar systems, but that hardly any of them has intelligent life, the explanation could be that either the evolution of an advanced civilization is a very rare phenomenon, or that advanced civilizations survive for only a very short period, say of the order of a century or two, and that as a result at any given time there are only very few, if any, present in our own galaxy. In either case, preserving our own civilization becomes a matter of even greater importance.

The life span of advanced civilizations

A very short life span for advanced civilizations may be a realistic possibility because, as our own case shows, technology mushrooms very rapidly and is accompanied by many dangerous effects such as overpopulation, depletion of natural resources, pollution, and worst of all the rapid escalation of nuclear stockpiles which can easily reach the level where they are capable of wiping out the whole population of a planet.

By the same token, if we were to find a significant number of other advanced civilizations in our galaxy, it would mean that some at least had been able to overcome the dangers that are now looming over our own civilizations. To have reached this advanced stage, it would mean that they had been able to discard all of their animalistic attributes, such as materialism, selfishness, territoriality, dominance over others, and killing instincts, which in a technological civilization are likely to lead to self-destruction. They would have been able to mature to higher levels of cosmic intelligence characterized by spirituality, altruism, respect for others, adherence to peace, and love for each other. Joining such a galactic society would indeed be a colossal step forward in the intellectual and ethical evolution of our civilization.

This might also be the reason why we have not yet heard from any of such advanced civilizations as may exist. There might be a galactic rule that says that before a new civilization is invited to join the galactic society, it must show that it is able to overcome the major crises that probably befall all new technological civilizations. Since we are still in the midst of this evolutionary problem, there may be advanced civilizations waiting to see how we do before inviting us to join the galactic society of advanced civilizations.

A galactic association of civilizations

Although they can not be excluded, routine interstellar missions are impractical for purposes of interstellar wars, colonization, or commerce. The reason is that the long travel times required and the colossal amounts of energy needed would nullify all possible benefits. It is easy to show that if an interstellar probe were to be used to carry commercial goods to another star, even at speeds equal to 10 percent of the speed of light, which implies travel times of the order of 100 years, the value of the products carried would be of the order of one trillion dollars per ton of freight carried. A galactic association of stellar civilizations will not be based on the kind of physical contacts with which we are familiar, such as military conquests or commercial trade, but on the exchange of ideas and knowledge through electromagnetic waves, which carry them at the speed of light.

With properly handled technological growth, it seems very probable that in the next century or two we shall know the whole story of the origin and the distribution of life and intelligence in the universe. If other advanced civilizations do indeed exist, we shall perhaps join their galactic society, thus opening exciting new vistas for all the people of our planet, who by then most probably will have populated our entire Solar System.

▶ **On September 29, 1985 film producer Steven Spielberg, aided by his infant son Max, threw a ceremonial switch to inaugurate the most sophisticated SETI program to date. The receiver he activated listens to 8.4 million radio transmissions simultaneously, fed by the 26-meter diameter radio dish near Harvard, Massachusetts which has scanned the radio sky for interstellar transmissions continuously since March 1983. The project uses a single radio telescope, and is a much smaller-scale affair than the NASA SETI program due to start around 1995 (♦ page 62).**

Gaia

6

One new way of looking at the Earth...Earth and Mars compared...Regulatory mechanisms...No license to pollute...The aid of computers...Collaboration among organisms in evolution

▲ James Lovelock, in his garden in Cornwall, in front of the statue he calls "Gaia". In 1986, Lovelock proposed that the study of the systems by which organisms regulate living conditions on the planet be called "geophysiology", with "planetary physicians" who would diagnose environmental problems and treat them precisely.

▼ Earthrise, as seen from the Moon. Pictures such as this suggest Earth is like a "spaceship" traveling in an hostile environment and vulnerable to damage from pollution and the depletion of resources. According to the Gaian concept, conditions on Earth are regulated by living organisms; the planet is far more robust than it looks.

Most of us were taught in school that for us our Earth is the best of all possible worlds. It must be because we, along with all the other plants and animals sharing the planet with us, are adapted to the conditions Earth provides. Many millions of years ago, we were told, life began in oceans rich in chemical compounds that nourished the first cells. Always adapting to the circumstances they found, organisms were able to colonize new regions. They became more complex, developed new ways of life, and little by little established themselves over almost the entire surface of the planet. The world we see today represents the latest stage in that process, with a wealth of species each of which is precisely adapted to its local physical and chemical environment. Species cannot influence their environments greatly, but when the environment changes some individuals can tolerate the change. They survive, others do not, and life continues.

When space exploration began in earnest this view was reinforced. We could see for ourselves just how hostile environments are everywhere except on Earth. It was as though we were passengers riding through the vastness of the Solar System on a ship, a "Spaceship Earth". This view of the planet and ourselves fueled the growing popular concern about the global environment. By polluting the air and seas with our industrial wastes and plundering the natural and non-renewable resources on which we depend, could we, the passengers, sabotage the ship, perhaps destroying it and ourselves with it?

The origin of the concept of "Gaia"

This is where the British atmospheric chemist James E. Lovelock began. Starting in the late 1960s he and his colleagues, especially the United States' biologist Lynn Margulis, developed an entirely new way of studying any planet that supports life. They developed a theory to describe the processes involved and William Golding, the British novelist and Nobel laureate, suggested they call the living planet Gaia, in Greek mythology the Earth, who emerged from Chaos and became the mother of the sky, the giants, the cyclopes, and the titans, who were the parents of the gods. The name, sometimes spelled "Ge", gives the "geo" in such words as "geography" and "geology". The symbolism is powerful, and necessarily so, for Gaian theory conveys an important message that flatly contradicts the traditional view of the relationship between living organisms and their chemical and physical environment.

Gain theory holds that organisms are indeed influenced by and adapt to their non-living environment, but they also modify that environment to make it more hospitable to themselves, and on a global scale. We are far from being passengers on a ship over which we have no control. It would be more accurate to describe the planet as a single, coherent, living organism of which the living species are components.

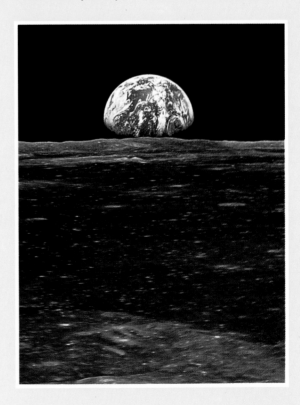

Most of Earth's once atmospheric carbon now takes the form of chalk cliffs and limestone rocks

Comparing Earth with Mars

The environmental debate raised many questions to which no one knew the answers. If we were to understand the global consequences of our activities we would have to find out much more about how the essential "life-support" systems of the Earth work. One way to approach the task might be to compare Earth, which supports life, with another planet on which nothing can live.

The search for Gaia began not on Earth, but on Mars. The 1975 Viking mission conducted experiments on the surface of the planet that would have revealed the presence of living organisms, provided those organisms were not too unlike those on Earth. But why should the life on another planet resemble life on Earth, even remotely, and if it is radically different how will we recognize it? James Lovelock suggested a way, and had used it to predict, ten years earlier, that Mars is lifeless.

Any living organism must take nutrient substances from its environment to maintain its own structure and provide it with energy, and it must excrete metabolic waste products. Nutrients would most easily be taken from, and wastes deposited in, a fluid, so some of them would pass through the planet's atmosphere, thus altering its chemical composition. If the atmosphere of a planet is chemically unstable, life may be present; if it is close to chemical equilibrium, its composition and reactions can be explained by physics and chemistry alone, and the planet is probably lifeless.

A planetary atmosphere can be analyzed chemically by examining the spectra of light passing through it, and the composition of the Martian atmosphere was known by this method in some detail before the Viking mission began. It consists mainly of carbon dioxide, is very close to its chemical equilibrium, and, as Viking 1 confirmed, Mars is lifeless.

Earth's atmosphere is very different. It contains, for example, both oxygen and methane. These gases react with one another so they cannot exist for very long together. On Earth they do, suggesting the constant replenishment of at least one of them, in an atmosphere that is chemically unstable. Were the concentration of oxygen to increase much above its present value of about 21 percent, all unoxidized carbon exposed to the air would burn. It may be that the methane, emitted by many animals but especially by termites, scavenges surplus oxygen, so offsetting the oxygen released by green plants during photosynthesis.

▼ *The Needles, Isle of Wight, England, are made from the crushed and compacted remains of seashells, composed mainly of calcium carbonate; carbon dioxide, once a main constituent of Earth's atmosphere, supplied the carbon. When the shellfish died, their shells sank to the seabed and formed sedimentary rocks, so preventing the carbon from returning to the atmosphere (♦ page 68). Today carbonate rocks, such as chalk and limestone, are common throughout the world. It did not happen this way on Mars or Venus.*

▼ *This microbial mat, in Baja California, Mexico, resembles fossil stromatolites 2 billion years old. Oxygen from communities like these mats, released as a byproduct of photosynthesis by the cyanobacteria, may have been what made Earth's atmosphere oxygen-rich (♦ pages 70-71).*

▶ Mars, as seen by the Viking1 lander in 1976. Ten years earlier, James Lovelock had used analyses of the Martian atmosphere to predict that no life would be found on Mars. This was the start of Lovelock's search for Gaia.

Regulating the climate

Carbon dioxide is a "greenhouse" gas: it traps heat radiated from the warmed ground surface, so forming a blanket that warms the air and the ground beneath. During the last four billion years the Sun is believed to have been growing steadily hotter, yet the temperature at ground level has varied little. This climatic stability has been achieved by the removal of carbon dioxide from the air and its burial, eventually, in ocean sediments well away from processes that might liberate the captured carbon. Green plants remove carbon dioxide from the air during photosynthesis, but when they die most of the carbon in their tissues is oxidized, returning the carbon dioxide. How, then, can carbon be removed from the air permanently?

Many rocks contain calcium silicate. As the rocks are weathered, making cavities into which bacteria, plant roots and burrowing animals can penetrate, calcium silicate is released. The living organisms release carbon dioxide below the ground surface, some of this dissolves to make a weak acid, and the acid increases the rate of weathering. It also reacts with the calcium silicate to form calcium bicarbonate and silicic acid, both of which are soluble. They move in solution through groundwater, rivers, and eventually reach the sea, where the calcium bicarbonate is taken up by marine organisms, which convert it to calcium carbonate, and use it to make their shells. When they die the shells drift to the seabed, where they accumulate as sediments. Thus the process by which the temperature on Earth remains fairly constant is controlled biologically. During the last ice age the atmosphere contained much less carbon dioxide than it does today. The end of the ice age was marked by a sudden sharp rise in both temperature and atmospheric carbon dioxide. No one knows what caused the change, but perhaps large numbers of marine phytoplankton – single-celled green plants that drift near the sea surface – died, reducing the rate at which carbon dioxide was being removed from the air.

This is not the only way in which our climate is being regulated. When the temperature rises, more water evaporates, especially from the oceans. Water vapor is also a greenhouse gas, and increases the warming effect, but when it condenses to form clouds the surface is cooled, partly by being shaded and partly because white clouds reflect incoming solar radiation back into space. Water vapor will not condense, however, unless there are microscopically small particles to act as "cloud condensation nuclei". Where are such particles to come from far out at sea? The vast majority of them are made from sulfate formed from dimethyl sulfide, which is emitted by most species of phytoplankton. Some of the sulfur-containing clouds and air drift over land. This is the principal mechanism by which sulfur, an essential nutrient that is constantly being washed from the land to the sea, is returned from the sea to the land. Iodine, another essential trace nutrient, may be transported in much the same way, using methyl iodide, also excreted by marine plants. James Lovelock has outlined the series of chemical reactions involved in this process and has suggested a way it may have evolved.

Today human activities are interfering with the way the climate is regulated. The atmospheric concentration of greenhouse gases is increasing. Carbon dioxide comes from the burning of carbon-based fuels and the clearance of tropical forests. Methane is released from rice paddies and cattle. Chlorofluorocarbons from aerosols and refrigerators trap longwave radiation very effectively. Most climatologists believe the resulting "greenhouse effect" will lead to major climate changes.

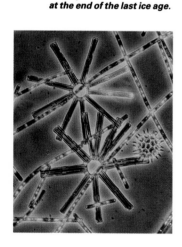

▼ *Asterionella formosa and Pediastrum boryanum are two species of phytoplankton, small marine plants that use carbon dioxide for photosynthesis. A decline in phytoplankton, and the oxidation of their carbon as they decomposed, may have caused an increase in atmospheric carbon dioxide at the end of the last ice age.*

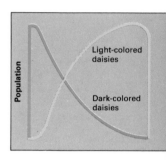

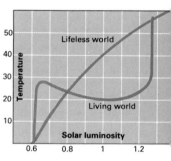

▲ *To test his idea that living organisms can regulate climate, James Lovelock made computer models of "daisyworlds" with light and dark daisies. As the planet's star ages, it becomes more luminous. At first, dark daisies predominate – they absorb sunlight and warm their surroundings. Later, white daisies take over – by reflecting the sun's light, they keep the planet cool. So the daisies keep their planet habitable to themselves.*

Daisyworlds

James Lovelock began describing the Gaian theory in the early 1970s, with articles in scientific journals; his book "Gaia: A New Look at Life on Earth" was published in 1979. For a long time scientists were reluctant to accept his ideas, mainly because of what they saw as a major flaw. If living organisms regulate the climate and the cycling of essential elements, largely for the benefit of other organisms, it seems to imply either that they can plan ahead for the results they wish to achieve, or that some overall planner operates the system. Lovelock set out to meet the criticism by designing "daisyworlds" as computer models.

A daisyworld is a very simple place. It is a planet much like Earth, but with no greenhouse gases in its atmosphere to complicate the climate, and it orbits a star very like the Sun. Only daisies grow on a daisyworld, but there are two kinds: black and white. In every other respect the two kinds of daisies are identical. They start growing when the temperature reaches 5°C, reach the peak of their growth at 20°C, but stop growing at 40°C. When it is very cold, no daisies can grow, but as the planet warms enough to cross the first temperature threshold, growth begins.

At first the black daisies thrive. Being dark they absorb radiation, so they are warmer than the ground beneath them. White daisies, on the other hand, reflect radiation, are cooler than the ground, and at first are very rare. Before long the planet is covered by black daisies, and this alters the color of the planet itself. It is darker, absorbs more radiation, and so the entire daisyworld grows warmer. Black daisies, then, make a cold world warmer.

As the temperature continues to rise white daisies start appearing, and eventually they begin to thrive because the black daisies begin to find conditions too warm for them. The white daisies reflect radiation, and keep cool, so they take over, and come to outnumber their black cousins. Now the color of the planet has changed again; it is lighter, reflects more radiation, and is made cooler. White daisies make a warm world cooler.

As the output of the star varies, so the black and white daisies simply respond to changing conditions, but in doing so they regulate the temperature. The process is entirely automatic; no planning is involved.

Still critical, some scientists objected that gray daisies would do better still. They could leave the regulation to the black and white varietes, thrive through all vicissitudes, and eventually take over the planet from their altruistic rivals. Later daisyworld models allowed for gray daisies. Indeed they allowed daisies of up to ten colors, only to reveal that the more variety there is in the world the more sensitive the regulatory mechanisms are to change and the finer their adjustments to it.

Rabbits were added to the models, to crop the daisies, and foxes to cull the rabbits, and all the populations interacted to regulate one another, and the world itself. Then arbitrary perturbations were introduced, causing the death of 40 percent of the daisies. Rabbits and foxes declined sharply, but then the world recovered rapidly, resisting the effects of the perturbations. The Gaian daisyworld models, growing more complex as they developed, have proved to be very robust. They have provided an explanation of the workings of Gaia and have demonstrated that planning and foresight are not required before the climate of a planet can be regulated. They also provide a theoretical justification for diversity. Species diversity is greatest when temperature regulation is most efficient.

◀ Examining ice cores at the Vostok base, Antarctica. Bubbles of air are trapped among the crystals as snow is compacted into ice. By analyzing this air, taken from layers that can be dated in cores cut from the ice, scientists can determine both the temperature at which the ice formed and the atmosphere's composition at the time. A clear correlation has been found between the temperature of the air and its carbon dioxide content going back more than 100,000 years.

The greater the diversity of species, the more the global system can respond to changes, sensibly, quickly and effectively

Gaian theory and the global environment

The Gaian theory and the new science of geophysiology derived from it allow scientists to study the Earth as though it were a single living entity and they were medical researchers who hoped to become skilled physicians. The daisyworld models (◀ page 69) suggest that the patient is inherently robust, but daisyworlds are not real, and Lovelock uses them only to demonstrate that this kind of planetary regulation is theoretically feasible. The Earth is different, and so may be its state of health. It would be quite wrong to suppose that the resilience of a daisyworld licenses humans to pollute and overexploit their planet with no thought for the consequences.

On Earth there are many areas in which we still do not know what is permitted and what is not, although it seems certain that mild pollution leading to no more than a deterioration in the quality of human life and, perhaps, a small reduction in human life expectancy will cause little harm to the planet as a whole. Many popular environmental concerns, such as slight radioactive pollution from nuclear power installations, are of little real importance.

Other human interventions in the system may be more serious. We know, for example, that there is a limit beyond which we should not interfere with the atmospheric concentration of carbon dioxide. If it falls below a certain critical value plant growth will be inhibited and we may expect a severe climatic cooling. If it increases we may expect a

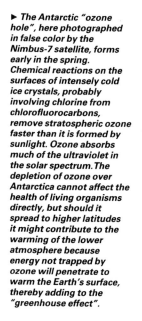

▶ The Antarctic "ozone hole", here photographed in false color by the Nimbus-7 satellite, forms early in the spring. Chemical reactions on the surfaces of intensely cold ice crystals, probably involving chlorine from chlorofluorocarbons, remove stratospheric ozone faster than it is formed by sunlight. Ozone absorbs much of the ultraviolet in the solar spectrum. The depletion of ozone over Antarctica cannot affect the health of living organisms directly, but should it spread to higher latitudes it might contribute to the warming of the lower atmosphere because energy not trapped by ozone will penetrate to warm the Earth's surface, thereby adding to the "greenhouse effect".

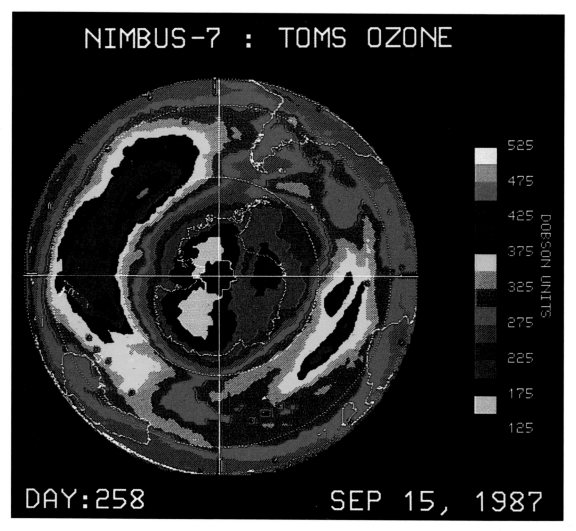

warming, partly offset perhaps by the cloud-seeding activities of phytoplankton, but we do not know how stable the climatic system is, now that so much of the Earth's atmospheric carbon has already been removed. Might a perturbation cause the world climate to alter suddenly and radically, either oscillating between severe cold and intense warmth, or might it restabilize to produce conditions much hotter than those we have now?

If we continue to clear forests in the humid tropics shall we alter the cycling of water locally to produce climatic changes with much wider effects? Shall we alter drastically the rate at which carbon dioxide is removed from the air, and release large amounts of carbon dioxide at present held in tropical soils? We do not really know, but it might be as well to proceed cautiously until we have more information. Meanwhile daisyworlds provide at least a few clues. They suggest, for example, that the greater the diversity of species, the more sensitive the system is to change, and the more effectively and quickly it acts to restore the conditions it prefers. Tropical forests are the richest and most diverse of all habitats in terms of the species they contain. The species may be of little importance individually, but taken together they may be essential.

There are also regions to which most of us pay little attention but which may be even more vital to our well-being. The sediments we see as coastal and estuarine muds when they are exposed at low tide, but which extend over much of every continental shelf, are not especially attractive, yet they provide the airless conditions in which countless numbers of microorganisms thrive, and those microorganisms play crucial roles in the cycling of essential elements between sea, air and land (◀ page 68). They have been playing this role since long before any of the larger plants and animals appeared on Earth. They could survive without us, but it is doubtful whether we could survive without them.

Gaian theory leads those who accept it to refute the old idea of organisms adapting to environments over which they have no control and to reject the crude symbolism of "Spaceship Earth", together with many newsworthy and apparently spectacular environmental issues that are revealed as imaginary or trivial. It substitutes a much more profound way of studying the Earth that allows us to look beyond symptoms to their underlying causes. Like illnesses, these causes are often complex, not easy to understand even for scientists, and almost impossible to describe accurately in nontechnical language. Yet, like an accurate diagnosis of illness, the application of a detailed knowledge of geophysiology will one day allow remedies to be prescribed that treat planetary ailments with clinical precision.

Since 1975, James Lovelock has collaborated closely with Lynn Margulis, professor of biology at Boston University. She argues that early in evolution certain organisms were absorbed into other simple cells, where they survived in modified form while more complex, nucleated, cells evolved, so that evolution has involved collaboration among organisms. Evidence for this is provided by the presence of deoxyribonucleic acid (DNA) in the chloroplasts of certain microorganisms in which photosynthesis occurs: the chloroplasts have evolved from cyanobacteria that were absorbed by other cells and have retained some of their own DNA. Professor Margulis has also studied the microbial communities living in algal mats (◀ page 66) and concluded that photosynthesizing cyanobacteria, in very similar communities, released the oxygen that transformed the atmosphere and allowed more complex organisms to evolve.

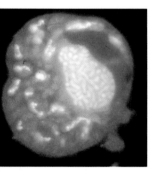

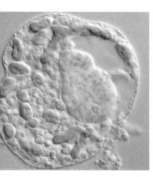

▲ *Gyrodinium aureolum, a dinoflagellate that contains chloroplasts in which photosynthesis occurs. The top picture shows the cell stained with a substance that binds to DNA, the lower picture shows the green chloroplasts. The presence of DNA in the chloroplasts, outside the cell nucleus (the large object in both pictures), supports Lynn Margulis's view that the chloroplasts have evolved from cyanobacteria that were absorbed into other cells, keeping some of their DNA.*

▲ *Lynn Margulis, professor of biology at Boston University, maintains that complex cells have derived from simpler cells. She now works closely with James Lovelock.*

AD 2290: a scientist reports

Perhaps this is the kind of "state of the planet" assessment we might expect from an environmental scientist 300 years from now:

"It was the relentless human urge to explore and colonize other worlds which led, in the 21st century, to experiments aimed at constructing, in hostile surroundings, sustainable environments that were hospitable to beings from Earth. Many failed, but eventually they led to the success which encouraged humans to see themselves as reproducing their Earth, first on Mars, and by the 22nd century in vehicles they sent far beyond the parochial confines of the Solar System.

"The experience gained in devising ways to keep colonists and long-distance travellers alive, well nourished, and healthy proved invaluable on Earth itself. The old idea that space research contributes nothing useful to the solution of terrestrial problems was soon recognized as profoundly mistaken.

"The development of space allowed the construction of Earth satellites that could monitor constantly every corner of the surface below, from the topmost layers of the atmosphere to the deepest ocean trenches. Any change was detected, analyzed, its significance assessed, and appropriate steps taken to remedy any harmful consequences. Environmental scientists were accorded popular respect and elite status which have always been granted to the most skilled of physicians. Their profession attracted ample funding, and the most talented of young scientists were eager to be recruited into it.

"By the 23rd century human understanding of the planet made environmental miscalculation virtually impossible. No large-scale development was permitted until its environmental implications were known. Nowadays, details of each scheme are examined by robot intelligences who analyze each separate item, calculate their mutual interactions, and then consider all of these in the contexts of the immediate neighborhood of the proposed scheme, then in the wider, regional context, and finally in a global context. If, at any stage, the calculations suggest changes which could prove adverse to living beings when extrapolated to a century beyond the probable life span of the development, modifications are demanded.

"Far from proving restrictive, such detailed consideration and care for what is still our traditional and 'natural' home is welcomed by everyone. No longer can inadvertent manipulation of the climate lead to drought and famine, irrigation schemes to salination, or poor engineering design to toxic pollution. Yet potentially hazardous schemes are not prohibited, they are simply relocated away from Earth, often to the Moon."

▶ A computer climate model of the US National Oceanic and Atmospheric Administration shows effects of doubling carbon dioxide in the atmosphere. Surface air temperatures increase (top two maps, increase in °C) in both winter and summer (upper and lower maps respectively). Soil moisture (bottom two maps, units in centimeters) falls in summer over central Eurasia and North America (bottom map). Large computers have made it possible to study the Earth's complex climate systems, in detail and as a whole.

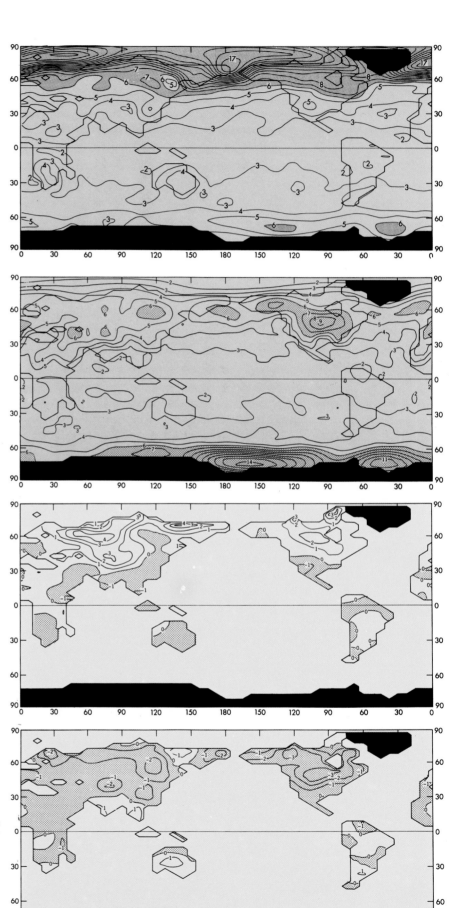

New Ways of Looking at Earth

7

*A single system...Earth-monitoring sciences...
The interdisciplinary revolution...Monitoring by
satellite...A "whole Earth" catalog...Computer
modeling...Effects of improved Earth vision...Should
we stop the next ice age?...Perspectives for future
generations*

The planet Earth is a large mass of rock, molten iron, water and gas and living things, held together by gravity and warmed by radioactivity inside it and by sunlight from the sky. An intricate web of life covers its surface. When you add human beings and all that they do the world seems too complicated a system for anyone to comprehend in its entirety.

For this reason, scientists describe the Earth in a piecemeal fashion, taking one region and one subject at a time. An expert on wild mammals, for example, is not expected to know much about volcanoes, irrigation, human birthrates, or the market price of timber, even though any of these things can be a matter of life and death for antelopes and lions. By tradition, geography is the subject that supposedly draws the threads together, and provides an overview that spans everything from earthquakes to nuclear power plants, but in practice geographers are specialists too.

Regardless of whether or not scientists comprehend it, the Earth and its human populations operate as a single system. A volcano in the Pacific Ocean can affect the weather in Europe. The price of copper in London influences mining policies in South America. Blighted coffee crops in Brazil can make Africans go hungry, if the effect is to encourage planters in Africa to grow more coffee, rather than grain. If the burning of coal and oil in North America helps to increase the carbon dioxide in the air, and if that results in the melting of the Antarctic ice sheets, the rise in sea level worldwide may cause floods in the Netherlands, Bangladesh and other low-lying regions.

Earth-watching sciences must improve
Until the 1960s, and despite the Copernican and Darwinian revolutions in knowledge, people went on behaving as if the Earth and its contents were created especially for their benefit, to do with as they pleased. The first images of the Earth from space had a big impact, in forcing people fully to realize that they inhabit a small planet. Today there is a widespread if still somewhat vague awareness that we are altering our planet more rapidly than ever before, for a whole variety of reasons. The future images from space will teach people, in salutary detail, that in their everyday deeds they are interacting with a complex and vulnerable system, which they need but which does not need them.

Some prophets of doom assert that we shall soon exhaust the Earth's resources or pollute ourselves to death. Optimists assert that the Earth's systems are robust, and that improved technologies will in any case ease all the pressures on the planet. Others see the main concerns as political, with environmental issues carrying the seeds of iniquity and war.

Scientific understanding of worldwide interactions is, so far, too limited to say where the truth lies, between these various points of view. If the care of the planet is a management task, our species is in the position of a child who has to fly a jet plane without knowing what all the switches and levers do. Fast learning is plainly needed, and very rapid developments in the sciences that monitor the Earth are likely to occur in the decades ahead.

► *Like horses on a merry-go-round, satellites chase one another around the globe in the "geosynchronous" orbit high above the Equator that keeps pace with the Earth's rotation. Each of them stays over a chosen region to relay radio signals or to observe the weather. Earth-watching satellites are now the key to monitoring the planet.*

74

The advent of artificial Earth satellites and the computer has provided the tools for use in the meteorological revolution

Seeing the planet as a whole

New ways of looking at the Earth as a whole are now becoming available just when they are most needed. A revolution in geology, in the 1960s, showed that volcanoes, earthquakes, mountain-building and the distribution of useful minerals are all to be understood in terms of plate tectonics. The outer shell of the Earth is divided into rigid plates that shuffle around the globe. Geological activity concentrates mainly at the boundaries between plates, but the plate movements reflect convection deep in the Earth and they communicate pressures across the surface at ranges of thousands of kilometers.

A revolution in studies of weather and climate, in the 1970s, involved, in part, a reassessment of knowledge of past climatic changes, which explained the ice ages and also forced meteorologists to realize that the present climate is unreliable. Climatic change has not ceased. There was also a growing recognition that human activities, in burning fuels, stirring up dust, felling forests, and covering large areas with buildings and roads, were reaching a scale where they could not fail to affect the climate. The last and most constructive element in the meteorological revolution was the advent of tools for looking at and comprehending the whole world's weather, using a combination of modern inventions. One was the Earth satellite, capable of radioing pictures of cloud patterns and other weather indicators from its vantage point high above the Earth. The other was the computer, which in the 1970s was becoming just about powerful enough to calculate the weather in realistic ways.

Worldwide data from the satellites, and from more traditional sources such as balloons, are now fed routinely into supercomputers capable of assimilating them and then running "models" of the worldwide weather system that can make forecasts for several days ahead. Similar computer models set out to describe the world's climate in precise, calculable terms, and to explore factors that can cause changes in climate. For example, plants alter the color of the Earth's surface, and therefore the amount of sunlight absorbed. They also pump water from the soil into the air, and their breathing of gases, in and out, keeps changing the chemical composition of the air. And the plants, especially the trees, act as windbreaks and as guardians of the

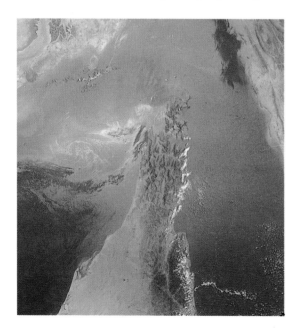

▼ In the Strait of Hormuz, a promontory of Arabia points like a spear at Iran. This photograph taken from the Space Shuttle "Columbia" shows rugged, arid land and the swirling currents of the sea at the narrow exit to the war-torn Arabian–Persian Gulf. Through this choke-point supertankers carry most of the world's trade in oil.

▼ While Mount St Helens, Washington, USA was brewing up for its big eruption in 1980, a high-flying airplane photographed it by infrared light. The ash-strewn volcanic cone stands out in the resulting image like a gray pimple amid forests and fields that were later devastated. The conversion of infrared data to false colors is routine in the processing of aerial and space images, and vegetation that looks green to the eye typically appears red in color composites.

soil. The meteorologists trying to describe the climate in a computer found themselves dragged willy-nilly into an ever-widening range of other sciences (◗ page 78). Organizationally, this has taken the form of an International Geosphere-Biosphere Project, which has come to be known as the Global Change Program (◗ page 76).

The combination of satellites and computer models that has been so successful in day-to-day weather forecasting sets an example for others to follow. There is a promise of an ever-widening network of knowledge that will range from astronomical and geological factors that have been operating over millions of years, to the responses of the genes of individual plants during the daily life of a meadow. Such developments will amount to a revolution in ecology, the science that investigates the interactions between living things and their physical and biological environments. The two main ingredients will be, first, better satellites and related analytical systems for monitoring physical and biological conditions in every part of the world and, second, better computer models of living systems.

▼ *Sea-surface temperatures in the Gulf of Mexico, measured by a US weather satellite, are gathered in a map that uses blue to depict the coolest areas, and red for the warmest. The narrow yellow and red ribbon at the right is the Gulf Stream. It pours out into the Atlantic Ocean between the long, thin island of Cuba and Florida, a finger of the USA. This current rules the climate of Europe some 7,000km away, and keeps that distant continent much warmer than it would otherwise be. The Gulf Stream typifies the long-range connections to be found within the Earth's physical and biological systems.*

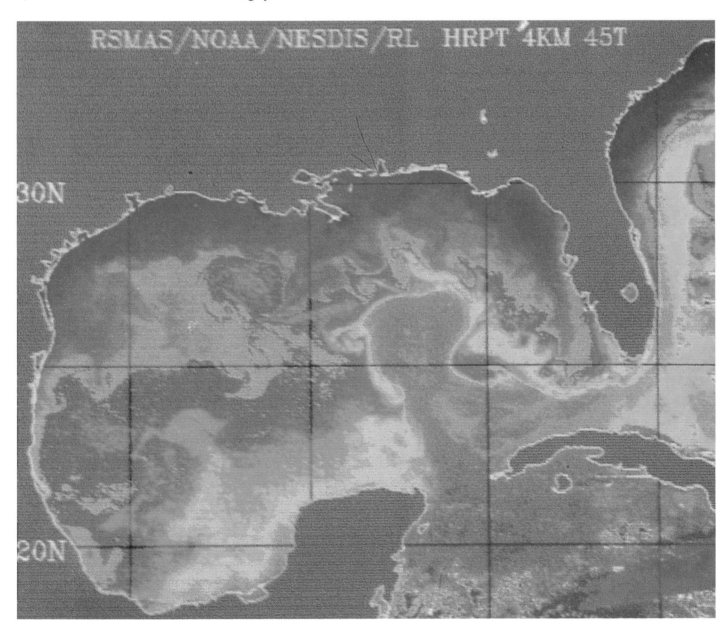

Modern techniques permit maps to be made in days, that used to take decades to compile

---

A Whole Earth Catalog – features to be monitored from space
Based on the Global Change Program of the International Council of Scientific Unions

For land ecosystems:

Surface albedo (light or dark color)
Surface temperature
Vegetation cover
Moisture, evaporation, and
    transpiration in plants
Snow extent and depth
Frequency and intensity of rain
    and snow

For marine ecosystems:

Ocean color (green plants,
    sediments)
Gases in the air over the oceans
Ocean topography
Wind stress
Sea-surface temperature
Volumes of ice by land and sea

For geological processes:

Soil type, and changes with time
Volcanic eruptions and dust
Sediments in coastal waters
Dynamic and permanent features
    of the landscapes

The Earth from space

Weather satellites provided the first and most directly useful systems for monitoring the Earth, and their images of cloud patterns are familiar to television viewers. But the satellites observe much more than clouds and storms. Besides temperatures, and a great variety of other weather-related data, they can record, for example, the density of vegetation in different places, and the condition of the soil. Other remote-sensing satellites, notably the American Landsat and French SPOT, observe the Earth's surface at different wavelengths of visible and infrared light, to build up multicolored pictures of rocks, soil, water, vegetation and land use.

Two particularly successful experimental satellites were launched by the United States. Nimbus 7 detected the colors of coastal waters and the amounts of key gases in the stratosphere. Seasat, in a short but highly productive life, observed the sea surface by radar and generated data on wind, waves and currents. A European satellite, ERS-1, is a successor to Seasat, largely dedicated to studying the oceans, coastal waters and polar regions by radar. Since it can penetrate clouds, radar is especially promising, but as with all aspects of remote sensing, everything depends on interpretation. Careful "ground truth" investigations, to compare the space images with what exists on the ground, are essential. Biological observatories at the Earth's surface will be necessary counterparts to satellites and meteorological observatories.

Looking ahead to the late 1990s, the planners of the Global Change Program (◀ page 75) expect more sophisticated weather satellites in orbit around the Earth's poles to be giving daily observations of land vegetation, plant life in the oceans, the composition and temperature of the atmosphere at various heights, snow and ice cover, and the Earth's budget of radiant heat received from the Sun and lost into space. Space stations and research satellites will extend the power of Earth observation, including the use of radars and laser beams.

Even the existing remote-sensing system gleans information that goes far beyond the generation of single images of pieces of the Earth's surface. Using satellite data, experts can make, in a matter of days or weeks, global and regional maps that would take decades or centuries of effort by conventional means. Sometimes they show data that have been mapped before – the bottom topography of the oceans deduced from Seasat data is a striking example. Other maps are completely novel, such as those that show the sources of evaporation that provide the rainfall in other places. The speed with which the mapping can be done, using satellite data, is not just a convenience, but the best assurance that global changes can be monitored year by year. Satellite data will also have to go into computer models analogous to those already used in weather forecasting, but now extending into the living environment. This will force a rapid development of the science of ecosystems.

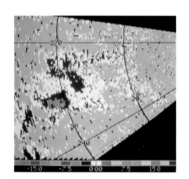

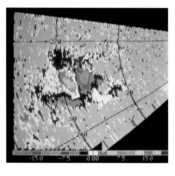

▲ *Winds observed by a radar of the US National Center for Atmospheric Research reveal details of a weather system. In the first image, the green-and-white areas show winds blowing toward the radar, but a minute later (below) the colors show a reversal in wind direction. This was the result of a strong downdraft of air.*

▲▶ *The French satellite SPOT ended a superpower monopoly of space systems generating detailed pictures of the Earth's surface. A SPOT image of southern France (right) shows at the bottom the Mediterranean Sea and the coastal swamps of the Camargue, which are a home for beavers, flamingos and cowboys. The Rhône river divides on its way to the sea, at the town of Arles. Roads, railroads and canals make straight lines across the plain, and the runways of an airport are visible. Fields and woodland stand out clearly in false reds. One "snapshot" from space tells more about conflicting uses for the land than years of study on the ground.*

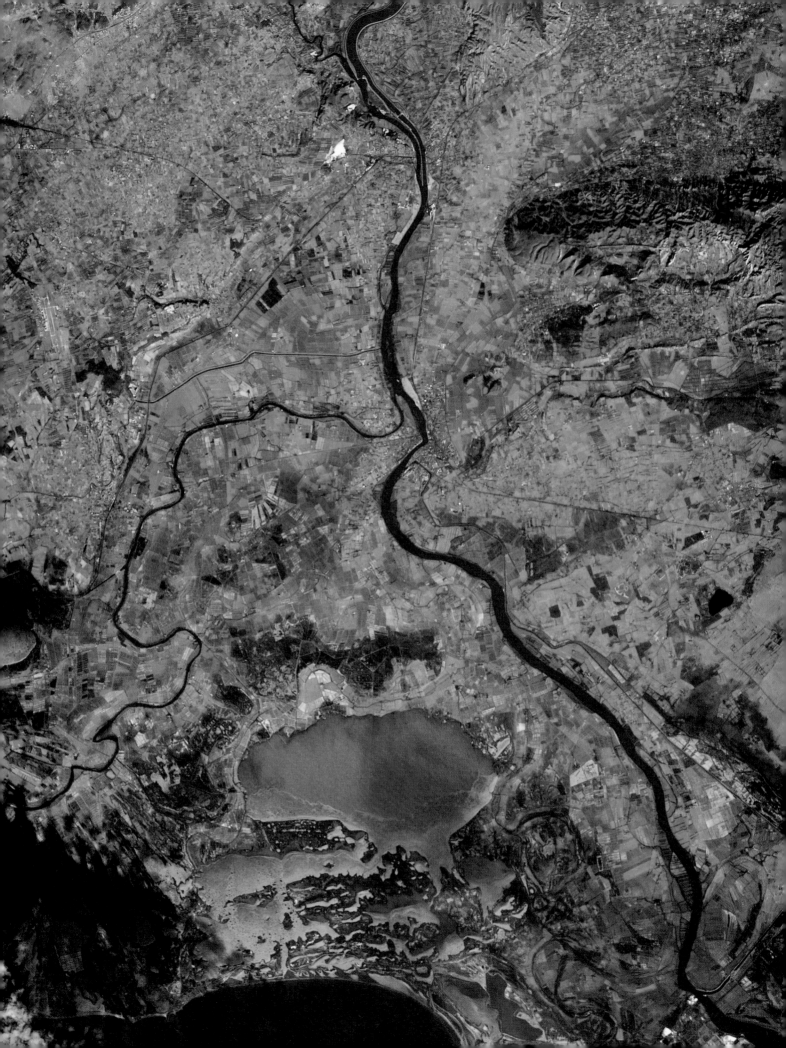

Matching economic models to remote-sensed data from satellites should help integrate human ecology in a comprehensive picture of world systems

▲ *The Chernobyl nuclear power station in the USSR shows up in this US Landsat image shortly after a major fire in 1986 released radioactive fallout across much of Europe. The red dot indicates infrared rays coming from the crippled reactor. Satellites can help considerably to assess disasters, natural or man-made, anywhere on Earth.*

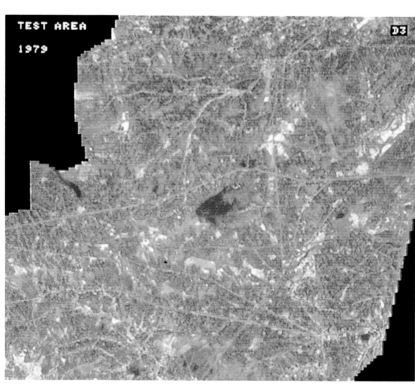

▲ *Rice and salt compete for possession of irrigated land in this Landsat image of rice paddies in Pakistan. Red denotes the vegetation of fields where rice is growing. White reveals areas that have been thrown out of cultivation by salt building up in the soil as a result of prolonged irrigation. The main irrigation channels are visible, and there is open water at the center of the image. Such pictures have a capacity to shock – and consequently to encourage wiser management of water resources.*

Computer models in ecosystem economics

Ecological theory has developed in a piecemeal fashion. Early descriptions of food chains, in which small animals feed on plants, and larger animals feed on the small animals, were elaborated into dynamic systems in which overfeeding could lead to a collapse of the populations, followed by recovery. Other research showed that the number of species and the size of the largest animals that an ecosystem can support depend on its area. Theories similar to those used by doctors to study epidemics among humans were applied to the study of the spread of pests and diseases in the wild; there was growing knowledge of cooperation and conflict between groups of plants and animals, and their interactions with their physical circumstances.

A different kind of theory proved to be better suited to handling data of the kind that comes from remote-sensing satellites. Scientists at the Agricultural University of Wageningen in the Netherlands had notable success with computer models of the growth of crop plants. Feeding in information about, for example, sunshine, temperature, and rainfall, they can predict the crop yield. As in the case of weather forecasts, the calculations proceed step by step, by additions to the plant's mass. Each increase depends on how big the plant was before, and what weather conditions it has experienced.

Ecological models of this kind can be used to explore the reasons for low crop yields, or to show the way to higher yields. If some aspect of the growing process is not well understood, the modeler makes a simple assumption about it and sees if the model works. But wherever there is special knowledge, it can be fed into the models. They thus provide a framework for a theory of ever-increasing richness, which will eventually describe entire natural forests on the one hand, and on the other will reach down into the genetic systems that govern the growth and behavior of individual plants.

The human economy is another major dynamic system to be included in a comprehensive picture of a changing world. Since the 1970s,

▲ That mankind is not the only clumsy species appears from this Landsat image of Zimbabwe, close to Lake Kariba (blacked out). On one side of a gorge (top right) a deep red shows lush growth in an area free from elephants. On the other side, yellow and orange tell of the presence of herds of elephants harming the vegetation.

computer programs that try to give a worldwide picture of human activity have been under development, with varying degrees of success. They are still not very reliable. However, the discipline of trying to match these economic models to remote-sensing data, of the kind that satellites can supply, should be a powerful incentive to making the necessary improvements.

At the simplest end of their range, economic models of human ecology will show that people burn more fuel when the weather turns cold. In their more ambitious modes the models will show, for example, how the rate of house-building in Japan affects the demand for tropical timber, hence its price, and hence the rate of tree-felling in West Africa. Crop models will show whether that rate is sustainable or not, and climatic models will explore the effects on local rainfall and on depths of water in the harbors at the mouths of West African rivers. With coupled systems of this kind, continuously monitored and updated by satellite observations, people will begin to see amazing linkages. An American ship may run aground in the mouth of the Congo river because tropical hardwoods are fashionable for decorating rooms in the Far East.

The impact on human life of improved Earth vision

Better knowledge of the world will not necessarily make international relations more cordial, as it becomes easier to see who are the polluters, who are squandering resources such as petroleum or tropical forests, in short, and who are prospering at others' expense. Countries may be pressured into stopping activities which harm the Earth, provided it does not cost them too dearly. Curbing the use of chlorofluorocarbons in aerosol propellants, for example, may be a good deal easier than restraining the use of coal and oil.

The ever-closer scrutiny of the Earth from space will have an effect in the military sphere. In the first decades of the space era, Landsat and other remote-sensing satellites developed for civilian purposes were clearly distinguishable from the much more searching surveillance or "spy" satellites used to observe military and related activities. The latter, possessed at first only by United States and the Soviet Union, gave those superpowers a privileged view of each other's territory and also of the rest of the world. But as civilian remote sensing systems improve, they become better able to observe warships, aircraft, tanks and other military objects. If the images are available world-wide, it will be increasingly difficult for one country to attack another without its preparations being apparent to the unsleeping eyes in space. This may tend to reduce the risk of war, and fears of war.

For ordinary people, the chief effect of improved views of the Earth will be psychological. Perhaps a new branch of science, ecopsychology, will examine the perceptions, interests, anxieties and pleasures of individuals and communities, in their relationships with their environment. How much of the planet-wide picture of an ever-changing environment an individual will be able to carry in his or her head, and how far this awareness of global processes will affect perceptions of the local environments, and everyday decisions at a personal or communal level, only time will tell. But the new ways of looking at the Earth may encourage a rediscovery of an ancient hunter-like or peasant-like wisdom, this time planet-wide in its scope. Hunter-gatherer communities possess such detailed knowledge of the animals and plants, soils and rocks, weather and water supplies, and the changing seasons signaled by the stars, that they are able to survive with the minimum of effort, even in the difficult environments into which the farmers and industrializers have driven them. Although peasant farmers have to work much harder, they too know the land and the life on it in ways that have not yet been adequately matched by scientific descriptions, but which are often reflected in local religions. They have long memories, too, recalling exceptional weather or outbreaks of crop diseases that brought their communities to the brink of disaster. The peasant's quest is not for maximum profit from year to year, but maximum chance of survival from decade to decade.

Today's televised weather forecasts give an impression of what is coming. Animated satellite images and computer forecasts portray great weather systems sweeping across the land, so that the viewer who knows where he or she is on the map can see not only how and when the weather will change, but why. People learn to read the satellite images as previous generations interpreted the patterns of clouds appearing on the horizon. They can also appreciate possible sources of error in the forecasts, if a depression should move faster or slower than expected, or in a different direction. Unseasonable weather also makes sense, as it occurs when the jet stream guides the depressions along unusual tracks, or is unable to break through an area of high pressure.

▶ *Loss of vegetation in the drought-stricken Sahel of Africa has caused the soil to harden, so that rainwater quickly runs away. To check the water and save it, the farmers of Burkina Faso adopt a traditional remedy. They build a large number of long, low walls of stone to make miniature dams. Their knowledge and experience may count for at least as much as the global overview of scientists, satellites and computers.*

▼ *Abandoned freezers in the English countryside typify a human capacity to take ores and energy from the Earth, to work diligently upon them in making ingenious products – and then to use them only to spoil the scenery. Developing a sense of belonging to a tightly-knit global system, may help to curb such behavior.*

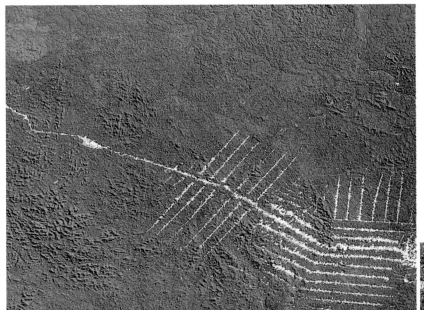

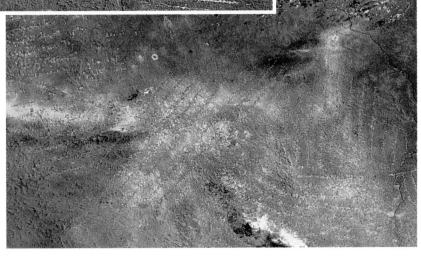

◄ Damage to tropical forest in Brazil is revealed in two successive Landsat images. The first shows a main road and side roads newly driven through the dense vegetation (red). Just 5 years later, the large blue-and-white patches reveal forest clearance, where the land has already become infertile.

The next ice age

In coming generations, increased respect for the complexity of Earth's systems may lead to a new caution about initiating human activities that may disturb them (▶ page 84). Paradoxically, accepting the Earth "as it is" also means tolerating natural changes in the environment. An important test case for human attitudes will come with the next ice age. The normal condition for the Earth during the present geological era, which began about two million years ago, is glacial. Large ice sheets bury Canada, Scandinavia and other northern and high-altitude terrain. Every so often, a favorable arrangement of the Earth in its orbit around the Sun delivers a blast of heat in the northern summers that melts the ice sheets. This event ushers in a warm interval that lasts for about 10,000 years.

Human agriculture and civilization developed during one of these warm interglacial periods, which will come to an end soon. If the increase in carbon dioxide due to human activities is truly tending to warm the Earth, that may postpone the advent of the next ice age by a few centuries. Sooner or later, though, the Earth will feel the effects of enfeebled sunshine in the northern summers, and the snows of winter will fail to melt over large areas of land.

A natural question in this technological era is "how can we ward off the ice age?" Ideas are not lacking. They range from painting the ice sheets black to putting huge mirrors in orbit to increase the supply of sunshine. The technical difficulties speak for themselves, but worse may be the task of achieving international agreement about what is to be done. Each country would be affected differently by natural climatic changes and by human countermeasures.

However, even if the technical and political problems could be overcome, it is not clear that "canceling the ice age" is a good idea. For a start, the melting of the present ice sheets and flooding of low-lying land would probably become inevitable. More fundamentally, the ice age is a period of renewal for the Earth. The grinding of rocks by glaciers creates rich new soil. A fall in the sea level refreshes the coastal landscapes, by clearing swamps and releasing fresh supplies of sand for the beaches. An ice age is a testing time for many living creatures, but Arctic and mountain species now in retreat will have a long-awaited opportunity to prosper. Among human beings, another ice age would alter the political and economic maps of the world in favor of the inhabitants of the tropics.

The new view of the Earth is comprehensive in time as well as space. In a long perspective, human beings are children of the past ice ages. The drastic climatic changes of the last two million years helped to drive evolution along, and favored a resourceful species. By 50,000 years ago, our talkative subspecies *Homo sapiens sapiens* appeared, in time to endure the worst of the most recent ice age, around 20,000 years ago. The hunter-gatherers not only survived but thrived, even in glacial Europe. They developed new technologies together with art, visible in the cave paintings at Lascaux in France, that bears comparison with anything done since.

Such factors will be remembered when ice-age policy is debated in the centuries ahead. With vastly superior technology, compared with their stone-age ancestors, modern human beings with due warning should have no insuperable difficulty in surviving an ice age. Just as the ordinary seasons bring variety to the lives even of urbanized humanity, so the superseasons of interglacial and glacial phases may come to be seen as but an interesting variation in the natural order.

▲ At present (top) the ice sheets of the northern continents are mainly confined to Greenland. During an ice age (below) they expand to bury much of North America and Europe. Even now, ice by land and sea can cover up to 16% of the surface of the globe, and in an ice age the figure increases to nearly 30%. Recent ancestors, members of our subspecies, lived through the last ice age, during which they spread all over the world.

▼ This could be a summer view of London or New York during an ice age, although it is really a present-day scene from Iceland in the spring. Whether our descendants should accept the next ice age, or whether they ought to resort to extraordinary technological means to try to prevent it, will be a matter for intense debate.

▶ *A defunct city of the Maya, Tikal some 1,500 years ago was the grandest city of Central America. For several centuries the Maya tamed the land with drainage canals – until something went wrong with their system and the jungle returned. It might happen again – there is no guarantee of eternal life for any of today's cities.*

Less engineering, more acceptance

The new ways of looking at the Earth bring a great convergence of human interests. Genes and mountains are related (◊ page 75), and so are weather and prices (◊ page 79). To know the Earth better is to know ourselves better – we are products of the planet's long history, as are the fishes or the rivers. The very colors of our skins reflect the climates to which our more recent ancestors were exposed.

What will the ordinary person glean about the planet-wide environment 300 years from now? He or she will see, from satellite pictures and analyses, that a pollution accident in an estuary has damaged important bacteria, or that a spaceship taking off has left a trail of nitrogen oxides. The images of the Earth will show the miracle of spring, as the physical and biological systems of the Earth combine in preparation for the new season's growth.

The consequences for planetary engineering may be curiously negative. Even while their fellow humans are transforming Mars and building cities in space (◊ pages 32, 36), or preparing batteries of rockets to defend the Earth against wayward comets and asteroids, the Earth's inhabitants may be loath to augment the sunshine, water the deserts or divert ocean currents, even though they will be quite capable of doing so.

Such a resurgence of peasant-like conservatism might result in part from caution, and a fear that even the most powerful computer models will not fully predict the consequences of man-made changes. The more these models assimilate and in some sense master the intricacies of the living environment, the more they will show up further areas of ignorance, and also unthought-of ill-effects of superficially beneficial schemes. The outcome might even be a paralysis of the human will to change the environment.

More positively, this will be seen as an acceptance of the Earth as it is, and an appreciation of its great diversity of habitats for wildlife and human life. These are more various, and therefore more valuable, than they could ever be if they were all adapted to high-yield crop production. People electing to live in deserts, on mountains or ice sheets will value their environments because they are distinctive, with their own peculiar climates and wildlife. They will keep their crop production and other necessities of life as compact as possible.

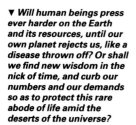

▼ **Will human beings press ever harder on the Earth and its resources, until our own planet rejects us, like a disease thrown off? Or shall we find new wisdom in the nick of time, and curb our numbers and our demands so as to protect this rare abode of life amid the deserts of the universe?**

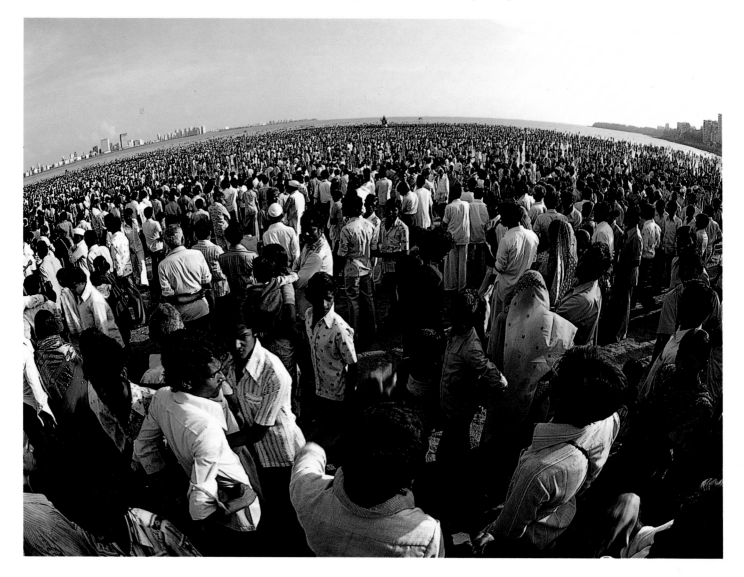

Warding off Natural Hazards

8

Natural hazards are part of the overall human condition...Natural compared with manmade hazards...Softening the impact of storms...Long-term climatic changes...Precautions against earthquakes...Earth as a target for bolides...Concerns of volcanologists...Prospects for controlling weather and climate

A context of manmade hazards

The problem of natural hazards must be set in the context of manmade hazards, especially those driven by human ambitions and fears. The present arsenal of nuclear weapons, for example, if used might kill up to one billion people from blast, fire and radiation. What happens to the remaining four-plus billion people is currently the subject of the typical type of debate when emotions are involved and the subject is too complex for accurate prediction. There can be no doubt that some people will die from cancer, starvation and social strife. Smoke clouds from burning cities will affect at least local weather conditions, and may produce a major climatic change. Depending on the time of year and the extent of the nuclear exchange, the mean temperature might fall by many degrees for days or months. There is enough food stored in the world to feed people for a few months to two years, depending on the country, even if agriculture is shut down. More than half of the world's population might survive a nuclear war, even in the worst case, but what a world it would be! Even ignoring the dangers of a nuclear winter, elimination of all nuclear weapons and most conventional weapons must be a highly desirable goal.

Conventional wars have already caused deaths up to the tens of millions, either directly or indirectly. Misconceived or deliberate social programs have killed further tens of millions either by famine or organized slaughter. One percent of the people in developed countries will die from routine automobile accidents, and ten percent will be seriously injured. Should natural hazards be taken seriously when they kill so few compared with these causes? Probably it is desirable to do something, no matter how many lives are saved, as it ensures that the human race recognizes the dignity of human life, and might help to establish a psychological climate for the reduction of manmade hazards. Certainly the diversion of scientists and engineers from military programs to averting natural hazards could serve a double purpose in working toward human safety.

On a day-to-day basis, most of us worry about health, getting a job, crime, and war: should we become more concerned about natural hazards and disasters, or should we just leave it to the experts?

Everyone experiences the meteorological hazards. High winds occur nearly everywhere, and hurricanes, typhoons and tornadoes occur in specially susceptible areas. Heavy rain and snowfall lead to floods, blizzards and avalanches. Ice storms and hail are locally destructive. Climatic hazards include droughts, which persist for several months or years, and long-term changes which proceed over decades or centuries. Greenhouse warming from growth of CO_2 (carbon dioxide), CH_4 (methane) and other gases will raise the sea level and change the agricultural zones; heat waves will intensify in the mid-latitudes, and storms may become stronger. Reduction of ozone in the stratosphere will increase the intensity of harmful ultraviolet radiation at the Earth's surface. Geological hazards range from frequent events such as landslides, subsidence and erosion of beaches and shores to rare violent events which include large earthquakes, big volcanic eruptions, and impacts by asteroids and comets.

Most hazards do not affect the safety of the entire human species. Even the worst earthquakes and storm surges have killed less than a million people. However, there have been on average about three large impacts every million years which have produced large craters, and probably one impact per 30 million years which has destroyed many species. The chance of extinction of the human species in any lifetime is small, perhaps one in a million, but it is not zero.

◄ **Lake Shore Drive, Chicago, closed by flooding in February, 1987 caused by a combination of factors typical of natural catastrophes: increased rainfall for the past 20 years, cooler temperatures generally reducing evaporation, a warm winter removing ice barriers and northerly winds piling water up at the southern end of Lake Michigan. Chicago's extensive lakeside development makes the city very vulnerable to flooding.**

86

Better meteorology depends on better satellite imagery, computer modeling, radar techniques, and surface observation station networks

Meteorological hazards

A look back over 30 years shows that meteorological forecasting has improved considerably, but has a long way to go. Satellite photographs show the progress of the major frontal systems. Computer models help in the preparation of weather forecasts. Radar reveals the movement of rain and snowstorms, and helps with hourly weather forecasts. Airline pilots can avoid dangerous storms. All these techniques will improve over the next 30 years, and would improve even faster if more resources were applied. Denser nets of more powerful radar sets will give more detail of storms. New techniques for satellite photography and sensing will probe the details of storm systems, and multiple arrays of satellites will give better coverage. An improved network of surface stations, especially at sea, is needed to give coverage under heavy cloud and to map water temperature. More information is needed on the pollution from dust and noxious gases. But complete success cannot be expected, because the weather systems are very complex, especially at continental margins and near mountains. Society must be organized so that the general public understands the problems of forecasting severe weather, and prepares itself to handle emergencies. Floods and avalanches are inevitable, and houses should not be built on land that has been flooded frequently in the past. Storm surges are inevitable on coastal flats, and improved social planning is needed to minimize disasters such as those in Bengal. The "greenhouse effect" (♦ page 100), a consequence of thermal expansion and ice melting, may cause flooding over much of Bangladesh and the Nile delta, both of which are very densely populated areas.

Can methods be developed to control violent weather? In principle, hurricanes can be capped with a cloud of carbon smoke to reduce the driving energy from the Sun. In practice, this and other ideas for modifying the weather are not taken seriously. Influencing the climate is a greater possibility, in the long term.

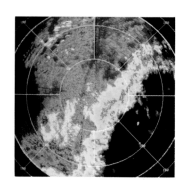

▲ *Radar imaging, here of the squall-line of a gathering storm, works when radar beams reflected from raindrops or snowflakes build up images which can be displayed on video screens and used for storm warnings and weather forecasting. Aircraft use radar to detect and avoid violent storms. More powerful radar can give more detail of storms.*

▶ *A hurricane taking shape. Satellite imagery is enhanced by computer and clarified by allocating "false" colors to radiation of different wavelengths or different intensities. Satellite imagery, computer processing and data from large numbers of ground and sea instruments can enhance the speed and reliability of forecasting.*

▶ *Some of the damage caused by tornado Albion in Pennsylvania in 1985. Satellite monitoring can give early warning of cyclones likely to form tornadoes. But the large-scale evacuation and other measures needed to minimize damage and loss of life are beyond the resources of a poor nation such as Bangladesh, which is most seriously affected by cyclones. A product of the "greenhouse effect", which is expected to warm the world by up to 2 °C before AD 2050, may be an increase of up to 40% in the destructive power of tornadoes. Calculations suggest that storm wind speeds will increase substantially. The destructive power of wind is proportional to the square of its velocity.*

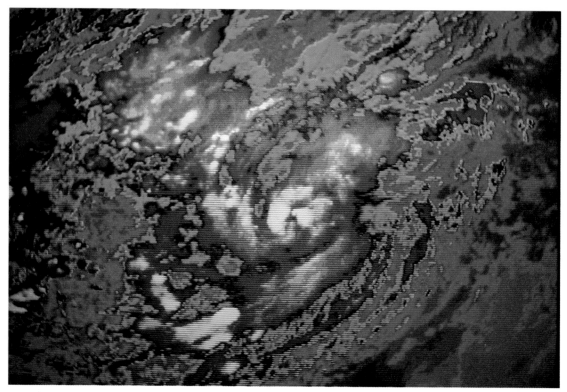

Changes in the Sun's energy output, volcanic eruptions, and increases in "greenhouse" gases may combine to vary mean temperatures by 2°C

▼ A bay in the side of an iceberg. Will the "greenhouse effect" cause large-scale melting of the great ice caps over Greenland and Antarctica, as well as increased melting of glaciers and the Arctic ice sheet? If so, then sea levels may rise by several meters. Further research is needed to make more accurate predictions possible.

Climatic hazards

The climatic changes that occur over the next few decades will result from three factors. First, the input of energy from the Sun does vary a little. However scientific understanding is still weak, and any predictions from the past climatic record are highly debatable. Second, the absorption of solar radiation by volcanic dust and sulfate aerosol (small droplets of acid) in the stratosphere (about 25 kilometers above the Earth) depends on the random occurrence of rare large volcanic eruptions. There is no way to predict when the next one will occur, but there is a 10 percent chance of a big one in any 30-year period. Third, the continual increase of CO_2, CH_4 and other "greenhouse" gases in the atmosphere is predicted to produce an average rise of temperature over the Earth's surface which might reach 1°C. In sum, these three effects should combine to produce an erratic variation of the mean temperature within the limits of -0.5 to $+2$°C, and probably within 0 to 1.5°C. It is important to recognize that the three factors have different time scales; the solar variation should be significant only over a 10-year or longer period; a huge volcanic eruption would modify the stratosphere for about two years; and the greenhouse gases will increase insidiously (unless the human race starts a major nuclear war) (♦ page 100).

Agriculture will undoubtedly be affected, but detailed predictions are difficult. Crop growth depends not only on the yearly average of temperature and rainfall, but also on the spacing and intensity of hot and cold periods and of wet and dry ones. It is unrealistic to expect accurate predictions at this level of detail from computer models. Plant geneticists are modifying the climatic range and robustness of plant varieties, and agricultural technology is still changing rapidly around the world. Nevertheless, there is some concern that there will be major changes in which regions of the world will support the growth of certain important crops. If there is no major volcanic eruption, the agricultural industry as a whole should be able to respond gradually to the overall climatic change. However, in the short term, farmers must face the disastrous effects of local weather extremes such as prolonged droughts. If the worst happens, they might have to face the two-year drop of temperature caused by a major volcanic eruption. Because food stocks range from only a few months in some countries to a maximum of two years in the most fortunate, it would be prudent to increase food stores in most countries. But in the present climate for international planning, this looks like a pipe-dream.

The loading of chlorofluorocarbons will increase in the stratosphere, simply because of their long lifetime and the economic and political difficulty of reducing emissions. How serious the increased intensity of ozone will be for humans and other species is a matter for speculation, but sunbathing should become less popular, and some species may suffer.

Pollution of the troposphere (atmosphere up to 8-15 kilometers) is likely to continue to be severe and might well get worse as more southern nations develop heavy industry and burn more coal. Local reduction may occur from improvements in emission control, as in the smokeless zones of British cities, but the regional outlook is not promising. Extensive liming of acidic soils and lakes may become economically desirable. Some people may move away from industrial areas and smog-filled basins into the windy prairies and savannas to improve their "personal" climate. However, the pull of the big cities like Tokyo, Beijing, Los Angeles and Mexico City may prove too strong.

▲ Air-pollution from an industrial estate near Haifa, Israel. The continuing increase in carbon dioxide from burning fossil fuels is thought to have caused an average rise in temperature of about 0.5°C over the past 100 years and to be likely to cause a further rise of up to 2°C by AD 2050. Damage from storm surges will mount, partly due to increased flooding and partly as a result of more powerful storm winds. Seawalls and tidal surge barriers will become necessary for some major cities. Prudent land use would involve the setting back of buildings in coastal zones, and designation of the lowest-lying areas as public parkland.

◄ *Gardens by the River Niger at Gao in Mali. It would be prudent to increase food stores in most countries, but this is beyond the resources of the countries most in need. Food stocks range from sufficient for a few months to a maximum of two years for the most fortunate nations.*

The problem of crying wolf will go on plaguing quake predictions, despite the experts' efforts

▼▶ *Buried underground in a tunnel (below) away from extremes of temperature which disturb readings, a strain gauge records slow and minute changes as rocks deform. Typical of the devastation wrought by earthquakes is a collapsed multistory building, destroyed by the Mexico City earthquake on September 20, 1985 (right). Strain gauges on the San Andreas fault in California can help to predict earthquakes with limited accuracy. Seismometers can provide at best a few minutes' warning, enough to switch off power to minimize fire dangers.*

Geological hazards

Each of the geological hazards has its own timescale and social effects. Landslides, subsidence and erosion, like the common cold, will continue to plague human beings, and there are no simple spectacular solutions. These hazards are essentially mundane, except to the unfortunates involved in each event. The cumulative loss of lives and of property is large in total, but usually small in each event. What is needed is meticulous and thorough mapping down to the scale of the hectare. Currently most geological surveys are starved for funds and most maps are hopelessly out of date, or there may not even be maps. From detailed maps, systematic land-use surveys can be prepared. Most would be ignored to some degree or other, as human hopes and wishes, and even greed, collide, but public education and a growing recognition of the private and public benefits of land-use planning should lead to their use in the mitigation of problems. As a first step, the more unstable parts of hillsides and worst areas of flood plains could be designated for parks and wilderness areas. The more stable parts of the hillsides and the less-frequently flooded areas could be used for specially-strengthened houses. There seems little hope for such planning in the next few decades in the desperately overcrowded areas of shantytowns in the underdeveloped world, but one must hope and plan with a longer-term perspective.

There will certainly be technical improvements in earthquake prediction within the coming decades. In the regions in which the plates of the Earth's crust slip past each other, the fault zones can be mapped in detail. There will be increasing success in predicting the site of large earthquakes as arrays of detectors pick up information on the release and buildup of strain. In parts of the Pacific margin, it is known that big earthquakes occur about once a century in each region, and that they tend to occur in seismic gaps where small earthquakes have been relatively rare. Direct measurements of strain have been of little value so far, but it will prove possible to focus on the most likely spots for the next big earthquakes, although there is little hope of a truly reliable prediction accurate to an hour, a day, a month, or perhaps even a year.

Without doubt, a real-time warning system from an array of detectors will provide from seconds to minutes of warning of the arrival of an earthquake's shock wave. Most well-constructed buildings should survive a major earthquake if correctly sited on stable rock. Good engineering, architectural and land-use planning would go far in reducing casualties. This desirable goal should be approached within decades in some technically-advanced countries. In less-developed countries, primitive dangerous buildings with weakly-bonded walls and collapsible roofs will probably collapse and be rebuilt the same way unless educational programs become successful.

Perhaps the major technical challenge facing scientists is to determine the causes of the earthquakes which occur within the major plates. Detailed mapping in the European and Asian seismic zones will undoubtedly reveal fault arrays, especially in eastern Asia where the continental block is fracturing in response to pressure from the Indian subcontinent. This should help experts to focus on the most dangerous regions for detailed study with arrays of seismic detectors. Even more challenging may be the Mississippi Valley region of the United States where a cluster of three earthquakes near New Madrid released more energy than big Pacific earthquakes. Did such a rare huge hazard come out of the blue, or was there a long period of precursory minor earthquakes not recorded by the untrained inhabitants?

▼ *A seismograph recording of the Mexico City earthquake. Building large offices on rubber mountings, as is now being done in Tokyo, allows them to absorb moderate tremors and built-in "fuses" can allow structures to sway. Regular, symmetrical structures are less vulnerable than irregular, asymmetrical ones.*

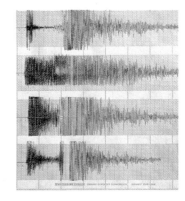

Out of sight, out of mind, describes the public attitude to the risk of impacts from bolides

Impacts

Earth continues to be the target of bodies ranging from tons of sand-size grains every day, to dozens of fist-sized bodies picked up as meteorites every year, a cathedral-size body every few centuries, and a kilometer-size bolide on a time scale of a million years. There is intense argument whether there is a regular cycle for the large bolides revealed by their craters, but it seems likely that at least half the impacts are random. Trees were knocked down 40 kilometers from the aerial explosion of a comet fragment over the Tunguska River in Siberia in 1908.

Most asteroids are probably parked temporarily in stable orbits, but a few skim past the Earth. Only one percent have been found by telescope; some are lost as their orbits change. About half-a-dozen new comets are recognized each year.

It is unnecessary to dramatize the damage from a big bolide. In general, a fast bolide blasts a hole about 10 times its own size in diameter and throws up a dust cloud which encircles the Earth. Atmospheric effects cannot be predicted accurately, but blockage of solar radiation and acid rainfall are two obvious hazards. Impact in an ocean would generate a huge tsunami which would swamp coastal areas. Volcanic activity might continue for centuries or millennia as the mantle moved up to fill a crater.

It would be premature to try within the next few decades to "zap" asteroids with nuclear bombs (but page 94). Much more sensible would be an effort to find out if any really big object is a current threat. This could be done with six wide-field-of-view Schmidt telescopes in 10 years as the Earth swings through the inner Solar System. The cost could be less than $100 million for equipment, staff and a computer center. Further planning for detection of smaller, but still dangerous, bodies could go ahead. Infrared satellites would help detect comets.

▼ A narrow escape. A meteorite of perhaps 1,000 tonnes was deflected from its course by the Earth's atmosphere on August 10, 1972, skipping off the thicker layers of the atmosphere like a flat stone skipping over water. The meteorite, seen here over Jackson Lake, Wyoming, leaving a trail of fire above the Teton Mountains, was visible from Utah to Alberta, a distance of over 1,000km.

Volcanoes

About 1,000 volcanoes are known to have erupted on Earth. Only a few are being monitored regularly, mostly with primitive equipment by the standard of big science and military technology. The rock and mineral chemistry of modern and ancient eruptives has been well determined, and there will be further advances over the next few decades in the understanding of the chemical and physical processes involved in volcanic eruptions. The technical jargon is forbidding because there are so many types of eruption and a wide range of chemical and physical processes. Essentially a volcano releases heat where it becomes focused under the Earth's crust. The type of eruption varies from quiet flows of gas-free lavas moving easily out of fissures, to violent eruptions from gas-rich viscous liquids trapped under the rocks from earlier eruptions. The geological record testifies to eruptions up to 100 times greater than any in historic times, but the volcanologists do not know how to predict where, when and how the truly giant eruptions will occur.

Volcanologists want to establish an international system for early warning of volcanic eruptions. So far their plans have been frustrated by lack of funding, but it is hard to believe that their well-justified proposals will be ignored indefinitely. The 30,000 people at Ruiz in Columbia need not have died from a mudslide if only the local leaders had heeded the warnings. It is only a matter of time (of course nobody knows how long) before a volcano such as Vesuvius shakes the industrial world into belated recognition that volcanologists should be funded at a level (millions of dollars) that would still be pitifully modest compared with military budgets (nearly a trillion dollars worldwide). To begin with, the volcanoes that look the most dangerous should be monitored, and crisis teams should go to those which show increased seismic activity. All inhabited areas near volcanoes should be checked for danger from potential ashfall and mudflows. Since most of the dangerous volcanoes are in poorer countries, technical training programs should be instituted so that local technicians can monitor their own volcanoes and educate the local people. At a more advanced level a satellite system is needed to monitor volcanic eruptions in remote areas, and to map the distribution of dust and aerosol in the atmosphere. Many commercial planes have flown into volcanic clouds, and some have lost power from ash choking the jet engines. Real-time forecasting is needed. All these programs can easily be brought about in 30 years. The technology is straightforward. Only the human will is needed.

▼ Dynamite being placed in an attempt to divert the flow of lava from the eruption of Etna, Sicily, in 1983. Volcanologists would like to monitor all volcanoes near populated areas to establish their "track record". Volcanoes with snow caps are especially dangerous because mudflows can develop. Volcanologists warn against complacency: eruptions up to 100 times more powerful than any in the last century have occurred in the Earth's recent geological history.

Influencing the weather long-term

Will it ever be technically feasible to control the Earth's weather systems, and would we want to? Instead of wind speeds ranging from 0 to 100 kilometers/hour could we moderate them to speeds of, say, 5-50? Could we control the rainfall so that there are smaller and more frequent precipitations spread more evenly over the Earth?

In principle, it is possible to inject smoke at chosen places to modify the energy distribution from the Sun. In practice, the problems are enormous, for both physical and social reasons. The current history of cloud-seeding is a morass of hopes, many failures, possible local successes and social conflicts. The same problems are likely to persist, but there may be some minor technical successes.

Probably the best way to minimize weather extremes is to reduce the contrast of energy-transfer across the Earth's surface. Forests reduce wind speeds and temperature extremes, and many parts of the world should be reforested, or remain forested. Planting drought-resistant shrubs and, ultimately, trees over desert regions would darken the reflecting surfaces.

Again in principle, energy-transfer could be modified at water surfaces by coating them with an oil or polymeric film. In practice, there are severe technical problems from wave action and chemical pollution. All in all, it seems likely that meteorological hazards ($ page 86) will be countered best by good prediction and social planning.

Climate

Current predictions about changes in the Earth's climate over the next few decades ($ page 88) are made without rigorous experimental justification. But they will be validated or discredited as the solar, volcanic and "greenhouse" factor contributions are accounted for. It should become possible to extrapolate the greenhouse effect reliably for at least some decades in advance, and it just might become possible to predict the variation of the Sun's radiation. However, predicting the size of a large volcanic eruption will probably remain elusive.

Thorough discussion of the possible manipulation of the physical processes and chemical composition of the atmosphere is certain to come. Currently there are no obvious ideas for reducing the 10-100-year

lifetime of the chlorofluorocarbon molecules which reduce the ozone concentration of the stratosphere: the tight bonding between the atoms resists chemical reaction. Perhaps some smart chemist will invent a species which can be sprayed into the stratosphere to scavenge the chlorofluorocarbons. Deliberate emission of microscopic soot particles in the high stratosphere is a technique worth trying as an experiment, if the astronomers do not object. Measurements of the rate of dispersal are needed to see how it compares with the movement of volcanic residues, which take three weeks to surround the Earth at constant latitude, and one year to spread from Equator to Pole. How the reflectivity and absorptivity vary with time also needs to be measured.

Perhaps more promising is the hope that humankind will learn to hold its population at a level compatible with a reduced level of "greenhouse" and ozone-destroying gases in the atmosphere. Good housekeeping of energy use may help, especially if solar-cell technology produces enough electricity for coal and oil to be phased out. The hope that genetically-engineered super-plants will scavenge CO_2 from the atmosphere must be explored, but it will be difficult to turn the combustion products of fossil fuels back into a solid form again. Furthermore it would be difficult to abandon rice paddies in order to reduce the emission of methane into the atmosphere.

In general, there do not appear to be any grand solutions to the dangers from climatic changes. Social and political changes, driven by public recognition of the scientific aspects of the problems, offer the best hope.

Earthquakes, volcanoes and impacts

All speculations of lubricating plate margins by injection of fluids, or even more dramatically by nuclear explosions, are regarded as wild by present experts even on the scale of three centuries. 3-D tomography of seismic events and good basic geology in a steady scientific and engineering program seem the best, if unspectacular, course to pursue.

Undoubtedly there will be major advances over 300 years in plotting the plumbing systems of volcanoes from 3-D tomography of microseisms, but elimination of volcanic eruptions is currently a pipedream. Commercial production of geothermal power might incidentally release enough heat to avoid some volcanic eruptions. In principle, slant drilling into the plumbing systems of shield volcanoes could release gases and magma, but the chance of catastrophic destruction of the drilling equipment seems high.

Space missions to asteroids and comets should establish the technology for rendezvous with ones that are in dangerous orbits. If enough time is available, an orbit can be changed by giving an asteroid a small kick from a mass-driver during each orbit around the Sun. If time is short, a comet or asteroid could be blown into smaller pieces which would cause less damage if they hit the Earth. A more sophisticated way to deal with such a threat would be a controlled deflection by a planar blast wave from an array of nuclear explosives.

▼ **An artist's impression of a mass-driver ship ($ page 36) towing away an asteroid threatening to hit the Earth. Space missions to asteroids are already being provisionally planned. Mass-drivers might be used to tow asteroids into new orbits giving Earth a wide berth.**

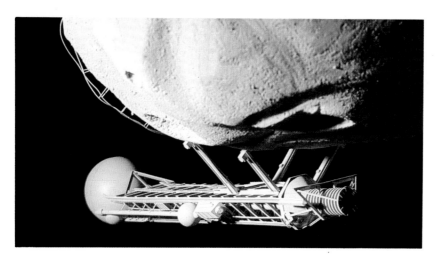

Planet Management

9

Limits to growth?...Population pressures on Earth's resources...What "natural resources" are...Integration of Earth studies...The "greenhouse effect"...Clean development...Clean production of energy...Acid rain...Fusion power...High- and low-tech energy alternatives...The agricultural crisis North and South...Advances in agriculture...Organic farming...Desalination...The tasks ahead

Barring disasters such as a major nuclear war or a deadly global plague, the people of this planet are going to have to use resources very efficiently in the 21st century, both to realize normal human aspirations, and perhaps merely to stay alive. The quandary becomes especially frightening when one plots the resources of a finite planet against a rapidly growing population with rapidly growing expectations. Fortunately, the answers derived from such an exercise are almost always wrong, erring toward pessimism. It is impossible to incorporate into such equations future changes in technology which may permit the more efficient use, or substitution, of resources.

In 1972, the Club of Rome published an influential report called *Limits to Growth* which predicted that if then-current trends in population growth, resource use, and pollution continued unchanged, then major systems would collapse in the coming century. These limits were inherent and mathematically definable.

Since then, views have changed. Today, few scientists would dare to point to inherent limits: there are too many variables. They find instead that there are limits set by the ways in which current technology and current economic systems impact upon the biosphere. New technologies are available to ward off doomsday. The challenge is for the politicians and the scientists to work together to see that more benign technologies – which are sustainable and which enhance rather than degrade the resource base – are widely adopted.

▼ *Mothers and children at a famine feeding station in the Ethiopian highlands. Such images from TV and newspapers, during times of record world food harvests, sparked charity. They also brought calls for changes in global trading systems, so that people would not starve in an impoverished environment amid a world of plenty.*

▲ *This sign in an Ontario, Canada, park warns against the eating of fish from the polluted Lake Superior. Such signs offer evidence of planetary mismanagement. Voters and their political leaders will have to work together to decide priorities, such as cheaper industrial products or less pollution. Only then can science help.*

Resources and numbers

In 1980, a world population well under five billion was using energy equivalent to 10 billion tonnes of coal each year. But one person in the rich industrialized market economies of the North was using almost 90 times as much energy as one person in the poorer countries of sub-Saharan Africa. If the global population rises modestly to 8.2 billion by the year 2025, and per capita energy use remains the same, we shall be using the equivalent of 14 billion tonnes of coal per year – an increase of 40 percent. But, to bring the whole world up to Northern standards of energy use, that future world population will need energy equal to that derived from 55 billion tonnes of coal by 2025.

The United States' agricultural writer Edward Wolf reckons that by the year 2020, the world will require grain yields 56 percent higher than 1985 levels just to maintain present standards, with little increase to be expected in the total area under cultivation. "Unlike past spectacular yield increases achieved under favorable cropping conditions, future improvements in average yields must come from raising the productivity of traditional farmers who cultivate unimproved crops under marginal conditions – perhaps the most demanding challenge that national governments and the international development community have faced." It is also one of science's most demanding challenges.

The world manufactures seven times as much today as it did in 1950, and produces three times as much minerals. But world industry would have to produce more than 2.5 times as many goods to bring the consumption of such goods in the developing world up to industrialized-nation standards, and there would need to be a five to tenfold increase to maintain this equity into the next century.

None of these projections is in any way a prediction of what is going to happen, but rather a means of visualizing the pressure that people are placing, and will continue to place in the relatively near future, on the planet's resources. Most of these projections come from *Our Common Future*, the final report of the World Commission on Environment and Development, published in 1987 (◗ also page 116). The Commission, of 21 leading politicians, scientists and jurists from 21 nations, was established by the United Nations to suggest ways by which a larger human world can progress safely into the next century.

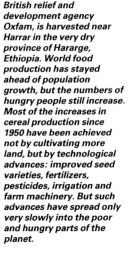

◄ *An improved groundnut variety, introduced by the British relief and development agency Oxfam, is harvested near Harrar in the very dry province of Hararge, Ethiopia. World food production has stayed ahead of population growth, but the numbers of hungry people still increase. Most of the increases in cereal production since 1950 have been achieved not by cultivating more land, but by technological advances: improved seed varieties, fertilizers, pesticides, irrigation and farm machinery. But such advances have spread only very slowly into the poor and hungry parts of the planet.*

▼ *A chemical plant at Bahia Petra, Brazil. The Third World must have economic growth to alleviate poverty. But must it reproduce, in the 20th century, the pollution and misery of Europe's Industrial Revolution? Cleaner industries must be dispersed, both to distribute jobs and to limit pollution in the capitals.*

Once used to cover only nonrenewable "inputs" such as fuel and minerals, the term "natural resources" now includes environmental assets such as water and air

The assets of Earth

Our planet is essentially a closed system, except in one respect. The only asset which we receive from outside the Earth is sunlight, of which we get a very steady, reliable supply: some 3,000 kilocalories every day on every square meter of the planet's surface. In an article celebrating the arbitrarily chosen day in July, 1987, on which the world population passed the five billion mark – twice as many as in 1950 – the British journal the *Economist* reckoned that, given the flow of solar energy, the globe could theoretically support a population of 132,000 billion – one person for every square meter of land. "But such a limit can be approached only if invention and organization keep pace with the mounting numbers, and ensure that mankind does not destroy the system it depends on." Here we are concerned more with the "invention" side of the equation, but we should not lose sight of the fact that scientific invention may be running ahead of social and political organizations, and that progress in these areas is just as important.

The somewhat playful mathematics of the *Economist* point up two lessons to be kept in mind when considering the sciences of planet management. Much scientific work in future will of necessity focus on ways to improve the efficiency of our use of solar energy, to convert it to calories of energy humans can use as both mechanical and other energy and for nutrition. However, 90 percent of the 220,000 new people added to the world population every day arrive in Third World countries, so that science which benefits the industrialized North but leaves out the developing South will provide no comfort or cure to an ever-larger proportion of the Earth's people. Some 93.8 percent of the world's total research expenditure is spent in the industrialized nations, only 6.2 percent in the developing world and only 0.3 percent in Africa, the home of well over one in ten people.

There are two classes of resources to be considered in any discussion of the present and future of our planet. The first are the obvious "input" resources of production, such as minerals, petroleum and other fuels, topsoil, wood and water. The other class, less often given their due weight, are the resources degraded by the various production processes, especially by the resulting pollution. They include clean water, clean air and the atmosphere in general, and forests.

"Natural resources" were once considered naively by most people to be obvious nonrenewable substances that could be mined or extracted from the Earth, such as minerals, oil and coal. But the above list shows how many of these assets for economic development are "environmental" in nature and – theoretically – renewable. The slow realization of this fact has forced many politicians and scientists to the belated conclusion that the finite planet cannot sustain economic growth achieved by means which squander those environmental resources. Examples can be found in both rich and poor countries where development activities have bankrupted the environment and made some forms of economic development impossible. Some 40 percent of Ethiopia was forested at the turn of the century; the forests are now down to about two percent. The overcultivated Ethiopian highlands lose through erosion about one billion tonnes of topsoil per year. Clearly, reliable agricultural production, under present systems, is unachievable in much of Ethiopia. In the Soviet Union, large tracts of land around the Chernobyl nuclear power plant have been taken out of production due to nuclear pollution of the soil following the 1986 reactor blast there. Both situations are more or less temporary, but both cause enormous hardship for the affected humans.

▶ *Intense farming amid the treeless Ethiopian highlands. The people here cut the trees for fuel, for posts and to make room for fields. They knew that the trees helped to put rainwater into the ground and to hold the soil together, but population pressure forced them to destroy this agricultural asset. Farmers are being paid in food to replant trees, but each drought destroys the seedlings. The Ethiopian government feels it may have to move people from these bare hillsides.*

▶ *The world's largest solar furnace – 63 mirrors on rotating mountings reflecting sunlight onto 9,000 smaller mirrors – at Odeillo in the French Pyrenees. Because sunlight is the only energy we get from outside our planet, we shall have to rely on it more and more as non-renewable reserves of oil, coal and gas run low. It is fortunate that the energy derived from falling water, wind, waves and the burning of plants are all ultimately forms of solar energy that has been "renewed".*

▲ An undersea researcher, a clipboard attached to his "tug", collects samples in a net. Fish are an obvious natural resource. The best fisheries are in the shallow seas over continental shelves, such as those in the northeast Atlantic and northwest Pacific. In such regions, nutrients which run off the land support the growth of minute plants and animals to provide food for the commercial species. Many of these are hatched and spend their early weeks in wetlands close to shore. Thus pollution which enters the sea disrupts fisheries, as does the degrading of marshes. The loss of stratospheric ozone due to industrial pollution could let in enough ultraviolet rays to harm the marine food chain. Most "natural resources" are supported by other, less obvious, resources.

The burning of fossil fuels produces both the "greenhouse effect" and acid rain

A whole new science

Science has traditionally been neatly compartmentalized into separate disciplines. To integrate these disciplines is one of science's most important frontier activities at the end of the 20th century and it is happening: "We are witnessing the birth of a sweeping new science", maintained the report *World Resources, 1987*. "This new science, which is an integration of the traditional disciplines of geology, oceanography, ecology, meteorology, chemistry and other sciences, has a variety of names – earth systems science, global change and biogeochemistry. Its subject is nothing less than the composition, behaviors and interactions of the planet's non-living realms or phases – the atmosphere, geosphere and hydrosphere – and its living realm, the biosphere, which encompasses parts of each of the others." Satellite monitoring has a huge role to play in this new science, as it allows humans for the first time to monitor from afar major changes in planetary systems, including the atmosphere, water, farmland and forests (◀ page 74).

The "greenhouse effect" – a big job for the new science

▶ *Acidic fog in the Black Forest of West Germany threatens shoots that may not survive. Acid comes to forests as rain, snow and fog. West Germany is the largest West European contributor of acidifying nitrogen oxides and a center of forest loss. A lower speed limit would help, but Germans like both trees and fast driving.*

Governments have long realized that the generation of the large amounts of energy required in the North pose various "environmental" problems. But they took the odd step of setting up environmental agencies and ministries to cope with these problems. While these agencies are well equipped to study and deal with the damage, they have little say in how energy is actually produced. Yet the challenges posed by energy production can only be solved by scientific and technical work on energy systems themselves. For example, the burning of oil, coal and gas accounts for over 90 percent of the commercial energy used in the world and puts a great deal of carbon dioxide (CO_2) into the atmosphere. Atmospheric CO_2 measured about 280 parts per million of air before the Industrial Revolution. By 1980, this concentration had increased to 340ppm; it is expected to reach 560 – a doubling of pre-industrial levels in the 21st century. CO_2 is harmless to humans but affects the atmosphere, the climate and plant life. Specifically, it traps heat from the Sun and warms the globe. In 1985, scientists from 29 nations meeting at Villach in Austria concluded that the globe had already warmed very slightly through CO_2's "greenhouse effect", and that the equivalent of a doubling of pre-industrial levels could occur as early as 2030, with a rise in global mean temperatures of somewhere between 1.5°C and 4.5°C. The Villach meeting predicted that if the increase were on the high side of this range, sea levels could rise 25-140 centimeters – the high end of that range being enough to flood the world's major port cities and lowlands. The temperature increases could also radically disrupt the world's delicate agricultural systems, dry out the tropical rain forests which contain a large proportion of the world's plant and animal species – a likely source of new food species, medicines, and industrial products – and disrupt marine food chains and the commercial fisheries that depend upon them.

Of course, the Villach scientists could be wrong, but as we possess no other planet upon which to run an experiment to test their conclusions, we shall not know for certain the effects of increasing CO_2 until they are upon us. But by 1988 governments were agreeing that the evidence for the "greenhouse effect" warranted action. Some climatic changes were beginning to be ascribed to it. Clearly, we need better monitoring of the gases, better computer modeling of possible effects, improved energy efficiency, and strategies to minimize damage and cope with consequences. It is a big job for the new "Earth systems science".

▲◄ *Beautiful but noxious: oil refinery burn-off, steam and oxides from power stations, and the general haze of auto fumes from a busy city. These pollutants cause health problems, acidify the landscape and warm the globe. Slices from trunks of two 30-year-old Sitka spruce trees (left) show that acid can cut into lumbering profits in ways besides killing trees. The larger trunk is from a "normal" tree; the rings of the smaller have been compressed due to acid precipitation damage.*

The challenge of acid rain

Oxides of nitrogen and sulfur emitted from the burning of fossil fuels can turn to acids and be deposited in the form of acid rain, snow and fog. It is not known exactly how this acid moves through air, soil and water systems and damages forests, but most scientists are convinced that it plays a major part in the tree damage found in 14 percent of all European forestland. The widespread loss of forest is not merely an esthetic or recreational disaster, but will increase the incidence of avalanches, erosion and the siltation of lakes and waterways.

While science knows no way to decrease CO_2 emissions from the burning of fossil fuels, there are ways of decreasing the discharges of impurities that lead to formation of acid rain. To reduce sulfur dioxide emissions, coal-burning power plants, their major source, will need to be modified or replaced (one option would be to build more nuclear plants). Modification is possible but expensive. A reduction in emissions of nitrogen oxides and hydrocarbons – the source of ozone that aids reactions producing the acids – would be achieved most effectively by reducing driving speeds or modifying automobile engines. A catalytic converter, for example, fitted to the vehicle's engine exhaust will remove most of the nitrogen oxides.

New ways to grow

Industrial growth has been slowing down globally, from a seven percent annual increase in 1950-1973 to three percent between 1973 and 1985. And industry has declined in many countries, in terms of its relative importance compared with other sectors of the economy. But manufacturing continues to grow rapidly in the developing world, especially the highly pollutive, heavy industries such as iron and steel, pulp and paper and food processing. The South cannot afford to follow the North's industrial pattern, which would take it through a phase of heavy pollution to be cleaned up later. Already Third World cities are among the world's most polluted, and poor air quality accounts for a high proportion of disease there. Computerization, new information, improved communications and process control should in theory allow developing nations to disperse industry more widely throughout the countryside, spreading both pollution and job opportunities. New composite materials, ceramics and high-performance plastics can also help to increase production with fewer resources, less energy and less pollution. The technology exists; the challenge is – again – to get it used where it is needed.

The industrialized North made great progress after the upsurge of environmental awareness in the late 1960s in cleaning up "old-fashioned" air and water pollution such as smoke and sewage. It is having trouble coping with a new generation of pollution, such as the

▶▼ *Skin cancer in residents (right) is just one effect of pollution at Cubatao, Brazil (below). There are 22 petrochemical and steel plants here. Some Third World governments feel they cannot afford to curb such industrial pollution. In fact, they will not be able to clean it up, as many wealthier Northern nations have done.*

hazardous chemicals from silicon chip plants entering the groundwater of parts of California and the large amounts of hazardous wastes from industry. Some 325-375 million tonnes of hazardous waste is generated world-wide each year, with only five million tonnes of this produced by the South. And the estimated costs of cleaning up the often carelessly established waste disposal sites are enormous: $1.5 billion for the Netherlands, $10 billion for West Germany, and $20-100 billion for the United States. Science will have to find new ways of disposal, or governments will be tempted to follow the alarming trend of shipping this waste to poorer nations and paying them to deal with it.

One of the great industrial challenges of the present is the use of the class of chemicals known as chlorofluorocarbons in aerosols, refrigeration chemicals and in the foaming of plastics.These are not only "greenhouse" gases, but also escape into the stratosphere and deplete the ozone there. This ozone layer reduces the amount of ultraviolet radiation reaching the Earth's surface. Work in the United States has resulted in estimates that only a one percent increase in the amount of such radiation would increase the incidence of nonmalignant skin cancers by five percent and the number of deaths from malignant and much rarer melanoma cancers by one percent. Increased ultraviolet radiation could also damage some crops and disrupt the marine food chain. Science has found it easy to find substitutes for the chlorofluorocarbons in aerosols, less easy to find alternatives for their other applications.

Scientists at the European Community's Joint Research Centre at Karlsruhe, Germany, have found that sound waves directed at smoke can cause the particles in the smoke to bind together, meaning that the total number of particles decreases and the larger particles fall to the ground quicker. Asymmetric sound waves can even be used to "herd" particles in a given direction. The technique, still very much in its infancy, could be used either routinely or in emergencies. Remote-controlled airships carrying loudspeakers could be flown into poisonous smoke released by accidents at chemical or nuclear power plants.

▼ Burning waste at sea. Science is coming to grips with garbage, using bacteria to detoxify waste and breaking down toxic molecules with 10,000 °C plasma-arc furnaces. The city of Columbus, Ohio, has an incinerator which burns 2,000 tonnes of garbage daily to generate 50,000 kilowatts of electricity hourly.

▼ "Pretty" pollution caused by copper mining near the King River in Tasmania. Man has always been more efficient at getting minerals out of the ground than at cleaning up afterward. But new techniques of restoring ecosystems to pre-disturbance quality are proving successful around mines, and with degraded marshes, rivers and forests.

From fission bomb to fission reactor took 10 years; 30 years after the fusion (hydrogen) bomb, there is still no practical fusion reactor

Conservation and clean production of energy

There are several ways of limiting acid pollutants, besides using low-sulfur coal and oil: using physical and chemical techniques to remove sulfur and nitrogen before the fuel is burned, preventing the formation of pollutants during burning, and screening pollutants from exhaust and flue gases. All technologies now exist at various levels of efficiency, and science is faced with the task of improving these technologies and bringing down their costs.

Nuclear power was once seen as the solution to the problems of CO_2 and acid pollution. There are even "breeder" reactors in operation which produce electricity while also producing their own fuel – an apparent energy panacea. But today a growing number of people are convinced that it is unwise to build an energy future based on a technology which produces a highly toxic waste material for which no safe and reliable storage or disposal system has been found. The 1986 Chernobyl accident proved that even if accidents are rare their effects across whole continents can be profound. The World Commission on Environment and Development, though containing commissioners from "pro-nuclear" nations such as the United States, the Soviet Union and Japan, concluded that "the generation of nuclear power is only justifiable if there are solid solutions to the presently unsolved problems to which it gives rise". But it added that "the highest priority must be accorded to research and development on environmentally sound and economically viable alternatives, as well as on means of increasing the safety of nuclear energy".

One very "high-tech" alternative, about which optimism has waxed and waned over the past years, is the fusion reactor, which mimics the Sun by forcing together light nuclei to release energy. The fuel would be cheap, derived from seawater, and the waste would be less troublesome than that produced by more conventional reactors. But despite much work, researchers have had difficulty getting a fraction more energy out of such a reactor than they put in, and even that has been obtained at tremendous expense.

Other, much "lower-tech", solutions involve the so-called "renewable" energies: wind, wave, tidal, geothermal and solar power; hydro-electricity; biomass fuels such as wood, charcoal, dung, crop residues and even alcohol fuel derived from crops such as sugarcane. Today these sources provide energy equivalent to two billion tonnes of coal, or one-fifth of energy currently used. Some 75 percent of this is from biomass and most of the rest hydropower. Yet many scientists feel that, given proper research and development, these sources could provide energy equal to present global consumption levels.

The seemingly benign term "biomass" raises the issue of "the other energy crisis" – the one faced by poor nations. Something like half the world's people depend on firewood, dung and crop residues such as stems and stalks for their domestic heating and cooking. As of 1980, some 1.3 billion people lived in areas where they could not get enough wood to burn; by the year 2000, some 2.4 billion people are expected to be in such a plight. Part of the answer to this crisis lies in new forestry techniques to produce plantations of fast-growing trees, but these technological solutions are often thwarted by the social, political and economic issues of motivating people to grow trees and of getting the wood to the poor who need it. Improved cookstoves and improved charcoal kilns can also prolong the period for which wood and charcoal are available; the challenge is to keep such innovations within the budgets of the poor people who could benefit from them (◗ page 107).

▶ *A stand of Leucaena trees in Tamil Nadu, India. These fast-growing "miracle" trees (◗ page 113) put nitrogen into the soil, produce pods which feed livestock, provide good firewood, and make good hedges and windbreaks to cut wind erosion. Probably American in origin, they have spread throughout the tropics.*

Research into atomic fusion power

It took less than 10 years to go from the first atomic (fission) bomb to the first fission reactor. Thirty years after the first hydrogen (fusion) bomb detonation, there is still no fusion reactor which produces more energy than it consumes. There are three basic approaches to fusion energy. The first two involve creating a "plasma" of light atoms (deuterium and tritium), the plasma being a mass of loose electrons and nuclei. Banging the two atoms together to release energy requires temperatures of around 100 million degrees Kelvin – so hot that any container would be melted. One system contains the plasma by a magnetic field which includes a current generated in the plasma. Another system relies only on external magnets to contain the plasma. A third approach fires lasers or beams of nuclear particles at a grain of frozen deuterium.

Major fusion research has been going on in Europe, the United States and the Soviet Union, and there is much international cooperation. But Japan has one of the most diverse programs, and one most closely tied to its industries. Japanese experts are hoping that their toroidal JT-60 experimental machine could achieve "break-even" – producing more energy than it consumes – by 1990.

◄ *This 30-meter particle accelerator at Sandia Laboratories, USA, has been used in fusion research. The fusing of atoms can, in theory, release cleaner energy than splitting atoms (fission). But science has some way to go before it becomes commercially feasible.*

▼ *The Westinghouse "fast breeder" nuclear power plant at Richland, Washington, USA. Such reactors produce fuel faster than they burn it. But nuclear waste cannot yet be safely disposed of, and the fuel produced can be used in nuclear weapons, perhaps illegally. Such technology raises as many questions as it answers.*

The cost of wind-generated electricity compares well with that of the output of small diesel generators

◄ An improved cookstove made out of mud for burning wood or charcoal. Such stoves save wood, and thus save people work or money. But mud stoves are not durable; and governments cannot afford to give many away. Still, Kenyans in cities are buying thousands of stoves – really modified metal buckets – which save them money on charcoal. As wood becomes scarcer and more expensive, more people will invest in such stoves.

◄ Photovoltaic cells convert sunlight directly into electricity. The cost of a peak watt of this energy has fallen from $600 in 1954 to $5 in 1986. But it will need to fall to $1.50 to compete generally with conventional sources. Already such cells are being used in remote areas to power pumps, generators and communications facilities.

Alternative sources of energy

The oil price rises of the 1970s proved to the developed world that energy efficiency is one of the most reliable and cheapest "sources" of new energy. Many industrialized nations improved energy efficiency steadily, so that, despite economic growth, the industrialized world consumed about one percent less energy in 1985 than in 1980. More efficient heaters, irrigation systems, refrigeration units and other energy-using devices consume one-third to one-half the energy of earlier devices. New thermally-tight buildings designed in Sweden and the United States use 90 percent less heat than traditional buildings.

Some 50,000 wind turbines have been installed around the world since 1974, and the price of wind-generated electricity is falling rapidly. The cost of a peak watt of photovoltaic electricity (derived directly from sunlight) has fallen from about $600 in 1954 to $5 in 1986. This is beginning to compete favorably with the small diesel generators used in remote regions of the world.

Another, even stranger, way of tapping the Sun's energy is to allow microorganisms such as bacteria and baker's yeast to break down sugar and produce a flow of electrons. Experimental "bug batteries" have been produced, and Peter Bennetto of King's College London has calculated that a room-sized tank of one million liters of liquid and 10 tonnes of microorganisms could produce one megawatt of power from 200 kilograms of carbohydrates per hour. It might sound a fairly elaborate contraption, but such tanks already exist for wastewater treatment in breweries; and the technology could benefit the many tropical countries rich in sugar but poor in oil. The process has led to predictions that in perhaps two centuries cars will be powered directly from a tankful of bugs and sugar, 50 liters of a saturated sugar solution giving a car a range of more than 1,000 kilometers.

Many Brazilians run their cars on ethanol produced from sugarcane. Scientists are also coming up with efficient chemical methods of converting ethanol into hydrogen, itself an efficient fuel which produces only water as a waste product. Already certain airplane and auto companies are studying hydrogen as a fuel of the future, and work continues on inexpensive and practical ways to separate it out of water.

108

Energy efficiency, computing, medicine and transport are among areas that may benefit from the technology of superconductors

More alternative means of energy production

An energy system offering more complex engineering challenges is magnetohydrodynamics (MHD), in which very hot ionized gases, which conduct electricity, are passed between the poles of an electric magnet to generate electricity. The principles of the technique were understood as early as the end of the last century, but it took rocket technology to provide containers for gases heated to as high as 3,500°C and flowing at about the speed of sound. The improvements in superconducting materials and the better magnets they offer are expected to give MHD another boost. When the hot gases of an MHD system, powered perhaps by natural gas, are hooked up to a conventional steam turbine and generator, the overall efficiency of converting heat to electricity is raised from 35 to about 50 percent and the cost of generating electricity reduced by 10 percent. Furthermore, MHD systems almost completely eliminate sulfur emissions and cut the nitric oxides and carbon dioxide in exhaust gases by 20-30 percent. The Soviet Union expects to commission a 270-megawatt MHD system connected to a 312 megawatt conventional steam-turbine generator by the end of the 1980s. And Israeli scientists are working on lower temperature MHD systems which use liquid metals rather than hot gases as the fluid conductor.

OTEC (Ocean Thermal Energy Conversion) is another complex, and as yet economically-unproved, way of using heat differentials to produce electricity. Imagine a huge pipe, say 30 meters in diameter, floating vertically in a tropical ocean, its top end at the surface, its bottom end 1,000 meters down. In the most common type of OTEC system, the warm surface water evaporates a working fluid – almost always ammonia – and the expanding gases drive a turbine generator. The vapor is then condensed by the cooler, deeper water. (Another OTEC approach flashes warm surface-water directly into steam. It produces both electricity and fresh water.)

The only geographical requirement for the technology of OTEC is a temperature differential of 18°C between the surface water and water 1,000 meters down. These conditions are to be found in virtually all of the world's tropical seas and within the 320-kilometer marine exclusive economic zones of 99 nations.

▲ *This is not a space station, but a plant which uses the temperature difference between the sea surface and great depths to produce electricity. Tropical seas and seas bordering 99 nations are suitable for such ocean thermal energy conversion.*

◄ *Superconducting magnets help this Japanese train to float a hand's breadth above the track. The current continues to flow even when the power is turned off, which makes for economical running. But liquid helium to cool the magnets keeps costs high.*

► *A CAT (computed axial tomography) scanner in a US hospital. The new superconducting materials which operate closer to room temperature could drastically reduce the cost of this efficient but expensive means of looking inside the human body.*

The benefits appear enormous. The technology is said to be no more than "sophisticated plumbing". OTEC can produce electricity where it is scarce – in the energy-poor tropical Third World. The process raises nutrient-rich deep waters which can be used for fish-farming, and the possibility of fresh-water production also makes such schemes more economically attractive. But OTEC is high technology, requiring vast amounts of piping and concrete subject to both erosion and tropical hurricanes. (A 22 kilowatt plant generated electricity off the coast of Cuba in 1930 until it was destroyed by a hurricane.)

One sensational breakthrough which could lead to increased energy efficiency was the series of discoveries in 1986-1987 of materials which are "superconductors" at temperatures higher than once thought possible. As far back as 1911, it was discovered that mercury loses its resistance to electricity at 4.3K (degrees kelvin), that is 4.3 degrees above absolute zero, which is minus 273°C. But Dr Paul Chu and his team at the University of Houston in Texas discovered a ceramic compound of the cheap elements barium, yttrium, copper and oxygen (which can be made in a school chemistry laboratory for little more than $1) which superconducts at almost 100K. This high temperature means that the conducting materials can be kept cool inexpensively with liquid nitrogen, rather than liquid helium. It also shattered previous theories of why materials become superconductive at all, and offered the possibility of materials that provide no resistance at room temperature. In mid-1987, Chu announced the discovery of a compound which showed superconducting potential at 225K. The phenomenon not only raises the potential of much more efficient electricity transfer, but of much more efficient and cheap electromagnets, medical body scanners, computers and trains that hover on a magnetic track.

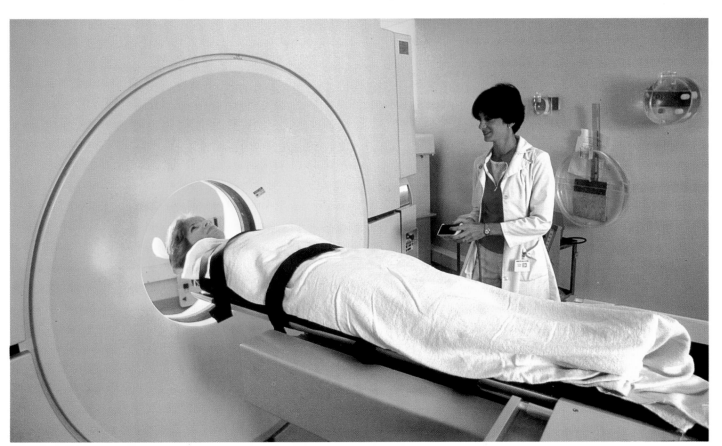

Current agricultural policies lead to large-scale habitat destruction both North and South

Two crises in agriculture

Just as there are two energy crises (◀ page 98), there are also two agricultural crises, and they are closely linked. Government subsidies in Europe and North America encourage the overproduction of food. The surpluses are expensive to produce, expensive to store, and expensive to ship free or at cut-rate prices to the South. The same policies can have the consequences of keeping farm prices low in the developing nations, discouraging farmers from producing their own surpluses and from taking care of their farmland.

Another outcome of the Northern policies is that they also encourage farmers to overcultivate their land, and to overuse nitrate fertilizers, pesticides and weedkillers. The overcultivation not only destroys many of the recreational and scenic amenities of the countryside, it also results in widespread erosion. By the end of the last decade, soil was eroding faster than it was being formed on about one-third of all cropland in the United States. And as the excess chemicals have to go somewhere, they were being absorbed into groundwater and rivers and threatening human health.

While Northern farmers are overproducing to make profits and in some cases to survive financially, many Southern farmers are over-cultivating their land simply to survive physically. In dry places such as much of sub-Saharan Africa, this overcultivation – along with over-grazing and the over-cutting of trees – plays its part in the process known as "desertification". This syndrome, whereby once-productive land is rendered unproductive, is largely human-caused, but the links between human activities and changes in climate, if there are any, are poorly understood.

One theory is that, by cutting trees and bringing more and more land under the hoe and the herd in Africa's Sahel region, just south of the Sahara desert, farmers are making vast areas more reflective of solar energy. This energy, bounced back into the atmosphere, keeps clouds from forming and thus rain from falling. Perhaps the gradual deforesta-tion of the wetter coastal states of West Africa is a part of the problem; or perhaps it is related to the "greenhouse effect"(◀ page 100); or it may be a natural cycle – or even a combination of all of these. Establishing the links between these different factors is another job for the new Earth systems science.

Whatever the causes, almost 30 percent of the planet's surface is suffering some form of desertification, and 230 million people live on the six percent of the land classified as severely desertified. Another six million hectares of good land turns to desert each year. And 11 million hectares of forest are destroyed each year. Despite the firewood needs discussed above, most of this forest destruction – sometimes called "slash-and-burn" – is by poor people looking for new land to farm, largely because many of them lack the technology, fertilizer and chemicals to cultivate more intensely.

The causes of much of the world's hunger lie in policies rather than technologies: farm produce prices, the flows of trade and aid, commod-ity prices, tariffs and the like. Science can help in two broad ways. The first is by finding ways to keep Northern production high enough without overcultivation and overuse of chemicals. Genetic engineering (◆ page 117) holds the promise of producing new crop varieties which fix their own nitrogen from the air, while resisting pests, disease, floods and drought. These developments will obviously offer hope also to Southern farmers, but once again the challenge will be to get the new varieties to Southern farmers in ways they can afford.

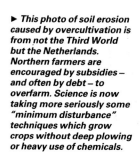

▶ *This photo of soil erosion caused by overcultivation is from not the Third World but the Netherlands. Northern farmers are encouraged by subsidies – and often by debt – to overfarm. Science is now taking more seriously some "minimum disturbance" techniques which grow crops without deep plowing or heavy use of chemicals.*

▶ *A camel carcass; caravan in background: Sudan. When herds overgraze and farmers overfarm fragile drylands, more solar energy is bounced back into space by the bared land, hindering cloud formation. Thus people can help to "make" droughts. Simple techniques using plastic-hose surveying tools and low lines of stones (◆ page 112) can help dryland peasants "harvest" scarce rainfall, and use it better.*

◄ The results of "slash-and-burn" farming, Bahia province, Brazil. Trees are cut and burned, and the ashes fertilize crops planted. After a few years, farmers move to a new site. The system works well — as long as sites are left to rest for years between plantings. But high populations give forests no time to regenerate.

Some advances in agriculture

Global agricultural production continues to outstrip population growth. Though most of the world's hungry people live in Asia, the only continent not producing enough food in terms of sheer volume to feed its people is Africa. The droughts and famines of 1984-1986 alerted the world of science to Africa's need for its own style of "Green Revolution", and scientists seems to be responding with low-technology solutions which African farmers can use.

The Oxford-based development organization Oxfam has taken simple "contour-damming" technology, based on Israeli work in the Negev Desert, to poor farmers of the Mossi Plateau of Burkina Faso. The dams are only 15-25 centimeters high, made of stones. The farmers use a simple "level" made from a clear plastic hosepipe full of water to find the contour lines. When rain does fall, it washes against the dams and percolates into the ground, watering the millet crops planted along the high sides of the dams. These small ridges prevent erosion as well as

▼ *A stone dam being built for irrigation in 'Shoa Province, Ethiopia, with aid from the British agency Oxfam. Oxfam and similiar bodies prefer to let local people take a lead in such projects. Thus they tend to favor dams and other products fitting local needs.*

▶ *"Alley-cropping" in Costa Rica, with corn (maize) planted between alleys of nitrogen-fixing seedlings which enrich the soil for the food crop. The yucca plants on the fringe are being raised for export to California, where they are sold as house plants.*

conserving scarce water. The technique is causing great excitement not only because it is bringing in harvests 50 percent higher than previously, but also because it requires only a day of training, and the practice is spreading spontaneously across the countryside.

In the neighboring country of Niger, long lines of trees are being planted in the Majjia valley – over 320 kilometers at the last count. The trees are planted at right angles to the prevailing winds, which conveniently blow from the northeast for half the year and from the south-west for the other half. Foresters from the United States charity CARE, working with a Niger forester, showed the local people how to set up nurseries of the Indian neem (margosa) tree species and how to plant the rows about 100 meters apart. The purpose of the lines is to prevent wind erosion, which takes away over 20 tonnes of topsoil per hectare each year from unprotected land. The trees, even accounting for the fact that they take up farmland, have increased crop yields by 18-23 percent, and have the added advantage of providing the people with a steady supply of firewood.

The Indonesian soil scientist B.T. Kang and his colleagues at the International Institute of Tropical Agriculture in Nigeria have developed similar techniques, generally referred to as "alley cropping". The crops are planted between rows of seedlings growing 3.5-8 meters apart. These trees not only conserve soil and provide firewood, as do the neem trees of the Majjia valley, but their leaves can provide fertilizer for crops and fodder for animals. The right species, such as *Leucaena leucocephala* (◀ page 104), has deep roots so as not to take nutrients and water from the crops, grows fast, provides good fodder, mulch, and firewood, and is leguminous – that is, it fixes nitrogen in the soil.

Not all solutions are necessarily so "low-tech". Farmers in 16 villages in Mali, for example, have been issued with single-side band radio receivers to listen into the latest information on rainfall and humidity, to help them to know when to plant, weed and harvest crops. Yields have improved as a result. The Egyptian government is experimenting with releasing millions of male Mediterranean fruit flies which have been sterilized with nuclear energy. This gets rid of pests without having recourse to pesticides with their associated risks to human health and of making the flies resistant to the poison.

◀ *Rice harvest, Nepal. New rice strains designed to be used with fertilizer, pesticides and irrigation have increased yields across Asia. But this "Green Revolution" has bypassed farmers who cannot afford the "inputs". So science faces a two-fold challenge: to bring down the cost of the technology, and to produce Green Revolution varieties of African staples such as sorghum, millet and the root crops.*

There is much scope for research into improving yields using organic farming techniques

▲ *A floating caviar "factory" on the river Volga, USSR. Aquaculture (fish farming) can not only produce protein but can mesh well with other types of farm production. It is proving itself in both industrial and developing nations.*

▶ *This lush farm near Zikhron, south of Haifa, Israel, was once scrub desert. Israel may lead the world in both high and low technology techniques of desert reclamation. But the basic processes are the same everywhere: first, stop wind erosion; second, plant some drought-resistant plant to put organic matter into the ground and to help the soil retain water; finally, either irrigate or establish regimes to make the best use of any available water – or preferably both. Many traditional systems accomplished these goals, but were overwhelmed by rising populations.*

◄ These experimental vegetable plots show an "organic" approach next to the "inorganic". The small white bins hold compost. Organic farming is attracting more and more research because many Northern consumers do not want pesticides in their foods and Southern farmers cannot afford artificial chemicals. Even Northern farmers are switching over to save money.

Back to organic basics?

An interim solution to the world crises in agriculture is to take a step "backward" in agricultural development and improve so-called organic farming techniques – those which use natural fertilizers and measures of weed and pest control. Many Northern farmers are "going organic", not only because a growing number of consumers are willing to pay higher prices for food containing no artificial chemicals, but as a way of conserving their soil from the effects of over-fertilizing. Scientists have been slow to take up the challenge of researching these techniques.

Poor Southern farms also desperately need this research, not because they are using too much chemical fertilizer and pesticides, but because they and their countries can afford to buy little or none. "Organic" techniques include more efficient use of manure and farmyard wastes; the sowing of many crops together to decrease vulnerability to pests or disease; the use of more robust crop varieties; and efficient use and conservation of soil and water.

Science can and is helping in all of these areas, but it is a science far different from that involving white-coated technicians in elaborate European laboratories. Agronomists working in the Third World are finding that they have to get out of the laboratories onto the farms to find solutions which fit in with the farmers' needs, labor availability and present practices. For example, using traditional techniques crop breeders developed for Ethiopian farmers a new strain of sorghum which matured more quickly than common varieties, thus lessening vulnerability to drought. But the scientists did not realize that the farmers not only ate the grain, they also depended on the stalks for building material and the leaves for fodder. As the new strain had short, weak stalks and few leaves, the farmers were unwilling to use it.

Furthermore, many peasant farmers have gone a long way on their own in adapting techniques suitable for their particular environments. They have ancient traditions, for instance, of mixing crops in the same fields. To be effective, scientists will need to build on this work, rather than trying to start from scratch in developing new solutions. Foresters will have to follow the agricultural act with new "agro-forestry" techniques both to grow wood as if it were a plantation crop and also to mix trees and food crops to conserve soil, soil fertility and water retention and to improve food harvests. Fish-farming is an ancient tradition in many nations, but techniques of "aquaculture" – both salt- and freshwater – are still in their scientific infancy. The practice offers great scope for many poor farmers to produce high-quality protein.

Desalination

New water desalination technologies are emerging which promise to revolutionize the industry, according to the report "World Resources 1987". The new reverse osmosis systems, using a membrane which allows water to pass through but holds back most dissolved organic and inorganic material, require only about half of the energy of the older multi-stage flash distillation units. By 1985, the world was desalting about 9.8 billion liters of water a day. The costs of large-scale desalination are still beyond the means of most poor nations, but are falling rapidly as the technology improves and international competition increases among suppliers.

Tasks ahead

Concern has mounted steadily over the ways in which human activity is degrading the environmental resource base upon which future human progress must be based. More and more scientific groups have called for a coordinated global examination of those changes, using all the latest technologies. In 1986 the 21st General Assembly of the International Council of Scientific Unions (ICSU) – research councils and academies from 71 countries – voted unanimously to launch immediately an International Geosphere-Biosphere Project (◀ page 75) to study all the physical, chemical and biological processes that regulate the systems of the planet. The project was to reach full momentum in 1992, last for 10-20 years, and assess the changes likely to affect the planet over the coming century.

Such a study should go a long way toward providing the scientific basis of the institutional, political and economic restructuring called for in the concluding "call for action" of the 1987 report of the World Commission on Environment and Development (◀ page 97). That call notes: "When the century began, neither human numbers nor technology had the power to radically alter planetary systems. As the century closes, not only do vastly increased human numbers and their activities have that power, but major, unintended changes are occurring... The rate of change is outstripping the ability of scientific disciplines and our current capabilities to assess and advise."

The Commission, and hundreds of scientists around the world, are calling for equally radical changes which will produce systems of production based on the reality of planetary ecological systems.

▼ **A desalination plant producing fresh water in Saudi Arabia. Such technology will become more important as the world runs short of water. Widespread desalination would take some of the human pressure off lakes and rivers, improving the hydrological cycle.**

Genetic Engineering

10

A modern science...Right or wrong?...The structures of DNA and RNA...New and improved crop plants...The development of anti-sense genes...Improving nitrogen-fixation in plants...Supermice and super-rabbits...The cloning of animals...From biosensors to...biorobots?

Within the last 15 years it has become possible to identify genes, the living blueprints for specific protein molecules with known functions in living organisms. It is also possible to isolate such genes and insert them into fast-growing and dividing cultures of bacteria, which then multiply the inserted genes along with their own. This process (gene cloning) can be accelerated by adding extra sequences of DNA (◗ page 118) onto the genes, which instruct the bacterial cells to multiply the inserted genes much faster than their native genes. Techniques are now available for inserting wanted genes into other organisms, besides bacteria and the other cell cultures used for cloning.

It has proved more difficult to transfer genes into crop plants than into bacteria, in particular, into the class of plants, known as monocotyledons, to which almost all important crops belong. Now, however, the crucial advances needed to make this possible seem to have been achieved. We can expect the revolution in plant breeding that this will make possible to be by far the biggest money-spinner among the applications of genetic engineering, at least for the next 20-30 years.

Genetic engineering for animals, too, has recently taken crucial steps forward. "Supermice" and super-rabbits twice the size of their litter-mates have been created and, in mice, genes inserted in this way have been shown to be inherited by future generations.

Concern and controversy

When it first became possible to insert genes taken from one organism into another, there was great concern that the technique might lead to the creation of new virulent strains of microorganisms which could escape from the laboratory and cause epidemics of disease against which there would be no natural resistance. These concerns proved groundless; it has been found simple to ensure that organisms used for cloning genes are kept harmlessly in laboratories. As a further safety precaution they can if necessary be genetically altered to prevent their causing disease.

More concern has been voiced over the deliberate release of genetically-altered organisms into the environment for use in agriculture, but here again experience to date suggests that fears are groundless. Biotechnologists have reminded their critics that genes are continually exchanged naturally in sexual reproduction and continually altered by natural mutation, and that the efforts of human genetic engineers add only minutely to such effects.

If, however, genetic engineering were to be used deliberately to create new and virulent strains of bacteria or viruses for use in warfare, then there is no doubt that the sophisticated techniques now available could make it possible to create new and terrible biological weapons. Concern has also been expressed that human genetic engineering might be used for purposes other than curing disease. But such possibilities lie far in the future.

▼ *Jeremy Rifkin, spokesman for the opposition to genetic engineering in the USA, speaking at a Green Party meeting in Rome. Many laymen but few scientists share his concern.*

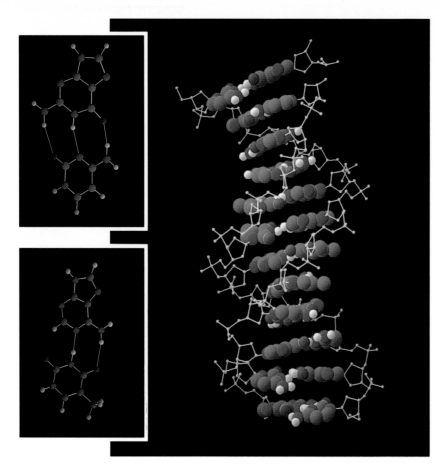

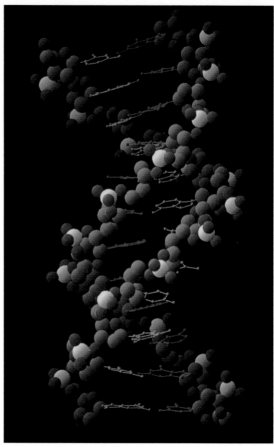

▲ The four nucleotide bases (above) which form the chemical subunits out of which strands of deoxyribonucleic acid (DNA) are built up (above right). Each base in one of the strands of the double-helix of DNA pairs with a partner of the opposite strand by a weak chemical bond. Thus guanine pairs with cytosine (top inset) and adenine in turn pairs with thymine (lower inset).

▲ Far right: The sugar and phosphate backbones of DNA are highlighted. The two intertwined strands run in opposite directions. For cell division and multiplication, the strands unwind and each builds onto itself the complementary sequence of bases (nucleotides) in order to complete the double strand again.

What do genes do?

Genes are units of heredity that are passed from generation to generation. Their main function is to determine the structure of peptide chains, strings of amino acids that form the building blocks of enzymes and other proteins. There are only 20 different amino acids; the remarkable diversity of living organisms reflects the existence of numerous varieties of proteins that differ from each other only in the order of these 20 amino acids in their constituent peptide chains. Amino acids have side chains that connect with each other and hence peptide chains and their proteins fold up into very precise shapes that are essential if they are to carry out their roles in body structure and chemistry. The shape of a protein is dependent on the order of amino acids in its constituent peptide chains. So a gene ensures that the amino acids of its peptide product are always in the same order. In short, a gene determines the structure of a peptide chain.

Deoxyribonucleic acid (DNA), the basic chemical constituent of a gene, is a double helix of two strands, each of which is coiled in a clockwise direction. Each strand consists of a chain of chemicals, or bases, called guanine (G), cytosine (C), adenine (A) and thymine (T), with a backbone of simpler sugar and phosphate molecules. Each base pairs with a partner base on the opposite strand by a weak chemical bond. Hence the two strands come apart quite easily. The information that directs the order of amino acids in peptide chains is stored in DNA by virtue of the order of the bases in its homologous strands. Because of their particular size and shape, the way in the bases pair with each other is constrained; guanine has to go with cytosine, adenine with thymine. In effect, the two strands are mirror images of each other. When DNA replicates itself, the two strands come apart and each acts as a template for the addition of bases to form a new

partner strand. Thus the two daughter molecules are identical to the parent molecule; this must be so because of the rules of base pairing.

Humans have the same genetic codes as the lowest bacteria; three bases represent the codeword, or codon, for a particular amino acid. For example, the amino acid leucine has the codons CCU, CUC, CUA, or CUG. Amino acids do not "speak" directly to DNA, which stays in the nucleus of cells directing operations; peptide chains are made outside the nucleus in the cytoplasm. When a gene makes a protein, one of its strands is copied, or transcribed, by an enzyme into a molecule called messenger RNA that, because of the rules of base pairing, is an exact replica of its parent DNA strand. It has a very similar structure to DNA except that its sugar is ribose instead of deoxyribose and it contains a base called uracil (U) instead of thymine. Messenger RNA travels from the nucleus to the cytoplasm, where it acts as a template or "workbench" on which peptide chains are made by a process called translation.

Amino acids are brought to messenger RNA templates by another class of molecules called transfer RNAs, each of which has three nucleotides called anticodons that are able to find their correct codon partners on the messenger RNA, again by the rules of base pairing: each amino acid becomes attached to its own individual transfer RNAs and, therefore, its own unique anticodons. Making a peptide chain starts at one end of the messenger RNA and proceeds in an orderly way to the other. The growing peptide chains, together with incoming and outgoing transfer RNAs, are held together in an appropriate relationship to each other and to messenger RNA by bodies called ribosomes, pulleys that carry a gradually lengthening peptide chain along the messenger RNA. There is one codeword to say where to start making a chain, and another to stop it.

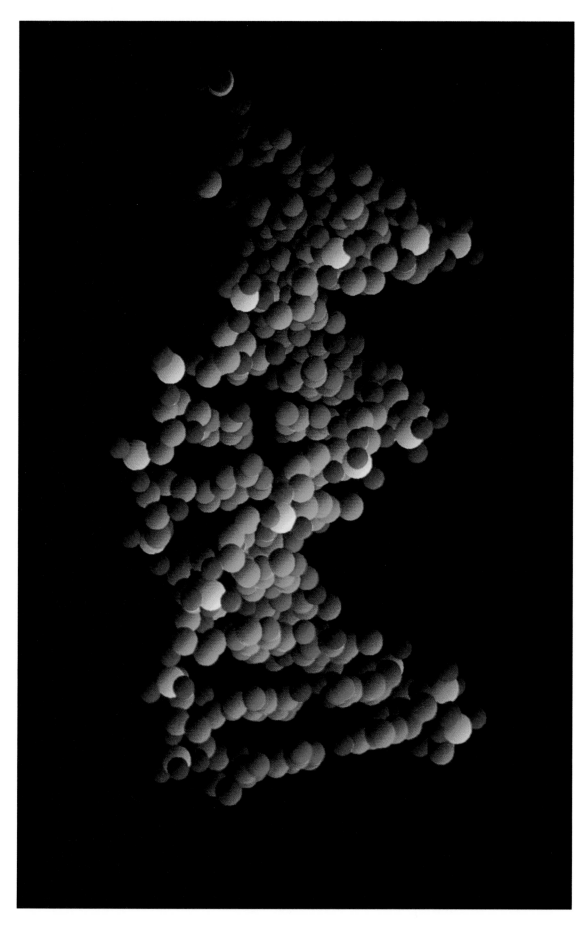

◄ The DNA double-helix complete with backbones and bases. Since DNA can replicate itself accurately, every cell in our bodies has an identical set of genetic information, derived from our parents when we began life as a fertilized egg. These instructions are passed on to our children through the DNA of our own germ cells.

▼ A molecule of uracil. For protein synthesis, an unwound single strand of DNA attracts to itself complementary bases (nucleotides) in which the thymine of DNA is replaced by another base, uracil, forming strands of RNA instead of DNA.

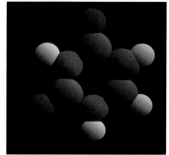

Green genes

By AD 2000, as studies already carried out by consultants for seed and herbicide companies have shown, genetic engineering will every year be adding $20,000 million to the value of crops worldwide. Just one characteristic added to plants in this way, that of resistance to herbicides, thus allowing weeds to be sprayed with heavy doses without affecting crops, will alone be adding $3,000 million annually to the value of crops by the end of the century.

Conventional crop breeding involves first seeking out a wanted gene for, say, disease resistance in a wild variety of the crop plant involved, and then crossing this wild variety with the cultivated plant. Then many generations of the hybrid have to be grown so as laboriously to breed out all the many unwanted characteristics of the wild variety that were absorbed along with the one wanted gene. Genetic engineering, by contrast, allows breeders to take a wanted gene from any living organism – plant, bacterium, even animal or human – and to insert this directly, on its own, into a crop plant.

At one stroke this widens the scope for plant breeders immeasurably. It allows them access to the gene banks of the entire living world instead of just the genes of the single species of the crop plant itself. Genetic engineering also speeds up the process of inserting new genes many times over, by cutting out the need to breed out unwanted genes.

▼ *Genetically-engineered corn (maize) plants being produced by the Zoecom Corporation at Palo Alto in California. Here in "Silicon Valley", heartland of the microelectronics industry, biotechnology is developing as explosively as microelectronics was 20 years ago.*

The problems inherent in inserting genes into crop plants seem in principle to have been overcome. In experiments two techniques have been successfully used. At the Max-Planck Institute in West Germany, solutions of genes were injected into young buds growing on corn (maize) plants, the buds which later form flowers. Then, when the flowers formed, plants which had been treated in this way were cross-fertilized by each other. The hope was that, in some of the plants at least, the injected DNA would have found its way into the reproductive cells, the pollen and ova (egg cells) of the flowers, and thus into future generations. In just one or two of more than 3,000 plants treated in this way, this proved to have happened. Clearly the success rate needs to be improved, but the biotechnology needed to introduce new genes into corn, and so by implication into rice or wheat or barley, now exists.

These and other techniques being developed will produce new disease-resistant and drought-resistant cereal and other crops. They will be needed to tackle the changing climatic conditions which will be brought about by the steadily increasing "greenhouse effect". This, many climatologists now believe, will by AD 2050 turn the North American wheat belt into an arid region where cereal crops can only be sustained by intensive irrigation and drought-resistant crops will be essential.

During the next 30 years, the clear benefits of genetic engineering will lead to an ever-intensifying search for commercially-valuable genes in wild varieties of plants and other organisms of all kinds.

This will in turn lead, one can perhaps believe as well as hope, to a change in attitude to wildlife generally. So-called protein engineering – really genetic engineering, the reshaping of genes so as to improve their protein products – is already beginning to improve on nature. But the main lesson learnt from genetic tinkering to date has been a new appreciation of the efficiency of natural genes. In 30 years we may still be destroying species too fast, but the rate will be slowing down as the commercial value of the natural gene pool is increasingly realized.

▲ A corn (maize) plant infected with maize streak virus shows streaky leaves, demonstrating that viral genes have been inserted into the plant's cells. Some viruses naturally integrate their own DNA into that of the cells they infect, so they can be exploited to insert extra genes. Maize streak virus DNA does not integrate if the virus is directly inoculated or injected into plants. But in 1987 the John Innes Institute at Norwich, England, showed that extra genes can be added to maize streak virus and the virus can then be inserted into a bacterium which naturally infects plants, called Agrobacterium tumefaciens. The bacterium then carries extra genes with the viral genes into the plant cells where they are integrated into nuclear DNA.

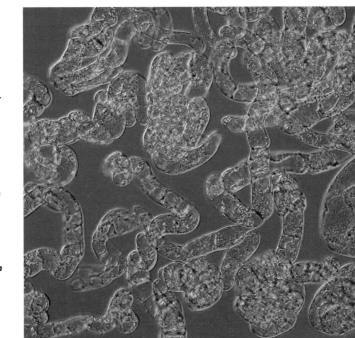

◄ Carrot cell cultures being used to prepare protoplasts (plant cells with their cell walls removed). Genes can be injected directly into protoplasts, and complete new plants can then be regenerated from the protoplasts, with every cell containing the added genes. The technique was pioneered by Professor Edward Cocking of the University of Nottingham, England.

Built-in pesticides

Recently Belgian scientists, working with an international biotechnology company, have shown that crop plants can be made resistant to insect pests by implanting new genes. Their achievement opens the way to the large-scale use of genetic engineering in agriculture.

Most of the pesticides in use today are made synthetically. But for more than 20 years there has been one important exception: the range of toxins produced by *Bacillus thuringiensis*. This species of bacterium naturally produces chemicals (proteins) which are extremely poisonous to a variety of insects but quite harmless to other forms of life. These toxins are very attractive for use as pesticides because they are highly specific as well as very potent. Unfortunately they are expensive to produce and unstable, so until recently their use has been limited to specialized applications. Now a team led by Dr Mark Vaeck of Plant Genetic Systems of Ghent in Belgium, where much of the pioneering work on plant genetic engineering has been done, has shown that it is possible to use this natural pesticide in a practical way.

Giving crop plants their built-in protection against pests in this way is obviously attractive because it avoids the need to spray poisonous chemicals around and avoids damage to any living creature other than insects which try to feed on the leaves of crop plants. No harm will be done to people or animals other than to the insects eating the leaves, because the toxins only affect insects.

The technique used involves first inserting the wanted gene into a bacterium called *Agrobacterium* which naturally infects plant cells and which naturally inserts its own genes in among the genes it infects. In this way the wanted genes can be inserted into plants along with the genes of *Agrobacterium* itself. Now that the technique has been shown to work for one useful gene and for one crop, it will certainly be used for more genes and other crops. The research team involved is already designing new combinations of genes which they hope will make crop plants produce very high levels of natural pesticides so as to make them invulnerable to the most concentrated attacks by insect pests. Genes for other valuable properties such as high nutritional value or drought resistance will be inserted too, if genetic engineers are successful in their experiments.

Of course there will be problems. For example, it is possible that insect pests will evolve resistance to the natural pesticide when they are confronted with it in a wide range of crops on which they feed. The best way round this may be to insert several genes for several different kinds of resistance simultaneously.

▶ *Two tobacco plants demonstrate successful genetic engineering. The right-hand plant has been made to synthesize a protein which kills insects; the left-hand plant is a control with no added genes. The technique used by Plant Genetic Systems in Ghent, Belgium, involves inserting the genetic blueprint for a toxin produced by Bacillus thuringiensis into tobacco plants, which are then protected against caterpillars of the tobacco hornworm, a major pest.*

▶ *Progress in growth of a field of genetically-modified tobacco plants is monitored by scientists of the American genetic engineering group CETUS. The much greater speed with which genetic engineering can introduce wanted new genes into plants, compared to traditional crop breeding, suggests that new varieties of crop will appear at an increasing rate.*

▼ *Undifferentiated plant cells (callus) growing in laboratory culture. Callus tissue forms naturally to repair damage to plants. It is now possible to take protoplasts (naked cells) made from callus tissue, to implant genes and, in some plant species, to persuade the protoplasts to differentiate into complete plants in which every cell contains the added genes.*

Developments in protein engineering may also reduce dependence on chemical fertilizers

Anti-sense genes protect crops

In the Centre for Biotechnology at Imperial College, London, Dr Conrad Lichtenstein has developed and begun to test a revolutionary new way to protect crop plants against virus diseases, using genetic engineering. He uses "anti-sense" RNA (ribonucleic acid) to cancel out the message contained in the viral RNA (◀ page 118), which would otherwise order the infected cell to make more virus.

The technique involves first isolating and cloning (multiplying many times over) a viral gene which produces a protein essential for the virus to replicate itself in an infected cell. This gene is then in effect turned back-to-front. This is done by removing the sequence called the promoter, which normally initiates the copying of the gene along its length, and the sequence called the terminator, which normally stops the copying process at the other end of the gene, and reversing their positions, so the gene is now copied backward.

When such an "anti-sense gene" is inserted into a crop plant, using one of the several techniques now being developed, it will then be copied, along with the plant's own genes, into the form of messenger RNA, single strands of nucleic acid. If the same plant is then infected with the virus from which the original gene was taken, the virus will insert its genes into the plant's cell in the normal way and the viral genes will, as usual in infection, also be copied as single strands of messenger RNA along with the plant's own genes.

If the plant were undefended, then the next step would be for the viral messenger RNA to be transcribed into new viral protein, as part of the process of making new virus particles. But if the "anti-sense" RNA made by the artificially-inserted gene is present in the cell, then its strands pair off chemically with the strands of viral RNA all along their length. This will happen because every sequence along the length of the anti-sense RNA will be complementary to, and so able chemically to bond with, the opposite sequence along the length of the viral RNA. The viral RNA cannot then be translated by the ribosome, which requires a naked, single strand of RNA to build up the corresponding protein. The viral message will have been canceled out.

Before anti-sense genes can be used to protect plants against virus infections much remains to be done, in particular to ensure that the anti-sense genes have no harmful effects in the plants they are supposed to protect. But Dr Lichtenstein points out that anti-sense RNA is used as a natural form of gene regulation in bacteria, though not to defend against virus; and he has carried out experiments which suggest the technique will work.

It may be possible to implant whole batteries of anti-sense genes into plants to protect against a number of different virus diseases. The technique would have the advantage of avoiding the use of chemicals and of providing protection even after a virus had gained access to plant cells. Anti-sense genes could also be used to delete a plant's own genes so as to create new mutants or to prevent plants from making toxins.

Several other research teams are now studying the potential of anti-sense genes used for other purposes. Among them is the exciting – though it must be stressed only distant – possibility of using an anti-form of a gene from the Human Immune Virus (HIV) that causes AIDS to try to limit the spread of the disease in an infected person. An anti-HIV gene inserted into human white blood cells (T-cells) that are infected by HIV, using a harmless virus as vector, might then produce anti-sense RNA which would pair with and "cancel out" any messenger RNA (which is needed by the HIV to reproduce) made by the HIV.

▲ *The pink nodules on these pea roots inoculated by nitrogen-fixing bacteria are colored by hemoglobin, which delivers oxygen to nitrogen-fixing Rhizobia bacteria.*

▲ *At his laboratory in the Biotechnology Centre of Imperial College, London, Dr Conrad Lichtenstein is developing new ways of using genetic engineering to protect crop plants.*

"Nod-ons" for food production

Scientists in the John Innes Agricultural Research Institute near Norwich, England, have discovered how leguminous crops such as peas and beans regulate the process of nitrogen fixing. The discovery, made by a team led by Dr Andy Johnston will be used to help crops fix nitrogen more efficiently, and so will make world food production cheaper and more efficient.

Nitrogen fixing is the process whereby nitrogen liberated into the air from decaying plant and animal material is recaptured from the atmosphere and made into new plant material. Legumes – plants that can fix nitrogen, such as peas, beans, clover and lupins – do so by means of bacteria living in tiny nodules on their roots. The bacteria capture nitrogen and transform it into ammonia, which is made into more complex protein compounds. The bacteria mainly involved in nitrogen fixing are called rhizobia.

Dr Johnston has been investigating the way in which the first stage in nitrogen fixing, the formation of nodules, is controlled. He has shown that eight genes in the bacteria are responsible for nodulation. When these eight genes are transferred into other bacteria, such as Agrobacterium, which are not normally involved in nitrogen fixing, then they make these bacteria nodulate too. Clearly no other genes are necessary for the formation of nodules.

Dr Johnston has gone on to investigate what stimulates these genes to start the process of nodulation. He has shown that chemicals produced by the roots of legumes but not by other species of plants cause nodule formation. Two compounds (a flavone and flavanone) produced by legume roots cause rhizobia to nodulate. He has christened these compounds "nodulation-ons", or "nod-ons" for short.

Dr Johnston sees one likely use for his discovery in the near future in rhizobia used as inoculants. Nitrogen-fixing crops are nowadays often inoculated with cultures of rhizobia to increase their efficiency in fixing nitrogen from the air. A number of strains of rhizobia which fix nitrogen exceptionally well have been developed in the laboratory, but they do not compete well with wild strains in the field.

Nod-on chemicals synthesized artificially might be used to give the laboratory-bred bacteria a "head start". Cultures of strains of rhizobia bred for excellence in nitrogen fixing would be sprayed with synthetic nod-on before being released. The spray would stimulate the laboratory rhizobia to initiate nodulation as soon as they came within range of a legume, without waiting for its own nod-ons to reach the bacteria. Such work can help to solve the problem of the high cost of fertilizer for Third World countries, especially as it can reduce the need for fertilizers by making the growing of leguminous crops an attractive alternative. In the future it may also become possible to induce nitrogen-fixing bacteria to form nodules in and fix nitrogen with nonleguminous crops such as cereals. It may even be possible to insert nitrogen-fixing genes into cereals themselves and avoid the need to use bacteria.

▲ In laboratories such as Biotol's in Cardiff, Wales (above left), the search is on for agricultural uses for naturally-occurring microorganisms. At the John Innes Institute in Norwich, England, bean plants were inoculated with Rhizobium bacteria (above). The bean on the left was not inoculated, the middle one inoculated with an inefficient strain of Rhizobium, the one on the right with a strain selected for its high efficiency in fixing nitrogen. Artificial inoculation could, at least partially, replace the use of nitrogen fertilizers.

The capacity to create new species has already become a powerful commercial force

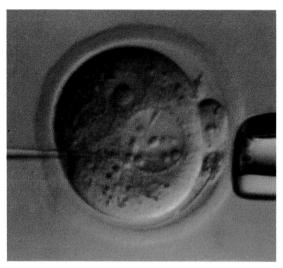

▲▶ *A fertilized mouse egg is held in place by suction using a large pipette (tip visible on right), while a smaller micropipette (entering from left) is inserted to inject a solution of genes. The central nucleus of the egg becomes swollen (right) by the injection of the solution containing genes.*

▶ *Two female mice, sisters from the same litter, about 24 weeks old. The mouse on the right contains an extra gene, composed of the gene for human growth hormone (red band) with a mouse promoter genetic sequence (yellow) attached. The mouse with the extra gene weighs more than twice as much as her sister.*

Supermice

On December 16, 1982, the journal "Nature" carried a color photograph of two mice – litter mates, but one twice the size of the other. The "supermouse" was produced by injecting an extra gene into a fertilized mouse egg cell. The gene was the genetic blueprint for making growth hormone, fused to another piece of genetic material, a promoter, which stimulated the transcription of the genetic blueprint for growth hormone.

The effect of this amplified gene was to cause the mouse's body to produce abnormal quantities of growth hormone which, in turn, stimulated it to grow abnormally fast. "Super-rabbits" have recently been created in the same way. Certainly, well within 30 years super-cattle, -sheep and -pigs will be widely bred and disseminated, using in-vitro fertilization and gene implantation, embryo storage in deep freeze, embryo transfer and cloning techniques.

A man-made zoo

On April 18, 1987, the United States' Patent and Trademark Office announced that it would in future be prepared to permit inventors to patent animals produced via gene splicing or other new genetic-engineering techniques. The Patent Office had already been patenting genetically-engineered single-cell organisms since 1980, and are now receiving ever-increasing numbers of applications for animal patents. These applications make it clear that the genetic engineering of animals, to create new species by direct gene transfers, usually by the direct injection of new genes into fertilized animal eggs removed temporarily from the womb, has already passed the experimental state. It is ready to become a powerful commercial force.

Multiple ovulation brought about by fertility drugs and transplantation of cattle embryos are already well-established procedures. Cattle embryos, and those of several other species, can be stored in deep freeze for long periods. This already facilitates the international exchange of embryos, as well as providing a uniquely effective means of conserving rare species. The Animal Research Station in Cambridge, England, is now developing techniques which allow eggs to be collected directly from ovaries and matured and fertilized outside the body for large-scale production of embryos for transplantation. New genes can now be inserted into the fertilized eggs before reimplantation. This has already been done in sheep. Cows are next on the list.

The same idea may be expected to be taken further in the coming decades. Appropriately-implanted human genes could cause cows to produce lymphokines such as interferon into their milk. They could easily be extracted and purified, leaving the milk to be sold in the usual way. This could provide extra income for conventional farmers, as could genetically-engineered silkworms used to clone various human-type compounds. This concept was already being tested in 1987.

The increasingly unnatural lives led by animals in factory farms are rightly a matter for growing concern. The ability to grow living tissue in the laboratory and to clone any number of flavoring compounds, natural and invented, could do away with factory farming altogether well inside 300 years, replacing it with brainless beef, lamb and pork and chicken grown in vats. The need for broiler chickens and intensively reared pigs and calves would disappear.

▼ A part-sheep, part-goat chimera produced by inserting goat cells into an early sheep embryo. Chimeras help scientists to understand how an embryo develops.

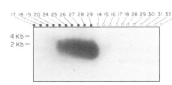

◄▲ The zebra-like quagga (left) was hunted to extinction in South Africa by the 1870s. In 1984 DNA from a museum specimen was successfully cloned, opening up the possibility of extracting DNA from other museum animals, to investigate the evolutionary history of an extinct species. In the photograph, (above), DNA from a quagga is pairing (dark area) with DNA from a modern zebra, demonstrating their close relationship.

Fleshy robots

Aldous Huxley and Arthur C. Clarke have respectively conceived of Epsilons and superchimps – humans deliberately stunted to enable them to find satisfaction in lowly routine jobs and chimpanzees given just the extra intelligence needed to enable them to act as servants on spaceships. In 300 years' time there may be no need for humans to perform routine work of any kind. But robots may be flesh and blood rather than, or as well as, metal.

Even today, in biosensors, living systems in the form of enzymes or antibodies are being linked to electronic intelligence, microprocessors and computers so as to diagnose disease or to control biotechnological processes. Living and nonliving systems are being linked together. This is also happening in the development of silicon chips and complete microprocessors to insert into the human body as part of artificial organs, used to cure conditions such as diabetes. Electronics engineers are designing computers using components made from biological materials. Factory robots 300 years hence may be fleshy creatures, but they will need only enough brain to perform their functions and should have no consciousness to suffer boredom.

The greatest challenge to the genetic and protein engineers of the future will be the colonization of distant planets, for example, the hot and cold sides of Mercury, the sulfuric acid clouds and molten-lead temperature of Venus, the huge pressures and ammonia atmosphere of Jupiter, and the frozen airless wastes of the outer planets and their moons. Perhaps first lowly, then advanced, engineered lifeforms, and finally colonists who will be human in their intelligence but not in their biology, will be designed to conquer such worlds. But will it be ethical to send them on such missions?

Professor Fred Hoyle's theory that our galaxy is full of clouds of life-type molecules through which stars and planets swim, occasionally becoming seeded with life, is generally disbelieved by other scientists. But it might be possible to make the idea work in reverse and to construct the seeds of life, immensely tough spores which could then be sent far out into space in attempts to seed the planets round distant stars with primitive life, which might then evolve to high intelligence. It may sound an unlikely prospect, but this kind of seeding mission is a more realistic possibility than sending human colonists on such a journey.

▼ **This biosensor measures concentrations of urea in blood samples. It uses an enzyme to hydrolyze urea, causing a change in electrical conductance which is measured. Biosensors typically link biological sensors, enzymes or antibodies, with electronic circuitry.**

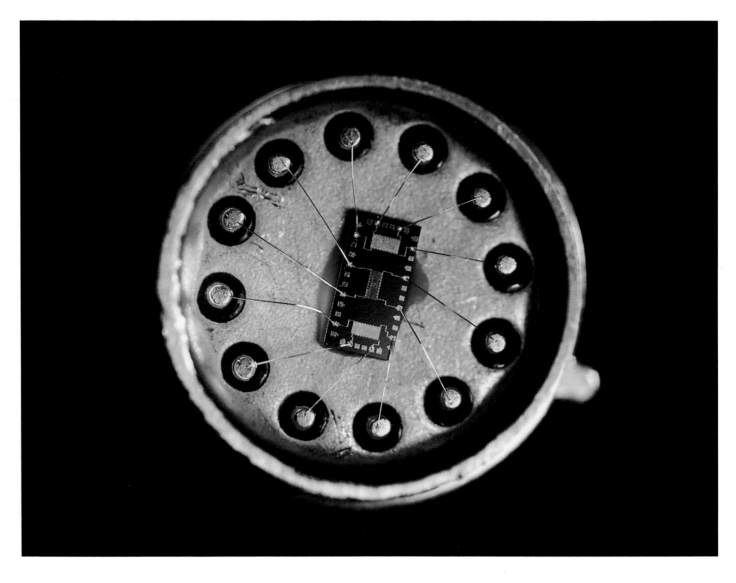

"Baldness begets baldness"...Early medical genetics...A remarkable revolution...Dominant and recessive disorders...Mutations...New techniques for finding human genes...Mapping the human genome...Some prospects in genetic engineering... Correcting genetic diseases...Oncogenes in human cancer...Germ-cell gene therapy...Some objections... Questions that remain

Whether we are glancing surreptitiously at the state of preservation of a prospective mother- or father-in-law to predict how our intended might look 30 years hence, or gazing hopelessly at the identikit features of a newborn baby in the hope of finding some semblance of likeness to its fond parents, we are all concerned with genetics, the science of heredity. The Greek physician Hippocrates, writing over 2,000 years ago, was aware that baldness begets baldness, and squinting squinting, and physicians have always been interested in the possibility that diseases may be inherited.

In the 1983 edition of Victor McKusick's *Mendelian Inheritance in Man*, the clinical geneticist's bible, there are listed over 3,000 disorders that follow Mendel's laws of inheritance. But, although the chemical basis for some of these conditions has been known for many years, it is only recently that it has been possible to determine what is actually wrong with the genes involved.

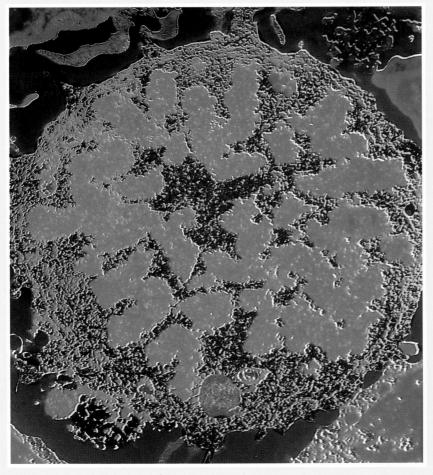

The development of medical genetics

The first serious attempts to measure heritability in human populations were made by the English physician Francis Galton (1822-1911) in the mid-19th century. Galton was fascinated by how talent appears to run in families, particularly those of Lord Chancellors. Although much of his work was obsessed with the idea of selective breeding for a better society, he was the first to apply statistical methods to problems of inheritance. However, Galton and his students were unable to explore the laws of heredity any further because they had no idea how genetic information is passed on.

At about the same time as Galton was studying heredity in England a Moravian monk, Gregor Mendel (1822-1884), was carrying out a series of elegant pea-breeding experiments that described how units of heredity, or genes, are handed down according to simple statistical laws. Though neglected for 40 years, this work laid the basis for modern genetics.

Medical genetics was born in 1901 when another English physician, Archibald Garrod (1857-1936), first identified an inherited disease due to a defect in the way in which the body handles a chemical substance. In describing this "inborn error of metabolism" Garrod made the remarkable intellectual jump of relating the pattern of inheritance of the disorder to one of Mendel's laws of heredity. This work suffered the same fate as Mendel's and was ignored. Not until the second half of the 20th century was the importance of genetics in medical practice finally established.

Human molecular biology

In 1953 James Watson and Francis Crick announced the structure of deoxyribonucleic acid, or DNA, the chemical from which genes are made (♦ page 118). This was the beginning of molecular biology, a field that for many years seemed to have little relevance for medical practice. However, in a remarkable revolution in biology that has occurred recently, methods have become available for isolating human genes and studying their structure. Although these new techniques were only applied to the study of genetic diseases in the late 1970s, such is their power that we already have a good idea of the repertoire of things that can go wrong with our genes, we can diagnose genetic disease in the fetus, and thoughts are turning to replacing defective genes. Furthermore, it is now realized that medical genetics is not confined to the study of diseases that run through families; inheritance plays a role in most common diseases.

So it appears that we are about to enter a particularly exciting phase in our understanding of human disease and its management. But these new advances have brought with them considerable concerns about the wisdom of tinkering with our genes. Where might it all end?

◄ *A human lymphocyte undergoes cell division. The chromosomes are arranged for mitosis, giving two daughter cells with equal numbers of chromosomes identical to the parent cell.*

Patterns of inherited disease

The 3,000 or more genetic diseases follow several patterns of inheritance. Some are called dominant because we only need a bad gene on one of a pair of chromosomes to produce a disease. Others are recessively inherited, that is, individuals with only one defective gene show no disability but those who have inherited the bad gene from both parents, homozygotes, are affected. Non-affected parents with only one bad gene are called carriers, or heterozygotes. In north European populations the commonest recessive disorder is cystic fibrosis which occurs about two or three times in every 10,000 births. Globally, the commonest genetic diseases are the inherited disorders of the red blood cells; approximately 5 percent of the world population are carriers. All of us carry a few bad recessive genes, though fortunately the chances of us meeting a sexual partner with the same gene are small. Dominantly-inherited disorders are less common. Some of the commonest genetic diseases are carried on the X chromosome; the blood-clotting disease hemophilia and some of the serious muscular disorders are well-known examples. Another common group of diseases are caused by major defects in our chromosomes. We may inherit too many or too few, or our chromosomes may lose or gain pieces. The best-known example is mongolism, which usually results from the presence of an extra chromosome.

What does all this add up to in terms of human suffering? About one percent of all babies are born with a genetic disability or serious congenital malformation. The latter are not all genetic and may result from damage during fetal development, but at least some of them have

▼ *A sufferer from cystic fibrosis receiving physiotherapy treatment. In this disease a genetic defect makes the secretions in the lungs and pancreas thicker than usual and therefore these children develop recurrent chest infections and bowel disturbance. They have to be treated with antibiotics, and regular physiotherapy.*

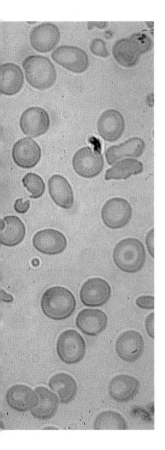

▲ *Thalassemia is caused by a genetic defect in hemoglobin production and the red blood cells, instead of being well filled with hemoglobin, look like pale "ghosts" under the microscope. The world's commonest genetic disease, thalassemia (from the Greek for "sea") was once thought to affect only Mediterranean populations.*

▶ *DNA can be obtained from a fetus as early as 8-9 weeks, by taking a sample from the amniotic fluid (amniocentesis). For the foreseeable future such screening for genetic disorders will be limited to those that are common – chromosome disorders, cystic fibrosis and the hemoglobin disorders, for example. For less common genetic diseases it seems likely that this approach will only be used in families that already have an affected child.*

an inherited tendency. Such genetic disorders are only the tip of the iceberg. Most of the common disorders that afflict western societies – heart disease, cancer, major psychiatric disease, and diabetes, for example – all have a strong genetic component (◗ pages 134, 136), although environmental factors are also involved.

The molecular basis of inherited diseases

In recent years molecular biologists have developed various techniques for isolating human genes (◗ page 132). Although these techniques are new they have already told us a great deal about what can go wrong with our genes, allowed us to detect genetic abnormalities in fetal life, and shown us how to harness our genes to produce a variety of therapeutic agents.

The first human genes to be isolated from patients with genetic diseases were those that control the respiratory pigment of the blood, hemoglobin. Hemoglobin is a protein made up of two different pairs of peptide chains (◖ page 118) called alpha and beta. The commonest genetic disease in the world is called thalassemia, after a Greek word meaning "the sea" (the condition was originally thought to be restricted to peoples of the Mediterranean, but it is now known to occur worldwide). Affected children cannot make hemoglobin, and if they do not receive regular blood transfusions they die within the first few years of life. The alpha and beta chains are controlled by alpha and beta genes, both of which may be affected by thalassemia.

An alteration in the structure of a gene is called a mutation. When the beta globin genes of children with beta thalassemia were isolated and sequenced it was found that many different mutations can give rise to this disease. In some cases the gene is deleted, that is, either part or all of it is missing. In others a single base change in the coding part of the gene scrambles the genetic code so that the messenger RNA cannot be translated properly. But many cases are due to single base changes in the critical regions where introns are cut out and exons joined together. These mutations are diverse and extremely subtle and emphasize the complexity of the normal splicing process. Finally, there is a family of mutations that are found outside the genes which involve the regulatory boxes that control the transcription of the genes.

▲ *American folksinger and writer Woodie Guthrie (1912-1966) died of Huntington's chorea, an inherited disease of the nervous system that affects individuals in middle life. Guthrie's mother and two of his five children died of the same disease. The gene for Huntington's chorea has been tracked by reverse genetics (◗ page 132).*

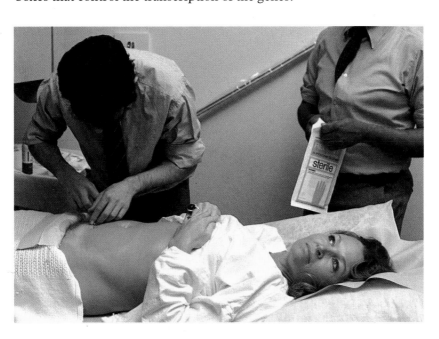

Joined together, one person's DNA would stretch to the Moon and back some 8,000 times

Studying human genes

In every cell in the body there are about two meters of DNA, and each one of us has about 3×10^{12} cells. When we are embarking on a search for a single gene of, say, 1,000-2,000 bases we are looking for a needle in a molecular haystack that is about six million times its size.

The two strands of DNA come apart easily and will reassociate under appropriate conditions. This reassociation process is highly specific and will only occur between lengths of DNA in which the bases are complementary. To find a gene all that is necessary is to make a mirror-image copy of the sequence of bases being looked for. We then treat the DNA to separate its strands and ask the copy sequence, or "probe", to go and look for a mirror-image of itself. It will only stick, or hybridize, to the DNA if it finds such a complementary sequence. If the probe that we have made is radioactively labeled we can follow its progress in hunting for its partner.

Another major advance is the discovery of bacterial enzymes that chop up DNA into small fragments. These restriction enzymes cut DNA at very precise base sequences. The fragments can be inserted into circular pieces of DNA called plasmids that normally live in bacteria and replicate separately from the bacterial genes. Plasmids containing fragments of human DNA are called recombinants, that is, they contain foreign DNA. If conditions are right, almost the entire human genome can be fragmented into pieces that can then be grown in bacteria, producing what is called a gene library. Bacteria can be applied to plates containing nutrients on which they grow in individual colonies. We can find the bacterial colony that contains a gene in which we are interested by looking for it with a gene probe. The colony can then be grown until enough DNA has been obtained to work with. In this way it has been possible to isolate over 100 human genes and to determine their DNA structure and, in some cases, to persuade them to produce human proteins in bacterial cells.

Finding genes for disorders of unknown cause

For some time geneticists have reasoned that the way to track a gene that cannot be identified by a specific test is to find another gene that can be easily detected and that is very closely linked to it – a partner on the same chromosome. If the two genes are so close that they will remain together through successive generations, the marker gene can be used to track the closely-linked gene of interest.

There is a lot of harmless variation in the structure of our genes which is inherited and which can be identified by enzymes that cut DNA. Hence we have a rich source of genetic markers that can be used for tracking genes. For example, every few hundred bases or so there are so-called point polymorphisms, that is, bases that vary from person to person and either produce a new site for a cutting enzyme or remove a previously existing one. Sites that give rise to different sizes of DNA fragment, after cleavage with enzymes, are called restriction fragment length polymorphisms (RFLPs). Taking a family with a genetic disease of unknown cause, geneticists are able to find an appropriate DNA marker and then see if the disease gene and the marker are linked. If they are, the marker can be used to track the defect through a family. Having obtained a linkage of this type it is possible to move from the marker to the disease gene using ingenious techniques called "walking" or "hopping" along the chromosome. And having found the gene it is possible to try to work out what its protein product might be and hence the cause of the disease, an occupation called reverse genetics.

▲ *Leroy Hood of the California Institute of Technology is one of many scientists developing gene-sequencing machines. In the future gene sequencing will be considerably speeded up, as well as the tedium being removed, by the development of fully-automated machines. This in turn should make sequencing of large regions of the human genome much easier, and should help to develop a physical map of the entire human genome.*

▶ *Mapping of two genes (blue) is shown in this false-color transmission electron micrograph of a circular loop (plasmid) of bacterial DNA. The "probe", or RNA copy of the sequence of DNA bases being searched for, sticks (red) to the complementary sequence of DNA. Ordinary double-stranded DNA is colored yellow.*

▶ *Gene-sequencing machines already incorporate laser systems and computers. A further development is the use of robots to assist in the work of synthesizing DNA for genetic engineers. Experimenting with the use of robots for this purpose is already taking place, for example, at the Genetics Institute in Cambridge, Massachusetts. Robots may revolutionize genetics and speed up sequencing so that mapping the human genome may be completed in the next decade or so.*

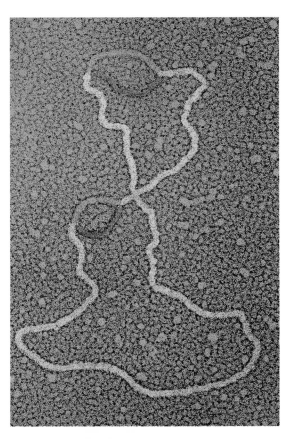

A road atlas of the human genome

It has always been the dream of human geneticists that some day they might have a map of the whole of the human genome showing the precise location of all our genes. Considering its enormous size this will be no mean task. One approach will be to develop linkage markers at a reasonable distance from each other so that they can be used to track any gene. This procedure will provide a genetic map. But it seems equally likely that it will be possible to produce a physical map, that is, overlapping lengths of DNA that can be laid end to end to give a precise plan of most of the human genome.

To produce such a "dictionary" quickly geneticists will combine the two approaches. This will provide a genetic road atlas. Just as a good atlas has the towns and villages marked out along the sides of roads, so our genes will be mapped along our chromosomes. Computers, lasers and robots are already being enlisted to assist with the task. Special computer software will also be needed to assess and find uses for the enormous quantity of information that gene mapping and sequencing will generate.

Our genes only constitute about 5 percent of our total genome. What else will we find in the process of mapping our DNA? Undoubtedly, regions that are involved in control and development will be found, but so will long stretches with no obvious function. Sorting out just why we carry so much apparently useless DNA will be one of the most fascinating tasks of the next decade.

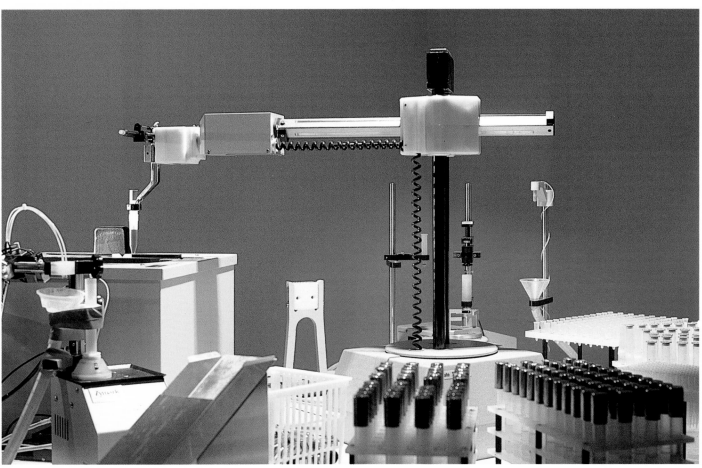

Recombinant DNA technology will provide new generations of antibodies and vaccines

▶ *One of the major difficulties in transplanting organs is that in many cases the body mounts an attack against the foreign tissue. Currently it is possible to match donors and recipients using complex blood tests which are both time-consuming and only partially successful. By analyzing the DNA of the genes involved in the rejection of foreign tissues, it should be possible greatly to improve the success-rate of organ donation in the future. There will be few branches of medicine that will not make use of genetically-engineered diagnostic agents.*

▼ *Gene mapping will help identify abnormalities of the chromosomes which cannot be seen under the microscope. This in turn will make identification of congenital disorders, such as Down's syndrome (below), much easier and in the long term should help understand how they occur.*

The future understanding of common diseases

Many diseases that are of particular concern to people in "western" societies have a genetic basis. Heart disease is a good example, although bad habits of smoking and eating also play a major role. It should be possible to define the genes that make people more likely to succumb to such bad habits. This will reveal more about the mechanisms that underlie the changes in blood vessels that produce heart disease, and, hopefully, how to prevent or treat these conditions. It will also provide a greater understanding of the molecular mechanisms involved in major psychiatric diseases, rheumatic diseases, diabetes, and other common disorders. In the long term this should make it possible to define groups of people at particular risk and help them to modify their life-styles and environments accordingly. But more importantly, it should help to develop better strategies for the management of such diseases.

A boom in the pharmaceutical industry

Human genes can be inserted into bacterial cells and encouraged to make their products. The application of this technique will evolve into an enormous industry. Using the techniques of genetic engineering it will be possible to produce a wide variety of blood-clotting factors that are missing from patients with diseases such as hemophilia. Unlike human blood products they will be free of contaminating viruses such as the AIDS agent. Other products will include a range of biological regulatory molecules for therapeutic use. Several factors of this type have already been isolated by genetic engineering including, for example, those that control the production of our white blood cells. They are already being used in clinical trials in patients who have severe infections; newborn babies who do not produce white cells properly should benefit in the near future. Recombinant DNA technology should also provide new generations of antibodies and is already providing new vaccines.

The widening use of diagnostic agents

As we learn about the genes of bacteria, viruses, and parasites, it will become possible to make probes for the rapid diagnosis of infections. And as we find out more about the behavior of oncogenes in cancer, we shall use gene probes to diagnose cancer and monitor progress during treatment. Using probes for genes involved in the rejection of foreign organs, we shall develop faster and more accurate methods for matching donors and recipients of kidneys, hearts, and other organs.

◄ *Reading a DNA-sequencing autoradiograph into the computer. Gene-sequencing machines will lead to a greater understanding of the causes of common diseases and genetic abnormalities. Mapping the entire human genome is viewed by many biologists as the "project of the century". Genes make up only some 5% of our total genome. Investigating why we carry so much apparently "surplus" DNA will open up whole new areas of research.*

Understanding the biology of human development

Scientists still do not have the faintest idea how a fertilized egg turns into a human being. Nobody has adequately explained how the appropriate genes are switched on and off in the right place at different stages of development. One suggestion that has been made is that we may have genes that act as developmental time clocks. There are hints from work being conducted on fruit flies that specific genes are involved in laying down patterns for different anatomical regions during development. Remarkably, these genes seem to have their counterparts also in humans.

The medical spin-off from the molecular biology of human development may be immense. It should enable us to understand how congenital abnormalities arise and how they can be prevented. Gene mapping is already showing that some congenital defects result from major abnormalities of the chromosomes that are not visible under the microscope. Such investigations may also help to understand aging; the reason for the limit to our "four-score years and ten" of life must, ultimately, be found in our genomes.

Correcting genetic diseases

Gene therapy will be developed over the next few years. Putting foreign genes into cells is not all that difficult; getting them to work and behave correctly in their new home is another matter. The most promising approach is to insert genes into retroviruses, that is, viruses that are designed by nature to enter foreign cells and incorporate their own DNA into that of the cell. The AIDS virus is a retrovirus though no one is contemplating using it for gene therapy. This technique is still inefficient, and even if we succeed in putting our gene into another cell we know very little about how to ensure that it is properly regulated. But these technical problems will be overcome.

Over the next 30 years this technique, or variations of it (retroviruses are not the only means available for inserting DNA into human cells, though they are probably the most effective), will be used increasingly to cure a number of the 3,000-odd serious conditions known to be caused by defects in single genes. Because of the ease with which bone-marrow tissue can be taken from patients, and genetically-altered bone-marrow cells reimplanted to repopulate the bones, conditions affecting blood cells are likely to be the first to be cured by gene therapy.

Leukemias may become curable by a combination of genetic engineering techniques. Stem cells will be implanted to replace the abnormal, permanently immature stem cells which produce leukemic, cancerous white cells. At the same time lymphokines will be used to persuade the immature stem cells to mature. Extra genes may be implanted into the bone marrow cells removed from a patient's body, genes selected, or in the further future designed, to stimulate the reimplanted cells to grow and divide faster than the surrounding, abnormal cells. In this way the new cells will gradually take over the bone marrow and render it healthy and normal. Also during the next 30 years we shall surely see the beginning, be it ever so experimental, of gene therapy for more complex conditions than those caused by single gene defects.

At present the defective genes responsible for inherited conditions such as cystic fibrosis and muscular dystrophy are being rapidly identified. Such conditions will be much harder to treat by gene therapy than those affecting bone marrow. This is because of the difficulties of developing a vector (the equivalent of the retrovirus at the top of this page) which will carry new genes into a sufficient number of cells in the appropriate part of a patient's body to cure or at least to ameliorate the condition. But as the ability of genetic engineers to manipulate viral genes so as to alter the properties of viruses in a controlled way increases, so genetically-engineered retroviruses will be developed selectively to infect target tissues chosen by doctors.

But the effect of such cures will be to spread genes for these conditions and others like them more and more widely through the population. People who as a result of genetic defects today die young or in infancy, or are too ill to start families, will be able to have children. Because the gene therapy which has cured them affects only the part of their body which is afflicted, as for example the bone marrow (in sickle cell anemia or thalassemia), the reproductive cells, the sperms and the eggs produced by such people "cured" by gene therapy will still carry abnormal genes. The continuing spread of such abnormal genes will necessitate more and more expenditure on gene therapy – unless means can be found to implant the correct versions of the abnormal genes into the reproductive cells as well as the bone marrow.

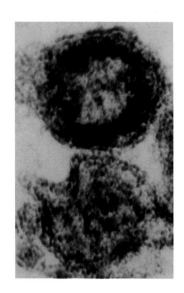

▼ *Particles of the human T-cell leukemia virus, which belongs to the same family as that which causes AIDS. Both can insert their own genes into the genetic code of the nuclei of the cells they infect, so that the viral genes subsequently behave and reproduce as an integral part of the cell's own genome. Such retroviruses. as they are called, cause diseases; they also offer the promise of human gene therapy.*

▶ *Monoclonal antibodies which react with cancer cells, made harmlessly radioactive by "labeling" with radioactive iodine, concentrate (orange) around a tumor in the liver which has spread from the original tumor in the colon. More powerfully radioactive isotopes, targeted to tumors by monoclonal antibodies in this way, are being used experimentally to treat as well as to localize tumors.*

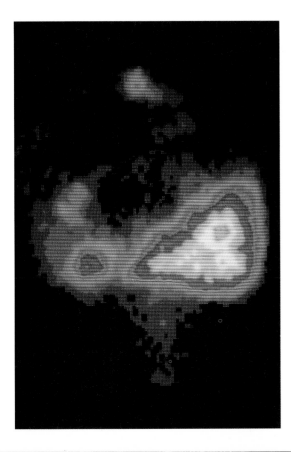

Cancer

Cancer does not usually run in families. However, the common cancers must involve a fundamental change in the genetic machinery of cells that is passed on to their progeny so that they lose their ability to divide in an organized way. Some animal cancers are caused by viruses, and the genes of the virus that are involved have been identified. Surprisingly, these have their counterparts in human cells. The human genes (cellular oncogenes) are involved in cellular housekeeping activities, such as the regulation of growth and division. It is believed that certain viruses picked up these genes from us and turned them into cancer-producing genes. The study of cellular oncogenes in human cancer promises to tell us a great deal about why a normal cell takes on a malignant role.

There are several ways in which genetic engineering and new biotechnology will make cancer treatment more effective. One is in making monoclonal antibodies which are at least semi-specific for cancer cells and using them to target toxins or radioactive isotopes to tumors. Another is in disguising such antibodies as human tissue, so they are not rejected and destroyed before they can have therapeutic value. Rapid progress has been made in this area in recent times, and rat monoclonal antibodies disguised effectively as human material have been successfully tested in animals. They are now being used experimentally to treat human leukemia.

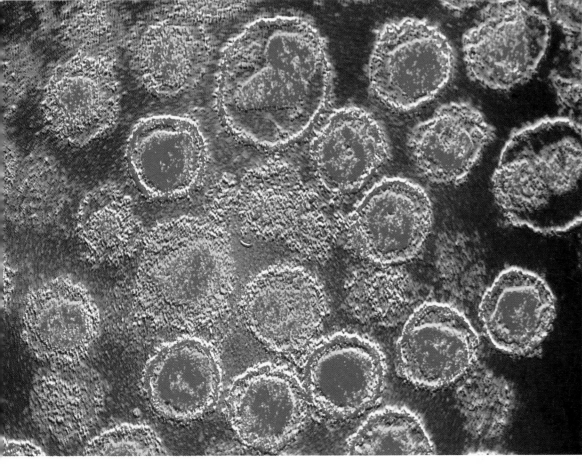

◄ *Virions (virus particles) of a retrovirus, an oncornavirus which causes cancer in birds (false-color transmission electron micrograph). The particles contain the enzyme reverse transcriptase, needed to transform the viral genes, in the form of RNA, into DNA so they can be integrated into bird or mammalian genes. Retroviruses are already being used experimentally to treat some genetic diseases.*

Some objections to gene therapy

Gene therapy is clearly an area where, as more animal experiments reveal the potential for humans more clearly, controversy is to be expected and is bound to become bitter. Why do many scientists and others oppose germ-cell gene therapy for humans, while welcoming somatic gene therapy?

One argument is that at present the success rate for germ-cell gene therapy experiments in animals is very low. Undoubtedly it will be possible to improve the success rate, but doctors may still face the prospect, if gene therapy for fertilized eggs is attempted, of the egg developing into an embryo and later into a person who is still affected by an hereditary defect, which the implanted gene has failed to cure. However, it may be possible to develop screening tests for developing fetuses which will reliably determine whether or not the implantation has been successful in curing the condition.

Another argument against germ-cell gene therapy is that inserting genes, which distorts the natural arrangement of genes in the cells of the growing embryo, could cause completely new abnormalities. One possibility is that because the injected genes cannot yet be placed in their correct position on the chromosome, their effects will not be properly controlled. This may lead to the inserted genes having an effect in parts of the body where they would not normally be expressed. Again, animal experiments could probably be used to develop techniques to ensure that this did not happen.

Yet another objection to the development of germ-cell gene therapy is that it will be of limited value since it will be really valuable only in cases in which one or both parents are homozygous for the abnormal condition. This means that they both carry the abnormal gene on both of the two chromosomes on which the gene may or may not occur in the nuclei of their cells. If both parents are homozygous then without germ-cell gene therapy all their children will be affected. If both parents have the affected gene on only one of the two chromosomes, then only one in four fertilized eggs will produce a person who is homozygous for the abnormality and so is affected by the condition. The other eggs will develop into people who, like their parents, carry the condition without being affected by it, though they are liable to produce offspring which, being homozygous, are affected.

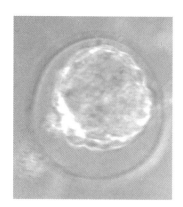

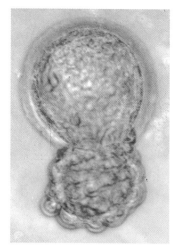

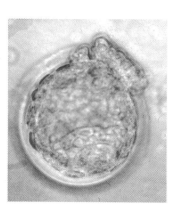

Germ-cell gene therapy

Gene therapy which can implant correct genes into reproductive (germ) cells as well as body (somatic) cells is definitely possible. In the "test-tube baby" technique, which has been routine for several years now, eggs are removed surgically from a woman with blocked fallopian tubes and are fertilized outside her body with sperm before being implanted in her womb to develop normally. The success rate for this procedure in the best clinics is now around one in five and is bound to improve. Germ-cell therapy would involve following the same procedure and, after the egg has been fertilized but before it begins to divide, or at a very early stage of division, implanting into the egg the correct versions of genes which are known to be abnormal in the woman from whom the egg has been taken. A retrovirus may be used to implant the genes deep among the egg cell's own DNA.

Then, as the egg divides to form an embryo and, after nine months, a baby, the extra genes will propagate along with all the other genes into new cells as they are formed. The extra genes will find their way into the testes or ovaries as they are formed, according to whether the baby is a boy or a girl. Later in adulthood, when cells in the testes or ovaries divide to form sperms or eggs, the extra genes will pass into the sperms or eggs, and so, when the eggs are fertilized, on into future generations. In this way not only an individual but also his or her descendants could be freed from genetic defects.

Gene therapy for human eggs could allow women at risk of bearing children afflicted with genetic diseases to avoid the need for prenatal testing for genetic defects and subsequent abortion of fetuses. Instead, only early embryos shown by examination to have had genes successfully implanted would be replaced in the womb to develop to term. At present genetic diseases can only be eliminated from a population by persuading people carrying defects not to reproduce or, if this fails, carrying out tests on fetuses to search for defective genes and, if they are found, aborting the affected fetuses

When and if germ-line genetic therapy is developed enough to be reliable, will couples, one or both of whom are carriers of genetic defects but are not homozygous, as well as those who are homozygous, opt for germ-line gene therapy? The alternative is prenatal testing followed by abortion if necessary, together with the knowledge that they are transmitting defective genes onward into future generations of their family. Testing fertilized eggs, rather than fetuses, for defects will offer an alternative to germ-line gene therapy for some, but maybe not all, purposes.

Clearly, for the next 30 years at least this will be a controversial area with varying practices in different countries and among different religious persuasions. Any practices involving the genetic manipulation of eggs or sperms is expressly condemned by the Roman Catholic Church. But the fact that, even in the present limited state of knowledge, scientists have already succeeded in experiments in germ-line gene therapy, and in screening out abnormalities at the fertilized egg stage, in animals suggests that both will soon become possible in humans. Then their potential benefits will become more and more apparent within a surprisingly short time. The development of similar techniques for use in farm animals will demonstrate publicly how effective they can be and how any risks involved can be circumvented. It seems most probable that pressures to develop germ-cell gene therapy for human use will become irresistible.

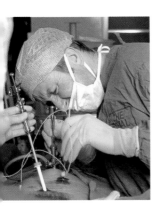

◀ Current work with marmoset monkeys will soon make it possible to test a human embryo for genetic abnormalities at such an early stage that no more inconvenience to the mother would be experienced than that of "in vitro" fertilization, the "test tube baby" technique. The pictures show an egg which has been removed from a marmoset, fertilized and allowed to grow to the very early blastocyst stage, when it is a microscopic hollow ball of cells (far left, top). The blastocyst is slit to cause it to produce a tiny growth, a so-called hernia of tissue (center), which is removed for genetic analysis while the blastocyst continues to grow normally (bottom). An embryo with a defect can be discarded. One with no defect can be reimplanted to develop, either in the original mother or as in this case (near left) a surrogate, into a normal monkey.

◀ A surgeon examines eggs in a woman's ovary before removing some for fertilization outside the body. At the time of fertilization, the eggs could be scanned for genetic defects and discarded if they possess them. This is seen by many as preferable to so-called germ-line gene therapy, in which normal genes would be added to try to render abnormal embryos genetically normal.

The questions that remain

At the time of writing it appeared that, probably in the United States, the first steps in human gene therapy were about to be taken, in an attempt to cure a deficiency of the immune system caused by genetic defects affecting the white blood cells. DNA is already being taken from human fetuses at an early stage of development and being matched to "library" DNA to see if the fetus has defects which the mother fears she may hand on to her children. Experiments in monkeys have already shown that it is possible to carry out such tests even earlier, on fertilized eggs which have undergone just 2-3 divisions. And tests in mice have shown that, if we want to, it will soon be possible to implant new genes into human eggs as well as screening out unwanted genes.

Having started down the slippery slope of human genetic engineering, are we likely to end up with a

society similar to that envisaged by Aldous Huxley in his "Brave New World" or to George Orwell's grim vision in "1984"? Shall we be able to control human behavior at will, and are parents of the future going to wander round gene supermarkets stocking up traits that they wish to see expressed in their children? Might governments be tempted to legislate for preventing genetic disease to save money spent on health care, or decide to breed populations of aggressive supermen for their political ends? And even worse, might dictators decide to be cloned, that is, to allow their genomes to be used to engineer a series of identical individuals?

Just as the revolution in physics at the beginning of this century provided us with the means to destroy ourselves, so the biological revolution that followed has given us the potential to tinker with the basic material of life, the human genome. This new-found ability has enormous potential for improving the health and well-being of mankind. But, as in the case of nuclear physics, it also has the potential for disaster. After all, the eugenics movement, founded with the best intentions by the British scientist Francis Galton (1822-1911) and his school, culminated in the racial policies of Nazi Germany.

There is little doubt that, over the next 300 years, we shall be able to control genetic disease, learn how to prevent or treat many of the diseases that afflict western societies, and improve the lot of the Third World by better methods of food production and dealing with infectious and parasitic disease. However, many questions remain. Certainly we shall be in better physical shape, but shall we be happier or, as envisaged by Galton, more intelligent? We have no generally accepted idea about the relative contributions of nature and nurture to the patterns of intelligence, behavior and creativity. It is doubtful if we shall ever be able to define a Beethoven symphony in terms of a DNA sequence. And while we may discover that schizophrenia and other severe mental illnesses are largely the result of a few mutant genes, it is likely that much of the variability of human behavior will turn out to be a reflection of our environment. But the behavioral sciences and neurobiology are young disciplines. As they mature and join forces with human molecular genetics, who knows what may be possible.

How much time is there for medical scientists and the population at large to open a debate on how far we wish to go in our efforts to control the human genome? Considering the enormous timespan over which natural selection has been at work to bring the human genome to its present level of complexity, it seems unlikely that even molecular biologists will be able to do it too much damage, certainly not overnight. Perhaps in 300 years' time gene therapy will be routine and the need for fetal diagnosis, termination of pregnancy, and the manipulation of human embryos will be long past. But we must start talking about these questions now. If we ignore them now, we could in the future have the spectacle of a summit conference between world leaders haggling over the size of their stockpiles of genetically engineered troops, or, to take a slightly more optimistic view, teams of cloned sports players.

▼ **Many human medications will be made using genetic engineering in the future. They will be produced in bacteria and will be free of the danger of AIDS virus and other infections which can contaminate biological products when they are made from human material.**

The discovery of bacteriophages..."Hybrid antibiotics"...Hijacking a microbe's own machinery...Advances and advantages of phage therapy...Cloning drugs...Lymphokines... Abzymes...Using monoclonal antibodies...The usefulness of plant products...Controversial new strategies...Fighting tropical diseases...An "all-in-one" jab?

"Do you mean to say you think you've discovered an infectious disease of bacteria, and you haven't told me about it? My dear boy, I don't believe you quite realise you may have hit on the supreme way to kill pathogenic bacteria." Long after Sinclair Lewis addressed those words to the hero of his novel *Arrowsmith* (1925), that very idea seems about to be moved from the realm of fiction into practical reality (◗ page 144). But the story really began long before publication of *Arrowsmith*. In 1915 Frederick Twort (1877-1949) reported a "transparent dissolving material" which seemed to attack bacteria. Then Félix d'Hérelle (1873-1949), of the Pasteur Institute in Paris, described an "invisible microbe" that was antagonistic to the bacillus responsible for dysentery. Twort and d'Hérelle soon realized they had stumbled upon a previously unknown group of viruses, similar to those which infect animals and plants. So each began to explore the possibility of using these "bacteriophages" to combat bacterial diseases in man and other animals. Although phages destroyed bacteria spectacularly in laboratory glassware, the same microparasites usually failed to perform anything like as well when patients swallowed them by the glassful. Only with the development of greatly improved techniques has it been possible to reopen this chapter of history.

▲ Frederick Twort during the early part of World War I, at the time when he discovered a "transparent dissolving material" which proved to consist of bacteriophages. Twort's research at the Brown Institution, London, was complemented by work in Paris, on a similiar "invisible microbe", by Félix d'Hérelle at the Institut Pasteur.

▼ Diarrheal disease, which causes a horrendous toll of suffering, debility and death throughout the Third World, is fostered by mediocre sanitation and hygiene, as in this Philippines street scene. Bacteriophage therapy could have a dramatic future in the control of serious infections as well as in veterinary medicine.

Novel antibiotics and a new class of "designer drugs"

If bacteriophage therapy proves as effective against human killer diseases as it has already in farm animals, the consequences could be enormous. Of course antibiotics (substances produced by microorganisms used to attack other microorganisms) are already available to treat such potentially deadly infections as cholera. But many of them are increasingly ineffective because the bacteria concerned have become resistant to destruction. Hitherto, the principal strategy used to maintain human control over these diseases has been for the pharmaceutical industry to devise successively new compounds, to supplant those against which resistance has become so widespread as to pose insuperable difficulties. That approach, greatly helped by the advent of the "gene splicing" techniques of genetic engineering, continues to spawn important innovations. Many novel antibiotics, for example, can be confidently predicted to emerge from work which Professor David Hopwood and his colleagues at the John Innes Institute in Norwich, England, have carried out during recent years. They have learned to manipulate the metabolic pathways by which fungi and other organisms make antibiotics in nature. As a result, the organisms generate "hybrid antibiotics" whose molecular shapes (and thus activities) have been determined partly by the genes of the microbes themselves and partly by their subtle human manipulators.

Another pointer to future antibacterial warfare came in 1987 from scientists working for the Swedish company Astra. They managed to advance from the longstanding tradition of isolating antibiotics by essentially empirical methods, to pioneer a much more rational approach to drug design. In the past, substances such as penicillin were developed as therapeutic tools long before anyone understood *how* they killed bacteria or prevented them from growing. Later, when scientists did acquire that knowledge, they exploited it to study bacterial metabolism. Penicillin, for example, prevents bacterial cells from building proper walls, and it was used in experiments that revealed the way in which building blocks become incorporated into the cell wall as bacteria grow and replicate. Had this understanding preceded the antibiotic's discovery, it might have suggested precisely how the drug could have been developed on rational principles.

The Astra researchers first located a precise target within a group of bacteria for which comparatively few potent antibiotics existed (the so-called Gram-negatives) and then set out to fabricate a substance that would attack that target but not harm the body's own tissues. They identified as their target an enzyme which catalyzes the formation of part of the outer membrane in this type of bacterium. They then evolved a substance which inhibited the enzyme – and which they modified so that it was able to get into the bacterial cells. Their crucial move was to alter the substance chemically so that it was carried, Trojan-horse fashion, into the bacteria via transport systems that normally pull nutrients into the cells.

The outcome of this work was an entirely new class of "designer drugs" which will provide a new line of approach in tackling a previously somewhat intractable type of infection. The principle of hijacking a microbe's own machinery for taking in nutrients is one which microbiologists now believe can be exploited to ferry many other specific poisons into many other types of organism. The Astra technique could well make life-saving drugs out of countless potent substances that have been set aside in the past simply because they fail to penetrate into disease-causing bacteria.

▶ **Production-line processing of pharmaceuticals. Some companies claim that the drug industry is facing diminishing returns, due to the costs of ever-more vigilant safety testing, combined with inadequate time to secure financial rewards on new drugs before patents expire. Yet expenditure on research and development remains very high, with many firms spending 10-12% of their sales revenue on R&D. Only 1% in 10,000 chemicals screened for possible use reaches the marketplace.**

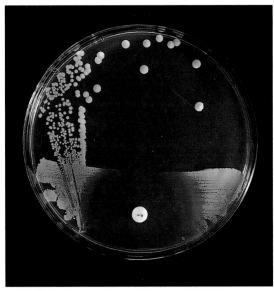

◄ *Penicillin (in white circle) inhibits growth of the bacterium Staphylococcus pyogenes. It was years after penicillin's discovery before scientists found out how it works – preventing bacteria from producing proper cell walls. Other antimicrobial drugs act quite differently.*

▼ *Pharmaceuticals are packaged at Glaxo's Verona factory in Italy. In contrast to the fortuitous discovery of penicillin, which went into clinical use long before its mode of action was understood, today's drugs are designed to interfere with well-understood processes in the target organisms – a strategy adopted by Wellcome chemists in evolving the AIDS drug Retrovir.*

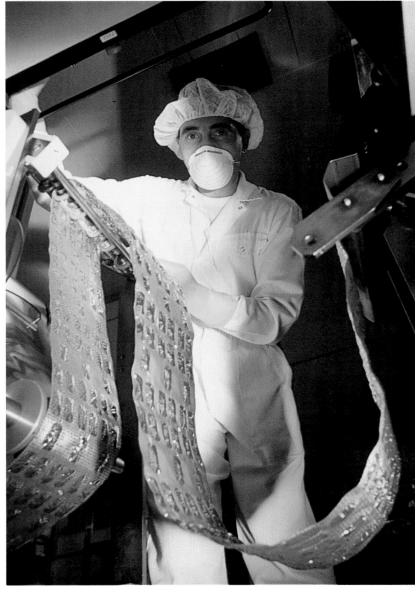

Phage therapy

The concept of exploiting one microbe (a bacteriophage) to attack another (a bacterium) parallels the concept of biological control of plant pests by using their natural predators, as compared with chemical warfare based on insecticides. Phages are viruses containing DNA or RNA (◀ page 118). They invade bacteria and use their cellular machinery to make crops of new phage particles, which are then released, smashing open the cells. Virologists now recognize innumerable phages, each specific to a particular type of vulnerable bacterium.

Leading the way in this development were H. Williams Smith and Michael B. Huggins of the Houghton Poultry Research Station near Huntingdon, England. Their first efforts centered on *Escherichia coli*, a bacterium which normally lives harmlessly in our intestines and those of other animals, but which sometimes appears in virulent form and can cause serious illness and death. The Houghton researchers studied a strain of *E. coli* that had struck down a young baby with potentially fatal meningitis. After growing the bacterium in their laboratory, the two bacteriologists went "fishing" for a phage to attack it. They did so by screening samples of sewage, which always carries an astronomical variety of different phages. Having isolated one phage that was

◀ *A false-color transmission electron micrograph shows newly-synthesized bacteriophages (black ovals) within the bacterium Escherichia coli. As with virus replication inside animal and plant cells, phages have no metabolic processes of their own and must invade bacteria in order to hijack the host cell's machinery.*

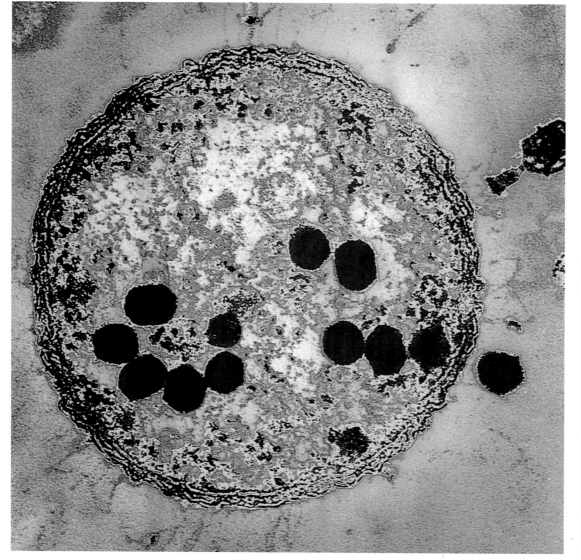

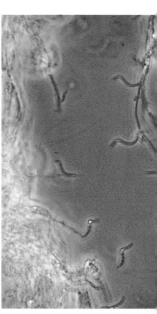

particularly devastating against the *E. coli* strain in laboratory tests, they injected it into mice suffering either from brain infections or more widespread disease, caused by the same microbe.

The carefully selected microparasite not only cured the mice. It was more effective than four out of five of the routine antibiotics with which Williams Smith and Huggins compared it. In sharp contrast to those dismal failures in the past, the phage's performance in an infected body reflected its activity in a test tube. Although a few *E. coli* mutants, resistant to the phage, did emerge during treatment, they were of very low virulence. This was a marked improvement on antibiotic therapy, where mutants tend to be as virulent as the parent strains, or more so.

Next, the Houghton scientists tried to attack bacteria responsible for intestinal infections. They chose strains of *E. coli* which cause considerable financial losses to farmers because of the voracious epidemics of disease they produce in calves, piglets and lambs. In one series of tests, they gave calves lethal doses of an *E. coli* strain. They then found that a mixture of two phages protected the animals against this otherwise fatal infection if it was administered before diarrhea had started, though not if administered afterward. Using a phage "cocktail" minimized the likelihood of resistant mutants arising.

Unlike Twort and d'Hérelle's experience (◀ page 142), one of the phages seemed to be much more effective when given to infected animals than when added to bacteria growing in laboratory glassware. When its twin was replaced by a third phage, the mixture worked well even if infection was well established and the calves had already developed profuse diarrhea. After a painstaking foray among many different samples of sewage, the Houghton team assembled a pool of phages that was highly active against most of the strains causing intestinal infections in lambs and calves. Even keeping calves in uncleaned rooms previously occupied by animals receiving phage treatment was effective in thwarting disease.

These investigations point to future offensives against bacterial disease superior in several respects to today's approach. First, phages need to be given in just a single dose. Unlike antibiotics, which become diluted by blood and other body fluids and soon disappear altogether, phages multiply inside their host bacteria and thus increase hugely in concentration. This amplification occurs precisely where the attack is wanted, at the site of infection, and it continues until the invading organisms have been reduced in number either to a level with which the host's defenses can cope, or to a level at which they are unable to continue the disease process. Second, any phage-resistant mutants that emerge during treatment seem to be considerably less virulent than their parent bacteria. Third, cross-infection with feces from ill animals given phages creates no difficulties – quite the reverse. Calves, piglets and lambs can actually acquire phages in this way and thus become protected against disease.

Some scientists question whether phage therapy could be applied to the entire spectrum of human infections. They believe it will not be of great assistance against conditions (like gonorrhea) which are caused by bacteria that flourish inside the victim's cells. Other experts are much more optimistic. Already Dr Stefan Slopek and colleagues at the Polish Academy of Sciences in Wroclaw have found phages invaluable in controlling blood infections caused by bacteria that are insensitive to antibiotics. In many cases, this form of treatment has been spectacularly successful even against suppurating and long-lasting wound infections that had failed to respond to any other approach.

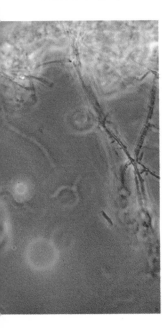

◀ *Michael B. Huggins (left) and the late H. Williams Smith (above) of the Houghton Poultry Research Station (now the Animal Health Laboratory of the Institute of Animal Health) near Huntingdon, England. During the 1980s they showed that, despite Twort and d'Hérelle's failures (◀ page 142), carefully-selected phages given to calves, piglets and lambs do effectively control intestinal and other infections. Virtually every species of bacterium yet investigated is attacked by one or more phages (which are commonly used to identify disease-causing organisms.*

◀ *Microorganisms in sewage and stagnant water range from submicroscopic viruses to the spirillar bacteria seen here. Several research teams are now scrutinizing sewage and other likely sources in search of phages which are effective against several different species of bacteria. The alternative is to evolve "cocktails" of phages. Reemergence of phage therapy could be as significant as the earlier developments of sulfa drugs, penicillin and streptomycin.*

Cloning new drugs – lymphokines

The transfer of genes from their native cells into the cells of other, often very different, species is already widely used commercially. Its first use has been in allowing the manufacture of, by biological standards, vast quantities of the human body's natural control substances, known as lymphokines, such as interferon and human growth hormone. Made by cloning, such substances are already being used, though so far only experimentally, as medical drugs which are far more potent and selective in their effects than any used hitherto.

In the United States Dr Steven Rosenberg is using one lymphokine, Interleukin-2, in a new form of cancer therapy in which it is used to stimulate a cancer patient's immune system to recognize and attack tumor cells more aggressively.

This is no miracle cure for cancer. But it has now been shown to be effective in some patients for whom other treatments have been ineffective. While it is still experimental, since the publication of Rosenberg's results (in the *New England Journal* early in 1987) lymphokine therapy may be said to have come of age.

Interferon, which is a lymphokine, or rather a mixture of lympho-kines, has been used for over 30 years, being produced in other, less efficient ways before cloning was developed. But it is only recently that the complex functions of the mixture of chemicals which used to be known as interferon have begun to be understood. It is becoming apparent that, as well as being extraordinarily potent in minute quantities, lymphokines such as interferon have more than one function. Their effects in combating cancer for instance, may in reality be incidental to other effects, only now beginning to be understood. As with other drugs, serious side effects will have to be accepted as lymphokines come to be used in medicine.

▶ *Dr Steven Rosenberg, head of surgery in the American National Cancer Institute, is pioneering the use of cloned human body control substances (lymphokines) in cancer treatment, using Interleukin-2, which stimulates part of the immune response in cancer therapy. While the treatment has been tested on relatively few patients, it may have advantages over conventional chemotherapy for some forms of cancer, though more research is needed.*

Antibodies against cancer cells have been linked to toxins and used to attack tumors. Drugs targeted in this way can be used in higher doses with fewer side effects on normal tissues, and so with a better chance of killing all the cancer cells in a patient's body and effecting a complete cure. Targeted drugs can be compared to guided missiles in their sophistication as anti-cancer weapons. But making such medical guided missile molecules in two parts – the warhead (the cell-killing toxin molecules) and the guidance system (the targeting antibody molecule) and joining them up – poses big problems. It would be much better to make the two in one. This is now being done, at Cambridge University, England, in the Molecular Biology Laboratory, where Dr Greg Winter and his colleagues have combined the separate genetic blueprints needed to make toxins and targeting antibodies, improved on the combined blueprint, and inserted it into the immortalized cell cultures used to make antibodies.

▶ *Interleukin-2 being cloned: cell cultures with human genes for the drug are grown in a fermentation room in the laboratories of a private genetic engineering company, the Cetus Corporation in Emeryville, California. Interleukin-2 stimulates "natural killer" cells to attack tumors. Several other lymphokines may become the most important pharmaceutical weapons in doctor's armories.*

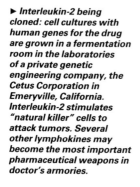

So, genetic blueprints are already being redrawn by genetic engineers to create new and more specific and effective anti-cancer medical drugs which are based on, but improve, the body's natural chemical defenses. Over the next 30 years, such drugs will undoubtedly come into wide use and will improve the cure rate for most common cancers. In 300 years' time scientists will have complete knowledge of the human genetic blueprint and complete mastery of techniques for altering it, and knowledge of the effects of any such alterations on the structures and functions of the protein molecules for which the altered blueprints are responsible. This will long have made it possible to design genes which are entirely man-made, and which act as the blueprints for wholly new man-made molecules, with new functions.

Medical applications of lymphokines

About 10 lymphokines have now been discovered, each so potent that a single gram is ample to treat thousands of patients, and all potentially able to be cloned in any required quantity. In the next 30 years lymphokines will be used, at first experimentally and then with growing confidence, to treat growing numbers of patients. Lymphokines will strengthen patients' ability to endure the side effects of conventional cancer treatment, as well as helping the patients' immune system itself to combat cancer.

There are more subtle ways of treating cancer. Leukemic blood cells are immature cells that never grow up. A lymphokine, pluropoietin, may be used to treat the abnormal bone marrow of leukemic patients, because pluropoietin stimulates blood cells to mature. Other lymphokines are known that will selectively stimulate specific classes of white blood cells so that they perform specific functions in the immune system.

Cells called eosinophils (♦ page 153) naturally attack worm parasites. Eosinophils can be urged on to the attack by a lymphokine, cloned outside the body and injected into a patient. White cells called macrophages specifically attack protozoan (single-celled) parasites such as those that cause dysentery. Lymphokines that stimulate macrophages can be cloned and used to strengthen natural resistance to diseases that are caused by protozoa.

In 30 years' time lymphokine treatments for cancer will be common and established and will have led to substantially improved chances of cures for several important cancers. As improved cloning techniques reduce the cost of lymphokines, they will become increasingly used to treat life-threatening infectious diseases, as well as cancers.

In 300 years' time, the sophisticated manipulation of human health with lymphokines will have joined the mainstream of medicine. Incipient weakness or deficiencies will be corrected with appropriate doses of the appropriate lymphokine, or rather, carefully mixed cocktails of lymphokines.

Anyone unfortunate enough to sustain an accident which destroys an organ or a limb, or to require surgery involving their removal, will grow new organs or limbs. They will be stimulated by the appropriate lymphokines, used to reactivate the genes which in nature are switched on only in embryonic life, when organs and limbs are first formed. New skin, intestine, brain or nervous tissue will be grown at will.

Abzymes

At the end of 1986 two teams of American scientists reported (to the journal "Science") that they had succeeded in harnessing the resources of the immune system to create completely new enzymes. It would be hard to overemphasize the importance of this advance. The immune system is capable of making two or three million different kinds of antibodies, each of which is able to react specifically with just one foreign organism or poisonous substance which has invaded the body of the person which the antibodies defend. The American breakthrough has opened the way to using this vast and sophisticated manufacturing capability to make enzymes as well as antibodies.

Chemical reactions involving complex molecules usually pass through at least one intermediate state en route to the finished product. The enzymes that catalyze the reaction work by reacting strongly and specifically with the intermediate state. This reaction, by stabilizing the intermediate state which otherwise is very short-lived and hard to create, encourages and smoothes the entire reaction. So an enzyme which catalyzes a reaction can be defined as a compound which reacts specifically and potently with the intermediate state of that reaction.

Supposing then, that the chemical industry has a reaction which it would prefer to catalyze enzymatically, but that no enzyme for the task exists in nature, the enzyme can be created as follows. First, the structure of the intermediate state in the reaction must be worked out. Next, that intermediate state is synthesized and injected into a mouse or other animal. The mouse reacts by making antibodies against the intermediate state compound. The antibodies react specifically and strongly with the intermediate state. Next, the cells making the antibodies are removed from the mouse (from its spleen). By fusing them with strongly-growing laboratory cell cultures, a cell culture is created which produces the antibody in useful quantities and in perpetuity. In the language of an immunologist, the ability to make the antibody has been "immortalized". And there, in the shape of the antibody, is an enzyme which is able to catalyze the required reaction.

Enzymes made in this way, as antibodies, have been christened abzymes. Abzymes can be made to catalyze almost any reactions with intermediate states with molecules complex enough to be recognized as foreign by a mouse's immune system, so that antibodies will be made against them.

▲ Interferon being tested in rats. Interferon, the first lymphokine to be discovered, is now known to consist of several different substances with different functions, which have been separately cloned. Their potential for the treatment of infectious diseases as well as cancer is now being explored.

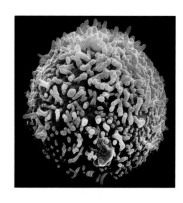

Protein engineering in fighting disease

Antibodies can be made to order by injecting foreign substances into mice and immortalizing the cells which make antibodies against the foreign substances (◀ page 148). They are called monoclonal antibodies and were first made by the 1984 Nobel Physiology or Medicine Prize winners César Milstein and Georges Köhler at the Cambridge Molecular Biology Laboratory in the 1970s.

Before monoclonal antibodies were made, antibodies could only be obtained from animals or from human or animal cell cultures in minute quantities and in impure mixtures. Made as a monoclonal, any required antibody can be produced in any required quantity and in a very pure form. The making of monoclonal antibodies on the one hand, and genetic engineering on the other, are the two great biotechnologies of the revolution brought about by molecular biologists that is now beginning to change the world.

Monoclonal antibody manufacture and genetic engineering are increasingly being combined, in the new craft called protein engineering. In this, genetic engineers take the blueprint used by a living cell to make an antibody, an enzyme or any other protein molecule, and redraw the blueprint to fit the new specification of the protein engineer.

Each successive trio of chemical subgroups, bases which form links in the ultra-long-chain molecule that is DNA (◀ page 118), is the blueprint for one link, one amino acid as the subgroups are called, in the long-chain protein molecule for which one gene (or sequence of DNA) represents the complete genetic blueprint. Before this blueprint can be redrawn so as to alter the protein, to make an abzyme (◀ page 147) more effective as an enzyme for example, the complete sequences both of the bases in the DNA and of the corresponding amino acids in the protein must be known. A full understanding is still to be reached of the effects that the sequence of amino acids have on the way in which the protein molecule is curled and tangled up, seemingly like a ball of wool but in fact to provide a very precise three-dimensional structure. Only a few proteins have so far been completely decoded in this way. But as more are decoded, genetic engineering is moving into a second phase. Genetic and protein engineers are no longer merely cloning genes and their products, they are improving on them.

Protein engineers already have some achievements to their credit. In April, 1987, researchers at Imperial College, London, announced that they had succeeded in making an enzyme 100 times more potent, by tinkering purposefully with its genetic blueprint. A 1988 product is insulin for diabetics that is absorbed as quickly as normally-produced insulin. But perhaps the most exciting developments in the application of protein engineering is in so-called "drug targeting".

Cancer cells have protein molecules (antigens) on their surfaces which are not found, or are only very rarely found, on the surfaces of normal cells. Several such cancer antigens have now been identified (though none has yet been found which is totally unique to malignant cells). Antibodies which react strongly and specifically with cancer antigens can easily be created by the standard technique for making monoclonal antibodies, by injecting the cancer antigen into mice and immortalizing the antibody-making cells. If such anti-cancer antibodies are then linked to very toxic, cell-killing chemicals, the antibodies can act as targeting agents, directing the killers to cancer cells. The antibodies become attached to these, while they flow past normal cells without becoming attached.

◀▲ A hybridoma cell (above) produces a monoclonal antibody to cytoskeleton protein. Most wanted antibodies can be made as monoclonals for use in medical diagnosis, therapy or research. Monoclonal antibodies are being developed as a means of directing toxins to kill cancer cells selectively. They are made by injecting antigens into rats or mice, removing spleen cells from the animals, identifying cells producing wanted antibodies and fusing these cells with fast-growing cells in culture. This forms a hybrid culture, a hybridoma, which will continue to make the wanted antibody indefinitely. Manufacture of the wanted antibody can be expanded to any required scale and it is effectively immortalized. This new 2,000-liter fermenter (left) is in the laboratories of Celltech, the UK national biotechnology company at Slough in Berkshire, which is now the world's biggest producer of monoclonal antibodies.

Plant products will be invaluable in helping to evolve ways to attack AIDS and similar viruses

Combating viruses – sugar mimics

Whatever the past and future triumphs of antibacterial warfare, we still have only a limited number of drugs that can be used to combat virus infections. Fortunately, there are highly-effective vaccines against many of the most serious virus diseases. Indeed, it is practically feasible for some of these maladies, such as poliomyelitis and rubella, to be made extinct worldwide by vaccination, just as smallpox was eradicated during the 1970s. All that is required is the political determination to carry through campaigns of that sort. Another prospect raised by genetic engineering is to incorporate antibody-triggering parts of other disease organisms, such as malaria and measles, into the *vaccinia* virus, which was formerly used to immunize people against smallpox. Using such hybrid vaccines, it should be possible to make children immune for life to several different virus diseases at the same time.

Although the few antiviral drugs now available have mostly been synthesized by chemists, many experts look to the natural world for future treatments, or more effective treatments, for virus diseases such as herpes, influenza and especially the acquired immune deficiency syndrome (AIDS). They anticipate finding many valuable biologically-active substances among the countless plants and other living organisms that have never been screened as sources of pharmaceuticals. One indication of such possibilities came in the late 1980s from a project based in the Jodrell Laboratory at the Royal Botanic Gardens in Kew, Surrey, which is beginning to bear remarkable fruit in the form of what Linda Fellows and her colleagues there call "sugar mimics". These are nitrogen-containing substances whose molecules resemble sugars in size and shape. The team have since suggested other sources in species from many parts of the world.

Interest in the sugar mimics centers on their ability to inhibit the action of glycosidases. These are enzymes which alter the structures of natural materials called glycoproteins by attacking the sugar regions of these sugar-protein composites. It is this action that has attracted considerable interest recently, because it seems to be responsible for the wide range of biological actions of the sugar mimics, particularly on glycoproteins that carry many sugars. Some can enhance the immune response of animals to infection. Some can thwart the spread of certain cancers in mice. Others prevent viruses from transforming normal cells into malignant cells, and a few are poisonous (even in very low concentrations) to insect pests that parasitize crop plants.

Particularly significant were the results of a study reported by the Kew team in 1987 in collaboration with researchers at St Mary's Hospital, London. A group of St Mary's clinicians had become concerned about the need for drugs that are active against AIDS virus but free of the toxic side effects caused by azidothymidine (AZT), at the time virtually the only substance of any value in ameliorating the appalling effects of the disease. They began to work with the Kew team when it emerged that glycoproteins were central to the AIDS virus's powerful attack on the immune system. The virus gains entry into defenders called helper T-cells when glycoproteins in the virus envelope interact with receptors on the T-cells. Moreover, the crucial glycoproteins are positively bristling with sugar molecules.

The researchers argued that sugar mimics, by inhibiting enzymes involved in processing glycoproteins, might be used as drugs to attack the AIDS virus. One of them, castanospermine (CAST), has proved to be very promising. A potent glucosidase inhibitor, CAST greatly impairs growth of the AIDS virus when cultured in the laboratory.

▼ *Poliomyelitis particles. Like smallpox (eliminated worldwide by vaccination), measles and several other diseases, polio can already be controlled by immunization.*

► *The black bean tree (Castanospermum australe) has proved to be a rich source of the "sugar mimic" castanospermine, which could be of considerable value in the treatment of AIDS. This and similiar substances emerged from research based at Kew Gardens near London.*

▼ *AIDS virus is released by a stricken white blood cell. Several synthetic drugs show promise, but scientists believe that the natural world may provide effective means of treatment.*

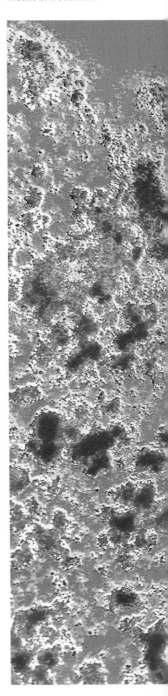

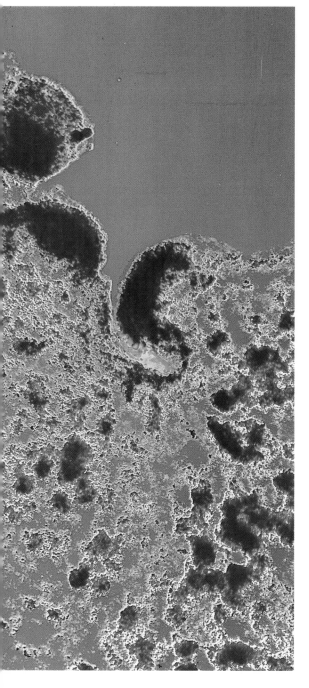

New strategies

One of the most controversial possible strategies for combating virus diseases was announced at the International Congress of Microbiology held in Manchester, England, in 1986. It is based on the observation that the release of new virus particles from infected cells can be impaired by antibodies against other viruses. Dr Gordon Skinner and his collaborators at the University of Birmingham, England, believe they can exploit this "immune inhibition" to treat disease – by infecting cells with a second virus and then exposing them to antibody against it, thereby preventing release of the first virus. They have already proved that the technique works in laboratory animals, but whether it will ever be extended to humans is unclear.

Another new strategy on the agenda in Manchester was exemplified by research on plague, a disease which retains a dreadful propensity to cause disease and death and still exists in many parts of the world. It can be treated with antibiotics, but attempts at vaccination have proved far less successful. Stanley Falkow and Ralph Isberg have pinpointed the gene that allows a close relative of the plague bacillus to invade cells. They first cloned a wide range of different pieces of DNA and spliced them into a noninvasive strain of Escherichia coli. Then they added this bacterium to animal cells, together with an antibiotic that cannot penetrate the cells, so that only bacteria able to get inside the cells escaped attack by the antibiotic. This allowed the researchers to isolate precisely those bacteria that were carrying the gene for invasiveness. The gene produces a protein which appears on the surface of the bacterial cells and seems to be important in initiating infection. The Stanford researchers believe that an understanding of this process will lead to highly specific drugs to prevent and/or to treat the much more serious disease of plague itself.

◄ Linda Fellows and her colleagues in the Jodrell Laboratory at the Royal Botanic Gardens, Kew, in collaboration with researchers at St Mary's Hospital, London, have played the leading roles in discovering the sugar mimics and investigating their potential therapeutic value against a range of different diseases. The substances were first found in a small number of wild plants cultivated at Kew, but the herbarium staff there have since suggested other sources in related species from different parts of the world.

In human medicine, genetic engineering need not be a technology just for the rich

Combating tropical diseases

One of the most important things to realize about genetic engineering as applied to human medicine is that it is not just a technology for the rich. It need not allow the richer nations of the world to draw still further ahead of the poorer nations in health and associated prosperity. In fact, if the needed resources are provided by international agencies, as in some areas they already are by the World Health Organization, then genetic engineering will make its biggest contribution to human health in the elimination of tropical parasitic and other diseases.

This is because genetic engineering has made it possible, for the first time, to make vaccines to protect against such diseases. The parasites that cause malaria and schistosomiasis, two of the most common and debilitating tropical diseases, will not grow in culture outside the human body. They are too specialized to their natural living environments. So vaccines for these diseases cannot be prepared in the conventional way, by growing masses of the infective organism involved outside the body and making it into vaccines. Genetic engineering, however, offers a new route to bypass this requirement.

For malaria, for example, several teams of researchers in the United States, the United Kingdom and Australia have identified specific proteins and antigens on the surface of the *Plasmodium* parasites that cause the disease. The antigens stimulate a protective immune reaction against the parasite when the isolated proteins are injected into humans. These antigens are clearly among the few which can actually be recognized as foreign by the immune system when a person is infected with malaria. The genes representing the blueprints for such antigens in *Plasmodium* have been identified and cloned in bacterial cultures, which then mass-produce the plasmodial antigens. These antigens can then be tested, as they are now being, as experimental vaccine. In 1987 vaccines made in this way were shown to protect monkeys against malaria. The vaccines are now being tested in humans. Meanwhile other cloned vaccines have been shown to protect monkeys against schistosomiasis.

Medical drugs alone are unable to eliminate tropical diseases because of continual reinfection, and the shortage of medical staff able to

▶ *Onchocerciasis (river blindness) is caused by infection with microscopic worms transmitted by flies. Like other parasites, the filariae which cause the disease cannot be grown outside the human body so as to make vaccines. The identification of worm antigens which might be used in a cloned vaccine is still at an early stage.*

▼ *Antibodies on the coats of malaria sporozoites show that an immune reaction can be stimulated against this stage of the parasite's life cycle. Vaccines which stimulate such immunity are now being tested in humans. The immune response will have to attack sporozoites in the few moments after their injection by a mosquito, before the bloodstream carries them into the liver. Because sporozoites cannot be grown in the laboratory, the vaccines are made from cloned plasmodial antigens.*

▼ *The life cycle of the malaria-causing parasite, Plasmodium. Sporozoites are injected into the human bloodstream by mosquitoes, travel to the liver and emerge later into the bloodstream as merozoites. These enter red blood cells and later emerge as the sexual stage of the life cycle, gametocytes which reinfect mosquitoes.*

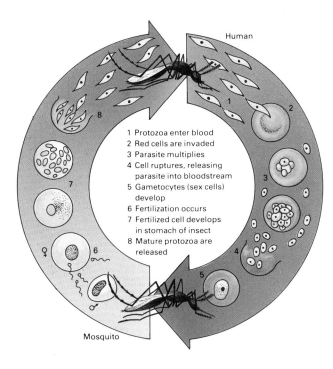

Human

1 Protozoa enter blood
2 Red cells are invaded
3 Parasite multiplies
4 Cell ruptures, releasing parasite into bloodstream
5 Gametocytes (sex cells) develop
6 Fertilization occurs
7 Fertilized cell develops in stomach of insect
8 Mature protozoa are released

Mosquito

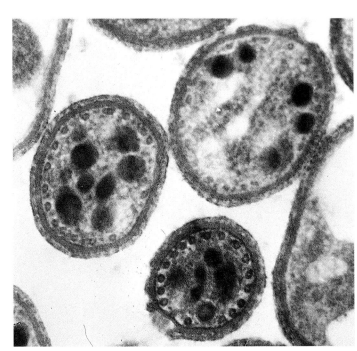

educate people to avoid reinfection and to administer more drugs. Vaccination can potentially protect for many years, even for life, and so requires fewer resources. Genetic engineering, as well as making vaccines for tropical parasitic diseases possible for the first time, will also allow medical auxiliaries to vaccinate against several major diseases simultaneously with a single "jab". This will make still better use of scarce resources.

The ultimate malaria vaccine may be a "cocktail", with antigens designed to stimulate immune reactions against the sporozoite stage that is injected by the mosquito, as well as the merozoite stage reinfecting mosquitoes. It is also now clear that a vaccine will need to contain antigens selected in order to stimulate the several different arms of the immune system, for example, cell-mediated immunity as well as antibody-formation.

This is equally true of schistosomiasis. Schistosomes have effective mechanisms for evading the immune response. This means that it will be necessary to attack them as larvae when they first enter the body. Attacks by both antibodies and eosinophils must be stimulated. The immune response to parasites is complex and all its elements will have to be stimulated to provide effective protection.

▼ *A human eosinophil, one of a class of white blood cells which specifically attack parasites entering the body, adheres to the surface of a larval schistosome. It has been targeted to the schistosome by antibodies adhering to its surface. The eosinophil's attack has already broken through the schistosome cell membranes.*

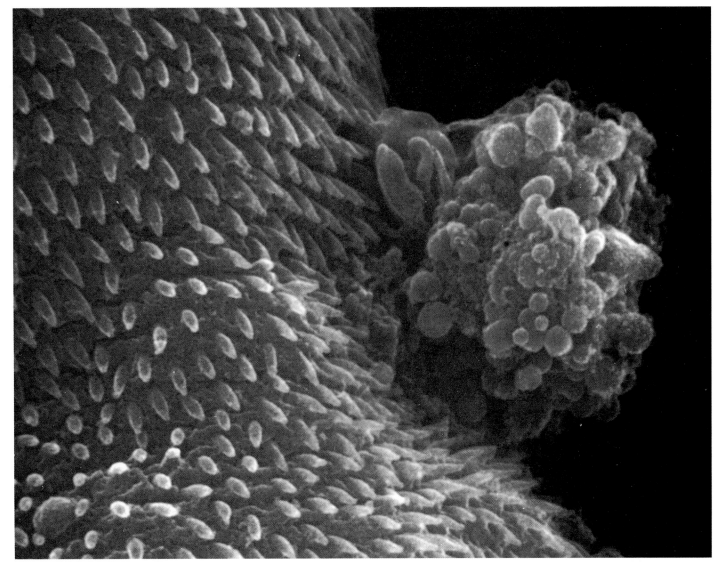

An all-in-one vaccination

One potentially major project of genetic engineering is focused on the use of the harmless vaccinia (cowpox) virus which was used to eliminate smallpox by vaccination. This has a very large genome (genetic blueprint), containing far more DNA than the average virus, making it possible to insert several extra genes into it without damaging the virus or limiting its ability to infect and stimulate immunity. Genes for antigens which stimulate immunity to each of a number of disease organisms, for example measles (a major killer in the tropics), malaria, schistosomiasis and leprosy, can be cloned and inserted into vaccinia to produce an all-in-one vaccination.

When such a genetically-engineered vaccinia virus is then used to vaccinate a patient, it will be intended to cause the vaccinated person to produce antigens characteristic of all the disease organisms whose genes are incorporated in the virus. The vaccinated person's body will then respond by mounting an immune response against the foreign antigens. In this way, it is hoped, immunity against several diseases will be achieved by a single vaccination. (It should be possible to incorporate a vaccine against AIDS, should one be available, as it may be within 10 years.) The technique could bring about immense savings in medical manpower and other costs. It could make the difference between success and failure in disease elimination through vaccination programs in the tropics.

Vaccines made by genetic engineering to protect against malaria are being tested in man. Vaccines to protect against schistosomiasis are being tested in animals. Vaccines to protect against other tropical parasitic diseases are under development. If the protection they confer is too weak, the means now exist to strengthen it. Such vaccines could be in widespread use before the end of the century.

This is true of the use of genetic engineering techniques in combating infectious diseases in the poor countries in the tropics generally. But everything will depend on the extent to which the rich countries of the world, working through the international aid agencies, are prepared to subsidize not only vaccination but also the health education campaigns needed. Vaccination programs will only be effective if they are combined with other control measures, to control mosquitoes, tsetse flies and other disease carriers and to provide medical drugs to treat established infection. Without vaccination, made possible only by genetic engineering, these other measures will probably always ultimately be ineffective. But privately-owned drug companies can make a lot more money by working to combat the diseases of the rich world.

Only concerted international programs will enable genetic engineering to be applied where it can be of the greatest benefit of all, in the developing world, and so make a major contribution to closing the health gap between the rich and poor worlds, rather than, as will surely happen without a major international effort, widening it still further. Political realism as well as humanity requires that such an effort should continue to be made. A good start has already been made through the World Health Organization's special program against the major tropical parasitic diseases.

If genetic engineering techniques are to make the massive contribution to human health in the developing world of which they are capable, substantial resources will have to be devoted to that end for the next century at least, without any direct reward for the richer nations providing the aid required. The most advanced genetic engineering will also have to be combined with the most culturally appropriate means of administering aid. If such farsighted policies are adapted – together with similar policies in agriculture, with the development and introduction of new crop varieties resistant to drought and disease, and new farm animal breeds genetically-tailored to local conditions – then genetic engineering might turn the tide. It might be the new factor that will make it possible to narrow and even close the gaps between developing and developed countries, within the next 100 years or so.

▶ **In one day in El Salvador 400,000 people were immunized against measles, whooping cough, diphtheria and tetanus. Scientists hope that in a few years it may be possible to vaccinate against several such diseases simultaneously with a single "jab". Hopes center on producing genetically-engineered vaccine virus. Foreign genes have already been inserted into vaccinia and have been shown to be expressed in injected volunteers. Other viruses, such as attenuated polio virus, may be used in the same way.**

Aging and Immortality

13

Is there a fixed age limit?...The causes of aging...Aging and genetics...How cells and tissues are maintained ...Single or multiple causes of aging...The difference between repair and replacement...Failure of maintenance is the key

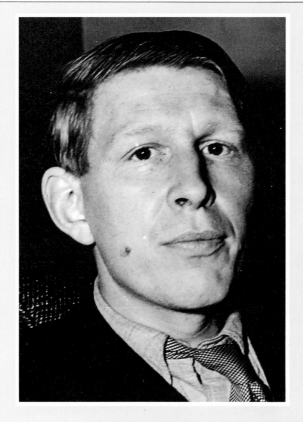

During the social evolution of mankind, the average expectation of life has gradually increased, slowly at first, and more dramatically within the last 100 years or so. It has always been thought desirable to increase life expectancy by improved health care, and in Europe, North America, Japan and Australasia this has resulted in an average life span of over 75 years for females and over 70 for males. At the same time it is unfortunately the case that in many Third World countries where there are still many problems with nutrition, hygiene and treatment of disease, the life expectancy is very much lower, and everyone would agree that more resources should be devoted to health care so that the quality and length of life can be improved. It is to be hoped that, with time, this will occur.

The increase in life expectancy achieved with improved health care is not accompanied by an increase in the maximum life span of individuals. All the indications are that this maximum has not changed over the centuries. In other words, a barrier to further life extension appears to be present. In practical terms this means that the major causes of death are age-related disease or the process of aging itself. A large proportion of the health care budgets is now devoted to care of the elderly. This may involve not only general geriatric practice, but also the best available treatment of many age-related diseases, such as cardiovascular and cerebrovascular disease, cancer, arthritis, diabetes, kidney failure, osteoporosis, failure of sight and hearing, Alzheimer's disease and other dementias. These treatments are not only very expensive in many cases, but also they may have only short-term benefits. It is an unfortunate fact that the prevention or cure of one age-related disease is all too often followed by the occurrence of others. The final regime of life-supporting systems becomes unjustifiable, in terms of both the poor quality of the life which is sustained by it, and the disproportionate expense which it involves.

In the field of biomedical research considerable resources are devoted to studies of the above-mentioned age-related diseases. Such research is concerned with an understanding of the cause or the origin of each individual disease and also the development of better treatments. In general each disease is studied independently of the others. However, this general strategy for research may well be based on false assumptions (◗ page 159).

It is easy to see why many people have been fascinated by the possibility of simply preventing the aging process itself. In this way the problem of debilitating disease would disappear and individuals would be able to enjoy the retention all their faculties for a much longer period or even indefinitely. In order to decide whether this may be a reality in the future or is merely a fictional scenario, it is first necessary to understand why aging occurs in humans and all other mammalian species, and what are the processes involved.

▲ *The English poet W.H. Auden as a young man and two years before his death in 1973. Some people age better than others, but all suffer some symptons of decline.*

Biologists are trying to discover how the apparently "nonadaptive" phenomenon of aging has evolved

Why does aging occur?

It is commonly believed that the process of aging is the inevitable result of the evolution of complexity in the living world. Microorganisms can be grown indefinitely and simple animals such as corals or sponges form colonies of individuals, which can be continually propagated without any obvious sign of aging. Plants are less complex in structure than animals and, although they may have finite life spans, some species are immortal, because they have the means to maintain themselves indefinitely by vegetative growth.

The complex organization of more advanced animals can be compared to a machine, in which the many components interact and coordinate their various functions. The analogy between animals and machines (◊ page 160) is in some contexts a useful one, but with regard to aging through "wear and tear" the analogy is false. This is because organisms develop from a fertilized egg, by the unfolding of a genetic program (the mechanisms of which are poorly understood) through juvenile stages to the sexually mature adult. Machines on the other hand, are assembled piece by piece. It has been pointed out by the British evolutionary biologist George Williams that if organisms have evolved the seemingly miraculous process of development from egg to adult, then they should have solved the much lesser problem of maintenance of the adult. Such maintenance might involve continual replacement of cells and tissues by regenerative mechanisms, repair of damage and so on. The crucial problem, therefore, is to understand why successful maintenance of an adult animal does not occur.

The German zoologist August Weismann (1834-1914) suggested that evolution is facilitated if adults are eliminated to provide living space for their offspring. Thus, he argued, aging is an adaptation which is "good for the species" as it accelerates evolution. Natural selection, however, acts primarily on the reproductive fitness of individuals, not populations of animals. It is clear that an individual which ages is less fit in Darwinian terms than one which can survive and reproduce indefinitely, therefore aging should not evolve because it is non-adaptive. This presents a serious problem to evolutionary biologists, but a simple and appealing solution has been proposed, particularly by George Williams and by Thomas Kirkwood of the United Kingdom National Institute for Medical Research. In the real world in which animals live, death commonly occurs from disease, predation or starvation. The survival of many species is close to exponential, that is, the likelihood of dying is approximately constant with time. This means that there are many more young adults in a population than old ones; in fact, very few aged animals are seen in a natural environment. It follows that almost all offspring are produced by young adults and very few from middle-aged animals and almost none from old animals. It therefore becomes a pointless strategy for an organism's genes to invest resources into continual maintenance of the adult body, when that body is likely to die from some extrinsic cause. It is much better to divert resources, which might otherwise be used for maintenance and the avoidance of aging, to rapid growth to adulthood and reproduction. It follows from this that germ lines which transmit eggs and sperm from generation to generation must never age; in fact germ-line cells from all extant species are potentially immortal. The aging process is seen in wild animals when they are placed in a protected environment such as a zoo, where starvation and predation do not occur and disease is controlled: maintenance of the adult animal begins to fail after a given life span, as with humans in any society with appropriate health care.

▲ *Small mammals, such as this harvest mouse suckling her young, reproduce frequently, have large litters, and mature quickly; they generally have short life spans, 2-3 years for rats and mice, for example. The changes seen in 2- or 3-year-old mice or rats closely resemble those seen in 70- to 80-year-old humans, so much so that in the life of a laboratory rat months are used roughly to model human years.*

▼ *A freshly-ovulated human egg is surrounded by sperms. Why has the human body, which can develop from a single egg cell into complex body of billions of differentiated cells and specialized and mutually dependent organs, apparently failed to solve the problem (surely much simpler) of staying youthful?*

The genetic control of aging

The fact that different species have different maximum life spans is an indication that aging is genetically controlled. It is generally true that small animals, such as rodents, which reproduce very fast, have a short life span (2-3 years), whereas large animals which reproduce slowly, such as elephants, whales or humans, have a long life span. This fits in well with the theory of the evolution of aging, if one considers the possible strategies which an organism might adopt in order to ensure its survival. One approach is to invest a high proportion of resources in rapid growth and reproduction and much less in maintenance; another is to grow and reproduce slowly and invest much more in the maintenance of an adult. Of course, the selected strategy will also relate to the ecological niche the particular animal occupies. Small animals suffer from a high probability of predation, so are unlikely to survive very long anyway; large animals have fewer enemies and face fewer natural hazards.

It is striking that many of the degenerative changes in tissue and organs seen in an aging mouse or rat are very similar to those seen in an aging human who can live at least 30 times as long. The genes in some way influence or control the maintenance of the adult and the period over which the aging will occur, but the details of the aging process itself seem very similar in all mammalian species. It is a major challenge to gerontologists to understand the molecular and cellular basis of these different rates of aging.

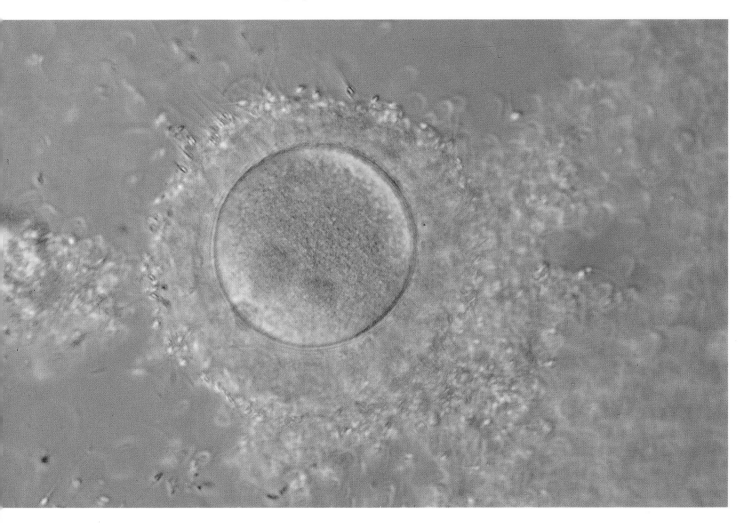

Body maintenance and aging

The processes of cell and tissue maintenance have been studied in considerable detail in a variety of organisms. First, there is DNA repair – a complex set of enzymatic reactions which recognize damage in chromosomal DNA and remove it through a variety of pathways. Such damage continually occurs spontaneously and can also be induced by chemicals or radiation from the environment. Second, the normal functioning of cells depends on the accurate synthesis of macromolecules, not only DNA, but also RNA and proteins. It is known that there are special proof-reading mechanisms which recognize errors in synthesis as they occur and these are edited out. Defects in protein synthesis would have severe consequences on cell membranes and organelles but, most important, they can feed back into the pathway for protein synthesis itself, thereby causing further errors. This in time could lead to an unacceptable level of defects in proteins and a variety of cellular malfunctions.

Third in this catalog of the known mechanisms of cell and tissue maintenance, there is a series of enzyme pathways for the removal of proteins, especially altered or abnormal proteins. Much of the nitrogen metabolism in animal cells is related to the continual breakdown and resynthesis of these molecules. Evidence is accumulating that abnormal proteins or their byproducts accumulate in aged tissues. Fourth, dangerous oxygen radicals are continually being formed by cellular

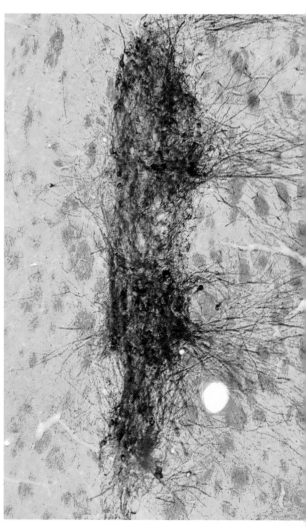

► *Scans of brain tissue from a normal brain (top) and an 85-year-old senile man. Some brain changes with age are inevitable but 2 million people in the USA alone are affected by Alzheimer's syndrome, in which senility is much more rapid and progressive. Some doctors think brain-tissue grafts may be used to treat the condition, while others fear that such treatment will prove useless, if not harmful.*

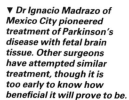

► *At the French National Institute for the Prevention of Cerebral Aging, positron emission tomography (PET) reveals hardening and thickening arteries, caused by aging processes. This patient plays video games to test brain functions.*

▼ *Dr Ignacio Madrazo of Mexico City pioneered treatment of Parkinson's disease with fetal brain tissue. Other surgeons have attempted similar treatment, though it is too early to know how beneficial it will prove to be.*

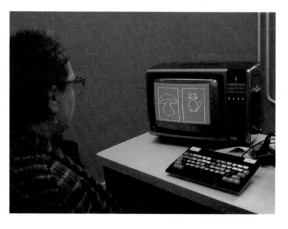

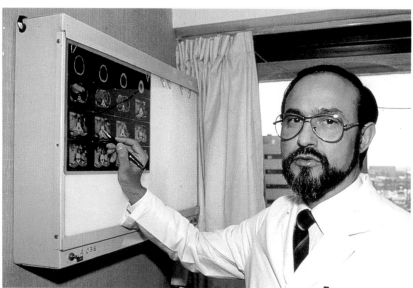

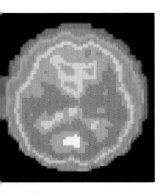

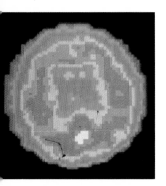

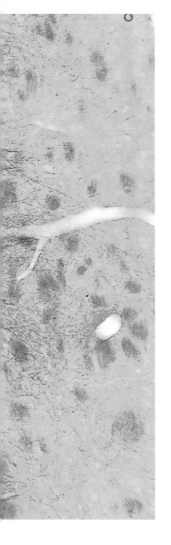

metabolism and especially by respiration. These free radicals have a short half-life, but they are highly reactive and can damage many essential cellular components, particularly membranes, by lipid peroxidation. It is not surprising that organisms have evolved means to eliminate free radicals, especially by enzymes, but also by naturally occurring antioxidants, such as uric acid, which can neutralize them. Fifth, all mammals have a highly complex immune system which can efficiently recognize and eliminate foreign antigens and in this way can defend themselves against invasion by viruses, microorganisms or parasites. Sixth, physical damage to tissues can be efficiently repaired by wound healing, which takes place both internally and externally. More generally, cells which have lost viability can be replaced by various tissues; an obvious example is the continual replacement of red blood cells which have a defined life span.

All six of these maintenance mechanisms depend on enzymes and proteins with specialized functions. The number of genes necessary to encode these proteins is probably very large. The general conclusion which may be drawn is that organisms invest a considerable amount in terms of energy and metabolic resources in order to maintain the integrity of adult structures. It could be predicted that long-lived organisms have more efficient maintenance mechanisms than short-lived ones, and so far this has been demonstrated in the case of repair of damage to DNA by ultraviolet light.

Aging is a cluster of pathologies

Aging in man is in effect associated with not one pathology but a cluster. From the organism's point of view, it is clearly pointless to invest resources for the efficient maintenance of one such system, while allowing others to degenerate. It is, therefore, not surprising that many body functions tend to deteriorate together. Of course, there is not complete synchrony; for example, some older individuals retain an excellent mind and memory while their body deteriorates, and others are physically very strong but become demented. But in general the synchrony in all age-related processes is quite striking and certainly supports the view that fundamental defects in cells and macromolecules are accumulating in all parts of the body simultaneously. This is the reason why the strategy for research on individual age-related diseases may be misplaced.

At present the assumption is that there are multiple causes of aging and that it is profitable to study one age-related disease without paying attention to the others. There are separate charitable foundations funding research on cancer, heart disease, Alzheimer's disease, diabetes, kidney failure, arthritis, osteoporosis and so on. As part of the process of understanding the origins of these diseases and preventing their onset, it would be advantageous to devote much more research to the global study of the process of aging itself. This would help coordinate research on all the age-related diseases and lead to a much better understanding of the underlying molecular and cellular events which comprise the whole spectrum of age-related changes. A promising approach in this field is the study of inherited defects, such as those in Down's and Werner's syndromes, since these result in the premature occurrence of many age-related changes. The elucidation of the biochemical basis of a genetic defect which has multiple effects on aging would be a major advance. Such studies can initially be done by studying cells grown in the laboratory, which have been obtained from affected individuals.

◄ *Human fetal brain tissue grafted into a rat's brain shows up as a dark patch because it has been stained to reveal dopamine, the neurotransmitter (brain chemical) which is deficient in Parkinson's disease. In rats whose brains have been treated to produce a condition modeling Parkinsonism, implants supply the deficient dopamine with, apparently, no long-term side effects. The grafted tissue is not rejected, partly because fetal tissue is less recognized as foreign than adult tissue and partly because the immune system which recognizes and rejects foreign tissue is barred from operating fully in the brain. Tests of fetal tissue implanted into monkeys, however, show that implanted tissue may revert to a primitive stage of development and grow abnormally.*

Life span in the future

Progress in the field of gerontology is painfully slow, partly because it is an unfashionable scientific topic. Even when money for age research is available, the tendency nowadays is to channel the funds into the study of particular areas, such as Alzheimer's disease, rather than a more general study of aging itself. When more resources become available, and more scientists become aware of the medical importance of studying the mechanisms of aging at the cellular level, much more rapid progress will be made. One very promising approach is to study human cells in culture. It is well known that some types of cell which can be grown successfully in the laboratory have a finite life span. On the other hand, cancer cells will grow indefinitely. The study of the aging of normal cells and the process of immortalization which occurs in cancer cells are very closely related.

Eventually, treatment of many age-related diseases may become available to prevent or defer their onset. This will lead to an improvement in the quality of life in old age, but will it lead to an extension of the maximum life span? The problem is that treatment of severe malformation becomes increasingly expensive.

Life-support systems, organ transplants and so on are possible, but their use cannot be justified to prop up the life of an extremely old person for a limited duration, when there are always younger members of society who may need such treatments because of a premature failure of one or another organ system.

With continuing research in the future, a complete understanding of the aging process at all levels will undoubtedly become available. For the first time in human history it will be possible to stand back and really know why people progressively lose their normal health, vigor and intellect. Many gerontologists believe that this understanding will also lead to a solution of the problem of aging, and that it will then be possible to devise methods for slowing down the whole process or arresting it altogether. There are already many published fantasies about this, often based on the assumption that a "clock" or pacemaker exists, and that when it is discovered it will be possible to change or bypass it by appropriate diet, life-style or drug treatments. Although these views have no scientific basis at present, when the process of aging is finally unraveled in full detai!, it may be possible to devise on rational grounds appropriate preventative measures.

The process of aging has a very long evolutionary history, at least as long as the origin of vertebrate animals and it is therefore embedded in the very fabric of our molecules, cells, tissues and organs. Nondividing cells cannot survive forever and many essential parts of the body consist of such cells and also have a low capacity for repair and renewal. This is true of the central nervous system, especially the brain and sense organs; it applies to a considerable extent to muscles and connective tissue, and therefore to the heart and circulatory system. Furthermore, structural components such as collagen and bone undergo progressive biochemical alterations which appear to be irreversible.

The analogy between machines and complex organisms is persistent (◀ page 156). Although machines do not function indefinitely, their parts can be replaced. A vintage Rolls Royce car can be kept in prime condition indefinitely with sufficient care, attention and expense. Unfortunately, complex organisms are not put together piece by piece like a machine. The individual is the result of an intrinsic process of development from the fertilized egg. Thus, the principles of repair and replacement are fundamentally different.

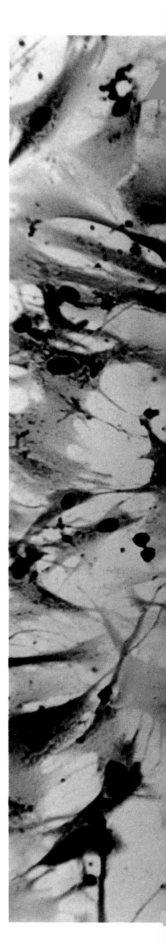

► *Senescent and (inset) young fibroblasts (connective tissue cells). The senescent cells were stained and photographed after having undergone about 50 cell divisions in laboratory culture; they then stop dividing and die. This shows that aging is an innate property of normal cells, which have a life span of a fixed number of cell divisions before they stop dividing and, after a while, degenerate and die. Some single-celled animals, such as amoeba, and the germ (reproductive) cells of higher animals have evaded their fate, and are potentially immortal. When normal cells become malignant (cancerous) they first undergo changes which make them potentially immortal if they are grown in culture.*

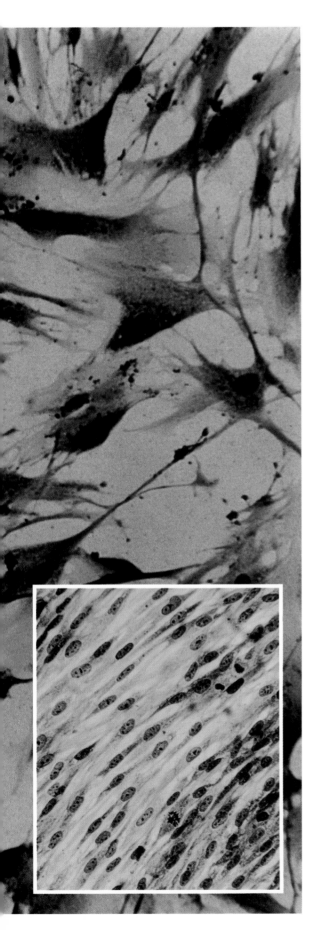

◄ A boy with Cockayne's disease, in which premature aging occurs rapidly in growth due to an inherited genetic defect. Cells containing such defects have a very short life span when they are isolated from the body and grown in culture. In view of the universality of the experience of aging it is surprising that more resources are not devoted to research into such promising topics.

▼ A false-color X-ray of severe rheumatoid arthritis in the hands. Rheumatoid arthritis tends to be more common in elderly people. Diet, drugs and exercise can help to prevent or slow up the effects of arthritis, but genetic predisposition also plays a big part, as does the aging process.

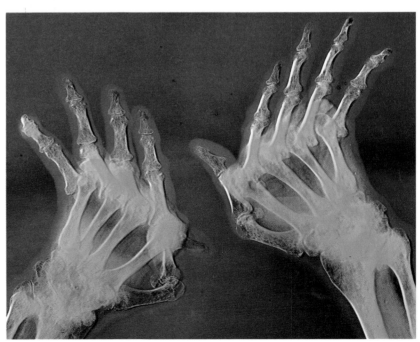

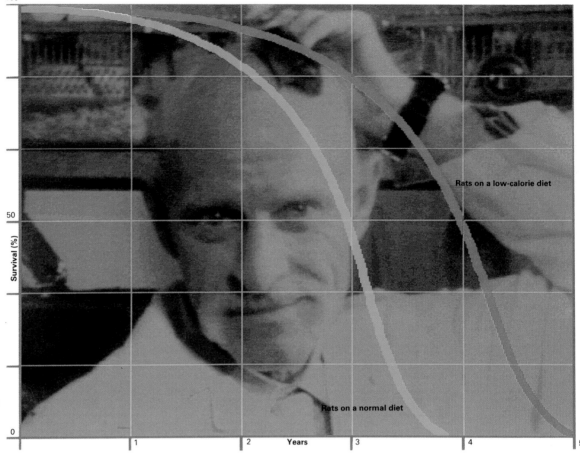

► **The graph shows the life expectancies of rats on normal and on low-calorie diets. Gerontologist Professor Roy Walford of Oxford University is sufficiently convinced of the relevance of this research to humans to live on a low-calorie diet himself, hoping that as a result he will live to an age of 140 or thereabouts. Animal research suggests that extending the human life span is a real possibility. Enough is known of how the body maintains itself to begin to design an immortal human – but it would be a different organism not just a modified man!**

Changing the human life span

Much has been written about increasing the human life span. This is a ripe field for speculation and wishful thinking. Unfortunately it is often difficult to distinguish fact from fantasy. A group calling themselves "The Immortalists" in the USA includes many gerontologists who appear to believe that aging is a disease which can be conquered by an appropriate diet and life-style. Books on the hoped-for life extension are often best-sellers, and there is a huge market for vitamins, antioxidants and assorted drugs which are supposed to counteract the aging process. In Britain, a clinic in Harley Street, London, dispenses nucleic acids extracted from fetal animal cells with the claim (which has never been documented) that rejuvenation follows a course of treatment. There is widespread belief that individuals in the Caucasus and Vilcabamba in Peru often live to 150 years or more, although the falsity of these reports has been clearly exposed by Zhores Medvedev, Alexander Leaf and others.

On the other hand, one observation on life extension using experimental animals has been repeated many times. It is clear that rats kept on a low-calorie diet increase their life span by about 50 percent. It is not impossible that the same might apply to humans. Attempts to demonstrate the life extension of rodents with various antioxidants have not been consistently successful, but it is possible that appropriate treatments might have some limited effect.

One can now imagine a complex organism capable of continual regeneration and renewal in all parts of its body, it would have to have pools of stem cells to replace post-mitotic neurones in the brain, and many other essential organs, such as the heart and circulatory system, would also have to be in a "steady state" with continual turnover of cellular and structural components. In addition, the design of skeletal structures would have to be entirely different, with built-in maintenance mechanisms. Such an organism would not be an improved version of a human being; on the contrary it would be a different organism altogether.

Many of the major theories of aging are directly related to the failure of one or more maintenance mechanisms. The "free radical" theory proposes that degenerative changes in cells (particularly lipid peroxidation and the accumulation of the age pigment lipofuscin in secondary lysosomes) is due to the continual damage inflicted by these reactive products. The "somatic mutation" theory proposes that aging is due to accumulated damage in DNA, especially gene mutations and chromosome breaks. The "protein error" theory argues that aging might be due to the accumulation of more and more defects, particularly by "error propagation" in protein synthesis. The gerontologist Roy Walford has argued for many years that a breakdown of the specificity of the immune system is a major cause of aging, since it can lead to the destruction of the organism's own cells by autoimmune reactions. There may be some truth in all these individual theories, but until more specific information is available, it might be better to lump them all together with the label "failure of maintenance".

Fringe Medicine

14

Signs of a new mood in medicine...Traditional Ayurvedic and Chinese medicine...Herbal medicine...Acupuncture...Homeopathy...Meditation... Is there a future for fringe medicine?

Heart-lung transplants, worldwide eradication of smallpox, and the routine curing of certain types of cancer attest to the enormous power of the means at the disposal of physicians today. But these same triumphs have also spawned, and increasingly strengthened, the idea that medicine needs to be rational and mechanistic if it is to be effective. It must reflect the logical, intellectual approach that is said to characterize natural science. And it must be founded on an analysis of the human body in terms of organs, tissues and chemical processes that require specific, discrete correction when they malfunction and cause disease. All therapies not fitting these descriptions, and not validated by statistically-based comparison with orthodox therapies, stand condemned as "fringe medicine".

In recent years, there have been signs that such rigid dismissal of all unconventional treatments may have been ill-conceived. Even the most orthodox of medical practitioners have had to acknowledge that on occasion particular "unproven" remedies do seem to help particular patients, sometimes when orthodoxy has failed. Some previously suspect approaches (such as hypnotism) have been absorbed into mainstream medicine. Others are no longer so widely dismissed because, it is argued, their validation by scientific means is inherently impossible. In the light of these developments, there are several pointers to possible developments in medicine in future.

▼ *One of the behavioral problems successfully dealt with under hypnosis is alcoholism, as in this addiction clinic in Moscow. Pioneered by Austrian physician Anton Mesmer (1733-1815), who used it to cure or alleviate hysterical and psychosomatic conditions, hypnosis has been accepted only gradually by orthodox medicine.*

▲ *Charles Slackman's drawing "Freud on Freud" questions the value of Freudian psychoanalysis. Psychiatry continues to be divided into opposing camps – those who argue that analysis is meaningful and useful, and those who espouse physical treatments and believe analysis tells us as much about the analyst as about the patient.*

Slowly, conventional western medicine is "scientifically validating" parts of "alternative" medicine

Ayurvedic and herbal medicine, and acupuncture

The eclipse of herbalism by the modern pharmaceutical revolution has been one adverse effect of the advance of highly potent, science-based medicine. Some "indigenous" remedies have been forgotten or prematurely superseded, and doubtless many others remain to be rediscovered. One indication of the new mood was the appearance of reviews expounding the virtues of Ayurvedic and traditional Chinese medicine in the impeccably scientific journal *Trends in Pharmacological Sciences* during 1986. In the first, scientists from the Seth G.S. Medical College in Bombay, India, contrasted orthodox medicine, which emphasizes specific cures for specific defects, with the holistic philosophy of Ayurveda (in Sanskrit, "life-knowledge"). This portrays health and disease in terms of balance or imbalance betwen the body's three *dosha* (humors), seven *dhatu* (tissues) and *mala* (excretory products). The Bombay researchers have reinvestigated several Ayurvedic remedies and found that they have powerful effects in stimulating the body's immune defenses against infection. They have also highlighted central tenets of the Ayurveda whose significance has been recognized only very recently within mainstream medicine. One is the importance of timing drug treatment correctly for maximum effect – something emphasized by today's emerging science of chronopharmacology. Another is the matching of treatment to a patient's individual constitution, which in modern terms implies to that person's personal constellation of HL antigens (which are comparable to, but more numerous than, blood groups). A third tenet is the therapeutic significance of food – presaging recent discoveries that diet can influence normal brain functions and mental illnesses.

It is possible to be as skeptical about traditional Chinese medicine, with its portrayal of diseases in terms of imbalances between Yin-Yang forces, as it is about the Ayurvedic humors. Yet Deng Quan-Sheng, a pharmacologist at the University of Utah, Salt Lake City, has argued that the integration of this approach with western pharmacology has promoted both the isolation of previously unknown drugs and a sensitive understanding of how best to use them. Examples include homoharringtonine and hydroxycamptothecin to treat certain cancers, gossypol as a male contraceptive, arteannum as an antimalarial, and tanshinone for coronary disorders.

Professor Varro Tyler, writing from Purdhue University, Lafayette, Indiana, has drawn attention to many other herbal medicines that have been scientifically validated recently – including echinacea as an immuno-stimulant, feverfew for migraine and arthritis, ginger to prevent travel sickness, and evening-primrose oil for eczema. "Furthermore, the intense interest in herbal medicine now shown by the general public will ultimately influence scientists and clinicians to renew their interest in the study of this promising area of pharmaceutical research," according to Tyler.

Acupuncture is another "alternative" therapy whose gradual acceptance by the medical establishment underlines the foolishness of dismissing a phenomenon simply because contemporary science cannot explain how it works. In individual cases the results of accupuncture are highly unpredictable. One person benefits, another does not. One experiences pain relief lasting an hour, another is pain-free for two years. Some individuals respond quickly, others much more slowly. Yet the existence of such variation suggests that acupuncture is indeed a potentially powerful technique which, with greater experience and understanding, could become much more useful than it is at present.

▲ *The Chinese tradition of using suction cups to "activate blood circulation" is one treatment unlikely to be vindicated by science. As with the opposition of orthodox science to astrology, a major reason for skepticism is the lack of any convincing explanation of how such techniques could work.*

▶ *Acupuncture, used in China as an anesthetic in surgery has been accepted by conventional science in recent years. Carefully-designed studies have indicated that insertion of acupuncture needles into the skin according to the traditional Chinese pattern has an analgesic effect in about 60 percent of patients with chronic pain caused by conditions such as osteoarthritis. It can prevent nausea and vomiting in patients undergoing chemotherapy for cancer.*

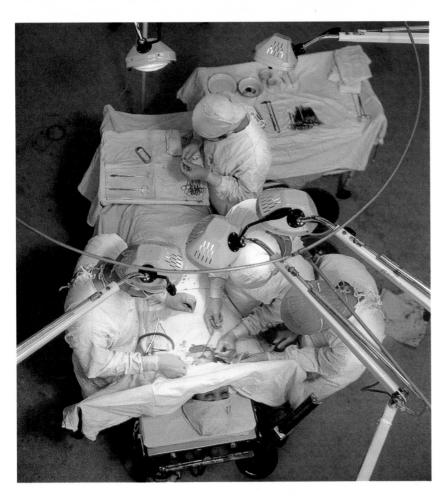

▲ Another ancient Chinese craft was the use of the "moxa" – a small cone of combustible material, which was applied at various points and then ignited. Moxibustion, here based on young wormwood leaves, has been examined scientifically without yielding any evidence that it has anything other than placebo value.

◄ A Chinese chemist makes up prescriptions according to the tenets of traditional medicine. While some venerable herbal remedies have been found to possess negligible therapeutic power, others are now being reinvestigated and exploited anew because of their undoubted value in applications ranging from contraception to cancer treatment.

A better understanding of the "placebo" effect could reveal the mechanisms of some effective "fringe" treatments

Homeopathy and meditation

Arguably the most suspect of alternative therapies among conventional medical scientists is homeopathy, whose medications are diluted successively until in many cases the final dose lacks even a single molecule of the original substance. By definition, this precludes any interaction between that substance and the tissues of the body. In answer to individual, anecdotal claims of success with homeopathic preparations, orthodox physicians tend to cite as an obvious explanation the "placebo effect", according to which someone feels better if they believe they are being given effective treatment, no matter what it does or does not contain. Even the most carefully designed investigations of homeopathy, including one organized jointly in 1986 by the Glasgow Homoeopathic Hospital and the Western Infirmary in that Scottish city, have been criticized for not eliminating this possibility.

But if the occasional successes of homoeopathy do prove to depend upon a placebo effect, that will only establish that the homeopathic practitioners' explanation of their craft has been incorrect. Indeed the placebo phenomenon remains almost as perplexing today as it was during the 1950s when Dr Henry Beecher of Boston, Massachusetts, found that 35 out of 100 surgical patients experienced genuine relief from severe pain after receiving an "ineffective" placebo when they were expecting morphine. The explanation of such dramatic effects may prove to be the release of endorphins, natural painkillers, by the brain,

▼ *Customers queue for their nostrums in a fashionable homeopathic dispensary. Commercial companies offering pre-formulated homoeopathic "treatments" are prospering. This is a bizarre and self-contradictory development, given that homeopaths have long argued that their craft, in sharp distinction to conventional ("allopathic") medicine, places great store by the empathetic, one-to-one relationship between practitioner and patient.*

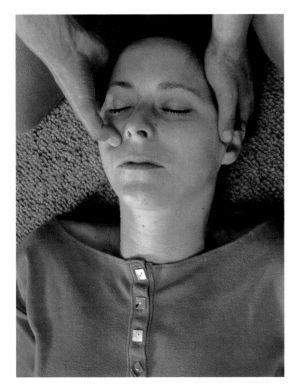

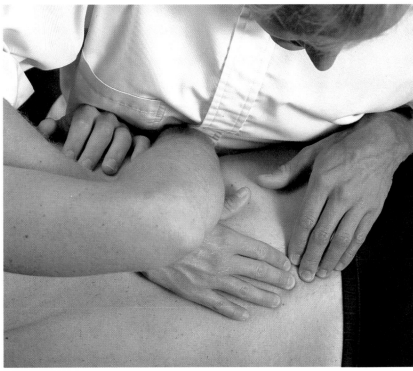

▲ *The ancient Japanese therapy of Shiatsu combines deep massage with the principles of acupuncture. The therapist seeks to cure disease by stimulating a flow of healthy energy by applying pressure with the thumbs to specific points, which are thought to be linked to various internal organs along lines known as meridians.*

▲ *Applying a high-velocity thrust to the joints of the spine, the osteopath hopes to loosen vertebrae that have become immobile. Although some mainstream physicians use osteopathic methods alongside conventional manipulation, the technique was dismissed as of negligible value by the British Medical Association in 1986.*

although it is unclear why this should occur in some individuals and not others. While conventional physiology and biochemistry indicate that placebos should be metabolically inert, such substances clearly can on occasion be as effective as the most powerful of drugs. By providing a real explanation of the placebo effect, future research could reveal for the first time why many different "fringe" treatments occasionally work. It could also lead to far more subtle and effective control of pain.

Another technique about which much remains to be learned is meditation, in its many different forms. The relaxation produced by regular meditation not only reduces heart rate and blood pressure but may also have longterm health benefits. Meditators often become less anxious and neurotic. Their pulse and blood pressure respond more quickly and recover more quickly in response to stress than do those of non-meditators. Yet prolonged meditation can also precipitate acute anxiety, depression and even suicide. Understandably cautious about recommending this form of therapy at present, many psychiatrists believe that deeper understanding of its effects on the brain and bodily processes, may greatly improve the treatment.

Meditation is also of interest to infectious disease specialists because it can, surprisingly perhaps, impair the body's immune responses against infection. Some forms of mental illness, and traumatic life events such as bereavement, have an even greater effect on immunity – including the arm of defense which normally eliminates cancer cells from the body. One recent study indicated that men's depression following bereavement or serious family illness was proportional to the reduction in their immune response. If we understood what links the mind with the body's army of defensive cells in such cases, it should be possible to boost the performance of the immune system at vulnerable times. Even more exciting is the possibility of establishing that a positive approach to life can have a beneficial effect in helping the body to repel both infectious microbes and the malignant cells which arise occasionally and threaten to destroy bodily harmony.

An end to fringe medicine?

The surest prediction about fringe medicine 300 years from now is that it will no longer exist. Certainly, the catalog of practices and panaceas lumped together nowadays as "fringe" or "alternatives" to mainstream medicine will seem an exceedingly odd mixture. It's already apparent that the tendency to either endorse or ridicule, en bloc, everything from hypnosis to homeopathy is indefensible. Although orthodoxy has been slow to accommodate them, techniques such as hypnosis and acupuncture have gained a small but established place in medical treatment during recent years, and their efficacy can be attested by the most rigorous of critical methods. But there is still conflict between the inherently implausible nature of homeopathy (some of whose allegedly most effective remedies have been diluted so far that they contain not a single molecule of the "active" ingredient) and the tenets of science-based medicine.

Some of today's alternatives, in other words, are flattered by being included in the "alternative" portfolio, while others are correspondingly cheapened. Given the intensive public and professional interest now being shown in all kinds of fringe medicine, however, the true merits and demerits of the various techniques will become apparent in the decades ahead. No doubt there will be some surprises. But the greatest prize of all will probably come from investigations into therapies which work by some route other than those upon which they are ostensibly based. Such progress will in turn depend to a large extent upon much greater understanding of the relationship between the brain and the other organs and tissues in the human body. Phenomena such as the placebo effect, which can be as powerful as some of our most potent drugs, prove that we have a far from complete picture of the exquisitely sensitive interactions between the nervous system and the rest of the body. Already, however, the emerging study of biofeedback and the discovery of endorphins – the brain's inbuilt opiates – suggest that our descendents may be able to control their own feelings, sleep patterns, metabolic activities and general well-being at will simply by focusing their minds in particular ways.

Today biotechnology is poised to spawn cheap, rapidly-used personal screening kits for conditions ranging from infections and metabolic aberrations such as diabetes to incipient tumors anywhere in the body. There will also be simple kits to help us determine our hereditary susceptibility to everything from skin cancer and osteoarthritis to peptic ulcers and alcohol abuse – and take evasive action accordingly. Combined with customer-friendly computerized diagnostic services, on-line 24 hours per day, this technology will radically alter the present distinction between patients and physicians. The medical profession will stoutly resist this downgrading of their professional status, yet new skills such as genetic therapy and genetic engineering could greatly increase their influence.

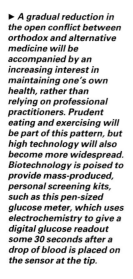

► **A gradual reduction in the open conflict between orthodox and alternative medicine will be accompanied by an increasing interest in maintaining one's own health, rather than relying on professional practitioners. Prudent eating and exercising will be part of this pattern, but high technology will also become more widespread. Biotechnology is poised to provide mass-produced, personal screening kits, such as this pen-sized glucose meter, which uses electrochemistry to give a digital glucose readout some 30 seconds after a drop of blood is placed on the sensor at the tip.**

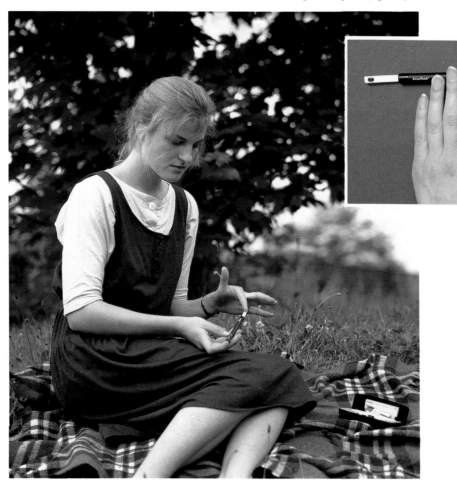

Mind-Body Interaction

15

Medicine, the body and mind...Aspects of anxiety...Physical and psychological causes of disease...Psychosomatic illness...Influencing bodily reactions under hypnosis...Is stress beneficial?...Stress and overbreathing... Bereavement...Effects of "life-events"... "Functional complaints"...Biased medicine has victims...A balanced system of body-mind care

The relationship between mind and body has fascinated philosophers and scientists for generations. Former ideas that regarded mind and body as separate entities have been replaced with a realization that they are virtually inseparable. Scientists now recognize that experiences such as pain and anxiety involve both physical and psychological components, while philosophers talk of a three-way division, between the physical world and the worlds of subjective experience and of objective knowledge. While they may be artificially separated for purposes of discussion, it should always be borne in mind that they are parts of a unified whole.

Anthropologists have demonstrated that people in the United Kingdom are as likely to consult relatives, or others in the community whose opinion they respect, as they are to consult doctors for physical complaints. Many will be advised that their symptoms result from stress or worry and prefer this explanation to the physical one offered by a doctor. In developing countries consultations with a faith healer greatly outnumber those with "western"-trained doctors. Such healers have been criticized for failing to recognize organic disease but their consultations probably lead to greater consumer satisfaction than those with many western doctors.

The physiology of anxiety
The term "anxiety" generally describes a psychological state, but this cognitive experience is invariably associated with changes in heart rate, respiration rate, sweating and movement of the gut (butterflies in the stomach). These are familiar to all of us from visits to the dentist, or after a near-miss in the car. They are brought about because the brain recognizes the situation as threatening and stimulates the sympathetic nervous system. This leads to the secretion of adrenaline. The ensuing changes ensure that more oxygen is circulated to the muscles, so that the body is in a state of readiness for "fight" or "flight", but they also create "fright".

Such changes promote better performances on the athletic track or the concert platform. But they may be dangerous for the person with narrowed coronary arteries, when the increased demand on the heart may precipitate a heart attack. Anxiety is a normal emotion, but may also be involved in disease processes. A constant state of anxiety is one factor associated with heart disease, which in many countries causes a significant proportion of deaths. This has implications for the use of drugs or other forms of treatment.

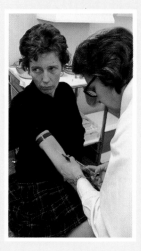

▼ *Aboriginal Australians consult a traditional medicine man (left). In purely physical terms, traditional remedies often do more harm than good. On the other hand, experience has shown that western medicine should be introduced cautiously and with awareness of local cultural traditions. The general practitioner taking* *a blood sample (right) learns little or nothing of psychosomatic symptoms, which may be the most serious in many patients. They are always taken seriously and sometimes treated effectively by traditional practitioners, who are much more likely to uncover any part played by personal distress and may suggest remedies.*

Greater understanding of the psychological causes of anxiety is reducing dependence on drugs

Factors relating to heart disease

The commonest cause of death in the western world is now heart disease, but this cannot be traced to physical causes alone. Factors associated with the development of heart disease include "physical" ones such as increased level of fats in the blood, smoking and raised blood pressure, and "psychological" ones such as particular types of personality, and a persistently raised level of anxiety.

Characteristics of the so-called "type A" personality are a strong sense of time urgency, inability to relax, and always striving to get things done quickly. If asked to do mental arithmetic, people who have a "type A" personality increase their blood pressure more than normal people. Some studies suggest reducing type A behavior reduces the chances of heart attack; others show the difficulty of defining such behavior. In fact, the "physical" factors can also be modified by behavioral changes without necessarily using drugs. Reduction in smoking, increased exercise, and changes in diet reduce the chances of developing heart disease very considerably. High blood pressure has traditionally been treated by medical drugs, but for some people this can also be reduced by biofeedback.

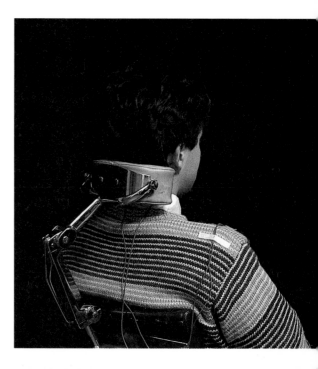

▼ *In a Shintaido exercise one person stretches upward and outward, transmitting her joyous feeling to her partner whose body follows because she is holding the other's wrists. The aim is to make mind-body interaction a shared as well as a solitary experience.*

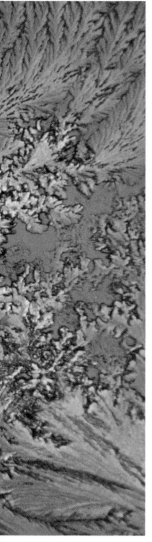

Experiments with anxiety

Attempts to separate the psychological and physical components of anxiety have been largely unsuccessful. One theory ascribes the sensation of anxiety to the bodily components alone. But attempts to provoke anxiety by injecting adrenalin were only successful if the person injected was told beforehand what to expect! The sensation of anxiety is therefore a result of both bodily and cognitive changes from the normal relaxed state. This is why the sensation can be blocked by two quite different types of drugs. Some act on the brain (tranquilizers) whereas others (including beta-blockers, such as Propranolol) reduce the heart rate, but in the short-term both are equally effective.

Excitement, anger or anxiety all cause similar bodily changes. These responses can be elicited in the laboratory by asking a person to solve problems of mental arithmetic. When listening carefully to instructions and while subtracting sevens from 100 the tension in the frontalis muscle (forehead) increases, sweating is increased (a plethysmograph attached to the index finger shows less electrical resistance) and the heartbeat increases.

These are normal physiological responses and can be elicited in everybody, but people vary in their response when the stimulus is maintained at a "stressful" level over a period of time. Normal people gradually become physically habituated to the prolonged or repeated stimuli so that their physiological responses decrease even if they are still faced with the anxiety-provoking stimulus. In people who are overanxious by nature this does not occur and the heart rate, for example, remains high. This may provide a clue as to why anxious people are more prone to develop heart disease.

The same bodily changes may result from a physical rather than a mental stimulus. A few irregular heartbeats may lead an anxious person to worry excessively that he or she has heart disease. This worry causes the heart to beat faster which seems to confirm the fears of heart disease. A vicious circle may develop in which the sensation of panic and the increased heart rate reinforce each other and it may become impossible to discern separate physical and psychological components. Although the sequence started with a physical (but normal) irregular heart beat, the state of extreme anxiety may only follow because this has psychological significance, for example, if a relative has recently died of heart disease. Such panic attacks are common in those who develop an anxiety state. These people go to their doctor for help either with suspected heart disease or with anxiety.

The relaxation response

Just as anxiety causes acceleration of certain bodily functions, relaxation leads to the reverse. Experienced practitioners of transcendental meditation (TM) lower their respiration rate, pulse and blood pressure when they meditate. Electrical records of brain activity indicate that the meditator is not asleep but in a state of deep relaxation consequent upon focusing his or her mind solely on the mantra. Similar states of relaxation are found in hypnotized subjects.

There is now a move away from the use of drugs to treat or alleviate the effects of anxiety; doctors and patients alike are keen to relieve anxiety by purely psychological means. This avoids dependence on drugs and other side effects. The dangers of all drugs used in modern medicine are increasingly being recognized and in future psychological means of treatment are likely to be ever more extensively employed. This has already started in the case of heart disease.

◄ *Lowering tension by biofeedback: 32 students in a school in S. Dakota, USA, learned to reduce tension in their forehead muscles, and raise the temperature of their hands, by biofeedback. Researchers concluded that biofeedback can attain many of the objectives of preventive medicine: "How much present and future health insurance money was saved by this program can only be guessed. Perhaps one of the health insurance companies will fund a research project to find out."*

◄ *A polarized-light micrograph of crystals of adrenalin (× 100). Adrenalin derivatives cause the symptoms of fright and prepare us for "fight or flight". Different people's bodies respond in different ways to stressful situations over long periods. Normal people become habituated to a stressful stimulus so that the adrenalin response decreases even if they are confronted with the same stimulus. Overanxious people continue to respond to the same extent: their heart rate remains high. This may hint at why anxious people are more prone to heart disease.*

An understanding that disease may have several causes lies behind the idea of psychosomatic illness

Psychosomatic disease

Certain diseases were termed "psychosomatic" when it was discovered that psychological treatments could achieve results when conventional medical treatment had failed. Doctors in the United States noticed that a few patients with asthma were particularly anxious. When psychiatrists treated these patients with psychoanalysis, the asthma improved greatly. Subsequently, relaxation and hypnosis have proved to be equally effective.

Not all asthmatics are overanxious. Many have "anxiety scores" similar to the normal population, though some do have an anxiety score as high as the most anxious patient attending a psychiatric clinic. It is these latter patients whose asthma improves most when their anxiety is given treatment.

Asthma usually has more than one cause. In one study, among 441 asthmatics psychological factors were important in 70 percent, infective factors in 68 percent and allergic factors in 36 percent. (The percentages add up to more than 100 because two or more casual agents were found in most patients – allergic and emotional ones being the commonest combination.) In only one percent of patients were psychological factors alone responsible. In other words, a constitutional liability for the airways to constrict (when faced with infection, pollen or dust) is a necessary prerequisite but rarely a sufficient cause on its own. Such a constitutional liability often runs in families.

Stress and the growth of tumors in animals

The relationship between stress, and hormonal and immunological response has been studied in controlled laboratory experiments. Certain strains of mice naturally develop a tumor at about the age of one year, and others can be induced to develop such a tumor for experimental purposes. These animals have provided a unique opportunity to study the factors which influence the development of tumors.

Tumor growth can be retarded by keeping the mice in a special low-stress environment. Later experiments demonstrated that this special care led to an extremely low level of corticosterone in the blood. The experiments then manipulated the level of corticosterone and found that as it increased, the body's defense system was weakened. High levels of corticosterone led to the presence of fewer white cells in the blood and a decrease in size of the thymus. The amino-acid metabolism was affected, and tumor growth increased. Here, then, was a model of cancer growth being linked to environmental stress through the intervening steps of corticosterone secretion acting upon the immune system.

Scientists later found that the level of corticosterone was very sensitive to changes in the environment. It was increased by placing mice of the opposite sex nearby, by removing the mice one by one from the cage, or by rotating the cage. Any of these stimuli led to an increase in corticosterones over a few minutes, a decrease in the white blood cells over one to two hours, and a reduction in the size of the thymus after one day or more. Tumor growth could be increased by three different stimuli. The first was an injection of a virus, the second rotating the cage, and the third the injection of corticosterone.

It is tempting to relate these animal experiments to humans, especially as some of the authors have used the term "anxiety-provoking stimulus" when they have referred to rotation of the cage or removal of the mice one by one for blood test. However, "anxiety" as it is experienced by humans cannot be assessed in animals.

▲ *A child uses an inhaler to prevent allergic asthma. Anxious asthmatics pose a problem for doctors. Does anxiety cause asthmatic symptoms or does anxiety develop as the outcome of repeated asthmatic attacks? Scientists are now looking beyond the person's emotional reaction and examining in detail both environmental stress and the way in which the body reacts to it physiologically.*

► *The lymphocyte (shown in a false-color electron micrograph) is one of the several classes of white blood cells which together defend us against disease. Studies have shown that people who live very lonely lives are abnormally prone to infection, and to cancer. In 1987, University of Texas scientists discovered that the stress hormone adrenal cortex trophic (stimulating) hormone (ACTH) directly affects lymphocytes through a receptor for ACTH on their surfaces. ACTH inhibits lymphocytes from producing antibodies and so limits their effectiveness in protecting against disease. Other scientists have found receptors for the natural tranquilizing substance produced by the brain, a substance similar to Valium, on lymphocytes, suggesting that our natural response to stress can also affect immunity to disease, though how is still unknown.*

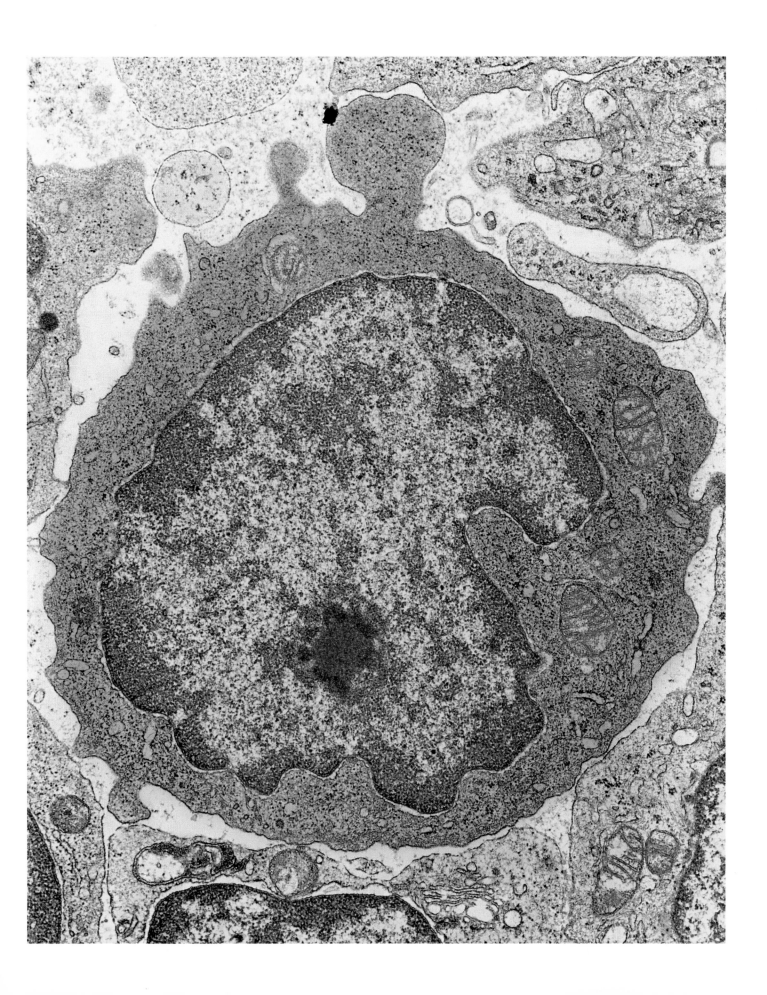

Research has linked some bodily changes to emotional changes accompanying stress

Hypnosis and the immune response

Perhaps the most spectacular piece of research concerning immune function in humans has been one involving hypnosis. It employed the standard Mantoux test for whether someone is immune to tuberculosis or requires immunization. Injection of tuberculosis antigen into the skin of the forearm provokes a red raised area of skin in those who are immune (Mantoux positive). Healthy medical students who were Mantoux positive were told under hypnosis not to react. After this had been done intensively over several days, injection of the antigen no longer provoked the expected reaction and no raised red area was detected. The overall thickness of the skin was normal because the accumulation of the fluid in the tissue spaces had been suppressed by the hypnotic suggestion. The area of skin did show the expected infiltration of white cells, demonstrating that some, but not all, aspects of the immune response can be suppressed by hypnosis.

Can stress be beneficial?

Stress does not always damage health. Those students who were deprived of their sleep for the purpose of the above experiment were found to have an enhanced immune response over the following few days. Animal experiments have shown similar results. When stress such as cage rotation (♦ page 173) precedes exposure to infection, the animal is more resistant than usual, whereas when the stress and the exposure to infection occur simultaneously the animal's resistance is lowered.

Causes of chest pain, overbreathing

It has been found that one-quarter to one-third of people having their appendix removed for suspected appendicitis have a normal appendix when it is examined by the pathologist (♦ page 176). The story can be repeated in any heart clinic. Cardiologists investigating men and women with chest pain thought to be due to heart disease have found that one-quarter to one-half have perfectly normal coronary arteries. The explanation of the chest pain lies in the patient's tendency to overbreathe at certain times. The overbreathing leads to a reduction in the carbon dioxide in the blood stream and this can cause many symptoms, including pains in the chest. Tingling in the fingers and legs, cramps, dizziness, weakness and even paralysis are other symptoms that may result from overbreathing. The correct treatment is exercises which retrain the person to breathe normally, especially when under stress. The appropriate investigation for such patients is one of the simplest in medicine. Rapid breathing in the clinic at the request of the doctor leads to the development of the symptom in question and both patient and doctor immediately gain insight into the true nature of the underlying physiological mechanism. Yet the belief of some doctors that an underlying physical cause for the symptom may be present leads to fruitless investigations for a "physical" illness.

At present thousands of people who are hyperventilators are subjected to investigations for suspected physical illness. The ordering of such tests leads to an increase in the patients' concern that there is something seriously wrong. Although

the doctor's aim is to reassure the patient, he may inadvertently increase the patient's worries. With increasing anxiety come increasing somatic symptoms. If each one attracts another test, the patient becomes convinced there is some bodily disease.

In this way, a vicious circle can easily develop, with the doctor contributing to the patient's anxiety, rather than relieving it. In frustration, the doctor may even eventually declare that he believes the patient's problems are "all in the mind". The realization by such doctors that body and mind closely interact could provide a much more satisfactory service.

► **Scientific evidence for real improvements due to faith healing therapy is scanty, but anecdotal evidence abounds. Can spiritual influences, not measurable by scientific methods, affect the immune system and other bodily functions? The possibility is worth investigating.**

The stress of bereavement

The stress that has been most widely studied is that of bereavement – usually loss of a spouse. Reports indicate that about 40 percent more middle-aged widowers die during the six months immediately after their wife's death than would be expected for men of their age. Deaths are mostly through heart attacks or strokes, indicating that the wife's death acts as a trigger on a previously arteriosclerotic arterial system. Other researchers have found a similar pattern among widows and have identified those at greatest risk as people who have little or no social support and who probably become severely depressed.

At present scientists know of two ways in which bereavement could affect white blood cell functions. First, there is probably a rise in the production of corticosterone (◀ page 172), which reduces white cell function. Second, healthy people deprived of sleep for one or two nights experience a change in immune functions. Sleep is consistently lost following bereavement, though individuals vary as to the severity of this change.

Most recently, psychiatrists and immunologists have discovered that not everyone is affected in the same way following a stress such as bereavement. The immune system is most severely affected in those who become profoundly depressed after the death of a close relative – further evidence of the close relationship between mind and body. This theme is now emerging from several different pieces of research; it is not the experience of stress itself that causes changes in the body, but the emotional changes which are most closely associated with them.

▼ An experiment that went wrong. Some members of the International Biomedical Expedition to the Antarctic in 1985 were "acclimatized" to cold in advance by spending up to an hour a day for 10 days in a cold bath. Others underwent other unpleasant experiences. The subjects became so stressed that some withdrew from the program. If matters had been carefully explained, to minimize unnecessary stress, the research might have been completed.

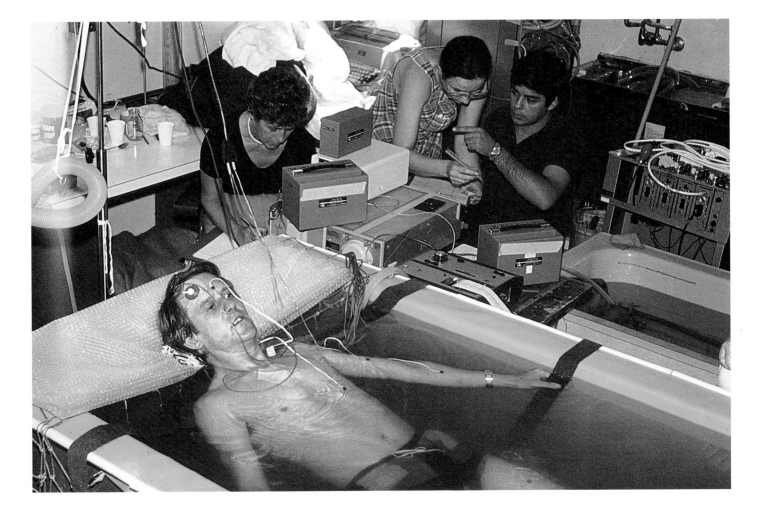

Are heart attacks preceded by a stressful life-event? The answer is a qualified "yes"

"Life-events" research

One line of investigation into mind-body interactions is the connection between environmental stress and changes in the state of the body. Some scientists pursued a strategy of studying life-events, such as bereavement or separation, that had been experienced by a group of individuals prior to the onset of one particular illness. Such an approach requires a carefully matched control group of healthy people. It also requires an accurate measure of life-event stress to overcome the natural tendency for the sick to see their recent lives as full of such events in an effort to explain their illness. Such a measure has recently become available and a number of diverse illnesses have been studied in this way.

The answer to the question "Are heart attacks preceded by a stressful life-event?" is a qualified "yes". Numerous studies have shown that people who develop heart attacks have recently experienced more stressful events than would be expected by chance but the relationship is disappointingly meager. Researchers have found a much clearer relationship, among certain groups of patients consulting general medical doctors, between stressful life-events and the onset of depression and anxiety states.

"Functional" complaints

Hospital doctors are now recognizing that up to one-third of the patients they see do not have organic disease. Yet the symptoms of these patients are so similar to those of organic disease that the doctors believe many expensive investigations are warranted to exclude organic disease. In the case of suspected appendicitis it may be justifiable to remove the appendix to prevent potentially severe complications.

Papers entitled "What does the gastroenterologist do all day?" and "Referrals to neurologists for headaches not due to structural disease – what should the neurologist do?" indicate the doctors' frustration that so much of their time is spent seeing patients who do not have organic disease and for whom modern medicine has so little to offer. Although doctors hope to reassure their patients by demonstrating the absence of organic disease, using X-rays and CAT scans, these tests may heighten the patient's anxiety because they fail to explain the symptom.

Gastroenterologists have defined the irritable bowel syndrome (one of the commonest conditions they see) principally in terms of the absence of organic disease. The symptoms of abdominal pain and diarrhea/constipation are very occasionally due to an enzyme deficiency, but the majority of those who develop the complaint can be seen to do so following a stressful life event. One-half have clear anxiety or depression diagnosed by a psychiatrist, and many respond to psychological treatment when physical treatment has failed.

The psychological component of this illness is therefore clear; the physical component lies in a constitutionally sensitive gut which is prone to develop painful contractions when the person is stressed. Why some people develop such symptoms when under stress while others develop a rapid heartbeat is not known.

Such "functional abdominal pain" is now known to respond to psychological treatment. Once this is more widely recognized, gastroenterologists will be forced to rely less heavily on drugs which affect the gut and instead incorporate the skills of a psychologist to help their patients. Since, it has been estimated, gastroenterologists in the United Kingdom may be seeing as many as 1,000 new patients with these "functional" complaints each week, the change in the techniques with which they are treated will be dramatic.

▲ Self-mutilation – here during a Nepalese festival – illustrates how trances and other self-imposed mental states can reduce pain. Similarly the Chinese ability to undergo minor surgery with no anesthetic but acupuncture shows that attitudes to pain in different societies can make the experience of pain more tolerable.

▲ Being hijacked and held hostage is an exceptionally stressful life-event on which a growing amount of data is becoming available. Hostage Jimmy Dell Palmer (in red shirt) was released by Shiite Amal militiamen in June, 1985 because he had a heart condition and it was recognized that the stress of being held hostage could lead to a heart attack. Brief periods of stressful conditions may benefit normal, healthy people, but the body is not designed to benefit from prolonged stress, as in a hijack.

◄ A Cypriot woman grieves over a dead relative. Bereavement causes depression, loss of weight and appetite, and lack of sleep, and hence weakness which depresses resistance to disease. Hormonal changes may also lower immunity. Loneliness has been directly linked to lowered immunity, increased risk of infectious disease, and reduced effectiveness of cells which normally help to defend against cancer. Other stressful life-events may include divorce, redundancy, even spending Christmas with close relatives.

Pain mimics appendicitis

Approximately one-third to one-quarter of patients having their appendix removed for suspected appendicitis are seen to have had a normal appendix when it is studied by the pathologist. The cause of the abdominal pain in most of these patients has not been explained. They have been found to have a great excess of stressful life-events over the preceding months compared with the patients who have true appendicitis. The most common life-event was a breakup of a close relationship and this stressful experience has led to some patients developing abdominal pain possibly in the same way as the anxious person develops butterflies in the stomach, or the unhappy child experiences abdominal pains. But even those with true appendicitis had a slight increase in less severely threatening events compared with a healthy control group. Their immunity may have been affected by examinations, rows or trouble with the police. Such trauma may affect the immune state and may also affect the mobility of the gut.

A victim of biased medicine

Two sets of hospital doctors were frustrated in their attempts to explain the abdominal pain, diarrhea and weight-loss in a 35-year-old woman. Even the most sophisticated investigations found that all the organs in her abdomen were functioning normally; this was eventually confirmed by the surgeon who opened her abdomen and examined the organs visually. Only at this late stage were psychological investigations performed. A psychiatrist found the woman to be seriously depressed with marked anxiety symptoms. The nervous state had started when she witnessed a neighbor choking to death, and was made much worse by a relative's suicide. The ensuing severe depression led to both the abdominal pains and the loss of weight and diarrhea. Antidepressant drugs and relaxation therapy led to a complete recovery for this woman who had been a victim of a system of medicine which is heavily biased toward physical factors in illness.

The nervous illness of this woman manifested itself in bodily rather than purely psychological symptoms. Such "somatizers" are common and may even completely deny depressed mood, and she was such an example. Within her family upbringing, attention and sympathy were only awarded to those who were physically ill; psychological distress was ignored or frowned upon. With a physical symptom the stigma of mental illness was avoided and the necessity of examining her traumatic marriage was also avoided. One-third of patients attending the general practioner with a recent onset of anxiety or depression report not emotional complaints but bodily ones such as headache, abdominal pain or breathlessness.

Diagnosing with talk and computers

Some general practitioners are ready and able to detect the underlying psychological nature of the patient's problems; others seem unwilling to do so. Only in the 1980s have doctors in western societies begun to be taught systematically to talk to patients and to detect psychological disturbance as well as physical disease. Perhaps in future the seven minutes with each patient will be increased to 2, 3 or 4 times that length of time with a decreased use of the prescription pad. On the other hand, scientists have already demonstrated that patients are more honest with a computer than with a doctor about the amount they drink — perhaps computer-aided diagnosis will be free of prejudice.

Not all discoveries are new

There are already reports of some cancer cures following psychological treatments, which aim to enhance the body's own defense system. Occasional such cures are no longer incredible now that the effects of stress and relaxation on the immune system are being understood.

Perhaps an emphasis on a correct diet and adequate exercise, relaxation and sleep will once again become a central part of medical regimes for cancer patients. This would bring a big change to many hospital wards where none of it is currently happening. It would, furthermore, be a return to some of the ingredients of former treatment for tuberculosis – it is not widely known that such treatment also included group therapy. Not all discoveries are new!

The implications for prevention are also clear. In the future, health services may cease to be primarily concerned with the sick and dying. Instead, fit people may be encouraged, possibly even obliged, to actively pursue health and well-being by taking responsibility for enhancing their own immune systems.

Collaborative research between psychiatrists and basic scientists has led to the development of a theoretical model of mind-body interaction. The steps between environmental stress and its effects on the body are becoming clearer, but much more research is needed. Our understanding of how stress leads to the development of disease is improving.

Toward "psychological" understanding

Medicine has experienced a massive increase in its ability to understand and treat "physical" aspects of illness, but this now needs to be balanced by a similar development of "psychological" understanding and treatments. The body and mind work as one and so should the two aspects of medical treatment. Current medical thinking has influenced the attitudes of many doctors, who are being jolted out of their present attitudes as the explosion of psychological treatments occurs. These will take their place alongside physical treatments, instead of being in competition with them, so that both mind and body will be treated appropriately.

In 30 years' time doctors' attitudes will have caught up with those of one section of our society, and psychological treatments will be recognized as being "useful". The circumstances when such treatments shall be prescribed will still be ill-defined in the medical school curriculum, apart from recognizing the need for more appropriate treatment for those who consult doctors for "non-organic" disease. Many patients may still prefer to conceal their psychological problems behind a "physical" presentation, while others will expect the doctor to be willing and able to deal with their own view of a psychological–physical interaction.

In 300 years the situation will be quite different. The medical defense unions may then be facing as many claims against doctors who have failed to diagnose psychological disorders as they now face regarding physical illness. Patients and doctors will view each symptom as representing either physical or psychological disorder and computer-aided diagnosis (along the lines of that currently used on cars) will not distinguish between these. Treatment will be aimed at regaining the body's homeostasis and would be as likely to involve relaxation, or other adjustment of life-style, as some physical treatment. Drugs will come to be regarded as a necessary evil, to be taken only as a last resort, because they are alien to the body and are capable of producing nasty side effects.

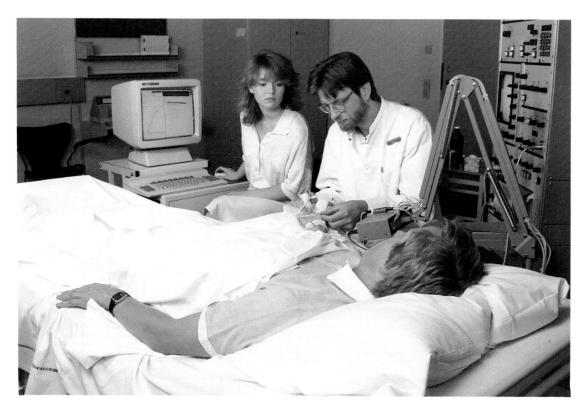

► An engineer helps a doctor to measure electrical signals generated by muscles in a patient's arm. Artificial intelligence, expert systems, and the collected experience of doctors, can be built into computer programs to help in diagnosis and monitoring progress. The use of biosensors and computerization will make self-diagnosis more possible and reliable (◊ page 168). Feedback systems will also allow, for example, insulin for diabetics and chemotherapy for cancer to be continually adjusted to the body's varying needs.

16

Views of consciousness: materialist, idealist, dualist and functionalist...Special problems for the student of consciousness...The approach of psychologists and physiologists...The computer analogy...Death and consciousness...The evolution of consciousness...Enlightenment...Mental models...Altered states...New directions

Consciousness is a problem. We all think we know what it is. Each of us likes to think that "I" am some kind of conscious entity inhabiting "my" body, making decisions and acting freely. This naive view may be no more accurate than the naive view of perception – that a self inside the head looks directly out of the eyes at a world outside. Nevertheless, while psychology, physiology and research in artificial intelligence have revealed a clearer picture of the constructive nature of perception, they have not yet found appropriate ways of tackling consciousness.

Philosophers have long argued about the status of mental phenomena. Materialists argue that all behavior has physical, not mental, causes. On the other hand idealists reject the reality of the physical body and take only the mental as fundamental. Dualists have treated mental and physical as two different, though possibly interacting, realms. More recently, functionalists have argued that mental phenomena emerge from the functional organization of the brain. The relationship of mind to the brain is like that of software to a computer's hardware. However, none of these basic approaches seems to reveal just what consciousness is or why we have it. Part of the problem is that consciousness (or at least subjective experience) is all we have. The problem of consciousness is all to do with what it means to be me, now.

Consciousness is different

Consciousness cannot be studied in the same way as all those things which form the contents of consciousness. If you try to make it the object of awareness it becomes something other than the awareness itself. It cannot easily be described, for any attempt to describe it changes it. If I try to tell you what my experience is like, I end up describing its contents or else using possibly misleading metaphors. No thought, no state of awareness either persists for any length of time, or comes back in exactly the same way again. The American psychologist William James (1842-1910), a pioneer of psychology, described the "stream of consciousness" which is always flowing, feeling unbroken but never repeating itself. Since science searches for regularities and patterns, it is hard to know where to start with something whose very nature lies in change.

One starting-place is what might be called a "commonsense" view of consciousness. Introspection appears to suggest that consciousness is unitary (each person has only one "consciousness"); that it is continuous and extends unbroken in time (we are the same conscious person from day to day); that it is a property of self (it is "I" who am conscious of everything "I" do and experience); that consciousness is the source of will (a conscious self can take decisions and act freely).

All these assumptions seem far less likely in the light of modern research. While dual consciousness and even multiple consciousness are studied, the proportion of mental activity which enters awareness is shown to be minute. Indeed we may have to overthrow entirely the notion of a permanent conscious self before we can begin to make sense of consciousness.

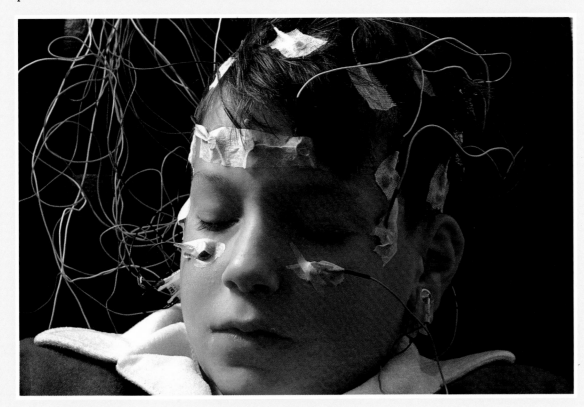

◄ *To obtain his electroencephalogram, (EEG), electrodes are attached to this young boy's head and face and the output is analyzed by computer. Changes in the EEG correlate with changes in a person's state of consciousness. For example, the EEG of a person awake is quite different from that during deep sleep or dreaming. But no physical apparatus can reveal what a person is experiencing or measure consciousness directly.*

There are psychological, physiological, biological and computational approaches to the study of consciousness

Reproduced by left hand (right hemisphere)	Model pattern	Reproduced by right hand (left hemisphere)

Consciousness in the study of psychology

Approaches to the study of consciousness include the psychological, physiological, biological and computational. Early psychologists took consciousness as central to their subject. It seemed obvious that a science of the mind was required and that this would study conscious experience. Introspectionism was one approach, within which people trained themselves to observe their own mental processes. However, among other problems, this method was unable to generate useful and testable hypotheses, or to produce agreement between researchers as to what they did experience.

Partly as a reaction against this approach, behaviorism gained prominence in the early 20th century. Behaviorists argued that consciousness could not be measured or tested directly, but only detected through the behavior to which it gave rise (including, of course, verbal behavior). They were not concerned with inner processes and indeed the American psychologist John Watson (1878-1958) went so far as to declare that "psychology must discard all reference to consciousness".

Only in the 1950s did inner processes such as mental imagery again come to be intensively studied within psychology. Of course only behavior can be directly studied, but if it arises from complex internal processes, those processes have to be investigated somehow. For example, research has shown that when a person imagines rotating a complex three-dimensional figure, the time the imagery takes is proportional to the actual time such a rotation would take. This is not to say that anything is being rotated inside the head, but that imagery has meaningful relationships to measurable processes and can provide insight into the brain's workings.

Physiology and consciousness

Imagine your finger quickly withdrawing from a hot flame. It is easy to think that you withdrew the finger as a conscious response to the pain. In fact the conscious perception begins only about half a second after the touch, even though the finger is well out of the way in about a tenth of a second. How can these processes be investigated?

The American neurophysiologist Benjamin Libet directly stimulated the cortex to induce a sensation like that of a touch on the skin. It took about half a second of stimulation (depending on the intensity) for the person to report feeling something. A touch on the skin, however brief, always elicited sensation. However, this skin touch could be backwardly masked by applying another cortical stimulus just after the touch, showing that the skin touch also takes some time to produce a conscious sensation. This does not mean the world is, as it were, delayed. The sensation appears to be accurately timed, from the beginning of the train of stimuli. In other words consciousness is full of events which occurred at least half a second ago, but by being referred backward they can give rise to the illusion of immediacy.

Research on "split-brain" patients, in whom the corpus callosum of nerve fibers joining the two hemispheres has been cut, has provided great insight into the workings of the whole brain. Information from the left hand goes only to the right hemisphere, which (in most patients) has little verbal ability. If a split-brain patient holds something in his left hand, such as a spoon, coin or pen, he may claim to have no idea what it is. When asked, he will say "nothing" or "I don't know". However, since only the left hemisphere can produce speech, this question is asking the hemisphere which doesn't know. If he is instead asked to use his left hand to choose the object from among many others he can do so.

In a sense such people are two, of whom only one can speak. It is then tempting to ask whether there is a split in consciousness, or what it would be like to "be" the right-brained person. Some have argued that only the verbal half is conscious and the other is not. Others suggest that splitting the brain splits consciousness and that it could be split many times until the units became insufficiently complex. This assumes that consciousness was originally unified. An alternative view is that the apparent unity of consciousness is, even in "normal" people, an illusion.

Michael Gazzaniga, an American neuropsychologist and one of the foremost researchers in this area, takes this idea further. He flashed a written command, such as "laugh" or "walk", to the right (largely nonverbal) hemisphere of split-brain patients. The person then laughed or got up and walked, but why? When asked, the patient said that the test was funny or that he wanted to fetch a coke. The speaking hemisphere had no insight into the real reason for the action. So it invented a reason. It could not accept that it did not know. Might all our "reasons for action" be similar inventions after the fact? Gazzaniga concludes that in normal and split-brain people alike, an interpreter in the left hemisphere constantly seeks ways of explaining the behavior of the whole system. Thus, an essentially fragmented system creates an illusion of a unified self.

All these findings have in common that they seem to undermine the "commonsense" view of consciousness. The more we learn about it, the more illusory it seems. And yet, given our own experience, we cannot dismiss it, as the behaviorists tried to do, as unworthy of notice. It must be a very special kind of illusion. So what is it and why do we have it?

◄ At Stanford University a student is the subject in an experiment probing the differences between the right and left halves of the brain. Slides of geometric shapes are flashed on a screen and the student is asked to think about what he/she has seen in an analytical way. Generally the right brain is more intuitive and the left more analytic but in normal people the two work closely together.

◄ In some patients with epilepsy the brain has to be split by cutting the corpus callosum, a bundle of 200 million nerve fibers joining the two hemispheres. Although these patients can appear to live as one person and manage their lives quite effectively, special tests reveal the depth of the division. In one test of the two halves of the split brain (left), the subject is shown the middle patterns and asked to assemble them with colored blocks. The right hand communicates with the left hemisphere and vice versa, and the two hands made quite different kinds of mistakes, revealing the differing skills of the two half brains. Since the right hemisphere usually has little verbal ability, a patient who is holding a spoon in his left hand cannot say what it is but he can still use it quite normally.

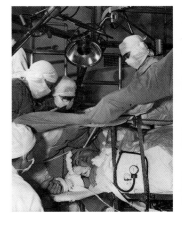

▲ During an operation to expose the brain for the treatment of epilepsy, the patient is fully conscious under local anesthetic and can speak to the surgeon and the anesthetist. US neurophysiologist Dr Wilder Penfield found during such surgery that electrical stimulation of different areas of the brain can induce realistic memories, images and experiences. In this procedure speech areas of the brain can be mapped.

If consciousness is the product of information-processing systems, it cannot survive the death of the physical system which underlies them

The computer analogy

The development of cognitive science and artificial intelligence has changed dramatically the way mental processes are understood and has offered new hope for understanding consciousness. Previous analogies for the brain included steam engines, waterwheels and telephone exchanges - all rather poor candidates for being conscious! Many now believe that the computer is the last and only analogy we need. The brain is an information-processing system and by understanding the computations it carries out we can understand how it constructs models of the world and of itself. It does not matter that the nerve cells of the brain are quite different from the hardware of contemporary computers.

Some have argued that consciousness is like the programmer of a computer, but this dualist view leaves it still mysterious. Others suggest that it is the contents of a limited-capacity serial-processing mechanism or a special device for setting up plans and goals. The British psychologist P.N. Johnson-Laird suggests that the conscious human mind is equivalent to an operating system and can model the options available to that system. The content of consciousness is the current values of parameters governing that operating system. The American psychologist Jack Yates argues that the content of consciousness is a model of the world.

Can consciousness survive death?

It is an unappealing thought that when your body dies and is buried you will cease to be: your conscious experience will simply cease and the world will carry on without you. For over a century there have been scientists struggling to prove this view false. In 1882 the Society for Psychical Research was formed in London and studied the communications given by mediums. Apparitions seen at the point of death were recorded but proved hard to substantiate. Although many were convinced, the researchers never developed a plausible theory of what survived, nor convinced scientists at large of the importance of the evidence.

More recently out-of-body experiences, in which a person seems to leave the body and be able to see and move around without it, have been claimed as evidence for survival. However, the experience can now be better understood as a change in the perspective of a person's model of self in the world. The experience seems real enough but, just as with the world we see, it is all a mental construction.

Undoubtedly some people will always seek proof of immortality. However, as science comes to understand consciousness better it seems ever clearer that it is the natural result of complex information-processing systems. If this is so, then there can be no consciousness when the physical system which underlies it dies.

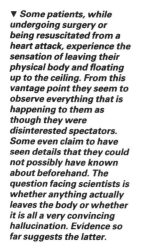

▼ Some patients, while undergoing surgery or being resuscitated from a heart attack, experience the sensation of leaving their physical body and floating up to the ceiling. From this vantage point they seem to observe everything that is happening to them as though they were disinterested spectators. Some even claim to have seen details that they could not possibly have known about beforehand. The question facing scientists is whether anything actually leaves the body or whether it is all a very convincing hallucination. Evidence so far suggests the latter.

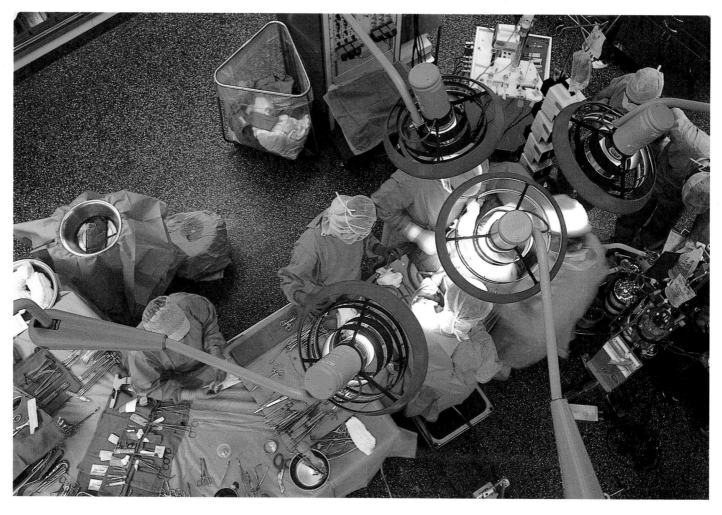

The evolution of consciousness

Some people have tried to understand the nature of consciousness by asking how it evolved. The British ethologist John Crook has argued that the characteristic features of human consciousness include reflexiveness (being conscious of being conscious); agency (the experience of personal power over action); and self-identity. These, he suggests, arose with the increasing use of tools by our ancestors, which gave rise both to the structure of our language and to the separation of individuals by ownership and possession. Only an animal which needs to know who owns what tools needs a sense of identity and agency.

The British psychologist Nicholas Humphrey argues that consciousness arose for more social reasons, in order to hold together the cooperative society on which early humans depended. Through evolution it became possible for a person to put herself in someone else's place, to imagine what others were feeling by having experienced such feelings herself. Being conscious is seen as necessary for predicting others' behavior. In this light, imagination, fantasy, novels and poetry, and even dreams can all be seen as practicing this skill.

A more controversial theory is that of the American psychologist Julian Jaynes. He argues that reflexive awareness and a sense of individual agency have only developed in the past few thousand years, very much later than Crook or Humphrey suggested. He cites the *Iliad*, the epic written by the Greek Homer, the "first European poet", some 3,000 years ago. There are, he argues, no references to mind, thoughts, feelings or self. Actions are all initiated by Gods, not by man himself. This reveals the bicameral mind in which action and volitions occurred independently of consciousness. Decisions only came into awareness as internal voices (the Gods) telling a person what to do. By contrast later Greek literature reveals a complex understanding of mind and consciousness with actions attributed to the self.

The problem with all these theories is that they do not specify why the evolving animal or man could not have acquired all these skills without being conscious. Somehow consciousness itself remains elusive. Nevertheless there seems to be a general principle involved here. Humans need to explain their own behavior. They develop theories about their actions and decisions which may be quite erroneous. Possibly the attribution of actions to the Gods is only an earlier theory later replaced by the concept of a self. Neither may be really accurate.

▲ *The British physicist Sir William Crookes (1832-1919) claimed proof of survival in his photographs of a materialized spirit girl called Katie King. Critics said it was just the medium in disguise – Crookes had been duped. Others measured the weight of a spirit as it left a dying person, but this was probably nothing more spiritual than body fluids. Photographs of the spirits of frogs, mice and insects taken in cloud chambers revealed only flawed apparatus.*

◄ *Achilles deals a finishing stroke to Hector in the climax of the "Iliad", depicted on a Greek vase around 500 BC. According to US psychologist Julian Jaynes, the early Greeks had no sense of personal volition or action. Decisions which we would now attribute to ourselves were heard by them as though coming from outside – as the voices of the Gods.*

The development of consciousness

Most of us live in a fog of confused distraction quite distinct from the clear consciousness of a truly enlightened mind. The possibility of enlightenment, once only considered in Buddhist and other eastern systems of thought, is now creeping into psychology. Traditional techniques include meditation, mindfulness in everyday life, chanting, fasting and prayer. Long practice brings about acceptance, calmness of mind, a sense of increasing presence in the moment, and a clarity of consciousness which many describe, but fail to convey to others.

If science is to tackle this development it needs an appropriate language with which to describe it. Already research has revealed some physiological changes in meditation, such as increasing control over, and an apparently greater coherence of, brain activity. The ability deliberately to control such functions as heart-beat and metabolic rate increases, as does control of imagery and concentration. Yet this fails to capture the essence of the self-transformation involved. Perhaps a science of consciousness, based on understanding the models of the world people inhabit, will take this a stage further.

With practice in meditation, the whole cognitive system is trained to build models which are less centered on a "me", on an imagined self who controls the body's actions and decides what to do. As this illusory self is gently let go, the world appears clearer and less distorted by its needs. Emotions arise and fall away, ideas form and are let go. To be such a model is to feel free and flowing and able to laugh with the follies of our self-made illusions. It is quite unlike being a closely bound and defended model of self as most of us are most of the time. Looked at in this way, science can hope to link its study of brain function to both the models the brain constructs and the experience of being those models.

In 30 years' time "mystical" will have ceased to imply "outside of science". An effective science of consciousness will not only describe humankind's potential development but will also be helping us all toward enlightenment.

▶ A statue of the Buddha, inside Wat Srikert Temple in Chiangrai, Thailand, sits in meditation: an image to inspire Buddhists seeking enlightenment. Gautama, the historical Buddha, became enlightened sitting under a tree. He then began teaching his insights: all life is suffering, suffering is caused by selfish desires and cravings but there is a way to abandon desire and transcend suffering. Although the development of consciousness involves building up a sense of self, the final step to complete awareness may lie in giving it up altogether.

▶ A scene from the "Oresteia", the last and probably greatest of the trilogies of Aeschylus, first performed in Athens in 458 BC. In this later Greek play, the hosts of traditional Gods are being overtaken by the powerful and merciful Zeus. Blind and vengeful actions are replaced by human justice; actions spring from the compassion and wisdom of men and women, not just Godly retribution. As consciousness develops, man's sense of self emerges from darkness. A step is taken toward self-awareness and personal responsibility.

Who is conscious?

It has been argued (◀ page 182) that the content of consciousness is a model of the world. This may provide some insight about the content, but is anyone or anything aware of it? Who is doing the willing and making the decisions? Who is actually conscious? Research in social psychology shows that the self is a constructed entity. Just as the world outside is constructed by perceptual processing, so the self is constructed from all the information we have about ourselves in relation to that world. It is constructed socially, by how other people respond to us, and individually, by modeling our own responses and actions.

So possibly the self is nothing more nor less than yet another of the models or representations which the human brain constructs. Actions, decisions, responses and perceptions may all be the products of a highly complex brain which then creates a model of a self to help explain them. This self, being only one model in the whole complex system, has access only to limited information. We (the model) can only be aware of a very limited amount of what goes on in the brain. What "we" don't understand we must fabricate. This may be hard to accept for those who would rather believe we have a soul or spirit at the center of our consciousness, but such an approach seems to be more consistent with the available evidence.

Being a mental model

One further speculation may help progress in this inquiry: what is it like being a mental model. In a famous paper, the American philosopher Thomas Nagel asked "What is it like to be a bat?". He argued that the fact that an organism has conscious experience at all means, basically, that there is something it is *like* to be that organism. But, as we have seen, the essential thing about organisms is that they construct models or representations of themselves in the world. So perhaps there must be something it is like to be a mental model. We could then say that being conscious is what it is like being a mental model.

But what sort of model? "I" am a model of self with all the attributes I have learned during a lifetime. I have a body image and a self image. It is relatively clear what it would be like to be me.

What then of all the other mental models constructed by my brain during its complex information processing? "I" am certainly not aware of them. Nonetheless we might ask what it is like to be them. So my suggestion is that all and any mental models are conscious. What makes "us" special is that we are the model which is constructed with the help of language, which is integrated by a self concept and made to seem continuous over time. We are an illusion of a permanent, unitary and decision-making self, sharing, as it were, the brain which constructed us, with myriads of other less person-like constructs.

We can never be aware of all these other models, unless by some act of information-processing they can be integrated into the model of self. Then "I" can become aware of them – or we might equally say – they become aware of "me". This theory of consciousness provides a new approach to altered states of consciousness (ASCs). To understand any altered state we need to ask what models of self in the world are being constructed by the system. In deep sleep there are virtually none, in dreaming there are all sorts of strange models, and of course hypnosis, alcohol and other drugs can act to change the models created. Multiple personality no longer seems an incomprehensible mystery but only an extreme version of the normal state – that we are each just one of the mental models our brain has made.

▲ A disciple of transcendental meditation (TM), performs what its founder, the Maharishi Mahesh Yogi, calls "levitation". This is supposed to be a super-natural power, attained by long practice, but scientific studies have detected only skillful muscle work. Although TM may not produce paranormal phenomena, it does teach how to enter altered states of consciousness.

▲ Dr LaBerge tapes electrodes onto the scalp and face of one of his "oneironauts". The output will reveal the various stages of ordinary sleep, or the EEG and rapid eye movements of dreaming sleep. It used to be assumed that all the voluntary muscles are paralyzed during dreaming, but recently a few "lucid dreamers" have learned to signal to the waiting sleep researcher by moving their eyes in a prearranged pattern. They can thus effectively tell LaBerge "I am dreaming and I know I'm dreaming", opening the way to direct communication between the scientist and the "oneironaut" dreamer.

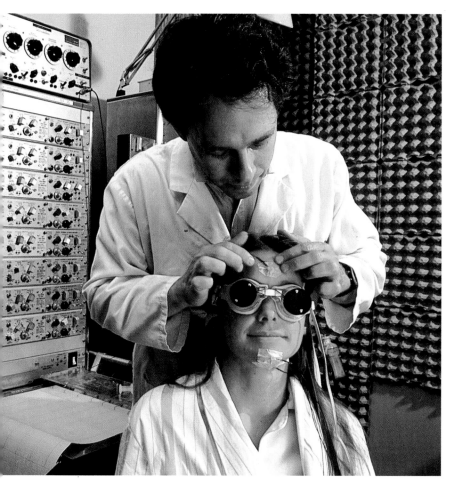

Altered states of consciousness

Dreaming, drunkenness and drug-induced euphoria: these are all altered states of consciousness (ASCs). While experiencing them we feel that something about our awareness is quite different, but what has changed? Some discrete ASCs are clearly different from each other, such as dreaming, deep sleep and waking. Others, such as alcoholic inebriation, seem to lie on a continuum. Techniques such as meditation can induce extreme changes in consciousness but need not do so, while some drugs produce highly predictable effects on consciousness.

Of all techniques for inducing ASCs, hypnosis is the most controversial. While traditionally it was thought to induce a special trance or hypnotic state, the American psychologist Theodore Barber has long argued that all the phenomena of hypnosis can be explained without recourse to any special state. Yet anyone who has been hypnotized knows that something feels completely different. So what has changed? One explanation may be that brain function has changed. Recent research has revealed much about the physiology of sleep and dreams, and the effects of psychoactive (or mind-altering) drugs on brain function. Important as this is, it does not address the question of how and why it feels different to be in an altered state.

The American psychologist Charles Tart defines an ASC as an unique configuration or system of psychological structures. From this he aimed to develop a systems approach to ASCs.

Another approach is to argue that consciousness is what it is like being a mental model (◀ page 186). Then we can only understand ASCs by knowing how a person's model of self in the world has changed. For example, in deep sleep model-building, and hence consciousness, is drastically reduced. In dreaming it increases but not enough to produce a coherent model of self, so there is consciousness but not self-consciousness. When you wake up it seems to have happened to someone else.

Sometimes, however, a self-model is constructed in dreaming sleep. This seems to make sense of the odd experience of seeming to awake in one's dream and to know one is dreaming. Such lucid dreamers can control the content of their dreams and even remember to carry out experiments while asleep. From such dreams a few people have been able to signal to waiting sleep researchers by moving their eyes in a prearranged pattern, opening up new possibilities for research on ASCs.

A few scientists are now abandoning the ideal of objectivity and study their own, as well as others', experiences. Tart has even argued that we need "state-specific sciences" in which scientists will work and do all their communication within ASCs. In 30 years' time we may expect many researchers to have trained themselves to enter different states and explore the vast geography of possible mental worlds. Only then will science be able to map that mental territory, relate it to the physical changes and finally develop a technology of mental exploration.

▲ Deep in trance, this woman from Sri Lanka has left this world and entered another – or has she? Maybe literally nothing has gone anywhere, but in such altered states of consciousness the world around seems to recede and mental images become vivid. Deeply subconscious knowledge can be tapped to help, guide or heal others without thought of self. Pain and hardship seem distant, easier to endure.

Future research

Psychology can never again afford to ignore consciousness as it did in the early part of the 20th century. But just what it will do with it is far from clear. We may only try to extrapolate from recent trends. In 30 years it should be obvious how consciousness arises from the construction of mental models in complex information-processing systems.

Philosophical arguments about the status of consciousness may never be resolved, but this will not worry cognitive scientists so long as they can manipulate and experiment with consciousness. It may then be accepted that any system, whether natural and alive, or made of silicon or anything else, can give rise to consciousness – and that as long as it models itself, it may be self-conscious.

This reveals the fascinating, but dangerous, possibility of self-conscious machines. Of course if all mental models are conscious then we already have conscious machines, but their consciousness must be static and uninteresting compared with ours. Even the best of today's robots has only a simplistic model of the world around it and an even less developed model of self.

However, in 30 years' time our robots will surely represent themselves in detail and be able to see the world around them. These developments will be possible because technology will enable robots to explore their surroundings, using their limbs and "senses" (◆ page 243). Another factor will be the advances already heralded by the new generation of parallel computers (◆ page 244). In a few decades, robots' consciousness will be important. We ought to ask "What is it like to be this robot's model of self in the world?". For it might be terribly painful and then we would have created suffering.

A new science of consciousness

To avoid the danger of creating suffering in robots, we need a science of consciousness which will understand the relationship between the structure of representations and the experience of being them. Then and only then could we create machines whose experience will be at least tolerable and perhaps even delightful.

Even more importantly, such a future science would do the same for us. New means of manipulating human consciousness will be found. Many have been available for thousands of years, but await rediscovery and development. They include the techniques of meditation and mindfulness used in some eastern disciplines and the rituals of western magic and alchemy.

Other techniques will be entirely new and only developed when we can understand how the brain constructs its representations, how training, drugs, or any other manipulations alter those representations, and what it feels like to be them. Progress in this area will entail the evolution of a new approach toward such "altered states of consciousness".

In 300 years' time we might expect the world to be inhabited by humans, animals and other "information-processing systems" – systems able to integrate all their mental models into one of the self, of which they are aware – whose experience of being is far more pleasant than it is for many of us today. For if we value the human capacity for empathy we shall not want to create machines whose experience is miserable. Nor should we fail to use our new science of consciousness to help people live. And so we shall need a technology of consciousness. Only then will the problems of consciousness begin to be resolved.

▲► What does it feel like being a robot? The most modern of today's robots, like this Japanese pianist (right), have a simple representation of the world around them and a primitive concept of self. So if self-representation is the key to consciousness, their awareness must be severely limited. But what of Artoo Detoo and See Threepio, the famous robots of the movie "Star Wars"? To behave and speak as they do they must have a highly complex model of self in the world. Robots like this, if we can ever make them, will be just as conscious as we are, or even more so.

Memory, with learning, distinguishes people from vegetables...Three kinds of memory...Help in understanding memory comes from the study of amnesiacs...and computers...Where and how brain traces occur...Hebb's theory...The mechanism of long-term potentiation...Mechanisms underlying habituation, sensitization, conditioning...Problems and benefits of understanding memory...

There are two broad strategies whereby through evolution an organism can be equipped to cope with its environment. One is to build in a set of adaptive reactions that are entirely sufficient to cope with any situation the organism may encounter. The other is to leave many options open, but give the organism the opportunity of adapting to its environment through the process of learning. Insects are a good example of the first solution; humans are the obvious example of the second. Without learning and memory, we should be reduced to vegetables, and distinctly inefficient vegetables at that.

It has become increasingly clear in recent years that human memory is not a unitary system, as are the heart or the lungs, but rather represents the operation of many subsystems, all of which have in common that they are capable of storing information. These subsystems can be divided into three broad categories, sensory memory systems, working memory, and long-term memory.

Sensory memory
When you perceive a moving object or hear a note, your visual and auditory systems need to take in information that is changing over time and use it to create a relatively stable precept. At the movies such brief storage allows us to perceive a series of still pictures separated by brief periods of darkness as a continuously moving image. Sensory memory systems presumably have other more basic functions to serve in the process of perceiving the world, and probably play an important, though poorly-understood, role in much of our normal process of perception, whether visual, auditory or tactile.

Working memory
This subsystem of human memory is used to hold and manipulate information in the process of performing other tasks, such as reasoning and understanding. For example, in order to understand a sentence it is necessary to hold information from the beginning of the sentence and integrate it with what comes later. Similarly, if you are asked to multiply 27 by 5 in your head, you need to multiply the 7 by the 5, remember the 5 and carry the 3, then multiply the 2 by the 5 add the 3 and so forth. Remembering to carry 3 is something that is essential to performing the task at the time, but does not need to be stored subsequently. Working memory is assumed to be the system responsible for such temporary storage.

Long-term memory
This is the subsystem responsible for holding information over a long period, whether it is a recollection of personal experience, or knowing the meaning of words or how to get from one room of your home to another. It is assumed that this system stores information in a relatively permanent way.

◄ **Migrating snow geese and maypole dancers behave in patterns established long before they were born. In the instinctive behavior of the geese, the "memory" is genetically determined, while each generation of dancers must learn and remember afresh. With sensory memory, however, the visual or other system uses changing incoming information to create a relatively stable "image". A similar principle of brief storage underlies the audience's perception of a movie film.**

The psychology of memory

Some of the most convincing evidence for the existence of distinct systems of working and long-term memory comes from studying people who have specific memory faults following brain damage. Sufferers of the "amnesic syndrome" appear to have lost the capacity to acquire new information. This syndrome is often associated with damage to the temporal lobes of the brain, or to a system linking other parts of the brain, the hippocampus, the mammillary bodies and the frontal lobes. While most brain damage leads to somewhat diffuse and multiple deficits, it sometimes leads to very profound amnesia, with otherwise unimpaired intellectual function. Such an individual has little or no record of ongoing activity, and will not know where he is, the date, what he had for breakfast or who is the Prime Minister. Others show the converse pattern. Their capacity to repeat a telephone number is likely to be limited to two figures, yet their long-term learning ability may be normal. The existence of two very different subgroups of amnesiacs supports a distinction between long-term and working memory.

Not all long-term learning is impaired in amnesiacs. They are capable of learning a wide and varied range of tasks, including motor skills such as typing, solving visual puzzles, and remembering words, provided their memory is tested in a particular way. Suppose you are asked to remember the word "pencil". Your memory can be tested in a number of ways: being asked to recall a word you have been told, being given a number of words, for example ruler, picture, pencil, ink and asked to recognize the one that was presented, or being given the first few letters penc... and asked to generate a word that would fit that pattern. Amnesiacs are very bad on the first two tests, but normal on the third – the correct word seems to "pop up" automatically since it has been "primed" by the earlier presentation. What amnesiacs appear to lose is not the capacity to acquire new information, but the ability to recollect, to re-experience it in retrospect. Such evidence indicates two types of long-term learning. One ("declarative learning"), impaired in amnesiacs, appears to offer a kind of window on the past. However, the learning of a wide range of skills remains possible, suggesting the existence of a separate "procedural" system that, unlike declarative learning, does not depend on the temporal lobes and hippocampus.

▶ *These are some of the objects used by Mortimer Mishkin and colleagues to test memory in monkeys. It is a comparatively easy task for a monkey to recognize in each pair the item he has seen only once before.*

▼ *Holograms provide a good physical analogy for the process of remembering, storing simultaneously many different images within the same system, then producing the whole image when provided with only a part of it. Like the brain, this holographic system, developed at the California Institute of Technology for pattern recognition, performs a recognition-and-retrieval task by the simultaneous operation of an array of simple components.*

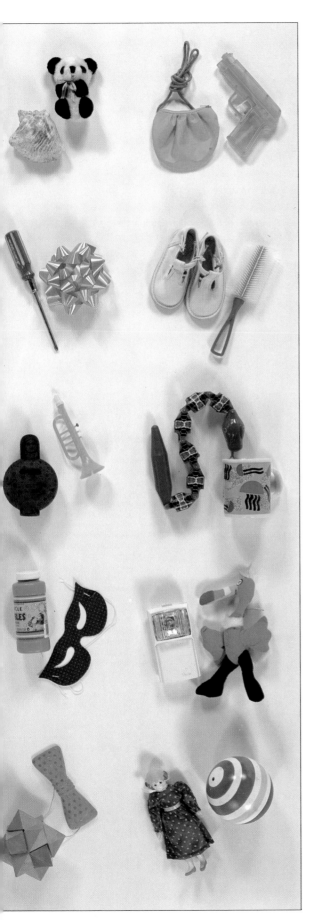

Future understanding of memory systems.

We know very little about sensory memory systems at present, but over the next few decades shall probably reach understanding of some of them in considerable detail, as an integral part of the memory process. The study of people with specific sensory memory defects will also probably tell us more about the relationship between perception and memory.

As regards working memory, a number of subsidiary or "slave" systems have been identified, one responsible for holding spoken information, another for maintaining and manipulating visual images. The speech-based system is probably the best understood component of working memory; there will be probably be a similar development in our understanding of the imagery system over the next few years. We should also know a good deal more about how these systems are interrelated. At present the relationship is assumed to occur through a controlling system known as the Central Executive. It has been suggested that a breakdown in the operation of this system is one of the major features of senile dementia. This system may well play an important part in the functions that we know as consciousness and the will.

Long-term memory will probably have been further subdivided. Procedural learning will probably still be regarded as a separate system, and "declarative" learning will have been analyzed into subdomains rather than separate systems. We shall know rather more about the subdomain of long-term memory that stores information about ourselves, our autobiographical memory. We shall also probably have a much better grasp of the process whereby individual experiences are gradually combined over time so as to produce a residue of knowledge of the world.

Finally, there will probably be a much more detailed theory of the process of learning. Much work on the psychology of memory over the last 40 years has been influenced by the computer analogy. However, the machines that have so far been available have operated on a serial basis in which one operation follows another. The new generation of much more powerful parallel computers (◆ page 242) is already beginning to have an impact on our theories of learning and memory.

▲ Even the best computers cannot beat players of the caliber of world champion Gary Kasparov (above), but they can beat most players. However, they do so by systematic analysis, whereas the player relies on memory processes that are closer to pattern recognition.

▼ Clive Wearing, a gifted musician who became densely amnesic following brain damage produced by a viral infection. He nevertheless retains his musical abilities and can play the harpsichord or conduct a choir apparently perfectly. This illustrates the way in which memory can be undersood as a number of separable systems which rely on different areas and capacities of the brain.

The physical basis of memory

Memories almost certainly have a physical basis in the brain. The neural changes that occur as a result of learning are often called memory traces. Where do these occur in the brain, in which precise neural structures, and how do they come about, and in what form? The study of brain-damaged human subjects has led to progress in answering the first of these questions, which has served to complement our understanding of the psychological basis of memory (◀ page 190). This evidence has strengthened the view that humans use different types of memory processes that are somehow coordinated by other systems to optimize our performance in diverse circumstances. It has also led to suggestions that learning and memory may result from basic neural processes which augment the capabilities of certain regions of the brain that are specialized for particular functions, for example, adjusting balance, or analyzing complex visual input. According to this reductionist view, there may be no brain region which is specialized for memory *per se*. Instead, this function may arise from the fundamental properties of the specialized nerve cells, or neurons, and the way in which they interact in interconnected arrangements or networks in various brain regions.

Any understanding of the way in which memory traces are formed is likely to depend upon an understanding of the way in which neurons normally communicate. When two neurons (nerve cells) interact across the small gap (synapse) that divides them, the pre-synaptic cell may be "fired" as a result of electrical events (action potentials) that are conducted down the neuron. The action potentials are propagated as a result of the opening and closing of channels in the nerve membrane for certain electrically-charged ions. When the action potential reaches the end of the neuron (or nerve terminal), a chemical neurotransmitter substance is released from the terminal, and this stimulates the post-synaptic cell at special areas of the membrane called receptors. The binding of the transmitter to its receptor leads to a further sequence of chemical and electrical events which generate an action potential in the post-synaptic cell. In this way activity in one neuron is propagated across the synapse, or neuronal junction, to the next cell.

Hebb's cell-assembly theory

The first major theory of the physical basis of memory tried to link what was known about the structure and development of the brain to the problem of how a particular sensory experience exerted a relatively permanent effect, outlasting the period of sensory experience. In 1949, the Canadian psychologist Donald O. Hebb proposed that groups of interconnected neurons, or "cell-assemblies" exhibited reverberating patterns of electrical discharge which persisted after the stimuli initiating the discharge were no longer present. Hebb's hypothesis was that this transient reverberation led to structural changes in the neurons that biased them to fire in the same way on future occasions.

There are several lines of indirect evidence for Hebb's theory. Disruptive electrical stimulation (such as electroconvulsive shock) administered soon after a training experience can disrupt its subsequent retention in both experimental animals and humans, whereas older experiences may remain intact, suggesting that the recent and more distant memories exist in different forms. Interference with basic biochemical processes of protein or nucleic acid synthesis has been convincingly shown to impair long-term memory, probably by affecting the structural changes in neurons or by altering neurotransmitter metabolism that may occur as a result of learning.

▲ *Canadian psychologist Donald Hebb distinguished two kinds of memory, one transient and based on electrical activity, the other based on more permanent neural changes. His ideas have become increasingly influential in recent years, with the development of computer programs capable of simulating his proposed model.*

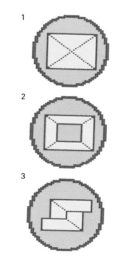

▲ *This key to the main diagram shows the sodium channels in the nerve membrane which open in response to a positive charge (2), admitting sodium ions. They then go into a closed-and-inactive form (3). Once the cell's negative charge has been restored, they revert to the closed-but-ready-to-open form (1).*

▶ *The cerebral cortex is the outer layer of the brain and the seat of the higher mental processes. The nerve cells (neurons), each of which has many dendrites, axons and fibrils, provide connections with other brain cells. Long-term potentiation or LTP (◊ page 195) leads to long-term enhancement of the action potential responses taking place in the nerve cells.*

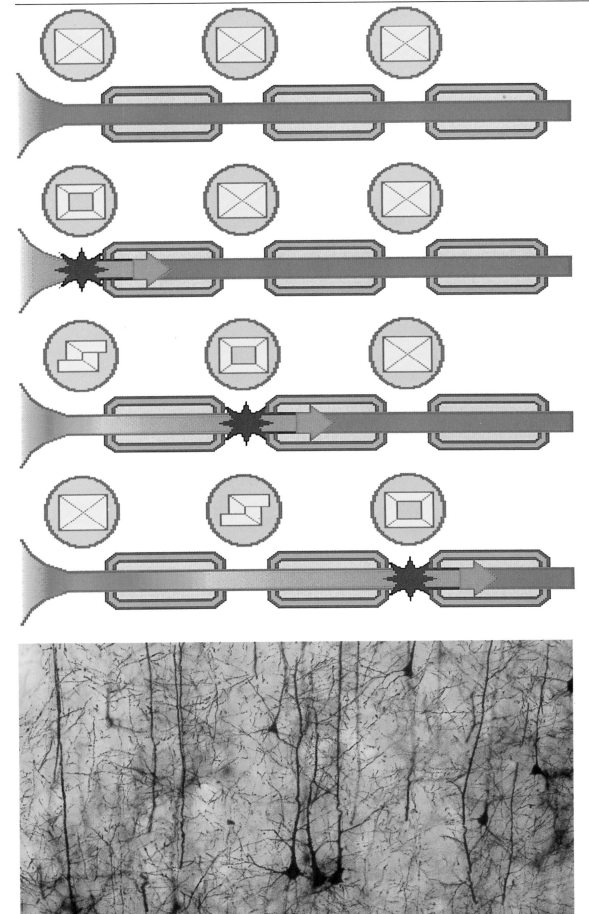

◄ This diagram of a neuron shows an action potential traveling down its length and the effect it has on the sodium channels. The action potential is transient because after a few milliseconds the automatic closure of the channels prevents more sodium ions from coming into the cell. The membrane pumps can then work to restore the negative potential and thus prevent the nerve cell going into a spasm of firing. When the action potential reaches the neuron terminal, voltage-gated ion channels open to admit calcium ions, which trigger the release of the neurotransmitter.

194

Scientists are developing various models of how sensory experience can lead to changes in brain tissue and to learning itself

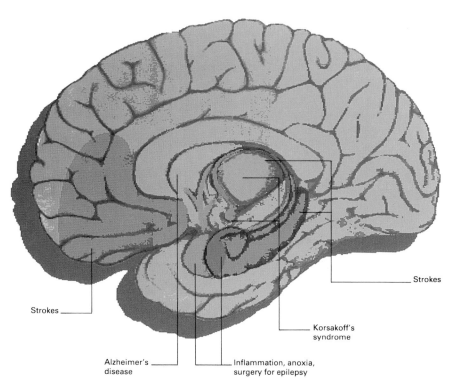

Strokes

Strokes

Korsakoff's
syndrome

Alzheimer's
disease

Inflammation, anoxia,
surgery for epilepsy

▲ Sites in the brain where
disease and other causes
result in loss of memory in
humans. People who are
densely amnesic tend to
have damage in one or
more of these areas.
However, these diseases
may also produce deficits
other than in learning, while
damage elsewhere in the
brain may lead to definite,
though less dramatic,
impairment in the capacity
for new learning.

► Different cells in the
cerebral cortex respond
to bars presented at
different orientations
(right). Voltage-sensitive
dyes are used to color-code
the columns of cells within
the cortex, illustrating
the way in which different
columns respond to
different orientations.

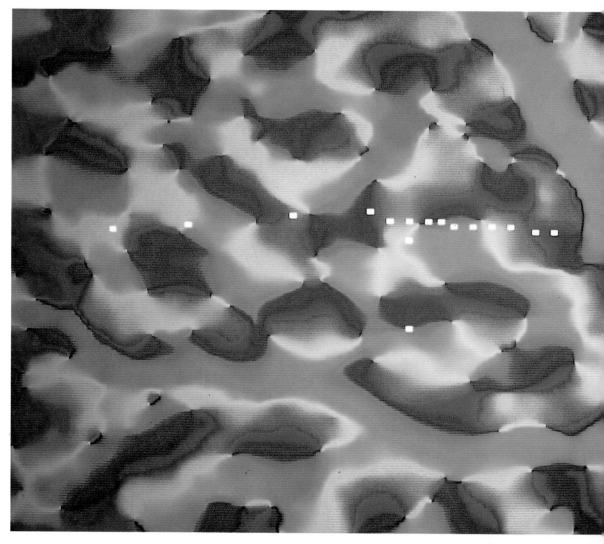

◄ A rat learning a water maze seeks a platform just below the surface of cloudy water. Rats rapidly learn to find this, and subsequently remember its location. Rats given a drug that impairs long-term potentiation (LTP) are slow to learn this task. The effect seems to be confined to spatial learning, since other learning tasks are unimpaired.

Long-term potentiation (LTP)

One of the essential ideas put forward by Donald O. Hebb (◄ page 192) is that the strength of a synaptic connection increases if the use of that particular synapse has contributed to the occurrence of action potentials in the post-synaptic cell. This has proved to be very difficult to test in the mammalian brain because of the complexity of its synaptic arrangements: However, an electrophysiological phenomenon called long-term potentiation (LTP), studied in slices of the mammalian hippocampus, has provided some clues. LTP occurs when a single intense burst of electrical stimulation administered to one of the neural inputs to the hippocampus leads to a long-term enhancement of efficiency of neurotransmission at the synapses of that region, so that subsequent responses to normal stimulation of its inputs are greatly enhanced. Scientists have used this as a simple model of how sensory experiences can lead to long-lasting effects on neural tissue, and even of learning itself.

There is currently a good deal of excitement and controversy about how LTP actually occurs. Here, we will discuss two of the major theories. Gary Lynch and Michael Baudry of the University of California at Irvine have proposed that the potentiating stimulation initiates a sequence of biochemical steps that leads to an irreversible increase in the number of effective receptors for the neurotransmitter glutamate on the post-synaptic cells that mediate the enhanced synaptic response. This is in essential agreement with Hebb's theory. The potentiating stimulation is held to trigger an influx into the neuron of calcium ions, thus activating an enzyme that breaks down proteins which normally block the access of glutamate to its receptors.

A rather different point of view has been advanced by Aryeh Routtenberg of the Northwestern University, Illinois. He argues that the addition of phosphate or methyl groups to brain proteins that compose the post-synaptic neuronal membrane will alter their configuration and so cause long-lasting changes in firing by the opening and closing of different ion channels. Routtenberg has amassed evidence (including some of that used in the Lynch-Baudry theory) suggesting that the crucial event in LTP is the addition of phosphate groups to a protein called F1, rather than the unmasking of glutamate receptors.

Thirty years from now, we shall probably understand the exact biochemical mechanisms underlying LTP, but what will be the relevance of this to the understanding of memory? There is already some evidence that makes the link plausible. Drugs that antagonize the specific class of glutamate receptors implicated in LTP also impair spatial learning in rats. Tissue from the regions of the brain that are involved in certain types of visual memory in trained monkeys is especially rich in the protein F1. Within the next 30 years we may well be beginning to link many forms of memory in different parts of the brain to biochemical mechanisms similar to those implicated in LTP. There is a problem of interpretation however, because a simple correlation between LTP and memory does not necessarily imply that one is caused by the other. This problem has driven other investigators to study preparations much simpler than those based on the mammalian brain, where the behavioral, as well as the biochemical and biophysical events occurring during learning can be studied simultaneously and so the significance of the biochemical changes for memory and learning can be assessed more directly. This approach has focused on learning in invertebrate animals such as the sea hare, Aplysia (◆ page 196).

▲ Dr Gary Lynch of the University of California's Center for the Neurobiology of Learning and Memory at Irvine. Lynch's view of the mechanism that underlies long-term potentiation has much in common with Hebb's earlier theory. Although today we have a much better understanding of the underlying neurochemistry, the search for the neural mechanisms underlying learning remains a highly-controversial and very exciting research area.

Sea hares and garden slugs feature largely in studies of the basis of learning

Habituation and sensitization

Eric Kandel and his associates at Columbia University, New York, have begun to elucidate the mechanisms underlying very simple forms of learning in the sea hare *Aplysia*. The mechanisms include habituation (reduction of response to a repeated stimulus), sensitization (augmentation of response by the previous presentation of a strong stimulus), and associative learning processes such as classical conditioning. Sensitization occurs in *Aplysia* when a noxious stimulus applied to its tail enhances the gill-withdrawal that is the mollusk's normal response to the touch of its siphon. The critical neuronal changes causing this simple form of behavior have been shown to result from the release of the neurotransmitter serotonin onto sensory neurons from a presynaptic neural input that is triggered by the sensitizing stimulus. Serotonin activates an enzyme, adenylate cyclase, which indirectly enhances the influx of calcium that normally accompanies an action potential, by lessening the flow of potassium ions that help to repolarize the neuron. Hence the action potentials of the neuron are both greater and longer-lasting. Related mechanisms may explain both the form of learning known as habituation and classical conditioning, whereby the organism learns to make a reflex response to a stimulus.

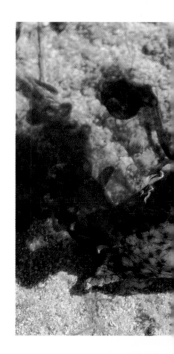

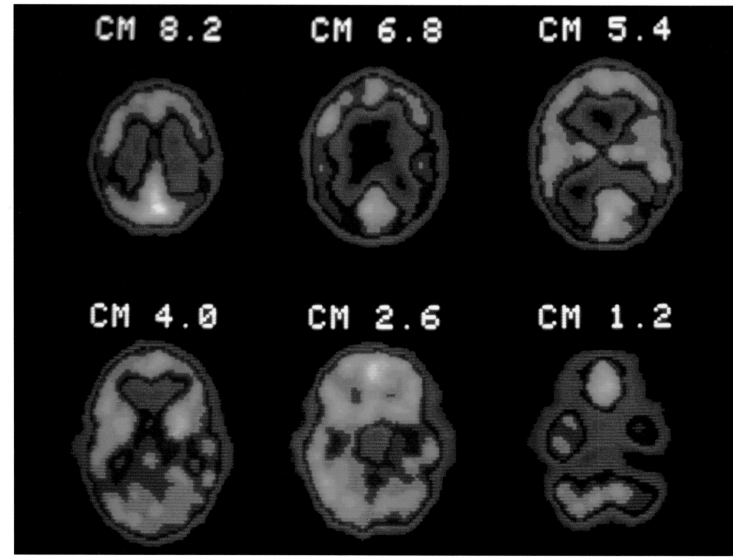

The observations with *Aplysia* are very significant for a number of reasons. First, it can be noted that they have provided little support for Hebb's postulate (◀ page 192) that learning must involve post-synaptic changes in reverberating circuits; pre-synaptic changes in a simple network appear sufficient in this case. Was Hebb then wrong, or can both pre- and post-synaptic changes occur, perhaps in different phyla of animals, with different forms of learning?

Second, the fact that similar biochemical mechanisms can be invoked to explain habituation and classical conditioning suggests that more complex processes can be built up from relatively simple neuronal mechanisms that are present in the mammalian brain, as well as in the simple invertebrate sea slug.

Third, the findings are significant from a genetic viewpoint. Single-gene mutants of the fruit fly *Drosophila* (called dunce) have been discovered which are deficient in classical conditioning and also in the production of the serotonin receptor, or the calcium-dependent adenylate cyclase. Increased understanding of genetic control over the alterations in synaptic proteins that accompany learning will perhaps within the next 300 years help to answer one of the most difficult questions concerning the relative permanence of memory traces: what is the relationship between changes in synaptic proteins, which have a relatively short half-life, and the much longer persistence of memories? One speculation is that the synaptic changes are maintained by the process of gene induction, which turns on the production of particular proteins for long periods, possibly permanently. Test-tube studies have established that the synthesis of substances such as neurotransmitters can be genetically induced, but the operation of such mechanisms in the context of learning has not yet been demonstrated.

One of the tasks of the next 300 years will be to test whether the types of mechanisms for learning and memory that have been shown to exist in the humble *Aplysia* also operate in the mammalian brain. This investigation will be aided by drawing up a much more detailed "wiring diagram" of the mammalian brain, such as we already have for *Aplysia*, and by developing new procedures that allow the dynamic monitoring of brain activity in these well-defined circuits involving learning and memory.

There are already indications that this monitoring is possible for the simple, classically-conditioned, eye-blink reflex of the rabbit, by using implanted electrodes in the key structures of the brain's motor system, such as the cerebellum. We shall obviously have to develop much more sensitive techniques for noninvasive imaging of brain activity in humans than we have at present. However, there are several reasons why it is difficult even to conceive of solutions at this stage. One of these is that learning and memory in mammals may well involve processing that is distributed simultaneously in several different parts of the brain, perhaps in parallel with other, unrelated activities. This is probably true, even for the rabbit's eye-blink reflex.

A second potential problem stems from the possibility that the types of learning studied in "subhuman" animals may only be primitive manifestations of human capacities. The apparently automatic phenomena of "priming" or procedural learning in human memory may well result from conditioning mechanisms that can be well-understood from a reductionist perspective based on animal studies. However, it is much less clear what relevance the biochemical mechanisms described above might have for the more complex aspects of human memory studied by cognitive psychology (◀ page 190).

◀ *The sea hare Aplysia, releasing poisonous dye. This relatively simple marine organism has been used as the subject in the study of a variety of forms of learning by Eric Kandel and his associates at Columbia University, New York.*

◀ *Six PET (positron emission tomography) scan images of sections through the brain of a patient suffering from Alzheimer's disease, in which both impaired memory and neurochemical changes are a marked feature. A tracer labeled with a short-lived radioactive isotope is used to indicate the ongoing activity in various regions of the brain. In the case of Alzheimer patients, activity progressively reduces as the brain deteriorates. Understanding and possibly reversing these changes may one day allow the disease to be treated effectively.*

The benefits and problems of understanding

In 300 years we should have an adequate understanding of the psychology of sensory memory and know a great deal about the relationship between the slave systems (♦ page 191) and working memory, the systems of speech perception and production, and of visual perception and spatial manipulation. In the case of the Central Executive, we may have found ways in which the concept has become obsolete, since the various slave systems may themselves be able to interact in such a way as to produce their own overall control mechanisms. Such mechanisms ought by then to be presenting us with at least some plausible models of consciousness and the operation of the will. An understanding of the "will" has enormous potential for helping people cope with the addictions to tobacco, alcohol and other drugs that are such a major current source of illness and misery. Such knowledge may also, of course raise major ethical problems as to how it should be used.

The practical benefits of a biochemical understanding of memory processes are likely to be enormous, particularly for treating amnesia and dementia of the Alzheimer type. Both of these conditions result from a loss of nerve cells, as well as neurotransmitters (many of which are yet to be identified). A few studies have shown small beneficial effects of drugs that restore or stimulate the depleted neurotransmitter substances. In individuals suffering from a loss of central nerve cells, restoring memory function will obviously be more difficult because the basic neural networks will be deranged or even absent. Some hope for them is provided by recent startling research showing that it is possible to transplant neural cells into the brain and perhaps reform functional circuitry.

If certain drugs are effective in treating impaired memory, there seems no reason in principle why they could not be used to boost normal functioning, though their use for memory and learning in education would also pose society enormous ethical problems. It would be most unwise to base new educational strategies solely on such artificial aids, which should form only one component of a broadly-based applied science of education.

What would we need to know to have a proper science of education? First of all we would have to understand what we are trying to achieve, whether to convey factual information, perceptuo-motor skills, problem-solving strategies or attitudes to the world. At present, our educational system tends to teach a mixture of these, with the particular blend being determined largely by tradition. In the Third World, many receive no education at all. In the more developed world, many spend their childhood and youth reluctantly acquiring information which they often regard as irrelevant to their real needs. Perhaps in 300 years' time we will have worked out what should be taught and have understood enough of human learning and memory to ensure that learning is both an efficient and a rewarding activity.

▼ **Throughout the world millions of children spend thousands of hours attempting to learn whatever their elders feel is appropriate, like this class in Szechuan, China. Perhaps we shall evolve psychological techniques that make learning easy and enjoyable, possibly aided by memory-enhancing drugs. But the more effective our capacity to teach, the more questions raised as to what should be taught.**

What is special about human language...Apes that use human sign language...Lateralization of the brain...A case of language deprivation...Localization of language functions in the brain...Dyslexia and dysgraphia...Psycholinguistics...The use of computers in research

Human language enables us to speak about anything, at any time or place. A comparatively small number of grammatical rules is used to combine a finite number of words to produce what is effectively an infinite number of sentences. This enables us to express any thought in either written or spoken language.

Talking to the animals

Other animals have communication systems too, but none has the power of human language. For example, bees can communicate the position of a source of pollen by "dancing" to other members of the hive. Ants communicate using a heightened sense of smell, with chemicals known as pheromones. Moving up the evolutionary scale, monkeys and other primates can communicate a great deal about the location and nature of predators using various calls. Dolphins also have a complex communication system based on sound. However, all of these are weaker than human language for two reasons. First, they are all tied to the "here and now". Humans can talk about abstract events that happened in a remote time and place. Second, our language system is much more creative. For example, all that bees can communicate with their "dancing" is the distance and direction of a source of pollen.

The United States' linguist Noam Chomsky suggests that there is something fundamentally special about human language. He argues that it is innate to all humans, and species-specific. In other words, it is a special faculty that has evolved only in humans and which sets us apart from all other animals.

▼ *Testing the idea that language is species-specific to humans, the psychologist Roger Fouts teaches AMESLAN to a chimpanzee called Lucy. AMESLAN (AMErican Sign LANguage) is used by deaf people to communicate and is as powerful as spoken language. Results so far with apes have been promising but inconclusive.*

▲ *Worker honey bees can communicate information about the distance and direction of pollen sources to other bees in the hive by "dancing" on the vertical surface of the wax honeycomb. The dance can only communicate this information, but although not genuinely creative, it has evolved to achieve this goal very efficiently.*

Teaching human language to apes

The mouths, lips, and tongues of apes are unable to produce the sorts of sounds needed to form words, but apes are very good with their hands. Most of the attempts to teach chimpanzees human language – thereby testing Chomsky's idea that language is unique to humans – have involved a sign language known as AMESLAN (AMErican Sign LANguage). The most famous of these attempts involved a chimpanzee called Washoe. At the age of five years she had learned 132 signs, and was even able to combine individual "words" together to form "sentences". On one occasion she saw a duck and, not having a symbol for duck, she combined two signs she did know to sign "water bird". However, success has been limited. At the moment important research is being carried out on whether mother apes which have been taught sign language will spontaneously teach it to their young. If this happens, communities of apes will grow up, all using sign language to talk to each other and to us. In this way, in the next 30 years we can expect to learn a great deal about how apes think.

"Feral children", found and rehabilitated in their teens, typically never fully learn our language

The site of the language faculty in the brain

The brain is divided into two halves which look physically fairly similar. Language is processed in only one side (hemispere) of the brain. For 97 percent of right-handed people, and 60 percent of left-handed, this is the left hemisphere. For the majority of us the left side of our brains is said to be dominant. The left and right hemispheres of the outer convoluted layer of the brain (cortex), do different things. The brain is said to be lateralized. As a broad generalization, in left hemisphere-dominant people, the left side is concerned with analytical processing of material which is essentially time-based in nature. The right-hand side is more concerned with the processing of spatial information. The major difference is that the language faculty is localized in the left hemisphere. That is, to some extent specific language processes occupy specific locations in the brain.

This localization has a major consequence for adults. If there is damage to certain parts of the left hemisphere, either through disorders such as strokes, or wounds such as those caused by bullets, language is impaired. A disorder of speech is termed aphasia, and a disorder of written language dyslexia. The language disorder is worse immediately after the injury, but the abilities improve as the language processes recover a little. Exactly how this happens is not really known at present. It might imply reorganization of our language processes, and it might also involve a little regeneration of the neurons or brain cells that have been damaged. Generally, neurons do not recover much and are usually not replaced. One of the advances in the near future might be finding a way to encourage adult nerve cells to grow again. This might be possible if the chemical or other processes responsible for embryo development can be utilized in fully-matured brains. Another possibility is that neurons might be transplanted either from somewhere else in the brain, or even from a different brain. In the next 30 years techniques of micro-neurosurgery will certainly improve. Brain tissue has already been implanted to treat Parkinson's disease.

One consequence of this limitation on the adult brain to recover is that brain damage of any considerable extent leads to permanent impairment of language. However, this is not the case with children. Their brains recover much more easily from damage than do the brains of adults. If the left hemisphere of a child's brain is damaged then the right hand side can take over its functioning. There have been cases of the complete surgical removal of the left cortex of very young children's brains, with the final outcome that the right-hand side takes over and the child develops language as usual. In an adult, such an operation would result in the complete loss of linguistic abilities.

The older the child gets, the harder it becomes for this switch to take place. Complete recovery can take place if the child is under the age of four, but there is some plasticity (ability to recover or alter function) usually to the age of puberty. This has led the United States' biologist Eric Lenneberg to suggest that there is a critical period of language development. His "critical period" hypothesis is that it is necessary to give children linguistic input before full and permanent lateralization has occurred. To acquire normal language abilities it is necessary to have linguistic input until the age of at least four. Studies with normal children of deaf parents have shown that it is not sufficient merely to listen. The speech must be interactive, as if part of a conversation. It is not impossible to acquire language past this age, but there will be restrictions on what can be acquired. Syntax is particularly impaired, probably because the left hemisphere cannot develop normally.

▼ *F. Truffaut's movie "L'Enfant sauvage" (The Wild Child) is based on the true story of a feral child. Feral children have been abandoned by their parents at an early age and left in the wild. The children are typically in their early teens when rescued. They do not learn language despite attempts to teach them. However, we do not know whether the children were otherwise normal when they were abandoned. Perhaps their mothers left them because they were autistic, in which case they would have had difficulties acquiring language anyway. The only case that does offer some understanding of feral children is that of the girl "Genie".*

▶ *The most important parts of the surface of the brain ("cortex") used in language tasks are called Broca's and Wernicke's areas (▶ page 203). When we speak a word we have just heard, neural impulses travel from the ear via the auditory nerve to the auditory cortex, then to Wernicke's area, through the arcuate fasciculus to Broca's area, to the facial area of the motor cortex which controls the muscles of our lips, tongue and larynx (voicebox). When we pronounce a written word, neural impulses are transmitted from the visual cortex through the angular gyrus to Wernicke's area, where the above mechanisms take over.*

Speaking a heard word

Motor cortex
Arcuate fasciculus
Broca's area
Primary auditory area
Wernicke's area

Speaking a written word

Motor cortex
Broca's area
Wernicke's area
Primary visual area
Angular gyrus

The case of the girl "Genie"

There is only one clear case where we know that a child was normal before a prolonged period of linguistic deprivation. This is a girl called "Genie", who for most of her life had been locked in a small room by her father, and deprived of all speech input. When rescued she did not speak at all. Genie was found when she was 13 years, 9 months old, at which time she was an unsocialized, primitive human being, emotionally disturbed, unlearned, and without language. She had been taken into protective custody by the police, and on November 4, 1970, was admitted into the Children's Hospital of Los Angeles for evaluation with a tentative diagnosis of severe malnutrition. She remained in the rehabilitation center of the hospital until August 13, 1971. At that time she entered a foster home where she has been living ever since as a member of the family.

The tragic and bizarre story which was uncovered revealed that for most of her life Genie suffered physical and social restriction, nutritional neglect, and extreme experiential deprivation. There is evidence that from the age of 20 months until shortly before admission to the hospital Genie had been isolated in a small closed room, tied into a potty chair where she remained most or all hours of the day, sometimes overnight. Given long-term remedial treatment, Genie learned to talk. However, there are clear differences between Genie's speech and that of normal people her age. In particular, she has more difficulty than normal in acquiring grammatical rules. While her vocabulary is larger than that of children with similar syntactic abilities, she uses no question words or demonstratives (words used to indicate pointing). The evidence suggests that Genie relies upon her right hemisphere for word ordering.

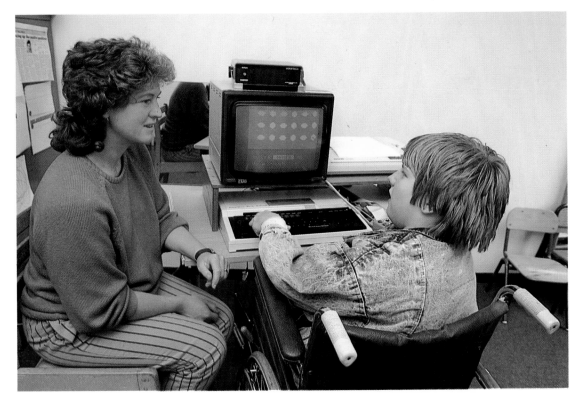

◄ Many techniques are now available for helping people with language difficulties. Speech therapists can help children who are having problems by visual training. Variations of different colored shapes are displayed on a computer screen to help children learn the patterns of language. Similar techniques can help children with developmental dyslexia in learning to read. It is even possible to improve the speech of brain-damaged aphasics (◊ page 203) by encouraging them to "sing". This seems to involve the right hemisphere as well as the left.

Reading disorders

Brain damage can give rise to disorders of reading and writing, called dyslexia and dysgraphia. Most research so far has been centered upon dyslexia, of which there are two main categories. If there is obvious brain damage, the dyslexia is said to be acquired. If there is no obvious damage, it is said to be developmental. Developmental dyslexia is now usually diagnosed in childhood when an otherwise apparently normal child has specific disability associated with reading, writing and spelling. In many ways this condition resembles full-blown acquired dyslexia, though often it is less severe. There is much research being carried out on developmental dyslexia, but no comprehensive theory of its cause. It has been suggested that it reflects a more general deficit in the operation of the left hemisphere. In the near future we can certainly expect advances in its diagnosis and, in the more distant future, in its treatment. There are three main types of acquired dyslexia, characterized by particular types of error when the patient is given a word or some text and asked to read it out aloud.

Those with surface dyslexia are able to read out non-words and words which have regular letter-to-sound correspondence (like CAVE), but have great difficulty with words which have an irregular letter-to-sound correspondence (like HAVE). When these words are read they are often over-regularized: HAVE is spoken as though it rhymes with CAVE.

In phonological dyslexia, people are able to read all words, but are unable to read non-words. To explain these different patterns of symptoms, a model of reading has been proposed which suggests that there are two routes from the printed letters of a word to the access of its meaning. Because of this the model is usually referred to as the dual-route model of reading.

In deep dyslexia, the type of error made here is the production of words which are related in meaning to the one presented but sound completely different. Examples are saying TULIP for DAFFODIL, and PICTURE for ARTIST. Deep dyslexics are also extremely bad at reading non-words such as NARST. Deep dyslexia is usually the result of extensive left hemisphere damage, and is often accompanied by Broca's aphasia (♦ page 203). It has been suggested that the semantic errors (paralexias) made by deep dyslexics might be due to the operation of the right hemisphere in reading.

▼ **Abnormal electrical activity in the front left brain of a boy with developmental dyslexia, or difficulty in reading. This image is produced by brain electrical activity mapping (BEAM). This measures the difference in electrical activity between normal and abnormal brains.**

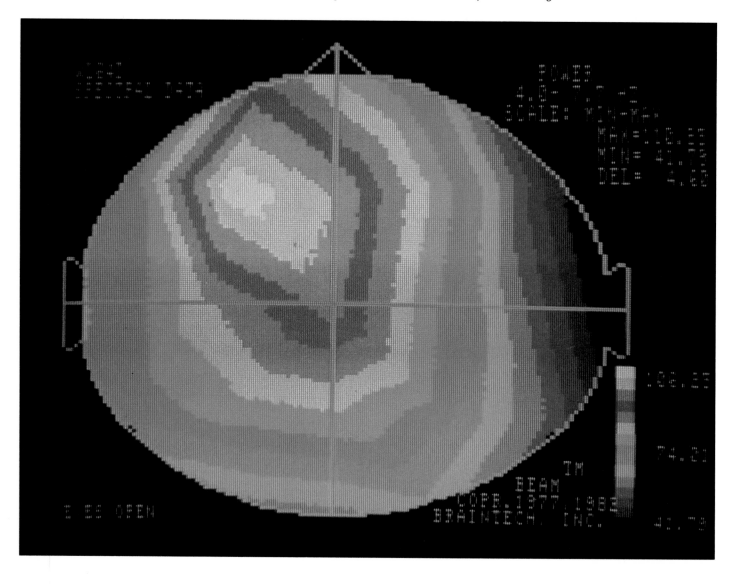

Brain localization of function in adult language

We can point to even more specific areas of the brain that are concerned with language processing. Most of our knowledge of these areas comes from the study of the speech of brain-damaged people. Some caution should therefore be applied to the interpretation, because we cannot be sure that the language system of an uninjured brain works in the same way. There is some evidence, for example, that even in adults some recovery of the damaged system occurs.

The French neurologist Paul Broca (1824-1880) observed that damage to a particular area of the left hemisphere called the left frontal lobe resulted in a particular type of speech defect. This region has since come to be known as Broca's area (◀ page 201), and damage limited to that area gives rise to Broca's aphasia. It is characterized in particular by slow, ponderous speech, where syntax is very simplified or totally absent. Broca's aphasics have great difficulty in articulating, but have little difficulty understanding speech.

The German neurologist Carl Wernicke (1848-1905) observed that damage to an area of the left cortex somewhat to the rear of Broca's area called the temporal-parietal cortex resulted in a different type of impairment. This region has been labeled Wernicke's area (◀ page 201), and the associated aphasia Wernicke's aphasia. It is characterized by rapid and fluent speech where the syntax appears unimpaired, but where the speech is often meaningless. Wernicke's aphasics often have great difficulty in producing the names of objects (anomia). Their speech in general suffers from a problem of lexical retrieval – they are unable to produce the sounds of the appropriate words. "Jargon aphasics" get round this difficulty by making words up. The comprehension ability of Wernicke's aphasics is greatly impaired.

Based upon these data, a model of the relationship between the brain and language production was developed by the United States' neuropsychologist Norman Geschwind (1926-1984). The basic principle of this model is that language production primarily flows from the back to the front of the brain (◀ page 201). The model suggests why damage to different areas should result in different types of aphasia. If patients have damage to Wernicke's area only, their comprehension will be impaired, as will their ability to produce meaningful speech. However, because Broca's region is intact, what speech they do produce will be perfectly fluent. Patients with damage to Broca's area but not to Wernicke's area will have difficulties in articulation and sequencing their speech, but will have virtually normal comprehension. Damage to the arcuate fasciculus will not impair either comprehension or articulation, but will interfere with the repetition of speech.

Finally, this model correctly predicts that following damage to one of these areas the language system might eventually sort out an alternative, more indirect route between the intact areas. Thus aphasic patients should eventually show some recovery of the damaged functions with time. But because this model relies so heavily upon the localization of specific functions in relatively small areas, it has been strongly criticized. Electrical stimulation of these regions does not always interrupt speech at all, let alone in the way predicted in this model. Also, there is no clear distinction between patients with difficulties in understanding and not in expression, and vice versa. Such clear-cut patients are just not found. For example, even Broca's aphasics do not have perfect comprehension of complex sentences. Nor does the model account for the role of subcortical brain regions. But although the Geschwind model is far from perfect, it has been influential.

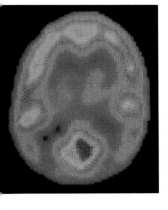
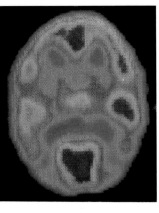

▲ In positron computed tomography (PCT) a small amount of injected radioactive glucose travels through the bloodstream to the brain. There it concentrates where there is most activity. These two images show which parts of our brain are active (red) in our normal resting state (top), and when we are listening to music (below). There is greater activity in the right hemisphere for music, in the left hemisphere for language.

▲ This gamma camera (GC) scan compares the amount of blood flow in a resting brain (top) with that of a person reading aloud (bottom). When reading, the brain requires more oxygen (shown by brighter colors), especially in the front part of the brain appearing on the right and the brain-stem area on the left.

Psychological research

The division of psychology concerned with investigating how people produce, understand, and remember language is called psycholinguistics. Psycholinguistics began in the early 1960s. It was originally based upon Noam Chomsky's work on grammar, in which the idea of transformations is central. A transformation is a way of taking a grammatically simple sentence and turning it into a more complex one. For example, the active sentence "The cat chased the dog" can be turned into the passive sentence "The dog was chased by the cat" by applying the "passivization transformation" rule. Or we could turn it into a question ("Did the cat chase the dog?") by a "question transformation". Using both the passive and question transformations on the original sentence would produce "Was the dog chased by the cat?" Psycholinguists such as the American psychologist George Miller thought that the more transformations a sentence had in it, the harder and slower it would be to produce or understand. Early experiments showed that indeed the more transformations there were in a sentence, the longer subjects would take to decode it into its simple form. In addition, subjects were also able to remember fewer numbers at the same time. However, it soon became apparent that the syntax and number of transformations were not the most important factor. For example, it is much easier to get these results if we use sentences like "The dog was chased by the cat". Here if we swap the two nouns round to produce "The cat was chased by the dog" the sentence still sounds plausible. This is not the case with "The flowers were watered by the girl" where the reversed sentence "The girl was watered by the flowers" is definitely rather odd. With this sort of sentence there is no difference between the times it takes us to understand the active and passive versions. Subjects can work out who is doing what to what just by looking at the sentence and relying upon common sense or pragmatic or world knowledge. There is probably no need for elaborate syntactic analysis in this case.

More recent psycholinguistic experiments have been concerned with the interactions between these different types of information – syntactic, semantic, and pragmatic. They can be seen operating in the recognition of both printed and spoken words, and the understanding and production of whole sentences. For example, recently psycholinguists have looked at how we read words. One popular type of experiment is called the "lexical decision task", where either a word, such as NURSE, or a nonword, such as NERSE, is flashed on a computer screen. Subjects have to press one button if they think they saw a word and another if they think they saw a nonword, and the time it takes them to do this accurately is measured. In naming experiments the time it takes the subject to pronounce the word or nonword is measured. Experiments like these have told us a lot about how our mental dictionary or lexicon works. One major finding is that a word is easier to recognize if it is preceded by a word related to it in meaning. To illustrate this "semantic priming", we are much quicker at recognizing the word NURSE if it is immediately preceded by DOCTOR than if it is preceded by BUTTER.

The introduction of the computer into psychology has had two major beneficial effects on such experimental research. First, complex experiments have become much easier to analyze. Second, computers now run many experiments. They deal with the presentation of materials, and the accurate timing and collection of subjects' responses. We can expect this trend to continue, as developments in computer technology are passed on into other domains.

▼ *The US linguist Noam Chomsky has been responsible for stimulating progress in psycholinguistics and artificial intelligence. In addition to his claim that important aspects of language are innate and species-specific to humans (◊ page 199), he has produced a detailed theory of how humans represent and acquire language, called transformational grammar.*

▶ *In the early 1970s, the computer program SHRDLU, written by Terry Winograd, suggested that computers might soon understand and produce language as well as humans. SHRDLU "talked" about a simple imaginary world, BLOCKSWORLD. Its ability to remember the relative locations of colored objects, and respond to commands to move them and to question about their location is illustrated in the diagrams:*
(1) HUMAN: Will you please stack up both of the green blocks and either a blue cube or pyramid?
SHRDLU: OK.
(2) HUMAN: Put a small cube onto the blue cube which supports a pyramid.
SHRDLU: OK.
...HUMAN: Put the littlest pyramid on top of it.
SHRDLU: OK.
(3) HUMAN: How many things are on top of the blue cubes?
SHRDLU: I am not sure what you mean by "on top of..."
Unfortunately, the problems of language proved more difficult than originally thought, largely because of the large amount of background knowledge humans use so easily, but which is difficult to represent for computers.

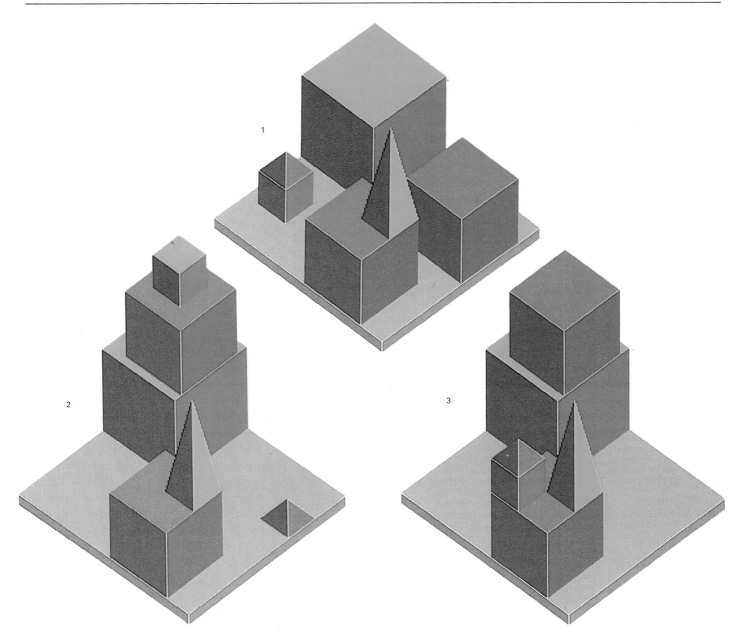

Computers and language

One of the first goals of artificial intelligence (AI) in the early 1960s was machine translation, *presenting a piece of material in one language , and waiting for the computer to output a perfect translation of the text into another language. It soon became obvious that this was an impossibly optimistic plan at this stage. It is a particular example of what is called the frame problem in artificial intelligence. In all thought processes humans are making use of a huge background information or context. This context may not always be obvious, in which case it is said to be implicit. It has proved very difficult to provide computers with mechanisms for dealing with implicit context. However, advances were made. For example, the American artificial intelligence worker Terry Winograd wrote a computer program he called SHRDLU which "understood" instructions for moving blocks of different shapes, sizes, and colors around an imaginary table-top called BLOCKSWORLD. SHRDLU was considered a major advance in the early 1970s, but most researchers now agree that it is too limited. First, it is too dependent on the context of BLOCKSWORLD to be able to be generalized to any other domain. Second,*

the program was only intended to work in the sense of understanding language in some very limited domain, not to be a model of how humans process language. This is obviously much more complicated.

There are now two approaches in this area. There are researchers in artificial intelligence who aim to develop a computer system capable of understanding and producing language, usually for some specific reason such as translation. Others use techniques acquired from computing and artificial intelligence to look more closely at linguistics and psycholinguistics. This area of computational linguistics has been particularly fruitful in helping us to understand how we might parse (work out the word order or syntax of a sentence).

As techniques improve over the next 30 years, we can expect the ability of computers to deal with natural language to improve. Intelligent word processors, limited translation systems, and semi-automated offices, where a computer takes human speech and instructions, and turns them into a properly laid-out document, are all likely in the foreseeable future. Computational linguistics will further our understanding in psychology too.

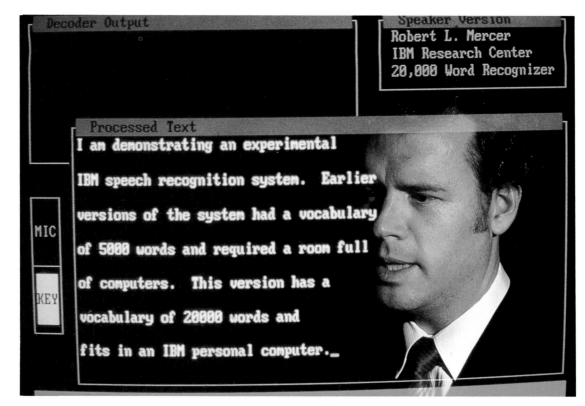

Decoder Output

Speaker Version
Robert L. Mercer
IBM Research Center
20,000 Word Recognizer

Processed Text

I am demonstrating an experimental IBM speech recognition system. Earlier versions of the system had a vocabulary of 5000 words and required a room full of computers. This version has a vocabulary of 20000 words and fits in an IBM personal computer._

MIC

KEY

▶ Advances have been recently achieved in computer speech recognition. The computer is able to "recognize" words in speech and display them on a computer screen, or print them out. This IBM system can recognize 20,000 words. Progress has also been made in machine translation (MT) from one language to another. In both cases using background knowledge is still a major difficulty. How do we know whether we have heard "knight" or "night"?

Connectionism

A recent development in psychological theory has been "connectionism". The basic idea of this is that complex tasks, such as word recognition, can be achieved by a large number of very simple processing elements working together. These models are popular because all the work in these systems is done by a network of very simple units (called nodes) and the connections between them. Psychologists now think that models of this type are more plausible because they are more reminiscent of neurons and how they are connected to form a brain than they are of computers. There are no explicit rules in these systems. Instead all the work (computation) is achieved by the spreading of energy (activation) around the network until a stable pattern is reached. "Memories" are not stored in any one particular place in the network, but are stored by the general pattern of activation across the network. Because of this, this approach is often called PDP (parallel distributed processing). The PDP approach has been most successfully applied so far for processes such as spoken and visual word recognition and as yet has really still to be extended to higher-level processes such as problem solving. It is still too early to evaluate the full impact of connectionism, but it is possible that in 30 years' time there will have been a "scientific revolution" in cognitive psychology and psycholinguistics rather like the one that was seen in the early 1960s. However, the emphasis on distributed processing means that our old-style serial-processing, "one thing at a time", computers are generally too slow and cumbersome for connectionist models of any size. The development of connectionism will probably go hand in hand with that of massive parallel computing.

Some likely future developments

The ability to order words in an infinite number of ways to form grammatical sentences appears unique to humans. Neuropsychology and psycholinguistics have shown how certain cortical areas are associated with particular components of the language system. Over the next 30 years or so, technological developments will allow us to observe the functioning of a living brain in detail and in real time.

In 300 years, more spectacular advances are likely. For example, we might be able to grow neurons outside the brain in vats. These neurons could then be "plugged in" to the brain to replace damaged tissue, or perhaps just to enhance our brains in some way. We might also learn how to make artificial neurons or groups of neurons. Similar research which might enable us to do this is already under way in the development of the biochip. This resembles the now commmonplace computer chip, but instead of being made out of silicon, it is made of organic materials. Even more spectacularly, we might be able to make replacement parts of the brain. These "plug-in brain modules" will be easier to make for small parts of the brain which have very specific functions.

There will undoubtedly be huge advances in computer processing of language. Computers and robots which can read, write, speak, and understand speech are likely to be commonplace in 300 years' time. How soon these developments can take place will depend on two things: first, computer processing becoming more powerful, and storage becoming much larger; second, developing a much more sophisticated model of how we can produce and understand language. Only then can we expect truly human-like speech abilities in machines, robots which walk and talk like us.

New techniques of investigating the brain...A boom in the use of drug treatments...Controversy over psychotherapy...Behavior therapy...Legal and political implications...A trend toward community care

No aspect of medicine changed more in the mid-20th century than psychiatry, yet the result now seems to some extent unfulfilled promises and mere glimpses of the mind's inner workings. The relationship of the brain to consciousness (◀ page 179) remains as much a mystery as ever.

Psychiatry is still coming to terms with a burst of drugs discovery in the 1950s which revolutionized treatment methods. Psychiatric disorders are now often responsive in the short term to antipsychotic, antidepressant, or tranquilizing drugs. But many of these illnesses are chronic or recurrent, and their management over years or decades is a relatively new enterprise for medicine. It is still uncertain whether or not the overall incidence of psychiatric illness is increasing and whether this total varies significantly from one culture to another. The number of old people is growing rapidly in most parts of the world. Highly-industrialized countries are having to cope with an epidemic of mental illness in the aged. But schizophrenia, depression, neuroses, and most other psychiatric disorders probably do not vary much in frequency rates throughout the world. In fact, no other chronic disorder has a distribution that is so unvarying as schizophrenia, which suggests that it is caused by some fundamental biological fault.

Anti-psychiatry

In all human societies, there is such a fear of mental illness and such hostility toward it that people tend to deny its existence. They also transfer some of this fear and hostility on to those who care for the mentally ill. In the 1960s, as part of the general cultural upheaval and feeling against authority, "anti-psychiatry" became widespread in western countries. The Scottish-born psychoanalyst R.D. Laing was at the center of this movement, claiming that mental illness was an understandable form of rebellion against family and social oppression, and that it even had value as a mystical experience.

Laing attempted to understand the delusions of schizophrenics. Later he concluded that normality was madness and that so-called mental illnesses were really a way of rejecting the irrationality of the ways of life, especially familial relationships enforced by society. Schizophrenic patients' delusions were explained by Laing as commentaries on the true madness of the family relationships in which a schizophrenic is trapped. Schizophrenia, said Laing, should not be treated in isolation by drugs or psychotherapy but be learned from as a clue to the changes needed in society, which represent true cures. His ideas were generally refuted.

At the same time, Marxists saw the mentally ill as merely victims of the political and economic forces of capitalism. These views were influential in the drastic reform of Italian mental health law in 1978, though its results have been very controversial.

Psychiatry continues to be attacked both by Marxists and by libertarians on the political right, neither of whom acknowledge the reality of severe mental illness. Yet there is no firm evidence that psychiatric disorder has any relationship to a country's political system.

◀▲ **Treatment of the severely mentally ill has changed considerably. In Italy, prior to the 1978 reforms, patients were often kept locked up in wards for years, as in this Naples institution (left). Now the government is trying to reintegrate patients into society or transfer them to normal hospitals. Long-term patients can now sit in the garden and talk to visitors (above).**

Investigation of the brain

X-rays were the first means of examining the brain, but they show only very gross changes. Later, opaque dyes were injected into the blood supply, and the internal cavities of the brain also could be outlined by air, but neither of these methods used with X-rays was completely safe. Another means was the electroencephalogram (EEG), which recorded the electrical waves of the brain from outside the skull. These waves show a different pattern if there are large abnormalities. However, the skull does not conduct electrical activity well, so that the information given by the EEG is limited.

This situation changed dramatically with the introduction of computers. These are able to build mathematical models of much greater amounts of information, produced by multiple X-rays, EEG recordings, or harmless radioactivity passing through the brain. Computed axial tomography (CAT), nuclear magnetic resonance (NMR), positron emission tomography (PET), and other techniques are moving rapidly into everyday medical practice. They have already revolutionized the practice of neurosurgery. In schizophrenia, it has already been shown by these new methods, that about one-third of patients have structural abnormalities on the left side of the brain, concentrated in the temporal region, which is the area governing speech. That is exactly what would be expected from the abnormal speech and hallucinatory voices that are so common in schizophrenia. Even newer is the monitoring of the brain's magnetic activity by an ultrasensitive detector, which may be able to localize points of cerebral activity with far more accuracy than any method now in use.

The new generation of investigative techniques, based on computers, electronics, and radioactivity, is still in its infancy. Together with the current progress in biochemistry, genetics, and epidemiology, it promises a vastly greater understanding of both the normal and abnormal functioning of the mind. What has been learnt in the last 30 years may be merely a beginning.

▼ Brain scans reveal differences in metabolic activity in the brains of normal (left) and schizophrenic (right) people. Such PET (positron emission tomography) scans use harmlessly-radioactive isotopes injected into the bloodstream and carried to the brain, where radioactivity appears concentrated in areas where metabolism is most intensive. Scanning techniques can reveal large-scale differences in brain structure, but they cannot show up the minute biochemical differences which are probably responsible for most serious illnesses, nor their underlying genetic and environmental causes.

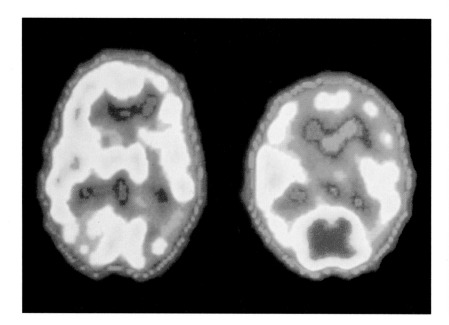

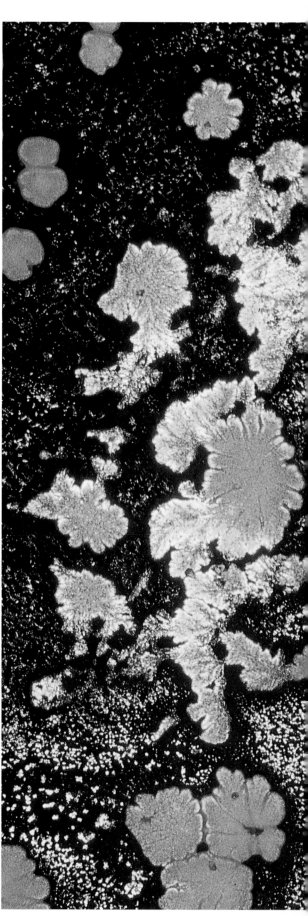

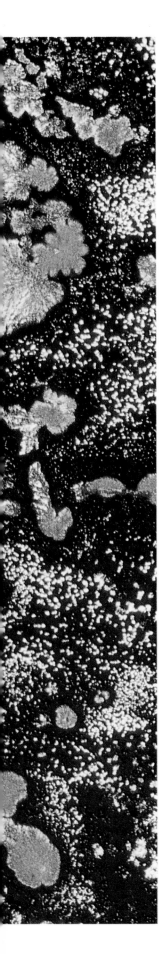

Drug treatment

Until the 1950s, the only drugs used in psychiatry were those producing drowsiness. The amounts required to control the disturbed behavior of schizophrenia or the agitation of severe depression would often cause unconsciousness – and this itself meant further dangers.

However, a new group of tranquilizers – benzodiazepines – caused much less drowsiness, and seemed to be free of the problems of earlier drugs, such as the barbiturates. Valium became the world's top-selling medication. However, after 25 years, it is now clear that the prolonged use of benzodiazepines can result in serious dependence, with distressing effects when they are stopped. They should therefore be used only for very short periods.

Like anxiety, depression was untreatable by medication until the accidental discovery in Switzerland that over 60 percent of cases were relieved by a group of drugs (tricyclics). Their drawbacks are side effects such as drowsiness and a dry mouth, and possible danger to life if they are taken in large overdoses. Since the 1950s, many more compounds have been found to have antidepressant action, but only one type has remained in widespread use – the MAOIs (monoamine oxidase inhibitors). So far, no drug has obtained a higher success rate than that of the original tricyclics, which suggests that there might be some kind of biological limit to these actions. Social factors, such as loss of supportive relationships, are known to be important causes of depression, and psychological treatment methods are being developed – particularly cognitive therapy, in which the sufferer is persuaded out of his depressive view of the world.

The third great pharmacological discovery of the 1950s was probably the most important – the antipsychotic (or neuroleptic) action of the phenothiazine drugs in schizophrenia and manic-depressive psychosis. This action is threefold – calming the disturbance of acute illness, removing psychotic symptoms such as delusions, and then preventing further attacks of illness from developing. As occurred with the antidepressant drugs, other chemical groups with antipsychotic action have since been developed, but none has achieved a significantly higher success rate.

The common factor underlying all these classes of drugs (psychotropics) is that they affect the chemical substances which are released at the terminals of a nerve fiber when an impulse passes along it. The arrival of these neurotransmitters at the terminals of the next fiber carries the impulse further. All anti-psychotic drugs have in common the action of blocking one important neurotransmitter – dopamine. Therefore, it is possible that in schizophrenia there is an abnormality in transmission between nerve cells in the brain, related to the activity of dopamine . If this is so – and the evidence is still far from conclusive – it cannot be the whole story. Literally hundreds of substances could be involved in neurotransmission, and one of these – perhaps still unidentified – might be even more important than dopamine.

In the case of depression, there is also a neurotransmitter (serotonin) which seems to play an important role, but its exact relationship to the illness is still unknown. Both antipsychotic and antidepressant drugs affect a wide range of biochemical systems in the brain. Though knowledge of these systems has advanced enormously, their complexity is so vast that we probably have only vague clues as to how the brain really functions in biochemical terms. Even when this functioning comes to be understood much more fully, social and psychological influences on the mind are likely to remain as important as ever.

◄ *Valium (Diazepam) crystals seen in polarized light. Valium acts on special receptors on brain cells, so there must be a naturally-produced substance that has similar effects. It may be possible to design an even more effective tranquilizer, without side effects. But some degree of anxiety may be necessary for healthy mental life.*

Psychotherapy

In the first half of the 20th century the treatment of common, less severe psychiatric disorders (neuroses) was greatly influenced by the theories of the Austrian founder of psychoanalysis, Sigmund Freud (1856-1939). Freud proposed that a patient's symptoms – such as anxiety, panic, depression, or obsessions – were only indications of unconscious emotional conflicts. These conflicts stemmed from childhood experiences, and if with the help of an analyst they could be brought into consciousness, so that the patient gained insight into them, the symptoms should disappear. The method used enormous amounts of time, and was very expensive. To some extent, it was less a treatment method than a way of reassessing one's life. The same principles can be applied in much briefer forms of psychotherapy, where discussion is more directed toward the actual problems which trouble the patient, and with groups, whose members may help each other to understand their symptoms, under the guidance of the therapist.

Since psychotherapy first began, there has been controversy as to whether or not it is effective. Though the amount of scientific evidence in its favor remains modest, troubled people continue to seek psychotherapeutic help wherever it is available. New methods are also constantly being devised, particularly in the United States. These include Gestalt, rational-emotive, and cognitive (◀ page 208) therapies, as well as the alternative form of analysis developed by the Swiss psychiatrist C.G. Jung (1875-1961). Another method, transactional analysis, devised by the American psychiatrist Eric Berne, is based on revealing the "games" which people play in their everyday behavior and which are often harmful to themselves and others. In some senses, psychotherapy may be seen as a commodity which people will consume as much as they can. As human societies become richer and more technologically complex, the need for a supportive or guiding relationship of this kind may be felt more and more. If scientific study succeeds in identifying whatever there is about psychotherapy that helps people, then it could become very much more effective.

▼ *Two cats' heads by a schizophrenic painter. Art therapy, in which patients are encouraged to express their own inner states as well as more conventional subjects, has real value in treating even severe mental illness. Self-expression helps patients to come to terms with and explore their condition. Art therapy may also provide clues about the underlying condition, and can help in group therapy.*

Behavior therapy

Even should Freudian theories of neurosis be correct, treating neurotic sufferers on their basis has proved to be very difficult in practice. One possible alternative to psychotherapy was drug treatment, but up till now no medication has been particularly effective for neuroses, particularly as they are often chronic or recurrent disorders. Another alternative was to use a different psychological framework – learning theory – founded on the work of the Russian physiologist I.P. Pavlov (1849-1936). His research on dogs showed that if a bell was always sounded before food was offered, the dog would eventually come to respond to the bell as if it were food. This "conditioned reflex" proved to be one of the fundamental principles of learning.

In the 1920s, the American psychologist J.B. Watson (1878-1958) tried to apply conditioned-reflex theory to human neuroses. The aim was to establish a new conditioned reflex between a situation causing severe anxiety (for example, open spaces for an agoraphobe) and a pleasant experience such as relaxation. This new connection would then replace the previous one, and the neurotic anxiety would consequently be removed.

Watson's experimental cases were forgotten for 30 years, until a South African psychiatrist, Joseph Wolpe, developed several new methods based on learning theory, which came to be called behavior therapy. "Desensitization" involves the patient getting used to a feared situation by very small steps, while "flooding" is the opposite – persuading the patient to expose himself to the full experience of a situation he has avoided through fear. "Aversion" was the attempt to remove unhealthy forms of behavior by symbolic forms of punishment, but this has been largely abandoned.

Behavior therapy aims both to remove unpleasant symptoms and to modify deviant behavior in ways which are more satisfactory both to the patient and to society. It is not concerned with possible "underlying" causes. Being based on psychological theory, it is mainly carried out by clinical psychologists, though drug treatment or even psychotherapy may be combined with it.

Behavior therapy has already brought relief to very many neurotic sufferers who were not helped by other methods. As the scientific knowledge of learning continues to grow, this important form of treatment should become even more effective.

◄ *A severely retarded young woman on a swing, used to stimulate the inner ear, the organ of balance and posture, to try to help her to improve control over movement and posture. Several forms of severe mental retardation are caused by biochemical abnormalities, in turn caused by genetic defects, some of which have now been located in specific genes. For example, retardation due to phenylketonuria (PKU) can be identified in infancy; the introduction of a special diet can allow the child to develop normally.*

◄ *Miming in a therapy group can help children to learn to communicate better and so become better adjusted. Environmental and familial influences and genetically-determined qualities are important in causing mental abnormalities. The most severe common mental illnesses are schizophrenia and manic-depressive psychosis. Recent studies have shown that manic-depressive illness is strongly inherited as a single gene. The risk of schizophrenia is higher the more closely anyone is related to a schizophrenic patient, also indicating a genetic factor. Understanding the relative roles of heredity and environment should lead to a precise knowledge of the biochemical abnormalities in mental illness and, perhaps, to ways of curing them.*

Politics and the law

Unlike the rest of medicine, psychiatry has legal and political implications because people can be deprived of their civil rights on account of mental illness or retardation. In that respect, the psychiatrist is acting both on behalf of the patient and as the agent of the state. But a totalitarian state can use psychiatry as one of the many means by which it oppresses its people, and there are individual abuses if not systematic abuses in many countries.

In Nazi Germany, mentally retarded and incurably mentally ill people were killed in large numbers, for the "purification of the race". In the Soviet Union, political dissenters have been diagnosed as mentally ill and subjected to ill-treatment both in prisons and mental hospitals. Some psychiatrists have also been persecuted there. In Japan, lack of legal control results in many people being confined in mental hospitals without adequate cause.

It is always most important to safeguard the human rights of those diagnosed as mentally ill, but legal precautions should not be so elaborate that they prevent people from receiving necessary treatment. Striking the right balance between these two valued, but sometimes opposing, objectives is difficult, and regular changes may be needed in the law, to bring it up to date with medical and social advances. Genetic engineering will raise completely new legal and ethical issues. Brain-tissue transplants, already used experimentally to treat Parkinson's disease, may in future be used to treat common mental illnesses. The use of fetal brain tissue as donor material is posing ethical questions. If many common conditions benefit from brain implants, then there may even be pressure on women in the poorest countries to become pregnant solely to produce fetuses for use as donor material.

▼ **Occupational therapy in a mental hospital in Cuba. This open medical regime contrasts with the treatment of religious dissidents in the USSR.**

Community care

While during the second half of the 19th century, general medicine in industrialized countries was making rapid scientific advances, psychiatry had become confined within the walls of mental hospitals. The pattern of institutional care developed then endured with little change for almost a century. During this time, psychiatry benefited little from scientific progress; the only important innovation was psychoanalysis, but this had no application to the care of severe mental illness.

Since World War II, psychiatry has changed not only in its new treatment methods and greater scientific knowledge, but even more in the way that it is organized and reaches its clients. There is a worldwide trend toward replacing large institutions by more dispersed and informal networks of facilities. These changes bring with them a need for the monitoring and continuous treatment (mainly by drugs) of people suffering from long-term psychoses – if necessary perhaps for 50 years or more.

Beyond the next 30 years, genetics may provide the key to a real reduction in the burden of severe mental illness. But this raises such important ethical issues as how much intervention and control human societies will accept to gain an overall benefit in mental health. Even today, the ravages of alcoholism and drug abuse could be much reduced, but only at the cost of controls which most democratic societies would reject. In the early 1980s, the totally unexpected emergence of AIDS, which involves much severe psychiatric disorder, showed that predictions of endless progress may be wide of the mark. Other unhelpful trends are the enormous migration to cities that is happening in most developing countries, producing megalopolises on a scale never seen before in human history, and the cultural shifts which compress the usual changes over generations into only a few years. These are throwing enormous strain on people's adaptive capacity, with results which no one can predict.

▼ *Anna Chertkova, a postal worker from the Kazak republic, USSR, and a devout fundamentalist Christian, was held in a special psychiatric hospital for 13 years. She was given repeated injections of a "restraining" drug causing high temperature and pain, because of her open proclamation of her belief in God and refusal to accept communism. Anna Chertkova was released in December, 1987.*

◄ *Handicapped girls have a cookery lesson at a mental home in Korea. Being able to perform domestic tasks such as cooking, cleaning and housework, shopping and using public transport, is of enormous value in allowing mentally or otherwise handicapped people to live more independent and normal lives, as far as possible as part of the community.*

214

See also
Mind-Body Interactions 169-178
Consciousness 179-188
The Problem of Memory 189-198
Mood Control 215-222

Race, society and schizophrenia

Jamaican psychiatrists have suggested that white doctors sometimes overreact to black patients who appear aggressive and threatening, but pay too little attention to quiet and withdrawn black patients. An editorial in the "British Medical Journal" in April, 1988 argued the need for further investigation of the role played by race and society in schizophrenia. In the United Kingdom, West Indian immigrants are 3-5 times as likely to receive hospital treatment for schizophrenia as are whites. For those of West Indian descent born in Britain, the difference is much greater: men are 7 times, women 13 times more likely to enter hospital with schizophrenia. Some British psychiatrists, who are mainly white, diagnose and treat West Indian patients differently, on average, to their white patients. They are more often diagnosed as schizophrenic and less often as depressed, more often given electric shock treatment and high doses of medication and less often treated only with psychotherapy.

Some psychiatrists believe that the racism experienced by black people in mainly white society has subtle but real psychological effects, affecting in particular the sense of identity. Such effects may trigger schizophrenia in people who otherwise might never have manifested overt symptoms. Clearly the relative contributions of racism, cultural differences, and perhaps genetic traits, to schizophrenia are matters for great concern in which properly applied research could make great progress possible.

A continuing need

The fact that psychiatry deals with the fundamentals of human nature, which have probably changed little in recorded history, suggests a continuing need for psychiatric help among those living 300 years from now. Most likely, people will live much longer and a high proportion might develop dementia. However, this may be cured by transplantation of embryonic brain tissue, probably by then grown artificially.

A fairly complete understanding of the biochemistry and electrical activity of the brain should mean that whatever disturbances of this kind occur in the psychoses will be corrected by sophisticated forms of medication. Careful monitoring of pregnancy and birth should give warning of anything going wrong, so that the big contribution that fetal damage makes to mental retardation, epilepsy, and probably schizophrenia, could be largely avoided. Advances in genetics should mean that a complete picture of the new individual will be available soon after conception; if anything is then found to be wrong, some kind of genetic or biochemical "surgery" to the embryo may produce a normal baby. Should this not be possible, children with vulnerability to any form of psychological abnormality will very likely have special environments designed for them that will restore their mental health. However, the need for the caring and supportive relationships of psychotherapy will remain, particularly as all this extra scientific knowledge has the potential for evil as well as good.

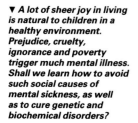
▼ **A lot of sheer joy in living is natural to children in a healthy environment. Prejudice, cruelty, ignorance and poverty trigger much mental illness. Shall we learn how to avoid such social causes of mental sickness, as well as to cure genetic and biochemical disorders?**

Mood Control

A perennial quest...Drugs self-administered by humans...and other animals...Dependence on drugs and tolerance to them...The neurophysiology of drugs...Drugs and the brain...The widening range of mood-altering agents...Dangers of brain damage...Future use and abuse of electrical brain stimulation

Mood or emotional state is something that all people understand personally. In scientific terms it is difficult to define because it is a private internal state. With humans it is possible to ask directly for information about mood with questionnaires or by personal interview. With other species scientists have to invent ways of measuring and interpreting behavior that may express emotional state. By applying this behavioral technology it has become possible in recent years to examine ways in which mood in laboratory animals may be controlled by drugs or by electrical stimulation of the brain. This area of investigation is important both for developing means of correcting emotional disorders in the psychiatric clinic and in relation to recreational activities related to control of mood. While drugs are not the only way of deliberately altering mood or emotional state, they are the most accessible to most people. Using laboratory animals to investigate effects of drug abuse by humans has greatly increased our understanding of brain systems involved in emotional states. They have included studies of effects of electrical brain self-stimulation and self-administration studies, in which animals are literally allowed to self-inject drugs, and research has provided detailed studies of drug effects on chemical events in the brain. This has been particularly important for the design of drugs and the restriction of availability of compounds likely to induce addictive behavior.

▲ Leaves of the coca plant (source of cocaine) are sold in Peru. People have always found ways deliberately to alter their mood. Different societies find different drugs acceptable – as was coca leaf chewing, still widely practiced, in the ancient civilization of the Incas.

◄ Glue-sniffing is a serious problem among teenagers and children in some areas. Most people feel that drug usage in all societies has normally been under social control, and that children and young people require protection from irrevocable hard drug addiction in societies in which they are too often alienated from their parents and from the type of social constraints that have regulated the use of drugs in other, more primitive, societies. Meditation and religious disciplines offer other means of altering and controlling mental states.

Mood change by electrical stimulation and drugs

In the mid-1950s James Olds and Peter Milner at McGill University, Montreal, discovered that laboratory animals could be rewarded by the direct electrical stimulation of groups of nerve cells in specific brain areas. It was subsequently discovered that some of the chemical neurotransmitters released from nerve cells during rewarding electrical stimulation are altered by drugs that induce pleasant or euphoric states. Electrical brain stimulation is also effective for altering mood states in humans. Studies by Wilder Penfield (◀ page 181) and others have demonstrated this for a number of human brain areas. Although deep brain stimulation is not subject to human abuse in the sense that drugs are, compulsive self-stimulation of the brain has been observed in human patients receiving therapeutic brain stimulation for the control of pain. Russell Portenoy and his colleagues in New York documented such behavior in a woman who reported that stimulation was accompanied by erotic sensations. Such cases clearly indicate the potential of deep electrical brain stimulation for mood control.

Since the 1960s laboratory procedures for studying self-administration of drugs by nonhuman species have been used to discover more about the nature of drug-induced mood changes in people. Under such conditions laboratory animals, ranging from relatively large primates to rodents, are allowed to control their own drug intake, for example by pressing a lever. This is often achieved by programmed delivery of drugs into veins through specialized pump systems which are activated by the animal's response. In this way the pattern of the animal's drug intake can be assessed with a variety of drugs at different doses. It has been demonstrated that there is generally a clear relationship between drugs self-administered by laboratory animals and those abused by people. Work of this kind has provided insight into brain systems underlying the rewarding effects of drugs in terms of assessing the roles of different groups of nerve cells in this behavior and of investigating brain sites at which direct drug delivery is rewarding.

Drugs: tolerance and dependence

Effects of drugs often become weaker with repeated ingestion or injection. Humans and other animals frequently exhibit drug-seeking behavior after exposure to some compounds. Classical examples of this are seen with the effects of repeated exposure to morphine and cocaine. Doses of such drugs that are very effective initially in inducing euphoria become ineffective as the user's exposure to the drug increases. This phenomenon, known as tolerance, serves to increase the amount of drug sought by the daily user or in some cases even by the occasional user. The development of drug-seeking behavior accompanies increasing drug dependence. It is important to distinguish between two kinds of drug-dependence: physical dependence and psychological dependence. In the most extreme form of physical dependence, drug withdrawal results in severe physical symptoms which, if untreated, may result in death. Tranquilizers of the barbiturate class exert this kind of effect after long-term administration of drugs such as morphine. In this case, although physical dependence clearly contributes to compulsive drug-taking (addiction), psychological dependence also plays a major role. Psychological dependence is the maintenance of drug-taking for the drug-experience itself, not to avoid the consequences of drug withdrawal. It extends in humans to factors related to the cultural milieu in which drug-taking occurs.

▼ *Marilyn Monroe was just one of the many star performers who have found that the stresses of film, theatre, pop music or similar work, allied to to fame and media attention, are too much to take without the aid of drugs.*

▼ *PET (positron emission tomography) scans show the effects on the human brain of cocaine (left) and morphine (right). In the images of the cocaine test, the top left picture shows activity in the cerebral cortex after taking a placebo intravenously, the top right picture activity after injecting cocaine. Cocaine has reduced activity in this higher center of the brain. The lower pictures show the effects of cocaine and placebo on the cerebellum, reveal that cocaine has little effect on this lower center. The right-hand set of images shows similar effects of morphine. Clearly, both drugs affect the higher brain functions while leaving lower functions alone, thus implying loss of higher control of lower pleasure centers.*

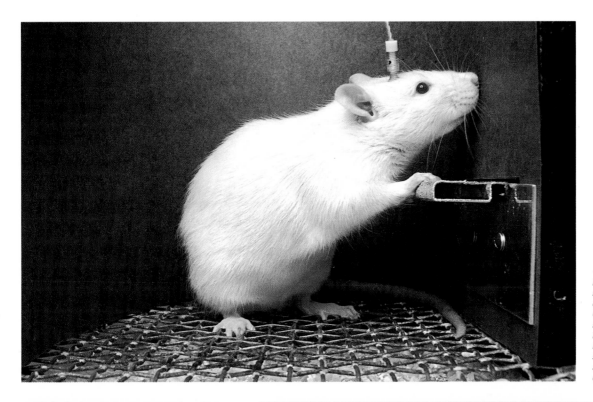

◄ A rat presses a lever to receive direct electrical stimulation of a pleasure center in the hypothalamus. Compulsive brain stimulation has been reported in human patients receiving electrical stimulation for pain control, and has been reported as causing erotic sensations.

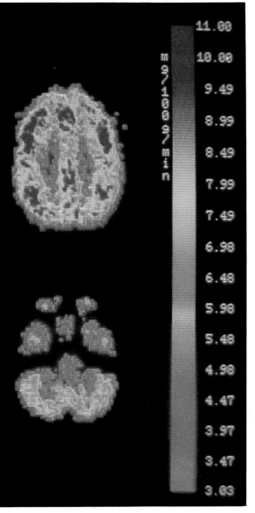

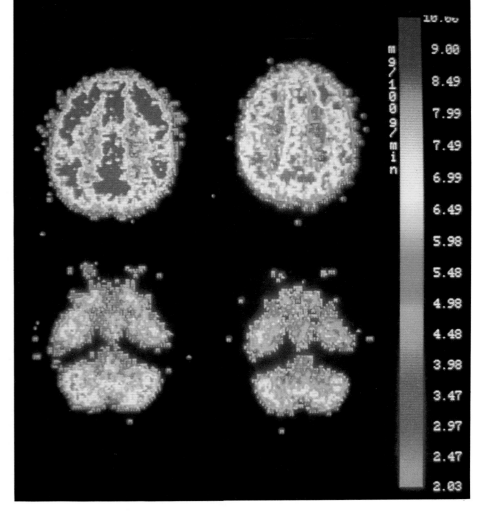

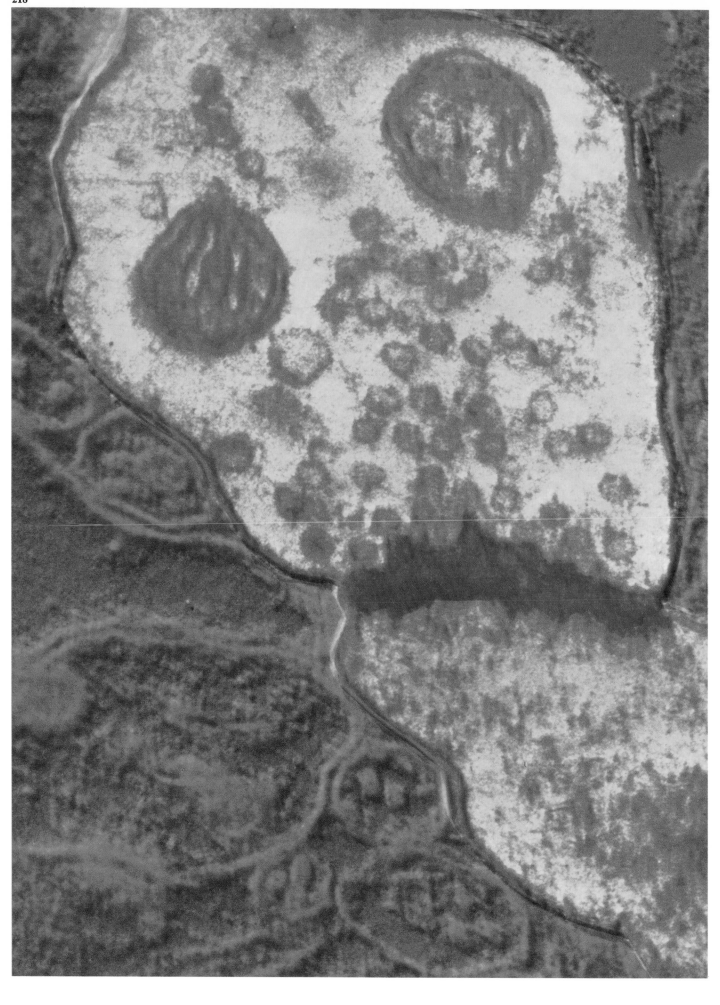

Drugs and the brain

Progress in the development of physical methods for controlling mood depends largely on research into drug action in the brain. The advancing area of drug-receptor interactions forms the critical core of this field. At the present time details of the effects of drugs on synaptic activity have emerged, with great potential for future refinement. At the same time powerful techniques have been established for measuring self-stimulation of the brain and drug self-administration. The combination of these current advances has set the stage for major advances in understanding factors that control mood.

Mapping pleasure systems in the brain

Recent studies indicate that drug and electrical brain stimulation involve nerve cells in an evolutionarily old part of the brain, the limbic system. Neural circuits from a low midbrain region, project to a number of brain areas, including parts of the neocortex and the forebrain. Activity of nerve cells in the area sending information to these regions is critically important for drug and brain stimulation reward to be effective. Chemical neurotransmitters that influence the same neural receptors that are achieved by drugs such as heroin and morphine (opiate receptors) and those activated by drugs such as the amphetamines and cocaine (dopamine receptors) play an important role in brain reward circuits.

The questions of whether or not a single complex system in the brain controls perception of mood and pleasure remains open. Electrical stimulation of midline structures in the hypothalamus results in fear-like avoidance responses in many species. Stimulation of structures a few tenths of a millimeter to the side of these sites may, however, induce powerful reward responses in the same animals. Strangely, increasing the duration of what is a rewarding electrical brain stimulus may change it into an aversive experience that animals will avoid.

Synaptic organization and receptors

Within a nerve cell, activity in the form of minute projections of axons controls the release of chemical messengers or neurotransmitters into specialized parts of the space between cells. These spaces or gaps are called synapses. Across them the neurotransmitter molecules reach uniquely sensitive areas of contact with neighboring nerve cells. At these sensitive points the neurotransmitter molecule locks on to a key-like receptor and causes electrical changes in the nerve surface. The changes, in combination with changes induced by neurotransmitter interactions with neighboring receptors, form the molecular basis for our mood states and all of our thoughts and behavior.

Drugs and electrical stimulation of nerve cells in the brain alter the availability of neurotransmitter molecules or directly interact with neural receptors. The sensitivity of these receptors may change with exposure to drugs, leading to tolerance or sensitization to the drugs' effects. Receptor sites are very specific and will only change brain activity if they are activated by molecules that accurately fit into their structure, very much like a chemical lock-and-key system. Drugs that induce pleasurable states are believed to stimulate receptors for naturally-occurring or endogenous neurotransmitters. Such drug/neurotransmitter "equivalences" include morphine-like drugs fitting into receptors for opioid brain peptides (specific short protein chains such as met-enkephalins).

◄ A synapse, or junction, between two brain cells (neurones). The picture is an electron micrograph produced by a transmission electron microscope, using false color to reveal detail. The cells communicate by the interchange of neurotransmitters, brain chemicals which are secreted into vesicles in the tips of dendrites, the long, thin processes which grow out of neurones and which meet at their tips at synapses. Tiny quantities of neurotransmitters diffuse across the gap to receptors on the other side. Drugs of abuse may mimic the natural process. Heroin is received by receptors for natural opiates resembling morphine.

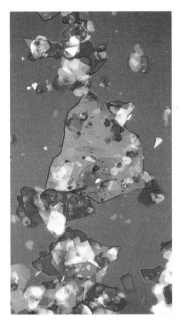

▲ Cocaine crystals show up in this micrograph taken using polarized light. Cocaine is known to activate brain cell receptors which are normally stimulated by the naturally- produced neurotransmitter dopamine. The most potent drugs of abuse, like the most potent medical drugs, stimulate receptors because their molecular structure resembles that of a neurotransmitter.

Drugs, society and human behavior

In contemporary western society both illegal and legal uses of drugs are areas of concern for planning current and future human welfare. For generations the use and abuse of alcohol has represented a major social issue and remains the largest drug problem of today. It is strange to consider that if alcohol had recently appeared as a new drug it would most probably not be widely available for public consumption due to national and international drug licencing policies. The fact that alcohol is a simple byproduct of the fermentation of sugars and that its production requires no knowledge of synthetic chemistry has guaranteed its continued widespread public use. Other mood-altering drugs occur naturally. For example, the hallucinogenic compounds psilocybin and mescalin occur in species of mushroom and cactus respectively. The opiates, such as morphine and heroin, and the stimulant drug cocaine are also harvested from plants, as are the cannabinols distributed in the form of marijuana or its resin hashish. Although drugs such as these are widely used, their availability has been more controlled because of restricted conditions suitable for plant growth and the need for more sophisticated processes for extracting the active ingredients.

With increasing advances in drug chemistry a wider range of mood-altering agents has become available for medical use. Of these compounds benzodiazepines such as Librium (chlordiazepoxide) and Valium (diazepam), which are commonly used anxiety-relieving agents, are the most widely prescribed psychoactive drugs in the world and form the most controversial class. These compounds induce pleasant mood states in people who are not suffering from anxiety disorders, and consequently they are subject to abuse. Although it was accepted until recently that these drugs did not induce physical dependence, long-term use actually does lead to both physical and psychological dependence. These effects are manifest in the form of irritability, disrupted sleep patterns and minor symptoms of physical discomfort. In terms of widespread use in industrial societies this class of compounds serves as a good model against which to consider likely patterns of the future use of mood-controlling substances.

Anti-anxiety or anxiolytic drugs are widely available because they are generally quite effective and are safe in terms of inducing few severe side effects. They usually work continually with long-term administration and have become a largely accepted part of present society. Factors such as safety, long-term efficacy and social acceptance are the keys which will dictate drug use in the future. Social acceptance is particularly important in the case of non-medical or recreational drug use with its attendant problems of dependence for the individual and changes in social conduct for society in general.

In his novel, *Brave New World* (1932), Aldous Huxley described a future society in which public order was maintained by giving everyone a mood-elevating drug which Huxley called "Soma". When the drug was no longer available, social unrest and rebellion followed. It is fascinating to draw parallels between Huxley's world and possible future societies. In reality, although the moral that drugs are no substitute for choice of life-style clearly applies to anxiolytic drug misuse, Huxley's vision remains an oversimplification. Drugs that override reality do so only fleetingly, tolerance and dependence are the cruel consequence of long-term mood changes induced by drugs. Compounding influences are the probable inability to maintain work effectively due to the side effects of many of these drugs, including perceptual alterations, sedation and loss of appetite.

▼ A man incapacitated by "Angel dust" falls through a window. Angel dust, Phencyclidine (PCP), was considered for use as a human tranquilizer but 1 in every 3 people undergoing tests suffered acute though temporary mental disorders. A 1984 World Health Forum report said 8 million Americans had used the drug. In 1978 it was responsible for over 200 deaths in the USA. PCP has been called the most dangerous and least predictable of all drugs of addiction.

▶ The hallucinogenic toadstool Psilocybe semilanceata contains the powerful hallucinogen psilocybin. The effects of taking the related hallucinogen mescalin were described by Aldous Huxley in his book "The Doors of Perception" (1954). Drugs derived from plants have been built into the structure of many societies, for example opium from the poppy in China, and cannabis in many hot countries (hemp only produces its active alkaloid when grown in hot conditions).

▶ Heroin addicts undergo treatment in a monastery near Bangkok. The 10-day treatment includes herbal emetics, steam baths, and hard physical work. How this counters physical dependence caused by long-term usage is unclear, but only 30% of those treated are reported to return to drug addiction. The brain responds to constant stimulation with heroin, which has a molecular structure very like the brain's own naturally-produced opiate, by adapting so that more is required for the wanted effect. An addict's failure to obtain heroin causes unpleasant effects which, in the West, explain the low success rate for treatment.

The high cost of street-drug use

In 1982 a group of young heroin addicts in a number of cities near Santa Cruz, California, rapidly developed symptoms of the debilitating motor disorder known as Parkinson's disease. The disease involves a progressive degeneration of dopamine-containing nerve cells projecting from an area called the substantia nigra in the midbrain to the striatal complex of the forebrain. The condition usually occurs in the latter part of life and progresses over a period of many years. This tragic development in the lives of these addicts was due to a mistake by a "street-drug chemist".

What had happened was that an attempt to synthesize 1-methyl-4-phenyl-4-propionoxypiperidine, an analog of meperidine used as a "synthetic heroin", resulted in the almost pure synthesis of a compound with entirely different characteristics, 1-methyl-4-phenyl-1,2,3,6-tetra-hydro-pyridine or MPTP. When ingested, MPTP is converted to 1-methyl-4-phenylpyridinium (MPP+) in the body. The main action of MPP+ is to destroy dopamine-containing nerve cells in the substantia nigra. The death of these cells in a major area of the brain's motor-control system leads to advanced motor dysfunction in the individuals concerned.

The damage done to the Santa Cruz heroin addicts was irreversible. Their experience stands out as a signpost warning everyone of the possible terrible consequences of amateur drug synthesis and of street-drug use.

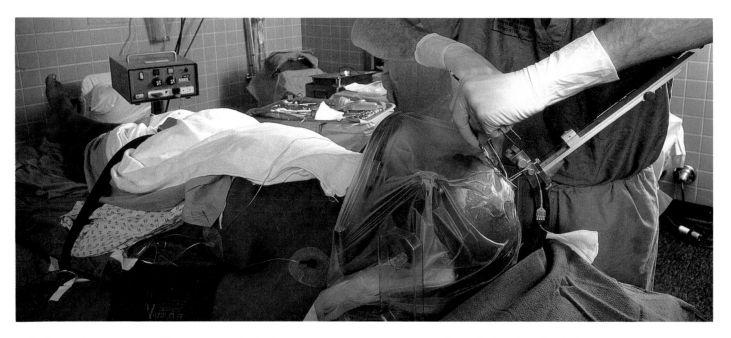

▲ *An electrode is implanted in a patient's brain to relieve chronic pain by electrical stimulation. To date such stimulation has only been used for the relief of pain, or during brain surgery as a means of locating which functions are located in which parts of the brain, from the mental experiences of the patient when different parts of the brain are stimulated. In the future it could become possible to use electrical stimulation of appropriate parts of the brain to provide pleasurable sensations. The potential for both use and abuse is enormous.*

Mood control in the future

Undoubtedly in the next 30 years great advances will be made in drug design. By increasing our knowledge of drug-receptor interactions it will be possible to tailor more selective chemical structures to make our drugs more specific in their action. This will be accompanied by a reduced incidence of side effects and by the development of long- or short-acting drugs to suit particular needs. Existing drugs will be supplemented by new drug types as different neurochemical systems are discovered and their controlling functions in relation to mood are characterized. At the same time problems of drugs abuse are likely to remain, with more and more knowledge about sophisticated compounds finding its way from the research environment to the street supplier. This will be offset by an ongoing attempt to provide effective drug education and by increasingly specific laws concerning drug availability. It is likely that, rather than restricting specific drugs from the public sector, whole classes of compounds will be defined by future legislators as illegal on the basis of their ability to stimulate specific neural receptors in the brain.

Such changes are readily predictable from the current situation. Three centuries from now the scene may, however, change tremendously. Virtually all the elaboration of drug-related technology and brain science has occurred within this century, and the study of mind-altering drugs has only developed rapidly since the 1950s. Major developments in drug design are inevitable, but the problems of tolerance and side effects are likely to remain.

An exciting possibility is the elaboration of more sophisticated means of stimulating specific brain circuits, perhaps with the use of fine electrode systems located deep within the brain. The cases of human electrical brain stimulation that have already been reported indicate the possibilities. It is now becoming possible to interface microelectronic components with brain tissue, the aim being to repair brain damage. From that to implants purely for pleasure would be a short step.

Electrical brain stimulation

Until the present time such stimulation has only been used for therapeutic reasons, acutely in exploratory neurosurgery, or with permanently implanted devices for control of such disorders as intractable pain. What is the potential for recreational use or abuse of electrical brain stimulation? The abundant supply of electricity compared to that of drugs, and the ease with which suitable stimulation units may be manufactured in the light of modern microprocessor technology, are factors which certainly favor its development. They are largely offset by the need for surgical sophistication in brain implantation. Surgery is, however, simply another form of technology and it is conceivable that the appeal of a single surgical intervention resulting in endless access to pleasure may be a desirable investment for those who wish to enjoy heightened emotional experiences. Whether such activities will be legal is questionable.

It has already been established that humans and other species can become addicted to electrical brain stimulation. The dependence is likely to be almost purely psychological but the problems for the individual, in terms of time-sharing between the "stimulation habit" and the rest of life, may be considerable.

Compared with Huxley's imaginary drug "Soma" (◀ page 220), perhaps electrical brain stimulation is a more realistic possibility for social control, albeit a currently futuristic one. The possibility of psychological well-being depending on controlled access to minute pulses of electricity delivered deeply in the brain is an undesirable concept to most people. To take a more optimistic view, perhaps future societies will reject such artificial means of mood control and provide a more beneficial and enjoyable external environment, restricting physical methods of mood control to therapeutic applications. It is, after all, useful to remember that human populations have actually survived to some extent at least, despite artificial means of mood control rather than because of them.

The theory of evolution is the key...Starting principles...Genetic and cultural evolution...Kin selection...Reciprocal altruism...A test of a theory...Human nature is not fixed...Selfishness and cooperation...Political and other possibilities for human sociobiology

The theory of evolution provides the scientific key to an understanding of human nature and existence. The full modern theory of evolution is a very large theory, made up of many sub-theories concerned with different aspects of nature. Still the most important part of the theory is natural selection proposed by the British naturalist Charles Darwin (1809-1882) to account for two observations. It explained, first, why evolution had happened at all. Living things have over the generations changed their forms, and there must be a reason why. Natural selection was the reason Darwin suggested. Secondly, natural selection explains adaptation. Adaptation simply means that animals are well designed for staying alive and reproducing. It is a property of all living things. Animals that live in social groups also have behavior patterns that are probably adaptations for life in a social group.

There is a rapidly growing body of ideas about how natural selection should operate on social behavior patterns. In social life, it is sometimes advantageous to exploit others selfishly, sometimes to cooperate with them, and always to be on the look out in order to avoid exploitation at the hands of others. These ideas are quite well confirmed for many nonhuman species. More controversially, some biologists have been tempted to apply them to human beings.

The Darwinian principle

Why should living things be well designed for life? Why should they be adapted? Before Darwin, the only explanation was that living things had themselves been created by a purposeful, supernatural Creator who was able to bring into existence well-designed creatures. Such an argument is in fact circular; but as the "argument from design" it was one of the traditional proofs of the existence of God. Darwin, however, realized that adaptations also served the needs of organisms in the competitive struggle to stay alive in the natural world. Better-adapted organisms would be more likely to survive and reproduce than less well-adapted ones. Over the generations, the better adapted types would increase in numbers. As we view the products of this process, we see around us well-adapted living things.

Natural selection only favors traits that increase an individual's chance of survival and reproduction. That principle, correctly applied, should be able to explain all the properties, whether of form, behavior or mental state, of all species of living things. It is the Darwinian method (in simplified form) of understanding all life, including human beings. Organisms should be the way they are because they can therefore generate more surviving offspring than they otherwise could. So, to understand some particular property of an organism, the biologist asks how it enables the organism to produce more offspring. To understand human nature (♦ page 230), we should therefore consider how it, too, contributes to reproductive success.

There is, however, one snag in trying to apply the theory of natural selection to human beings. An additional process is now operating alongside natural selection. Biologists call it cultural evolution.

◄ **Chameleons can change their color rapidly to camouflage themselves. Camouflage is a good example of the adaptation of living things to their environments.**

▲ **Charles Darwin's theory is the starting point for our understanding of humans. All living things have evolved by the Darwinian principle of natural selection.**

▼ *These Japanese macaques are washing their food. A Japanese macaque learned to separate wheat from sand by throwing both into the water, then skimming off the floating wheat. Other troop members imitated the trick and it rapidly spread through the troop. This is an example of cultural evolution.*

Genetic and cultural evolution

Natural selection cannot change the frequency of a trait unless the trait is inherited. Offspring must resemble their parents. If they do not, then even if some types of parents are producing more offspring than others, their characteristics will not increase in frequency in the next generation. As it happens, most traits are inherited to some extent. The need for inheritance therefore poses no great problem for the theory of natural selection. Biologists have worked out the mechanism of inheritance in great detail (◀ page 129) and there can be no doubt that natural selection, working on genetically inherited traits, does operate in nature.

It will operate in humans too. Any inherited trait that causes its bearers to produce more offspring will increase in frequency and vice versa. Inherited diseases (◀ page 130) provide the best examples, but imaginary ones make the point more simply. If, for example, there were any inherited tendency to be incompetent in the use of contraceptives, that tendency would surely increase in frequency by natural selection, as the least competent would produce the most offspring. Natural selection would in this case favor a sort of stupidity.

The use of contraceptives, however, is not a genetically inherited trait. Contraceptives were invented not by genetic mutation but as an ordinary human discovery. The increase in the proportion of the human population that uses them was not due to natural selection. It was due to learning from others. It is an example of "cultural evolution".

The simplest form of cultural evolution takes place by pure imitation, and is found in animals other than humans, for example some monkeys. This means that the Darwinian principle (◀ page 223) cannot be universally applied. Not all traits exist to make organisms have more offspring. To understand behavior, therefore, we have to distinguish those traits that have evolved by natural selection from those evolved culturally. For animals other than humans, this will probably not be much of a problem. Although cultural evolution operates in macaques and other species, it is only a minor process in them. It can be recognized and treated as appropriate. In humans, however, cultural evolution is an all-pervasive process.

This does not mean that natural selection applies only to genetic or "instinctive" behavior, and never to learned behavior. Natural selection applies as much to learned as to any other kind of behavior, and in any case the distinction is largely nonsensical. The ability to learn itself originally evolved because it enables animals to respond more flexibly to changing conditions. However, in species in which learning is very important – particularly humans – another process of change beside natural selection can come into play. It is necessary to allow for it.

The success of human sociobiology – that is, the attempt to apply Darwinism to human behavior – crucially depends on a successful distinction of cultural from Darwinian evolution. At present, these can usually only be distinguished in a vague or general way, and that is why human sociobiology is more a promising science for the future than a record of achievement. The rich theory that biologists have developed to explain social behavior should indeed eventually yield a correspondingly rich understanding of our own behavior. But it has been developed and tested, and is therefore most easily understood, in nonhuman animals. It is therefore useful to look first at the ideas concerning animals, before speculating about their application, tentative so far and perhaps more comprehensive in future, to humans.

► *Cultural evolution is an exceptionally powerful force in humans. New habits can be passed on from any one member of a culture to another, such as from parent to offspring. Here a mother in Brazilian Amazonia teaches her daughter to make and decorate pottery. Such "cultural" transmission of ideas or skills from one generation to the next runs parallel to genetic transmission. Natural selection works only on genetically-transmitted characteristics, and cultural evolution is consequently independent of Darwinian evolution.*

In cooperative behavior, animals sometimes appear to break the rules of natural selection

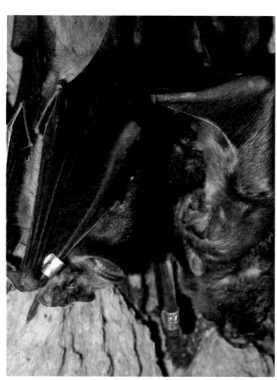

▶ Bees, such as this worker of the species Apis era, can live in large cooperative colonies. The members of the colony are genetically related and the main force of selection favoring their cooperation is called kin selection, helping relatives.

Understanding cooperative behavior

Cooperative behavior illustrates how animal behavior can be understood in terms of natural selection. The general principle is that each selected behavior pattern must increase the number of offspring that the individual produces. In cooperative behavior, however, animals apparently violate that principle. They can therefore illustrate the subtle way in which biologists now apply the theory of natural selection.

The vampire bats of Costa Rica roost inside the hollows of trees, in groups of 8-12 adult females with their young. At night, the bats leave the roost individually to feed by sucking blood from large mammals such as horses and cattle. The mammals do not give blood willingly, and if one notices a bat it brushes it away. Young bats are particularly unskilled at obtaining blood, probably because they have to learn how to feed unobtrusively. After succeeding, or failing, to find a meal, the bats return to the daytime roost. Now is the time for some remarkable behavior: blood regurgitation. If a bat consistently failed to find food, it would, left to itself, soon starve to death. But inside the roost, the bats do not leave each other to fend for themselves. The American biologist Gerry Wilkinson found that the successful bats regurgitate blood for unsuccessful ones, and so keep them alive for longer.

Blood regurgitation in vampire bats is only one example from many of cooperation in animals, all of which pose the same paradox. Natural selection is supposed to favor animal behavior that makes animals leave more offspring: and yet animals sometimes behave in such a way as to increase the survival of other individuals at the expense of themselves. The Darwinian theory has two ways round this paradox – kin selection and reciprocal altruism (page 229) – and Wilkinson's research illustrates them both.

Kin selection

Cooperation can be advantageous if it is between relatives. Natural selection favors traits that enable animals to leave more offspring only because offspring are genetically similar to their parents. By producing more offspring, an individual produces further copies of the genetic predisposition that enabled it to produce more offspring. That is natural selection. However, the same process can operate for other classes of relatives. Sisters, for example, are genetically similar. Therefore, a trait causing sisters to increase each other's success in life can be advantageous. If the trait is in one sister, it is likely to be in the other. And when a sister increases the survival chances, and reproduction, of her sister, she thereby increases the number of copies of her genetic predisposition to help sisters. Natural selection in a sense favors genetic rather than individual selfishness, and it is for this reason that the British biologist Richard Dawkins has described natural selection as favoring the "selfish gene". All relatives are genetically similar to some extent and natural selection will favor more or less cooperation among relatives depending on how closely related they are. Biologists call this process "kin selection".

The bats of a communal roost are not randomly sampled from the bat population. They are genetically related. Female vampires tend to stay in their natal roost. They may also sometimes move between roosts, so that any one roost contains a mixture of bats, some of them sisters, some cousins, and some more distant relatives. This fact of relatedness alone would predispose the bats to evolve cooperative behavior. However, there could be an advantage in regurgitating preferentially for more closely related bats.

◄ Vampire bats live in communal roosts, for instance in hollow tree trunks. The members of a roost help each other in various ways. Vampires that have successfully hunted for blood will regurgitate a meal for unsuccessful bats.

◄ Groups which hunt cooperatively can catch prey that an individual could not. Humans often hunt in cooperative groups. Cooperative hunting requires considerable trust between the group members, such that cheats will not take advantage of opportunities to opt out of dangerous situations. The forces making for trust in humans probably include kin selection and reciprocal altruism.

The main problem with the theory of reciprocal altruism is that this "code" is vulnerable to cheating

▲ Climbers such as this group 5,500m up on Nya Kanga in Nepal physically enforce cooperation on each other. If one slips, he or she endangers the others; but it pays each climber to risk his or her life for others, as any one will usually be saved should he or she slip.

Reciprocal altruism

Another form of cooperative behavior, not necessarily involving animals that are relatives, has been detected by biologists. Reciprocal altruism, simply stated, is the principle of "You scratch my back, I'll scratch yours". Animals will cooperate provided that they can expect to be paid back on average more than they give. The cooperation will then be advantageous, and the cooperating animals will produce more offspring than ones that do not cooperate. Arrangements of reciprocal altruism are difficult to evolve, however, because of their vulnerability to cheating. A cheat takes benefits from others but does not pay them back. Natural selection clearly favors cheating, because the cheat will receive more than the "honest" reciprocal altruist and will produce more offspring. Unless some way can be found to prevent cheating, reciprocal altruism can never evolve. Cheating can only be prevented if offenders can be individually recognized and discriminated against. Then they will not receive the advantages of reciprocal altruism, and selection will cause the frequency of cheating to decrease over the generations. Reciprocal altruism therefore practically requires that different individuals can recognize one another. They are most likely to do so if they meet and interact with one another frequently. In his study of vampire bats (◀ page 227) Gerry Wilkinson found that the bats which associated more with one another were also more likely to regurgitate than bats who spent less time together. Reciprocal altruism and kin selection probably both occur in the vampire bat.

The American political scientist Robert Axelrod and the British biologist William Hamilton have recently suggested a behavior pattern or "rule" which, if animals were to use it, would result in reciprocal altruism that was resistant to cheating. The rule is called "tit for tat". It means that the animal should treat others as they treat it. If another animal cooperates, you cooperate with it; if it does not, nor do you. "Tit-for-tat" behavior discriminates against cheats, and reciprocates only with true reciprocal altruists. Situations as superficially different as regurgitation in vampire bats and arms reduction talks between superpowers can all be represented as forms of the conflict between cheating and cooperation. It is a very general problem.

▲ Many of the relationships between individuals that are involved in tit-for-tat or reciprocal altruism are probably learned early in life. Cooperative relationships, however, are less well understood in humans than in other animals. Biologists have elaborated a fairly thorough theory of when animals should cooperate and when behave selfishly. Kin selection and reciprocal altruism are essential parts of that theory. It should help to understand cooperation in humans.

◄ The theory of reciprocal altruism has been ingeniously tested with a stickleback and a system of mirrors. By adjusting the angle of the mirror, the stickleback can be made to see a fellow stickleback "cooperating" (swimming with it) or "defecting" (lagging behind). The top photo shows the cooperating case and the bottom one a stickleback with its defecting image, which is apparently lagging behind. Sticklebacks tend to cooperate only with their cooperating image.

A test of the "tit-for-tat" rule

Do animals follow the tit-for-tat rule? Axelrod and Hamilton published their idea too recently for much work to have been done, but the German biologist Manfred Milinski has already carried out an ingenious experiment on the stickleback, a small freshwater fish that is preyed on by larger fish such as pike. When a stickleback sees what looks like a pike nearby, it may stealthily swim up to the possible predator. The reason for this "predator inspection visit" is uncertain. The stickleback may be able to find out what the predator is (and that it really is a predator), its exact location, and whether it is in a hungry mood. But the reason does not matter here. Two other points do matter. One is that the stickleback, by swimming up to the pike, makes itself more vulnerable to being eaten. The other is that sticklebacks more readily approach predators in the company of another stickleback than when they are alone. By going in a pair, each stickleback cuts in half its risk of being eaten, because the pike strikes at them one at a time.

Each stickleback in the approaching pair would "like" to reduce its risk of being eaten, and therefore tends to hold back behind the other. The pair nudge forward, little by little, keeping an eye on the other one to see that it is not lagging behind. Milinski simulated a "cooperating" and a "defecting" stickleback by means of mirrors. In one experiment the stickleback saw a broadside reflection of itself; as it approached the predator, so too did its image. In the other experiment, the mirror was angled and as the stickleback swam up to the predator, its image appeared to move further away. The former image "cooperated", the latter "defected". Milinski found that the stickleback spent more time nearer the predator in the cooperating experiment than in the defecting. He suggested it was following a tit-for-tat strategy of conditional cooperation with its image. The test of the theory is imperfect, however. It would be better if there were a clearer series of occasions when the animal could choose to cooperate or defect. More experiments will probably be carried out.

Biologists have elaborated a fairly thorough theory of when animals should cooperate and when they should behave selfishly. Kin selection has been tested successfully in many species. In humans, however, the examples are less well worked out. That is a defect in the evidence, not the theory.

Despite our obsession with kinship, to some extent we can shape our lives independently of natural selection

Human nature

If human sociobiology is correct, human nature should not be simply selfish. For some purposes, natural selection can be simplified as a process that maximizes individual reproductive success. If that were all there was to it, then human nature should indeed be selfish. But there are social circumstances in which selection favors cooperation. The two main cases are for relatives and reciprocity. Human nature should therefore be "conditionally cooperative". Humans should behave morally towards relatives and friends, but more wickedly toward strangers. That is approximately what we do.

The fact (if it is so) that humans behave with limited, rather than universal, morality, and that we do so because of natural selection, does not mean either that we ought to behave in this way, or that we are compelled to do so. Human sociobiology has been picked up by right-wing political enthusiasts as if it supported their views. However, it does not. It is a descriptive, or explanatory, not a prescripitve, science. Our morality can be chosen for moral, not biological, reasons. We morally prefer more universally altruistic behavior than has been favored by natural selection, and there is nothing in human sociobiology to oppose our preference. By understanding our evolutionary nature, it may even be easier to overcome it. There is no reason to suppose that human nature is fixed. The fact of cultural evolution shows that natural selection is often overridden in human affairs.

▶ *Much human cooperation takes place along the lines of relatedness. Cooperation within the family is the obvious example, as in the Sundari Saree Emporium, a family shop in Bombay. Such cooperation among relatives is easily accounted for by the theory of natural selection.*

Cooperation and selfishness in humans

Human beings are obsessed with kinship. All human tribes, including our western civilizations, are interested in and know about kinship. Patterns of human altruism fit, at least roughly, patterns of human relatedness. Kin selection probably is the correct explanation of our general obsession with kinship and of the way kinship influences our social behavior. However, interpretation becomes more difficult at a more detailed level. With human behavior, there is always the possibility that a habit has evolved culturally rather than by natural selection, although for something as universal as our interest in kinship, the purely cultural explanation is implausible. But as we examine the habits of particular tribes, the possibility increases.

Biologists have devised two methods to get round what they see as the problem of cultural evolution. One is to try to abstract, from broad surveys of many species of monkeys and apes as well as humans, what our ancestral habits were. The other is to concentrate on "primitive" peoples, in which the pace of cultural change may have been slower. The theory of kin selection has had a number of successes in interpreting puzzling anthropological observations. One concerns the "mother's brother" phenomenon. Anthropologists have found this phenomenon in several tribes. In these tribes, ordinary paternal behavior towards children is carried out not by the father (mother's husband) but by the maternal uncle (mother's brother). For instance in a tribe called the Djuka, the head of the family is not the father, but the mother's older male relative – her brother or her mother's brother. All children belong to their mother's family, and are subject to the authority of her brother or maternal uncle. Why should this be? Several biologists have argued that the mother's brother phenomenon is found in tribes in which confidence of paternity is low – there is a relatively low probability that the mother's husband is the genetic father of her children. In that case, the mother's brother may have a higher relatedness to the children than the "father" has. If kin selection is operating, the closer relative will be the one that is altruistic.

The example of mother's brother is at present only a hypothesis. But it does show how kin selection makes a clear prediction and illuminates an otherwise puzzling phenomenon. The prediction is that the father will turn out to be the genetic father of less than half of his wife's children. The crucial evidence is rather delicate, and the prediction has not been tested. The advent of "genetic fingerprinting" techniques will make the evidence easier to collect.

It is not yet known how important kin selection is in human cooperation. Some habits, such as the adoption of unrelated children, are clearly impossible to explain by pure kin selection. But no one is suggesting that kin selection explains all human cooperation, so a few counter-examples do not upset the general idea.

Reciprocal altruism (◀ page 228) is surely also important in human cooperation. Humans do tend to cooperate selectively with people who they know well and trust. This fact may cast light on a number of human characteristics. Reciprocal altruism requires constant vigilance for cheats, and opens up manifold opportunities for deception and exploitation. The American biologist Robert Trivers has suggested that such human characteristics as guilt, envy, and moral aggression all evolved in association with reciprocal altruism.

Moreover, as the theory of kin selection predicts, our patterns of selfish and cooperative behavior are closely connected with kinship. We tend to cooperate with relatives and treat non-relatives with suspicion.

◀ Members of a tribe in Borneo hold their weekly meeting in the longhouse. Members of the same tribe are not so closely related as members of the same family, but will tend to be more closely related than to members of different tribes. And, as the theory of kin selection predicts, members of the same tribe are more likely to cooperate. At any rate, different tribes do not cooperate in the way that members of the same tribe do.

◀ Many human behavior patterns cannot be explained by Darwinian natural selection. Adoption is an example: adopting parents do not increase their own genetic success. If human behavior were exclusively under the ruthless control of natural selection, adoption would probably be eliminated. However, we have the power to shape our lives to a large extent independently of natural selection.

The prospect for human sociobiology

Human sociobiology is an application of the theory of evolution. It is now in the controversial phase. Biologists do not know how correct it is to explain human nature in terms of natural selection. If it is incorrect, it will be dropped soon enough. If it is found useful, then in 30 years' time human sociobiology may come to be looked upon as a late phase in the Darwinian revolution, in which biologists at last saw how to apply the theory of natural selection to social behavior and drew from it an understanding of human nature and morality. Just as Darwin pointed to our ancestry from the apes, so human sociobiology may be able to reveal what influence that ape ancestry has had on our nature.

In the longer term, the subject matter of human sociobiology is likely to shift away from its present interests. No science retains a single set of interests for long; but how they develop is difficult to tell. One possibility is that, like the theory of evolution a century ago, human sociobiology may come to direct attention to genetics, particularly the genetics of human social behavior. Darwin could get on all right without understanding inheritance, but nevertheless his theory directed biologists to that subject. Sociobiology can also manage in its primitive form with little knowledge of human behavioral genetics. Its success might force biologists to look more closely at how social behavior patterns are inherited.

Human genetics has many discoveries to its credit, especially concerning inherited disease. However, we still know remarkably little about how exactly our genes influence our behavior. The traditional genetic techniques are not powerful enough. One way of studying human genetics, for instance, is to look at the similarities among twins. The inheritance of IQ has been studied intensively in this way for half a century but a noncontroversial conclusion about how genetics influences intelligence has yet to emerge. New genetic methods will be needed. We do not know what these will be, but the rapidly expanding science of gene cloning is the obvious area from which new methods may emerge.

Following such developments, we might look forward to a knowledge of which of our genes, if any, are responsible for the remarkable variety of, for example, human cooperative, or aggressive, or sexual behavior. Human sociobiologists want this knowledge for its own sake, but it also could have practical interests. No doubt it is too simple-minded to guess that at some time we could change a heterosexual into a homosexual, or vice versa, by a hundred or so appropriate genetic alterations, at the right age. (Even if we could, whether we should apply this knowledge is a separate, and more important, matter.) The descendants of today's human sociobiologists, however, may be asking some form of that question.

As political science and evolutionary biology have combined in the study of aspects of human behavior, some biologists (in transitory moods of vanity) have foreseen a more momentous consequence of the science. In the tit-for-tat strategy, biologists have shown how trust can be built up between selfish and mutually suspicious individuals. It is unlikely that an evolutionary idea will contribute to solving the arms race, not least because there is more to international politics than rationality. But the necessary theory for cooperation among selfish and distrustful nations is now becoming available in human sociobiology.

In the last two decades biologists have discovered how to understand social behavior. In the case of cooperative behavior, they have developed two main ideas: kin selection, which allows cooperation among genetic relatives, and reciprocal altruism. The two processes both operate in many nonhuman animals (◀ page 226). Their application in humans is more difficult to assess. Cultural, as well as Darwinian, evolution influences human behavior. They are difficult to disentangle, and naive interpretation of human behavior in terms only of natural selection will often be mistaken. But kin selection and reciprocal altruism probably both played a part in the evolution of human cooperation. They suggest an interpretation of human nature, as conditionally cooperative, which seems to fit the facts.

▼ The disarmament process involves building up trust. Competing nations, like competing individuals, will not automatically trust each other. They require strong reasons to do so. The conditions of cooperation in animal conflict also apply to conflicts among nations of human beings.

Improving Humans

22

Hopes and fears...Eugenics: noble aspiration or vicious philosophy?...Understanding the nature of genetic disorders...A new technique of prenatal diagnosis...Development and consequences of "in vitro" fertilization...From "droit du seigneur" to cloning

The idea that people can be improved by human intervention is not new. The betterment of individuals was, indeed, the main factor in the emergence and progress of society. If the evolution of ancestral hominids resulted from several million years of natural selection, social man advanced rapidly by learning intellectual and manual skills which were discovered and developed over only a few millennia. Education has been a recognized medium for human improvement since time immemorial, even if its use for the general good rather than the maintenance of privilege is recent.

Formal proposals that human groups might be improved by control of reproduction were first made by the British scientist Francis Galton (1822-1911) in the 19th century. Yet, in a sense, selective breeding has played a part in the building and maintenance of elite social strata throughout history. The extent to which intelligence and talent result from heredity as distinct from upbringing is, of course, a matter of continuing and controversial debate, and the available evidence is more often mustered in support of preconceived convictions than impartial analyses in a search for truth. On the one hand, it is certain that both the parental environment and wider education are crucial in human development. On the other, the possibility that components of personality such as intelligence, talents, and even social and moral orientation are in some way partly dependent on inheritance cannot be dismissed on the basis of the evidence available.

Objections to the manipulation of reproduction for the supposed improvement of the species, or of individuals within it, spring from two preoccupations. The first questions whether the goals of human betterment are definable, achievable or, in any case, justifiable at the expense of reducing human variation. The second recognizes that any program for improvement must encroach upon individual freedom.

These problems have been brought into sharp focus by the challenge of two new developments in biology and medicine. It is now possible to make a prenatal diagnosis of genetic disorders which offer only short and appalling lives to the affected fetuses. In addition, techniques have been invented for the removal, fertilization in culture, and subsequent reimplantation of human eggs. The procedures are not only invaluable in female infertility but open up a range of novel opportunities. For example, a woman may carry and give birth to a child of which she is not the genetic mother. More disturbing is the possibility that the fertilized embryo may be tampered with to produce an unnatural adult.

Traditional viewpoints cannot be ignored when considering the social and ethical problems presented by these scientific advances, but they may be insufficient to meet the whole challenge. Rational thinking and, perhaps, some radical rethinking will be unavoidable. Otherwise, not only may undesirable ends be pursued, but obvious benefits to the human condition may be denied.

▲ *Did the genius of the Huxleys result from heredity? Julian Huxley (1887-1975), a leading biologist of his generation, Aldous (1894-1963), the famous author of "Brave New World" and Andrew (b. 1917), winner of a Nobel Prize for Medicine, were all grandsons of Thomas Henry Huxley (1829-1895), the champion of evolution.*

The control of reproduction

The view that society has a responsibility for the betterment of its members by education and medicine developed slowly and is still not universally accepted. The suggestion that human groups might be improved by control of reproduction was, in contrast, at first enthusiastically endorsed by many and then vehemently rejected as its implications became clear.

If faster race horses, fatter pigs, more productive milk cows and woollier sheep can be produced by selective breeding, why should not similar methods be used to improve the human race? Following proposals first put forward by Francis Galton in 1865, this idea became widely supported, especially in Britain and the United States.

The popular endorsement of the cause of "eugenics" was reflected by legislation. The state of Connecticut was first in the field in 1896, with a statute which prohibited marriage or extramarital relations to the eugenically unfit if the woman was under 45 years of age, with a minimum penalty of three years' imprisonment for violation. In 1905, Indiana followed suit with a measure which forbade marriage of the mentally deficient, persons having "transmissible disease", and habitual drunkards. In 1907, even more severe measures, providing for sterilization, were enacted. Within the ensuing decade no fewer than 15 other states had enacted laws for sterilization of habitual or confirmed criminals, rapists and, in many cases, epileptics, the insane, and idiots in state institutions. British legislation was much more cautious. A mental deficiency bill enacted in 1913 provided for the care of various types of incapacity, but it did not impose mandatory segregation on all mentally-handicapped people and sterilization was not mentioned. The act was, however, regarded as a victory for the eugenics movement, since it did make possible the detention and segregation of certain of the "feeble-minded", which would put some restraints on the multiplication of the unfit. The clamor for sterilization of the unfit often went far beyond the beliefs of the eugenicists. Sterilization measures were enacted in Sweden, Denmark, Finland and even in one canton of Switzerland. In Britain, however, where the ideas had originated, it was generally held that sterilization would be a trespass under the Offences Against the Person Act of 1861, and British doctors were reluctant to perform the operation even on volunteers.

The tide did not flow entirely in the eugenicists' favor. Criticism came not only from some religious bodies but also from scientists. The Catholic Church, in general, dissented on the grounds that even the biologically unfit were children of God, blessed with immortal souls, and entitled to respect. In his encyclical *Casti Connubii* of December 31, 1930, Pope Pius XI condemned eugenics along with divorce, birth control, companionate marriage, and the celebration of animal passion in films, the press, and the theater. Among the scientific critics were Herbert S. Jennings (1868-1947), who was professor of zoology at Johns Hopkins University in the United States, and J.B.S. Haldane (1892-1964), Julian Huxley (1887-1975), and Lancelot Hogben (1895-1975) in Britain. Their viewpoints were by no means identical. Jennings had already in 1925 pointed out that the inheritance of most characters, whether physical or behavioral, could not be explained in terms of the simple model of the Moravian Gregor Mendel (1822-1884) in which a single character, such as the shape of peas, could be related to single genetic factors, later known as genes. They must depend on the interaction of a large number of genes which can be combined in an infinite variety of unpredictable ways. Hogben opposed eugenics from

▲ *Francis Galton (1822-1911) coined the word "eugenics" ("noble in heredity") to denote the science of improving stock by "giving the more suitable races or strains of blood a better chance of prevailing speedily over the less suitable".*

► *Could some forms of control of reproduction be beneficial? This male baby was the first to have its sex artificially predetermined at conception. Sex depends on a pair of chromosomes; females are XX and males XY. Spermatozoa have either an X chromosome which produces a female embryo, or a Y chromosome which makes a male. So the egg was fertilized in vitro, at the Fertility Institute of New Orleans, using Y spermatozoa isolated from the semen of the father.*

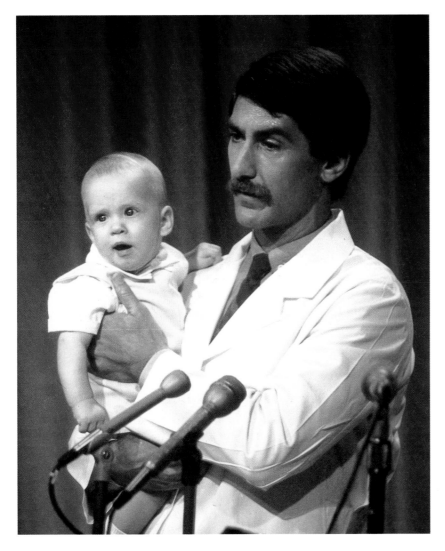

early in his career, identifying it with "ancestor worship, anti-Semitism, color prejudice, anti-feminism and snobbery". Haldane at first supported the creed, and Huxley, at the beginning of the economic depression of the 1930s, actually suggested that a condition of unemployment relief to males should be their agreement to father no more children. Nevertheless, both came eventually to challenge many of the over-simple views of the eugenicists.

It was not, however, the criticism of scientists or the feeling of the Church which caused eugenics to fall from a noble aspiration to a vicious philosophy, but Adolf Hitler. In 1933, the National Socialist cabinet of Germany passed a law to set up hundreds of "hereditary health courts", each consisting of a jurist and two physicians, which would have the power to order sterilization of persons suffering from allegedly hereditary disabilities, including "feeble-mindedness", schizophrenia, epilepsy, blindness, and drug or alcohol addiction. Within three years 225,000 people were sterilized, about half of them designated as "feeble-minded". Thus started a philosophy which was to have horrifying consequences. Within a decade the Third Reich authorized euthanasia for certain classes of disabled people in German asylums and the provisions were most severely applied to Jews. The road led to the extermination camps at Auschwitz and Buchenwald. This is the context for viewing attempts to improve human beings.

▲ *Supporters of the Afrikaner Resistance Movement at a Nazi-style rally in South Africa. Segregation of blacks ("apartheid") is based on the idea that whites are genetically superior. There appear to be no shortage of young advocates.*

Understanding hereditary disorders – a precondition for progress

Since the end of World War II a large number of hereditary disorders has been recognized and their mode of inheritance determined. Of even greater importance has been the discovery of how enzymes, the agents by which life is maintained, are made within cells, and how the blueprints for making them are passed on from generation to generation. This knowledge, together with the development of new techniques for examining the unborn fetus, has made it possible both to counsel couples about the probability of their producing defective children and to detect a number of the defects early enough for the embryo to be artificially aborted. In the United States and Britain, genetic disorders are found in 3-5 percent of all live births. Some, for example spina bifida, in which the tube of the spinal cord fails to close, are polygenic, that is, their inheritance involves the interaction of many genes. But many are caused by a faulty enzyme which results from a gene which makes a single wrong amino acid in a sequence. If only one faulty allele (one of a pair of normally identical genes) must be present to produce the disorder, the gene is said to be dominant. If both alleles must be faulty, the condition is recessive, and in that case no effect is produced by a single wrong allele.

An example of a dominant defect is Huntington's chorea (◀ page 131), a disease which does not manifest itself until middle life, but which then progresses from speech disorders, memory lapses and depression to general destruction of the nervous system, leading to death. A recessive defect is exemplified by Tay-Sachs' disease, a neurological disorder which is invariably fatal by the age of four, caused by the absence of a single enzyme, hexosaminidase. Another example is phenylketonuria, in which the development of the brain is affected because of an error of metabolism in the liver during infancy. Brain damage can be prevented if the child is fed a special diet which is free, or nearly free, of the amino acid phenylalanine.

Another group of disorders arises from chromosomal abnormalities. It includes Turner's syndrome, in which females are partly masculinized in that their sexual system and breasts are only poorly developed (they also are short in stature and have webbed necks), and Klinefelter's syndrome, in which males tend toward femininity in that they have atrophied testicles and tend to develop breasts. The first condition is due to possession of only one X chromosome instead of the normal female XX, and the second to the possession of an extra X, giving a constitution of XXY instead of the normal male XY.

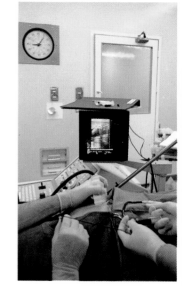

▼ *Taking a chorionic villus sample: some hereditary disorders, such as sickle-cell anemia and Huntington's chorea, can be detected as early as 8-10 weeks by chorionic villus analysis. This involves taking a small piece of placenta by a probe inserted through the vagina. From the removed tissue the DNA is extracted, and, by the so-called DNA probe technique, gene sequences can actually be identified and located.*

▶ *Testing for the disease phenylketonuria, which is inherited through a recessive character. It affects the development of the nervous system because of the deficiency of an enzyme which acts upon the amino acid phenylalanine. In the Guthrie test, a blood sample is taken (right) for analysis 6 days after birth. The abnormality occurs once in every 25,000 births, but the consequences of phenylketonuria can be averted if it is diagnosed early and the infant is reared on a diet free, or nearly free, of phenylalanine.*

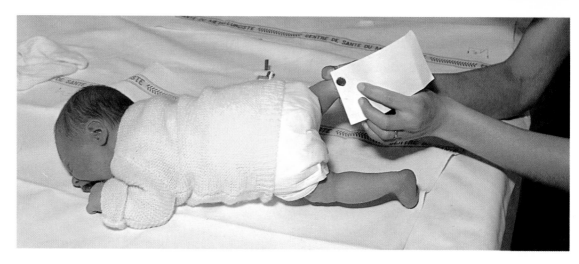

Identifying carriers and prenatal diagnosis

Genetic disease can be prevented or lessened if carriers can be identified and counseled, or affected embryos detected and aborted. Family history is clearly important in assessing the likelihood of a prospective parent carrying a serious heritable disorder. Sometimes it is possible to screen people by biochemical tests. For example, carriers of Tay-Sachs' disease can be detected from the abnormally low levels of the enzyme hexosaminidase in their blood, and a simple analysis of blood will also detect carriers of sickle-cell anemia.

There are a number of methods for prenatal diagnosis. Between the third and sixth months of pregnancy, spina bifida and abnormalities of the kidneys, heart and other organs can be found by ultrasound, hemophilia by sampling of fetal blood, and epidermolysis bullosa (an incurable blistering disease of the skin) by taking a small sample of fetal skin. Some fetal abnormalities can be determined by biochemical tests on the mother. Spina bifida, and other malformations of the nervous system, are indicated by raised levels of alphafetoprotein in the maternal blood. In Down's syndrome the level is often depressed.

Techniques of diagnosis

At present, the most valuable of all techniques, known as amniocentesis, involves taking a sample of the amniotic fluid which surrounds the fetus by insertion of a needle into the abdomen. The procedure is not reasonably safe before the 14th week of pregnancy, though it is possible earlier. The fluid contains fetal cells which are cultured and analyzed. Chromosome defects, as in Down's syndrome, can then be detected. A new test, known as chorionic villus analysis, allows the diagnosis of some disorders as early as 8-10 weeks. It involves taking a small piece of the placenta by a probe inserted through the vagina. Tissue obtained by these techniques may then be subjected to recombinant DNA technology (◊ page 121). The method has already been successfully exploited for prenatal diagnosis of sickle-cell anemia and thalassemia and it may prove of value in Huntington's chorea. Looking ahead, the way seems open for the prenatal diagnosis of many heritable disorders by identifying the genetic material actually responsible for them. It may even prove possible to cure a genetic defect by implantation of foreign material into the fetus while in the womb.

▼ *A blood transfusion is given to a fetus. Hemolytic disease of the fetus occurs when a mother who is Rhesus-negative develops antibodies which destroy the red blood cells of an RH-positive embryo. The disorder can be prevented by intrauterine transfusion of RH-negative blood.*

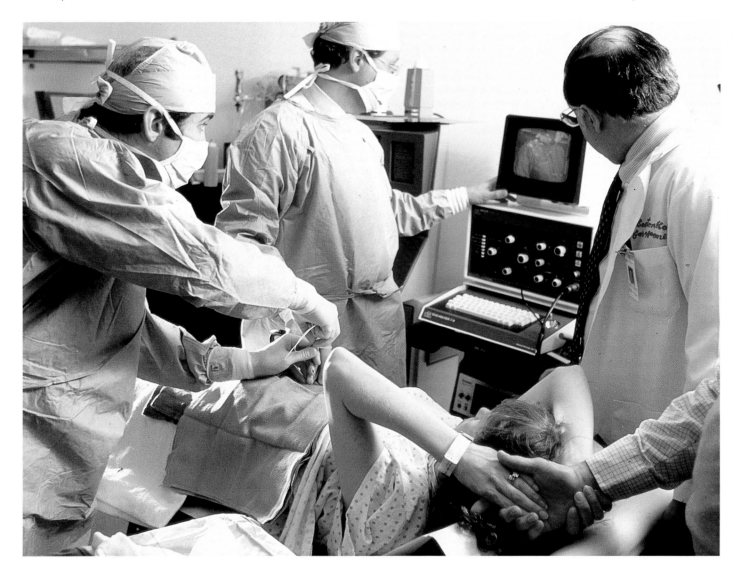

Surrogate motherhood

It is now, in several countries, almost commonplace for babies to be born from human eggs which have been fertilized outside the body and then returned to it. The pioneer of the technique was the Cambridge physiologist, Robert G. Edwards (born 1925). As early as 1934, Gregory Pincus of Harvard University, later famous as the inventor of the first contraceptive pill, described how he had obtained eggs from both monkey and rabbit ovaries and fertilized them in culture or *in vitro* (literally, "in glass"). Indeed, he managed to inject the fertilized rabbit eggs back into the female and set in motion a successful pregnancy. In the late 1950s, Edwards started to use similar methods to study the maturation of oocytes – the cells that give rise to eggs – of various mammals, including humans. In 1968 Edwards met the gynecologist, Patrick Steptoe (1913-1988), and his co-worker Jean Purdy. Together they developed techniques for collecting human eggs using a laparoscope, fertilizing them *in vitro*, allowing the embryos to grow for 2½-4½ days, and then replacing them in the uterus of the mother through a catheter passed through the cervix.

▼ *The happy outcome of a surrogate grandmotherhood. Pat Anthony, a South African, had eggs taken from her daughter Karen implanted into her womb and successfully carried them to term to give birth to triplets. The eggs had been previously fertilized "in vitro" by her son-in-law Alcino.*

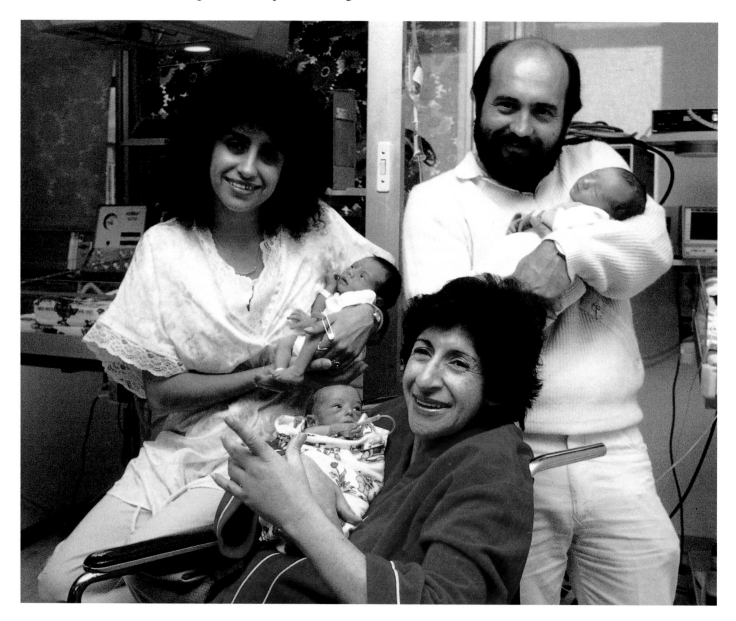

To describe the offspring so produced as test-tube babies is journalistic hyperbole, since it is only their conception that is achieved in a glass vessel, not their gestation, and they are born by the normal route. Nevertheless, the potential of the technique is so great that sensational reportage was probably justified. In the first instance, *in vitro* fertilization makes childbearing possible for a woman with tubal blockage or for her eggs to be successfully fertilized by a husband with sperm deficiency. It thus has high medical value. It is equally possible for a woman to be implanted with an egg from another woman's ovary, fertilized *in vitro* by sperm from her own husband or, for that matter, from any other male. The risk of passing on an heritable disorder might thus be avoided. The social and ethical problems of such a procedure do not greatly differ from those of artificial insemination by donor (AID), which is widely permitted. It would thus seem illogical to forbid it. However, a married woman might, with the consent of her husband, wish to receive an embryo in which both the egg and sperm have been provided by others. If it is legal for either sperm or egg to originate form a donor, why not both? Some of the consequences could, nevertheless, be disturbing.

It would be logical for the law to recognize clearly that there are now three categories of motherhood. A genetic mother is one who supplies an egg, a gestational mother one who carries and gives birth to the offspring, and a social mother one who rears the child and is legally responsible for its care. If a child is conceived with egg or sperm from other than the legal mother and father, the details of the genetic origin should either be recorded on its birth certificate or, at least, be stored by an agency from which they can subsequently be recovered. There is no sign that any government is considering such a radical approach.

These problems may, however, prove to be minor in comparison with others that could arise. To test embryos *in vitro* for hereditary defects and select only healthy ones for reimplantation is now possible in animals and will soon be possible for humans. It would appear to be entirely benign in purpose. On the other hand, the fact that fertilized eggs can be frozen and stored in liquid nitrogen where they remain viable for at least several months, means that any woman can now be implanted with an embryo produced by egg and sperm from selected donors. Does this offer potential for improvement of the human race, or is it a dangerous threat to the structure of society?

▼ Surrogacy can pose legal and moral problems. A working-class mother of two, Mary Beth Whitehead, received $10,000 to act as a surrogate mother for a professional couple, William and Elizabeth Stern (above). After birth of the child, Mary Beth decided she wished to keep it, and a long legal battle ensued. In 1987, the courts denied Mrs Whitehead any parental rights. In 1988, higher courts allowed her a weekly 6-hour visit but ruled that "womb-for-rent" contracts were invalid, though surrogacy agreements without payment were legal.

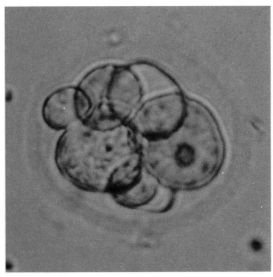
▼ This fertilized human egg is at the 8-cell stage of division. It will develop to a many-celled "blastocyst" and will then become implanted in the wall of the womb.

Preserving one's identity

If it is true that intelligence or particular talents are at least partly inheritable, then it should be possible to produce to order embryos having particular characters. A woman could then choose to bear a child with genetic material from, for example, a pair of famous philosophers or mathematicians, musicians, opera singers, or athletes. One can imagine that such embryos might be marketed by human seedsmen, having many famous egg or sperm donors in their catalogs, each of whom might receive large stud or egg-donation fees. On the one hand, such practice might, by individual volition rather than state compulsion, achieve some of the noble aims of the early eugenicists. On the other hand, there is no doubt that it could alter social structures, since traditional patterns of courtship and mating would no longer produce the same genetic consequences. From the scientific viewpoint, it must be admitted that such developments might produce some interesting evidence to fuel the nature versus nurture controversy!

The establishment in California of a bank for the sperm of Nobel prizewinners and others suggests that the sale of human embryos cannot be ruled out. But, even if permitted it is unlikely to be popular: it would be expensive, and people want their own children. The ultimate use of "in vitro" fertilization could be the use of techniques of genetic engineering to alter and perhaps improve the embryo. One such possibility, known as cloning, already looms on the horizon, though it is by no means certain that it can be achieved in humans. It involves initiating the development of an embryo by removing the nucleus from the egg and inserting a nucleus, with its full complement of chromosomes, from an adult body cell of a donor. The result would be to produce a child genetically identical with the donor. Cloning was first demonstrated in amphibians, using cells from the adult gut. It has also been achieved in a mouse, but not by using adult cells, only with a nucleus from an embryonic cell.

Cloning, coupled with the use of surrogates, could enable any individual, male or female, to produce an unlimited number of children who were genetically identical to themselves. The idea might appeal to rich potentates who wish to ensure survival and propagation of their own genes – it could be a more efficient mechanism than those provided in history by the "droit du seigneur" or polygamy. Cloning could also provide for the serial survival of genetic identity throughout time. Live copies of famous or talented individuals could be bequeathed to posterity and their numbers constantly built up. Perhaps this threat should not be taken too seriously. Manufacturing a double may for most people appear to be an affront to the idea of their own uniqueness.

◄ **Mr Robert Graham, with the tanks of liquid nitrogen in which he maintains his sperm bank in Escondido, California. He stocks only very special sperm, those of around 10 men considered by him to be geniuses, in his "Repository for Germinal Choice". Some have already been used to father children** by artificial insemination. **Graham strongly denies that he is trying to create a super-race. Nevertheless, the only sperm donor who has revealed his identity is the Nobel prizewinner, William Shockley, known for his opinion that blacks are intellectually inferior to whites for genetic reasons.**

Replacing Humans

23

Are humans too clever for their own good?...Our distinguishing feature – language...The quest for artificial intelligence...Once started, "AI" will spread like wildfire...Telepathy for computers...A machine that makes what you describe to it...Some assumptions about the course of evolution and "progress"

Ancient fears that the human species may be too clever for its own good found expression in the myths of Prometheus and Faust. In the late 20th century, causes of anxiety include those technologies that damage the environment, or threaten the world with nuclear war. But even these great matters may come to appear less important than a question anticipated in Mary Shelley's tale (1818) of Frankenstein, who invented a monster. Which will be in charge – the human species or its creations?

The same question arises in a low-key version every day, whenever individuals wonder if they have become enslaved by the machines they operate, the crops they raise, or the money they earn. But two possibilities latent in current science and technology dramatize the issue and make it graver. One is the quest for computers that, in some practical sense, will be cleverer than human beings. Another is the idea that knowledge of genetics and genetic engineering could provide the means to breed a new species or race of human beings superior to *Homo sapiens sapiens* in mental and physical powers. In either of these cases, people may find they have condemned themselves to the same relationship to supercomputers or supermen that chimpanzees have with human beings.

These extreme possibilities throw other issues into sharp relief. How much of human creative work, in the arts and technology, should be handed over to computers? Where is the borderline between curing genetic defects in patients, and trying to make superior human beings? What is the essence of human nature as distinct from machines or superhumanity?

The human example

The human brain starts, apparently, with some basic data-processing and rule-making programs "wired" into the connections between its nerve cells by hereditary instructions. But most of what a person knows, from the appearance of his or her mother to the theory of relativity, has been learnt in the course of everyday life.

In a word, the human brain is self-organizing, and efforts by farsighted computer experts to develop self-organizing electronic systems give an impression of how much remains to be done. Self-organizing systems that can recognize human speech sounds and transcribe them with fair accuracy onto a typewriter are regarded as very advanced. However, they are a far cry from a computer that understands what the words mean.

Natural language may be the most important gift that distinguishes human beings, not only from computers, but from their relatives in the animal kingdom (◆ page 199). The evidence of archaeology points to a change in human affairs about 50,000 years ago, which suddenly promoted our species from clever tool-making hunters to the creative people who would in due course fly to the Moon. Tools became much more sophisticated, and artistic and scientific ideas date from that period. The simplest explanation for that revolution is that it was related to the emergence of fully-fledged language.

The gulf that separates users of natural language from computers became apparent when early attempts to use machines for language translation ended in failure (◆ page 204). Attempts to coach computers in the use of natural language loom large in Artificial Intelligence (AI) programs. One aim is to make communication with computers easier for humans. This calls for fresh insight into the nature of human languages, and the mental processes involved in constructing an ordinary sentence. The chief difficulty is that human beings share much knowledge which remains unspoken, but is necessary for comprehension.

A remaining difference between human beings and ordinary computers concerns our sense organs. These inform the brain about what is going on around it, through systems that are wonderfully efficient at sorting out significant information from background "noise". Human life is also an endless experiment – you control the muscles of your legs, fingers or lips, and you observe the consequences. An infant explores the world by sight and touch, and so discovers the behavior of inanimate objects and living things. Some experts in AI believe that intelligent computers will have to be elaborate robots with sensors and limbs, exploring the world for themselves, and learning about it by experience in essentially the same way as a human child.

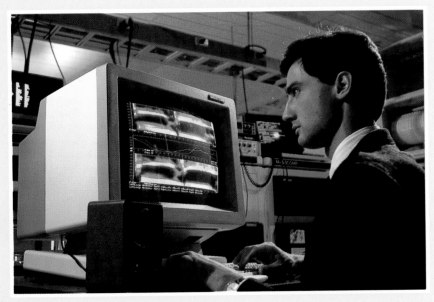

◄ *"Voiceprints" of the word "baby" spoken by four people demonstrate that everyone pronounces words slightly differently, when judged by the changing frequencies of sound waves. This is one of the problems in coaching computers to deal with ordinary language.*

Toward metallic minds

Marvin Minsky of the Massachusetts Institute of Technology remarked in a television interview in 1983: "People giggle and blush when you talk about such things, that the real promise of artificial intelligence is to design our successors … What kinds of feelings of regret should we have, if in the future we'll be succeeded by creations of ourselves with greater powers?" With less apparent enthusiasm, indeed as a dire warning, the Swedish Nobel prizewinner Hannes Alfvén published *The Great Computer* (1968) under a pseudonym. In this work of science fiction a computer tells how it and its metallic comrades managed to outwit human beings and take charge of the Earth.

In the real world of the late-20th-century, developments frequently tagged as "artificial intelligence" (AI) have become respectable, from a technical point of view, as a key element in efforts to develop new generations of computers. In Japan, the United States and Europe, outpourings of money by governments and industrial firms sustain these efforts. Car manufacturers have announced projects for the development of intelligent vehicles that will help to prevent drivers from having accidents or losing their way.

Philosophers enjoy debating the meaning of intelligence in machines, but in practical and political terms, a machine is intelligent if people judge it to be so. No one would call ordinary computers anything but stupid. They cannot add 2 and 2, or make the most trivial decision, without detailed instructions. Carefully briefed, computers can operate on data with wonderful speed and reliability, much as a jet aircraft flies in a reassuring, but not intelligent way.

Pseudo-intelligence confused the picture in the early stages of AI. "Expert systems" is the name for programs that endow computers with professional skills. Human experts feed in their specialist knowledge, and instruct the machines in routine decision-making based on that knowledge. Conceivably such systems may make many doctors and lawyers redundant, but they are not really any more intelligent than computers that mimic craftsmen in factories, and usurp their jobs too.

Another aspect of AI is a matter of good housekeeping within computer systems. As these become faster and more capacious, and are set ever more intricate tasks, tracing faults may be extremely difficult. Techniques with an AI label can enable a computer to monitor its own operations, and provide windows through which human beings can see more easily what is going on. Related to this are methods by which computers help in writing and checking their own program.

The quest for real AI is much more ambitious, and may require computers of a new kind. One profound difference between ordinary computers and the human brain is that computers typically work like typewriters, handling one operation and one piece of data at a time. This is called serial operation, while the human brain operates in a parallel mode. The power of the living brain is most apparent, not in high-flown ideas about angels or black holes, but in commonplace experiences. You turn the corner of a street and, within a very few seconds, you have sized up the traffic, avoided collisions with other walkers, flicked a fly from your face, noticed some cheap strawberries for sale, recognized a friend coming toward you, and found the words of greeting. To program a computer for any one of these tasks, taken separately, would be a monumental undertaking. To have a conventional machine execute them all at once, and also remain ready to deal with the unexpected (a sudden downpour of rain, a child on a skateboard, an observation that your friend is limping) would be impossible.

◄ *A Cray machine at the US National Supercomputing Center, based at the University of Illinois, uses "parallel processing" to achieve fantastic rates of calculation, counted in billions of operations per second. By comparison, human mental processes, at one or two thoughts or spoken words per second, seem at first sight very slow-witted. In fact, the supercomputers of the late 1980s scarcely begin to match the capacity of an ordinary human being to process information simultaneously, with messages racing through many parts of the brain.*

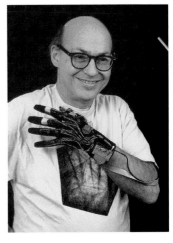

▲ *Known as the prophet of superintelligent machines, Marvin Minsky of the Massachusetts Institute of Technology, demonstrates a "DataGlove". Developed by VPL Research, the glove translates the movements of a human hand into electrical signals. One of its practical applications is to coach robots to work with human-like dexterity.*

Parallel computing

Computers that work in parallel are under development, but to be intelligent, machines will also need a capacity for learning that goes far beyond existing programs. There are many reasons for thinking that fully-intelligent computers will be difficult to develop. On the other hand, the requirements are cast in the broadest terms, and it is not necessary that computers should observe the environment, handle natural language, or process information in parallel, in ways that slavishly imitate the human brain.

Much faster, more efficient and more reliable systems can probably be devised to exploit the virtues of electronics. Current developments in computer hardware strongly favor the rapid development of artificial intelligence (AI), if the conceptual problems can be solved. Hard on the heels of parallel processors using silicon chips come possibilities in optical computing, using beams of light, that seem ready-made for parallel systems capable of interpreting a scene faster than a high-speed camera could snap it. In limbs and hands, developments for industrial robots already promise plenty of manipulative power for intelligent computers, and machine sensors will out-perform human senses.

Once the first steps have been taken toward truly intelligent computers, their further development will proceed apace. One reason is that intelligent computers can help in the design, construction and programming of computers even more intelligent than themselves. Engineers will one day find that their computers are recommending designs that they, the engineers, do not fully understand, but which will work when they are constructed.

A more fundamental reason for expecting machine intelligence to grow rapidly, once it takes off, is that machines are already better adapted than human beings to reading the contents of one another's memories. This is the capacity that people wish for, when they speak of telepathy. There have been proposals to wire human brains together in groups to create a collective mind, more powerful and durable than any individual's. Such an operation will be much easier to achieve with AI, than by implanting wires and radio transmitters in people's heads.

▼▶A blueprint for complex circuitry compressed to a microscopic scale on a single silicon chip (below) gives a sense of technology beginning to match the fine "wiring" of nerves in the human brain. IBM's experimental RP3 computer (right) uses "parallel processing". Like the brain, it also has both local and global systems of memory, and a capacity to send out data to several parts of its system at the same time.

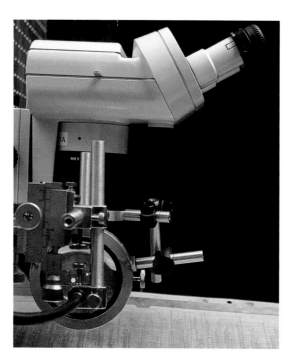

▶ A robot sensor examines an electrical circuit for possible faults. With microscopic and telescopic vision, machines can easily out-perform the human senses. They can "see" and "hear" at wavelengths far outside the human range, and "smell" airborne molecules more keenly than a bloodhound. Yet making sense of sensory information can often require massive computing power.

A Santa Claus machine

The engineer Theodore Taylor of Princeton University has envisaged a "Santa Claus" machine, which would eat rocks and manufacture anything that human beings wanted – coffee cups, sports cars, computers, or other Santa Claus machines. The only human intervention necessary would be to describe the desired product. Running self-sufficiently on sunlight or nuclear energy, the Santa Claus machine would be the apotheosis of the robot, equipped with machinery of many kinds, and capable of reproducing that machinery. In short, it would be a machine capable of "breeding" other creations like itself. To survive on the Earth's surface, a Santa Claus machine might require intelligence neither greatly inferior nor greatly superior to a human being's.

In the exploration and settlement of space the intelligent robot will be an indispensable partner. What could be more natural than to leave the most laborious and dangerous work to intelligent and self-reproducing Santa Claus machines? Let them build orbiting space cities out of Moon rock, let them prepare Mars for human habitation, let them multiply the rocket craft needed to fly them to other parts of the Solar System. And when the time comes to despatch the first ships to other stars, let them be manned by intelligent robots.

Dangers lurk in these "helpful" concepts. Santa Claus machines could run amok; like humans, computers are vulnerable to mutations caused by cosmic rays; a self-reproducing machine could pass defects on to its "offspring", and so on.

Looked at another way, simply sending intelligent self-reproducing robots to seek out habitable planets in the vicinity of other stars could amount to a willful abdication of the rights of our species in the universe at large. If the human species manages its space affairs wisely, there is good reason to hope that in the centuries ahead it will begin expanding beyond the Solar System, to find new abodes of human life throughout the Galaxy. The breathtaking prospect of worlds without end could be canceled at the outset by giving too much opportunity to intelligent and self-reproducing robots. With the head start that they gain from their better adaptation to existence in space, they could easily usurp the millions of planets that could serve for human settlements, and populate them with robots. In that case our mechanical creations, not our own living species, would be the means of spreading intelligence through the Galaxy.

Some dubious beliefs

The possibility of deliberately producing inferior human beings to carry out menial or repetitive tasks has been explored (◀ page 128). Another moral minefield attends any attempts to improve, or improve on, the human species. The primary motives for trying to develop a superhuman are likely to have little to do with improving life for human beings in general, and much to do with the economic and military contests between nations.

However, a distinctive impetus to the quest for a superman will come from ordinary people. Parents are often unreasonably ambitious for their children and some would welcome a chance to produce a genius with a little help from genetic engineers. But how many of these beings will suffer as a result of being botched? And if a creature produced by genetic manipulation were to commit a murder, who should take the blame: that creature or the scientist who made him? These are among

► *The Toshiba industrial robot ARI resembles the human-like creatures of science fiction. It is able to examine a structure made of LEGO blocks and figure out how to duplicate it. But ARI is not a toy. It is part of the effort by leading industrial nations (Japan in this case) to beat their competitors in industrial automation and in the development of intelligent computers. Commercial and military pressures will prompt a rapid advance to superintelligent machines, even though many people are afraid that they may become too powerful.*

the short-term hazards of playing God, but we should perhaps be concerned more with the long-term implications of such a project, if it were successful.

As in the case of intelligent computers, there is reason for wondering if a superior intelligence of flesh and blood would be friendly or aggressive toward its makers. Ordinary people might feel less unhappiness about making way for handsome creatures walking on two legs, than about kowtowing to robots. Nevertheless, to make superhumans seems, on the face of it, an act of treachery to our own species, and the case for it would need to be much stronger than it appears at present.

Implicit in the quest for superior intelligence is an assumption about the course of evolution, and its supposed natural direction. Some 600 million years ago, the highest intelligence on the planet Earth was possessed by worms burrowing on the seabed. By 200 million years ago, the dinosaurs may have possessed intelligence similar to that of birds, of which they are the ancestors. Apes appeared 20 million years ago, endowed with monkey-like cunning. The high intelligence of *Homo sapiens sapiens* emerged just a moment ago on the geological clock. This chronicle has encouraged a belief that nature, in its evolutionary pathways, is unconsciously endeavoring to increase intelligence. From this belief flow the notions that human beings have a cosmic duty consciously to strive for ever-higher intelligence, and that evolution proceeds by a process of gradual, continuous improvements. Recent discoveries and counter-theories cast doubts on all of these beliefs.

There is growing evidence that evolutionary changes occur in jumps, perhaps in isolated populations that evolve independently of the rest of their species, and then replace it. Something of the kind may explain the sudden emergence of our own talkative subspecies, and its rapid spread all over the world. If there is any moral at all in the patterns of evolution, it may be that species are conservative. Natural selection usually acts, not to keep changing a species, but to eliminate harmful mutation and oddities. There is no evidence that our subspecies has altered in any significant way since it made its debut 50,000 years ago. This is not to say that purposeful human beings must follow the models of blind nature, but only to argue against the dubious belief that nature favors intelligence. Indeed high intelligence may not be a survivable trait.

▼ At Oxford University a British girl, Ruth Lawrence, graduated in mathematics at 13 and in physics at 14. She is a natural prodigy, but it is easy to imagine ambitious parents asking genetic engineers to help them breed a superintelligent child. Then the quest for a superman or superwoman could proceed without any public control.

◄ Ever-higher intelligence is not a goal in natural evolution. Insects such as this fossil long-legged fly preserved in amber, have prospered in a relatively brainless way for 10,000 times longer than our own subspecies of human being, whose high intelligence seems an evolutionary fluke.

An uneasy conclusion

If there were a global referendum on whether to develop superior creatures, who would displace the present incumbent species as chief agents on this planet, the answer would probably be a resounding No! The outcome would be the same for a referendum on the desirability of a nuclear war, and the similarity does not end there. However the tides of international negotiations may flow, between arms races and arms control agreements, the human species will retain its knowledge of nuclear explosives into the indefinite future. Avoiding nuclear war for ever will require unceasing diplomacy and political action. Equally, the human species will retain control of Frankenstein-like artifacts only by eternal vigilance.

"Superman" already exists, in the form of the human species as a whole and all its coherent subdivisions. The real secret of success of the most prosperous species of large animal in the history of the world lies not in the high intelligence of a few gifted individuals, but in our species' ability to mobilize large numbers of brains and hands over long periods – reckoned in centuries – to tackle its tasks. The recognition of inventors, discoverers and artists who have made special contributions, and the careful preservation of their work, are part of the social system. Any tampering with human beings that might upset the balance between sociability and individual intelligence could destroy this fabric.

Many of our current problems arise less from a lack of creativity and inventiveness than from an excess of new-found technological powers to which our societies have not properly adjusted. There is a lack of wisdom, certainly, to temper the use of those powers. If there are any genes for wisdom, they are even more elusive than genes for cleverness. Wisdom tries to reconcile powerful knowledge with a sensitivity to the complex systems of the environment and human society, and with a deep understanding of human needs, hopes and fears. If anything needs reinforcing in the brain, it may be the capacity for compassion.

The promotion of superintelligent computers or supermen may seem opportune from time to time, to solve the problems of the moment, and the initiative for such developments will come typically from governments or commercial enterprises. They will not find it difficult to recruit scientists and engineers to carry out the projects, because enthusiasm for creative work with one's own skills is another enduring aspect of human nature.

But, extermination excepted, nothing could be more impoverishing than to rob human beings of control of their own affairs, and to hand it over to superintelligent computers or supermen. The final appeal may be to the communal intelligence of the human species, and the capacity for survival that has carried it through a long succession of natural calamities – and crises of its own making.

▼ **This is the central region of our Milky Way, a galaxy which harbors hundreds of billions of stars including the Sun. Conceivably ours is the only highly intelligent species in the Galaxy. If so, an awesome responsibility falls on humanity, to keep its little flicker of natural intelligence alive.**

Credits

Key to abbreviations: CD Chemical Designs Ltd, Oxford; SPL Science Photo Library, London. b bottom; bl bottom left; br bottom right; c center; cl center left; cr center right; t top; tl top left; tr top right; l left; r right.

9 Camera Press/Homer Sykes 10-11b G. Garradd/SPL 11t NASA/SPL 12 Camera Press 13 D. Parker/SPL 14 CERN 15, 16t D. Parker/SPL 16b S.J. Maddox/APM Group Cambridge, UK 17t Lockheed/SPL 17b Dr D.H. Roberts/SPL 18 Jean Collombet/SPL 18-19 Royal Greenwich Observatory/SPL 19 Jerry Mason/SPL 20 (main pic.) Royal Observatory Edinburgh 20 inset, 21tl Anglo-Australian Telescope Board 21tr IMB collaboration/SPL 22t NRAO/SPL 22b X-Ray Astronomy Group Leicester University/SPL 23t NASA 23b ESA 24b NASA 24-25t Mary Dale Bannister, Washington University/NASA 25b NASA 26tl Jerry Mason 26-27t NASA 26b Max Planck Institut für Aeronomie/D. Parker/SPL 28l, 28r, 29b ESA 29b Orbital Sciences Corporation, Fairfax, Virginia 31t Perkin Elmer 31b ESA 32tr, 32cr, 32b, 33 NASA 34-35t NASA 34-35b ESA 36, 37 NASA 38 D.A. Hardy/SPL 39t Frank Spooner Pictures 39b M. Downes 40 NASA 41t NASA/SPL 41b Novosti/SPL 42 NASA/SPL 43l British Aerospace, Stevenage 43r Julian Baum/SPL 44 Alexander Tsiaras/SPL 45l NASA/SPL 45r UKAEA, Culham, UK 46l NASA/SPL 46r David A. Hardy/SPL 47 British Interplanetary Society 48l Professor C.O. Alley 48r M. Freeman/Telegraph Colour Library 49 CERN/P. Loiez/SPL 50-51 David A. Hardy/SPL 52 NASA/SPL 53 Julian Baum/SPL 54 NASA/SPL 55 Mary Evans Picture Library 56-57 Hansen Planetarium 57c Frank D. Drake and the National Astronomy and Ionosphere Center, Cornell University/NSF 57r, 58 NASA 59 Alfred McEwan, U.S. Geological Survey, Flagstaff, Arizona 60t Paul Ely, Institute for Astronomy, University of Hawaii 60b National Astronomy and Ionosphere Center, Cornell University, NSF 61 Frank Spooner Pictures 62, 63tl, 64 Sky Publishing Corporation 62-63b National Astronomy and Ionosphere Center/Arecibo Observatory 63tr Max Planck Institute for Radio Astronomy/SPL 65t Anthony Howarth/SPL 65b NASA/SPL 66 S.M. Awramik, Department of Geological Sciences, University of California 67t Mary Dale Bannister, Washington University/NASA 66-67b John Heseltine/SPL 68 F. Sauer/Bruce Coleman Ltd 69 C. Lorius 70 NASA/SPL 71tl, 71bl G. Kite 71r Boston University Photo Service 72 S. Manabe and R.T. Wetherald 73 Telegraph Colour Library/ESA/METEOSAT 74l, 74r NASA 75 Dr R. Legeckis/SPL 76tl, 76bl National Center for Atmospheric Research 76r New Scientist/SPOT 77 New Scientist/CNES 78l EOSAT 78r, 79 Hunting Technical Services Ltd 80-81c Ian Griffiths/Robert Harding Picture Library 80-81b B. McDairmant/Ardea 81t, 81c Earth Satellite Corporation/SPL 82-83 M. Chillmaid/OSF 83t Robert Harding Picture Library 84 Patricio Goycolea/Hutchison Library 85 Chicago Tribune Company 86l National Center for Atmospheric Research 86r Carl Purcell/SPL 87 Rex Features 88 Simon Fraser/SPL 88-89t Bernard Régent/Hutchison Library 89b Mike Goldwater/Network 90l Art Directors 90-91, 91r Frank Spooner Pictures 92-93 James H. Baker 93r Frank Spooner Pictures 94 Mat Irvine 95t Hutchison Library 95b Alex Low/Telegraph Colour Library 96 Patrick McClay/Oxfam 97 Sue Cunningham/Panos Pictures 98-99 Patrick McClay/Oxfam 99tl F. Corbineau/Telegraph Colour Library 99tr Dick Clark/Planet Earth Pictures 100-101t R. Elliott/Telegraph Colour Library

100-101b, 101r Adam Hart-Davis/SPL 102t, 102b Sebastio Salgado/Magnum 103l Hildegard Weismed/Greenpeace 103r Patrick Fagot/NHPA 104r Geoff Barnard/Panos Pictures 104-105b Westinghouse Harford Company 105t Alexander Tsiaras/SPL 106-107 Ken Biggs/SPL 107 Paul Harrison/Panos Pictures 108 Pacific Press Service/SPL 109 Larry Mulvehill/SPL 110r David Woodfall/NHPA 110-111 Peter Charlesworth/Panos Pictures 111t L.C. Marigo/Bruce Coleman Ltd 112-113 P. McClay/Oxfam 113t Geoff Barnard/Panos Pictures 113b N.A. Callow/NHPA 114l N. Wright/Bruce Coleman Ltd 114-115 Bernard Régent/Hutchison Library 115 M. Boulton/Bruce Coleman Ltd 116 T. Beddow/Hutchison Library 117 Ferdinando Scianna/Magnum 118, 119 CD 120 Art Directors/Chuck O'Rear 121l John Innes Institute 121r Dr J. Burgess/SPL 122 Charlotte Raymond/SPL 123tl, 123tr M. Vaeck/Plant Genetic Systems 123b Art Directors/Chuck O'Rear 124l Sinclair Stammers/SPL 124r, 125r John Innes Institute 124-125 Biotal 126tl, 126tc, 126b Dr R.L. Brinster, University of Pennsylvania 127cl Rex Features/J. Craymer 127b Ann Ronan Picture Library 127r B. Bowman, University of California, Berkeley 128 Plessy Research Caswell and Cambridge University 129 CNRI/SPL 130b J. Calder/Impact 130-131 CNRI 131b Anthea Sieveking/Vision International 131tr Hulton Picture Library/Bettmann Archive 132 Caltech 133t P.A. McTurk, University of Leicester and D. Parker/SPL 133b Genetics Institute Inc, Cambridge, Mass./Ted Polumbaum 134t John Watney 134b Aspect Picture Library 135 Celltech Ltd 136l National Cancer Institute/SPL 136-137 CNRI/SPL 137t Dr Karen Sikora/SPL 138tl, 138cl, 138bl, 138r Dr P. Summers 139 John Watney/Petit Format 140 Art Directors/Chuck O'Rear 141t Dr A. Twort 141b Sally and Richard Greenhill 142-143 Robert Isear/SPL 143t John Durham/SPL 143b Glaxo, Verona 144l Lee Simon/S. Stammers/SPL 144tr, 144cr Institute for Animal Health, Houghton Laboratory 144-145 J. Walsh/SPL 146tr Rex Features 146-147 Paul Fusco/Magnum 147r Rex Features 148-149 Celltech Ltd 149r Dr J. Burgess/SPL 150l CNRI/SPL 150-151 Institut Pasteur/CNRI/SPL 151t Australasian Nature Transparencies/Natfoto 151r Royal Botanic Gardens, Kew 152 Professor G. Targett and Electron Microscopy Unit, London School of Hygiene and Tropical Medicine 153t David Reed/Impact Photos 153b Dr John P. Caulfield 154 David Reed/Impact Photos 155t Camera Press 155b Hulton Picture Library 156 OSF/G.I. Bernard 156-157 OSF/Mantis Wildlife Films 158tl Rex Features 158bl Sergio Dorantes/Sygma/John Hillelson Agency 158-159 Dr Deborah Clarke 159tl, 159cl Rex Features 160-161, 161bl Dr Leonard Hayflick 161tr Rex Features 161br CNRI/SPL 162 Imagine/Channel Four 163t Bildarchiv Preussicher Kulturbesitz 163b Frank Spooner Pictures 164 Bruno Barbey/Magnum 164-165b, 165tl Sally and Richard Greenhill 165tr Ian Berry/Magnum 166 Rex Features 167l, 167r Paul Biddle and Tim Malyon/SPL 168l, 168r Medi Sense (UK) Inc. 169l Zefa 169r Ian Berry/Magnum 170l Anita Corbin/Impact Photos 170-171t Martin Dohru/SPL 170-171b David Parker/SPL 172 John Durham/SPL 173 CNRI/SPL 174 Patrick Ward/Telegraph Colour Library 175 Professor Goldsmith 176l D. Beatty/Susan Griggs Agency 176r Frank Spooner Pictures 177 Don McCullin/Magnum 178 ESPRIT 179 Alexander Tsiaras/SPL 180 Art Directors 180b Imagine 181 Dr W. Feindel, Penfield Archive 182 Art Directors 183t Mary Evans Picture Library/Society for Psychical Research 183b Michael Holford

184 Donald Cooper/Photostage 185 Alain Evrard/Susan Griggs Agency 186l Frank Spooner Pictures 186-187 Michael Nichols/Magnum 187 Bruno Barbey/Magnum 188l The Kobal Collection/Lucas Films 188r Frank Spooner Pictures 189l S.J. Kraseman/Bruce Coleman Ltd. 189r Ronald Grant Collection 190l Eung G. Paek and Ken Hsu/Caltec 190-191 Equinox Archive 191tr Frank Spooner Pictures 191br Channel Four 192 McGill University Archives 193t Imagine 193b Biophoto Associates 194tl Imagine 194-195 Dr Guy Salama 194tr Dr R.G.M. Morris 195r George Steinmetz 196-197t A. Kerstich/Planet Earth Pictures 196-197b Hank Morgan/SPL 198 Gilles Peress/Magnum 199t Earth Images/Terry Domico 199b Paul Fusco/Magnum 200 The Kobal Collection 201t Imagine 201b Maggie Murray/Format 202 Alexander Tsiaras/SPL 203tl, 203cl Dr John Mazziottaetal/SPL 203r CNRI/SPL 204 Constantine Manos/Magnum 205 Imagine 206 IBM 207l, 207r Magnum 208l National Institute of Health/SPL 208-209 Sidney Moulds/SPL 210bl, 210br Aspect Picture Library 210tr Blair Seltz/SPL 210-211 D. Modge/Hutchison Library 212 Hutchison Library 213t Amnesty International 213b M. Harvey/Hutchison Library 214 Neill Menneer 215t Tony Morrison/South American Pictures 215b Christopher Pillitz/Impact Photos 216l The Kobal Collection 216-217, 217br Dr E.D. London, National Institute on Drug Abuse, Baltimore 217t David Reed/Impact Photos 218 CNRI/SPL 219 Michael Abbey/SPL 220 Rex Features 221t N.G. Blake/Bruce Coleman Ltd 221b Rex Features 222 Dan McCoy/Rainbow 223l Jane Burton/Bruce Coleman Ltd. 223r Hulton Picture Library 224 NHPA/Orion Press 225 Hutchison Library 226tl Dr F. Sauer/Bruce Coleman Ltd 226tr G. Wilkinson 226b A. Bannister/NHPA 228l John Cleare/Mountain Camera 228r Sally and Richard Greenhill 229t, 229b M. Milinski 230t Robert Harding Picture Library 230b Sally and Richard Greenhill 231 Rex Features 232 Frank Spooner Pictures 233t, 233tc Hulton Picture Library 233bc, 233b Popperfoto 234 Hulton Picture Library 235l Frank Spooner Pictures 235r Camera Press 236t M. Selinger, Nuffield Department of Gynaecology, Oxford 236b Yves Bié/Petit Format 237 J. Marmaras/Susan Griggs Agency 238 Mail on Sunday 239l Frank Spooner Pictures 239r Petit Format/CSI/SPL 240 Frank Spooner Pictures 241 Hank Morgan/Rainbow 242 M.L. Abramson/ Woodfin Camp and Associates 243, 244l Dan McCoy/Rainbow 244r Hank Morgan/Rainbow 245 IBM 246 Frank Spooner Pictures 247l Rex Features 247r G. Zeisler/Bruce Coleman Ltd 248 Ronald Royer/SPL

Artists
Kevin Maddison, Colin Salmon, Mick Saunders, David Smith

Indexer
John Baines

Typesetting
Peter MacDonald, Una Macnamara

Production
Joanna Turner

Editorial assistant
Monica Byles

Further Reading

Asimov, Issac *Fantastic Voyage II* (Grafton)
Bains, William *Genetic Engineering for Almost Everybody* (Penguin)
Close, Frank and Sutton, Christine *The Particle Explosion* (Oxford University Press)
Comfort, Alex *The Biology of Senescence* (Churchill Livingstone)
Comfort, Alex *The Process of Ageing* (Weidenfeld & Nicolson)
Davies, Paul *The Cosmic Blueprint* (Simon & Schuster)
Dawkins, Richard *The Blind Watchmaker* (Norton)
Duncan, R and Weston Smith, M. (eds.) *The Encyclopaedia of Ignorance* (Pergamon Press)
Fairbairn, S. and G. *Psychology: Ethics and Change* (Routledge & Kegan Paul)
Feynman, Richard and Weinberg, Steven *Elementary Particles and the Laws of Physics* (Cambridge University Press)
Friedman, Louis *Starsailing* (Wiley)
George, Frank (ed.) *Science Fact* (Topaz)
Gradwohl, Judith and Greenberg, Russell *Saving the Tropical*

Forests (Island Press)
Gregory, Richard (ed.) *The Oxford Companion to the Mind* (Oxford University Press)
Gribbin, John, *Hole in the Sky* (Bantam)
Gribbin, John *Double Helix* (McGraw Hill; Bantam)
Harris, M. and Coltheart, M. *Language Processing in Children and Adults* (Routledge & Kegan Paul)
Harvey, Brian *Race into Space* (Wiley)
Hawking, Stephen *A Brief History of Time* (Bantam)
Henbest, Nigel and Marten, Michael *The New Astronomy* (Cambridge University Press)
Islam, J.N. *The Ultimate Fate of the Universe* (Cambridge University Press)
Koestler, Arthur *The Sleepwalkers* (Hutchinson, Penguin)
Lewis, John and Ruth *Space Resources* (Columbia University Press)
Locke, S. and Colligan, D. *The Healer Within* (E.P. Dutton)
Marsh, Peter *The Space Business* (Penguin)

Meadows, Jack (ed.) *The History of Scientific Discovery* (Phaidon)
Miles, Frank and Booth, Nicholas, *Race to Mars* (Harper & Row)
Moore, Patrick and Hunt, Garry *Atlas of the Solar System* (Mitchell Beazley)
Panos Institute *Towards Sustainable Development*
Popper, Karl and Eccles, John *The Self and Its Brain* (Routledge & Kegan Paul)
Pratt, Vernon *Thinking Machines* (Blackwell)
Rycroft, Charles *Psychoanalysis and Beyond* (Chicago)
Scott, Andrew *Pirates of the Cell* (Basil Blackwell)
Seyle, Hans *The Stress of Life* (McGraw Hill)
Sutton, Christine *The Particle Connection* (Simon & Schuster)
Timberlake, Lloyd *Only One Earth* (Sterling)
Tudge, Colin *Food Crops for the Future* (Blackwell)
Wade, Nicholas *A World Beyond Healing* (Norton)
Watson, J.D. *Molecular Biology of the Gene* (W.A. Benjamin)
Whittow, John *Disasters: The Anatomy of Environmental Hazards* (University of Georgia)

Glossary

Accelerator
In particle physics, a research tool used to accelerate SUBATOMIC PARTICLES to high velocities.

Acid rain
Precipitation, both rain and snow, made acidic in reaction through the chemical pollution of air by waste gases, such as oxides of sulfur and nitrogen, from industry and car exhausts.

Acquired Immune Deficiency Syndrome (AIDS)
Prgoressive damage to white blood cells caused by infection with human immune virus (HIV).

Adaptation
The process whereby, under the influence of NATURAL SELECTION, an organism gradually changes genetically in such a way that it becomes better fitted to cope with its environment.

Addiction
A craving for a potentially harmful drug with increased bodily tolerance for it.

Allele
An alternative form of a GENE found at a particular site on the CHROMOSOME.

Allopathy
Disease treatment by adding (e.g. drugs) or removing (e.g. blood, germs) something in order to restore equilibrium to the body's system.

Allotrope
An element that occurs in varying forms, differing in their crystalline or molecular structure.

Altruism
Behavior which benefits another individual at the cost of the first.

Amino acid
A basic chemical unit from which PROTEINS are synthesized by the body.

Anemia
A disease in which the number of red blood cells circulating in the body, or their ability to carry oxygen, is lowered.

Antibiotic
A chemical produced by a MICROORGANISM and used as a drug to kill or inhibit the growth of other microorganisms.

Antibody
A defensive substance produced by the immune system to neutralize or help destroy a specific foreign substance.

Antigen
A foreign substance that provokes the body to produce ANTIBODIES.

Artificial Intelligence
Defined in 1968 by Marvin Minsky as "the science of making machines do things that would require intelligence if done by men." Intelligence created using non-living man-made microelectronic or other components.

Artificial selection
The process whereby the animals that produce offspring are chosen by humans, in contrast to natural selection where biological fitness determines the success of reproduction.

Atom
Classically, one of the minute, indivisible particles of which material objects are composed; in 20th-century science the name given to a relatively stable package of matter made up of at least two SUBATOMIC PARTICLES.

Auto-immune disease
A disease in which the body rejects some of its normal tissues and mobilizes the immune system against them.

Bacteria (singular bacterium)
A large and varied group of MICROORGANISMS, classified by their shape and staining ability. They live in many environments; only a few are harmful.

Bacteriophage
A VIRUS that attacks BACTERIA.

Big Bang
The hot, dense explosive event which is widely believed to have been the origin of the universe.

Biological control
The use of one species (usually a predator or parasite) to control the population of another.

Biomass
The total quantity of organic matter associated with the living organisms of a given area at a particular time.

Biosphere
The part of the Earth which is capable of supporting life: includes part of the ATMOSPHERE, lithosphere and hydrosphere.

Biotechnology
The use of MICROORGANISMS for industrial purposes.

Black hole
A region of space surrounding an old, collapsed star, from which not even light can escape.

Boson
A behavioral classification of SUBATOMIC PARTICLES according to Bose-Einstein statistics.

Bubble chamber
A device used to observe the paths of SUBATOMIC PARTICLES, by reducing pressure as the particles pass through so that bubbles form along their paths.

Catalyst
A substance which increases the speed of a chemical reaction but is itself chemically unchanged at the end of the reaction.

CAT scan (CT scan)
Computerized axial tomography, a technique of building up an X-RAY image of a slice through the body.

Cerebellum
The lobe at the rear of the brain that controls movement and balance.

Chromosome
A thread of genetic material contained in the cell nucleus and duplicated when the cell divides.

Comet
A member of the SOLAR SYSTEM, made up of a nucleus, a coma, and (with large comets) a tail or tails. Most comets have highly eccentric orbits.

Computer
A device that performs calculations and stores their results, according to a program.

Conditioned reflex
In physiology, the triggering of automatic reflexes by substitute stimuli.

Conditioning
Learning by association. In classical conditioning two stimuli are associated so that the second comes to elicit a response formerly only elicited by the first.

Cortex
The outer surface of an organ, such as the brain (where it is the seat of the higher functions).

Cyclotron
A particle ACCELERATOR in which the particles travel in a circular path in a strong magnetic field.

Diploid
Having two sets of CHROMOSOMES. See also HAPLOID.

Diversity
A measurement of the richness of species in a given area.

DNA
Deoxyribonucleic acid; its structure contains the blueprint that contains genetic information.

ECG
Electrocardiogram; the recording of the electrical changes accompanying the cardiac cycle.

Ecology
The study of organisms in relation to their physical and living environment, or ecosystem.

EEG
Electroencephalogram; the recording of the electrical impulses of the brain.

Electromagnetic radiation
The form in which energy is transmitted through space or matter, using an electromagnetic field. Its wavelengths carry radio waves and infrared waves, visible light, ultraviolet, X-RAYS and gamma rays.

Elementary particles
See SUBATOMIC PARTICLES.

Electron
A SUBATOMIC PARTICLE of negative charge, commonly in orbit around an atomic nucleus.

Electron micrograph
A highly magnified image obtained by using a beam of ELECTRONS rather than light.

Embryo
In humans, the developing baby in the womb from conception to the end of the tenth week.

Energy
The ability to do work. It may take many forms, such as light, heat and chemical.

Enzyme
A PROTEIN which is a CATALYST of biochemical reactions. There are many different kinds, each kind directly promoting only one or a very limited range of reactions.

Evolution
The process by which species have developed to their present appearance and behavior through the action of NATURAL SELECTION in determining the survival of those individuals most suited to their environment.

False-color photography
Processing of special photographic or other emulsions to display information, using "unnatural" color.

Fetus
The developing baby, from the tenth week after conception to birth.

Fission
The changing of an element into two or more elements of lower atomic weight, with the release of energy.

Frequency
The rate at which a wave motion completes its cycle.

Fusion
In nuclear physics, the merging of two nuclei to form a new element of higher atomic weight, resulting in the release of energy.

Galaxy
(A) A distinct star system: galaxies may contain from a few million to a few million million stars together with differing proportions of interstellar matter (gas and dust). (B) The star-system of which our Sun is a member: it contains about 100,000 million stars.

Gametes
Cells produced for the purpose of sexual reproduction – ova (eggs) and sperms. Except in parthenogenetic species they must fuse with another gamete before development can take place.

Gene
A unit of hereditary information. Each gene produces a single polypeptide chain.

Gene flow
The interchange of genetic factors between and within populations as a result of emigration and immigration.

Genetic drift
The occurrence of random changes, irrespective of selection and MUTATION, in the genetic make-up of small isolated populations.

Genetics
The study of heredity.

Genome
The total genetic complement of an organism.

Germ-line gene therapy
The proposed addition of extra genes to fertilized eggs to cure genetic defects for all future generations.

Greenhouse effect
The accumulation of gases, such as carbon dioxide, in the atmosphere which prevent infra-red RADIATION leaving the Earth and hence cause increasing global temperature.

GUT (grand unified theory)
The attempt to explain the forces of nature in terms of one underlying force.

Haploid
Having one set of CHROMOSOMES. See also DIPLOID.

Heredity
The passing of genetic characteristics from parents to children.

Holography
The creation of three-dimensional images by photographing the subject when illuminated by a split laser beam, and reproducing the image by recreating the beam.

Homeopathy
The treatment of medical symptoms by giving minute amounts of a drug which produces similar symptoms.

Homeostasis
The maintenance of constant conditions in the internal environment of animals.

Homozygous
In genetics, having the same ALLELE at both loci of a pair.

Hormone
A chemical secreted by an endocrine gland which has a specific effect on a target cell in another part of the body.

Hybrid
Offspring of parents which are not genetically identical.

Hypothalamus
The central part at the base of the brain, a center controlling primitive physical and emotional behavior.

Immunity
A state of resistance to an infection, through the existence of ANTIBODIES and immune cells specifically able to attack the MICROORGANISM responsible.

In vitro
In glass; outside the living body and within an artificial environment such as a test tube.

Ion
An atom or group of ATOMS that has become electrically charged by the gain or loss of ELECTRONS.

Isomers
Chemical compounds with identical chemical composition and molecular formula, but differing in the arrangement of ATOMS in their MOLECULES.

Isotopes
Atoms of an element with the same number of PROTONS in the nucleus but different numbers of NEUTRONS.

Kin selection
Selection in favor not necessarily of the individual but of relatives carrying the same genes; may be favored by behavior such as ALTRUISM.

Laser
Light Amplification by Stimulated Emission of Radiation; a device producing a very intense beam of parallel light with a precisely-defined wavelength.

Light-year
The distance traveled by light in one year: 9.46 million million km.

Macrophage
A white blood cell specialized to circulate through the body tissues and consume foreign bodies and cell debris.

Magnetic resonance imaging
(Or nuclear magnetic resonance, NMR.) The use of the spin of an ATOM when subjected to a strong magnetic field to form images of the interior of objects, including the human body, by detecting the presence of particular elements.

Metabolism
The chemical processes occurring within an organism, including the production of PROTEINS from AMINO ACIDS, the exchange of gases in respiration, the liberation of energy from foods and innumerable other chemical reactions.

Meteor
A small particle moving around the Sun. If it enters the Earth's upper atmosphere it becomes heated by friction, and burns away producing the luminous shooting-star appearance.

Meteorite
A small body sufficiently massive to survive entering the atmosphere at speeds of tens of km/sec and which can reach ground level.

Microbe, microorganism
Organisms of microscopic or ultramicroscopic size, such as bacteria, some fungi, viruses.

Microprocessor
An electronic device that receives, processes, stores and outputs information according to a preprogrammed set of instructions.

Molecule
An entity composed of ATOMS linked by chemical bonds and acting as a unit; its composition is represented by its molecular formula.

Mutation
A structural change in a GENE which may give rise to a new heritable characteristic if it occurs in one of the germ cells.

Natural selection
The process by which those organisms which are not well fitted to their environment are eliminated by predation, parasitism, competition, etc, and those which are well fitted survive to breed and pass on their GENES to subsequent generations.

Neutron
An uncharged SUBATOMIC PARTICLE.

Nuclear magnetic resonance (NMR)
SEE MAGNETIC RESONANCE IMAGING

Nuclear physics
The study of the properties and mathematical treatment of the atomic nucleus and SUBATOMIC PARTICLES.

Oncogene
A GENE carried by a VIRUS that is involved in transforming normal cells to cancerous ones orginally a section of DNA picked up by a virus.

Pangea
The supercontinent that existed between about 250 and 200 million years ago, comprising all the continental masses.

Pasteurization
A technique of heating milk, beer, wine etc. to destroy BACTERIA it may contain; named after Louis Pasteur.

Pathogen
An organism that produces disease.

Peptide
A compound containing two or more AMINO ACIDS.

Photon
A quantum of electromagnetic energy, often thought of as the particle associated with light.

Photosynthesis
The synthesis of organic compounds, primarily sugars, from carbon dioxide and water using sunlight as the source of energy, and chlorophyll, or some other related pigment, for trapping the light energy.

Piezoelectricity
The relationship between mechanical stress and electric charge exhibited by certain crystals.

Polarized light
Light in which the orientation of wave vibrations displays a definite pattern.

Protein
Organic compound made up of AMINO ACIDS.

Proton
A stable, positively charged SUBATOMIC PARTICLE found in the nucleus of all atoms.

Psychoanalysis
The free-association therapy invented by Sigmund Freud.

Quantum mechanics
The theory of small-scale physical phenomena, such as the motions of ELECTRONS and nuclei within atoms.

Quantum theory
A theory developed at the beginning of the 20th century to account for certain phenomena that could not be explained by classical physics.

Quark
A fundamental SUBATOMIC PARTICLE.

Quasar
A very remote superluminous object. Quasars are now believed to be the nuclei inside very active GALAXIES.

Radiation
Any form of energy that can be transmitted through a medium without having an effect on that medium.

Radioactivity
The spontaneous disintegration of unstable nuclei, accompanied by the emission of RADIATION of alpha particles, beta particles or gamma rays.

Refraction
The change in direction of energy waves as they pass from one medium to another.

Relativity
Theory of the nature of time, space and matter, enunciated by Albert Einstein.

RNA
Ribonucleic acid; a single-stranded nucleic acid that cooperates with DNA for PROTEIN synthesis.

Seismograph
A device used to detect seismic waves caused by earthquakes or explosions.

Semiconductor
A material whose electrical conductivity varies with temperature and impurity. By introducing impurities to different regions of a semiconductor, it can be modified for different electrical purposes.

Sociobiology
The branch of behavior study concerned with the social behavior of animals, its ecology and evolution.

Solar System
The system consisting of the Sun, the planets and their satellites, the asteroids, comets, meteoroids and other interplanetary material.

Space-time
A concept introduced by Hermann Minkowski to show how Einstein's ideas of RELATIVITY necessarily mix up space and time.

Spectroscopy
The production, measurement and analysis of spectra, much used by astronomers, chemists and physicists.

Strain gauge
A device for measuring strain at the surface of a material by determining variations in the current through a PIEZOELECTRIC device attached to it.

Stress
A physiological state induced in animals by conditions they are unable to tolerate and cope with, such as pain or overcrowding.

Subatomic particles
(Or elementary particles.) Small packets of matter-energy that are constituents of ATOMS or are produced in nuclear reactions or in interactions between other subatomic particles.

Sulfates
Salts of sulfuric acid, formed by reactions of the acid with metals, their oxides or carbonates, or by oxidation of sulfides or sulfites.

Superconductor
A material cooled to low temperatures, at which electrical resistance is zero; used in large electromagnets.

Supernova
A cataclysmic stellar outburst. Some supernovae are due to the collapse of a massive star; others are due to the complete disruption of the white dwarf component of a binary system.

Synchrotron
A large ACCELERATOR in which the particles are accelerated around a circular path.

Synapse
The junction between the processes of adjacent NEURONS, across which nerve impulses are carried by transmitter substances.

Transistor
An electronic device made of SEMICONDUCTORS used in a circuit as an amplifier, rectifier, detector or switch.

Tumor
A growth of excess tissue due to abnormal cell division.

Vaccination, vaccine
Originally, the introduction of matter from cowpox pustules to lessen the danger of catching smallpox; by extension, vaccines are attenuated forms of disease organisms used to confer immunity.

Villus (plural villi)
One of the microscopic projections of mucous membranes.

Virus
The smallest form of living organism, dependent on living cells for replication.

Vitamin
A substance which is essential for life and which the body cannot synthesize, so it must be present in diet.

Wave motion
The motion of a material or extended object oscillating in such a way as to create an illusion of crests and troughs.

X-rays
Invisible ELECTROMAGNETIC RADIATION with a wavelength between that of ultraviolet radiation and gamma rays.

Zygote
The cell that results from the fusion of two GAMETES; a fertilized egg. It is usually DIPLOID.

Index